Sociology for Midwives

Ruth Deery, Elaine Denny and
Gayle Letherby

polity

First published in 2015 by Polity Press

Polity Press
65 Bridge Street
Cambridge CB2 1UR, UK

Polity Press
350 Main Street
Malden, MA 02148, USA

ISBN-13: 978-0-7456-6280-0
ISBN-13: 978-0-7456-6281-7(pb)

A catalogue record for this book is available from the British
Library.

Deery, Ruth (Professor in maternal health), author.
  Sociology for midwives / Ruth Deery [and 13 others].
     p. ; cm.
  Includes bibliographical references and index.
  ISBN 978-0-7456-6280-0 (hardcover : alk. paper) -- ISBN 0-7456-6280-3 (hardcover :
alk. paper) -- ISBN 978-0-7456-6281-7 (pbk. : alk. paper) -- ISBN 0-7456-6281-1 (pbk.
: alk. paper)
  I. Title.
  [DNLM: 1. Midwifery. 2. Sociology. 3. Interpersonal Relations. 4. Nurse Midwives-
-psychology. WQ 160]
  RG940
  362.1982--dc23
                        2014019515

Typeset in 9.5 on 12pt Utopia by
Servis Filmsetting Ltd, Stockport, Cheshire
Printed and bound in Great Britain by
Clays Ltd, St Ives plc

For further information on Polity, visit our website:
politybooks.com

Sociology for Midw

Contents

Boxes, Figures and Tables

Boxes

Figures

Tables

Notes on Contributors

Sarah Church is a Senior Lecturer in Midwifery and Deputy Lead for the Centre for Family Life in the Institute of Health and Wellbeing at the University of Northampton. She contributes to a broad range of modules within the pre-registration and post-registration under-graduate midwifery programmes, concentrating mainly on: research methods; evidence-based practice, perinatal mental health and soci-ology of reproduction and childbirth. She has contributed journal articles and book chapters on issues within the sociology of reproduc-tion and childbirth. Her PhD focused on gender identity, and explored the reproductive identities and experiences of midwives and mothers. Current research areas include migration and midwifery, and espe-cially the experiences of Polish mothers and migrant midwives. She supervises doctoral students in a range of health-related topics and is the Lead for the Masters in Clinical Research programme.

Lorraine Culley is Professor of Social Science and Health at De Montfort University, Leicester, where she leads the Reproduction Research Group. Her research interests encompass work on: social and political aspects of infertility; ethnicity and health care; and user perspectives in health. In her work on assisted conception, she has completed a major study of access to infertility services for British South Asian communities and an ESRC-funded study of perceptions of gamete donation. She was recently the Principal Investigator on an ESRC research project, exploring the experiences of people who travel abroad from the UK for fertility treatment, and is currently leading an ESRC project on the impact of endometriosis on couples. Recent books include *Marginalized Reproduction: Ethnicity, Infertility and Reproductive Technologies*, Earthscan Books, 2009 (co-edited with Nicky Hudson and Floor van Rooij).

Deborah Davidson is an Assistant Professor of Sociology at York University in Toronto. Her research interests focus on reproduction, motherhood and life-course issues, particularly those at the begin-ning and end of life. Currently, her research projects include tattooing as memorialization, the use of the Internet for bereavement support, support during high-risk pregnancy, and support needs for immigrant parents of children with disabilities. Her teaching falls within the areas of health, gender, diversity and qualitative methodology.

Lorna Davies is a UK-qualified midwife who has worked in midwifery education for the last two decades. She is presently undertaking a doctoral thesis exploring midwifery practice within the broad framework of sustainability. Lorna is currently a Principal Lecturer in Midwifery in Christchurch, New Zealand. She is an author and editor of several midwifery textbooks, carries a small caseload as a self-employed midwife, and is a childbirth educator.

Ruth Deery is Professor of Maternal Health at the University of the West of Scotland. She is interested in applying sociological and political theory, action research and implementation science to the organizational culture of midwifery in the National Health Service in the UK. Her research has been in the maternity services with particular interests in organizational culture and change, public policy, emotions and care, and now the clinical improvement/patient-safety agenda in Scotland. Ruth is co-editor (with Billie Hunter) of *Emotions in Midwifery and Reproduction* (Palgrave), and co-author (with Deborah Hughes and Mavis Kirkham) of *Tensions and Barriers to Maternity Services: The Story of a Struggling Birth Centre* (Radcliffe). She is also co-editor (with Lorna Davies) of *Nutrition, Food and Childbirth* (Routledge).

Elaine Denny is Emeritus Professor of Health Sociology at Birmingham City University. Her research interests focus around women as recipients and providers of health care, in particular reproductive health, and she has published work on women's experience of IVF, the experience of endometriosis, and the occupation of nursing. Elaine has conducted qualitative research within Health Technology Assessment funded randomized controlled trials on a variety of women's health topics. She has also undertaken a collaborative research study, funded by Research for Patient Benefit, on endometriosis and cultural diversity, aimed at improving services for minority ethnic women. With Sarah Earle, Elaine has co-edited two editions of *Sociology for Nurses* and a third edition is in preparation.

Fiona Dykes is Professor of Maternal and Infant Health and Director of the Maternal and Infant Nutrition and Nurture Unit (MAINN), School of Health, University of Central Lancashire. She is an Adjunct Professor at University of Western Sydney and Visiting Professor at Dalarna University in Sweden. Fiona has a particular interest in the global, sociocultural and political influences upon infant and young child feeding practices. She is a member of the editorial board for *Maternal and Child Nutrition*, the Wiley-Blackwell published international journal (editorial office in MAINN), and a Fellow of the Higher Education Academy. Fiona is currently involved in projects in Scandinavia, Eastern Europe, Australia and Pakistan. Fiona is author of over sixty peer-reviewed papers and editor of several books, including her monograph *Breastfeeding in Hospital: Mothers, Midwives and the*

Production Line (Routledge) and *Infant and Young Child Feeding: Challenges to Implementing a Global Strategy* (Wiley-Blackwell).

Sarah Earle is Associate Dean for Research and Enterprise in the Faculty of Health and Social Care at the Open University, Milton Keynes. She is a medical sociologist of nearly twenty years' experience and she has a special interest in the role of sociology in health-care education and practice. With Elaine Denny, she is co-editor of the leading text, *Sociology for Nurses* (Polity Press). She has specialist expertise in the sociology of sexuality and human reproduction, and most recently has published (with Carol Komaromy and Linda Layne) *Understanding Reproductive Loss: International Perspectives on Life, Death and Fertility* (Ashgate).

Pamela Fisher is a sociologist with expertise in understandings of marginalization. Pamela's early research interests related to social and political transitions in eastern Germany in the wake of unification. The focus was on understanding how disrupted life biographies were reconfigured in ways that provided new meaningful orientations. Her subsequent research has continued to address social justice, citizenship and marginalization, primarily related to issues of health and well-being. Pamela is particularly interested in how health and well-being are enmeshed and intersect with issues of power and resistance. Another strand of Pamela's work focuses on critical understandings of professionalism within health and social care. Her work in this area is informed by the sociology of emotion and critical perspectives on ethics and values. Pamela's methodological expertise is in qualitative research applied to 'real-life' contexts. She is widely published in leading peer-reviewed journals.

Alistair Hewison is Senior Lecturer and Head of Nursing in the School of Health and Population Sciences at the University of Birmingham. His professional background is in nursing, with experience as a staff nurse, charge nurse and manager in the NHS in Birmingham, Oxford and Warwickshire. His current research and teaching activities are centred on the management and organization of care. His main focus at the moment is as Principal Investigator for a five-year project as part of the Birmingham and Black Country Collaboration for Leadership in Applied Health Research and Care (CLAHRC), examining service redesign in three acute NHS Trusts. In addition, he is working in partnership with colleagues at the Health Services Management Centre to investigate the organizational factors which contribute to failures in nursing care. He has written widely on health-care management and policy issues in papers published in scholarly journals and chapters in edited collections.

Bob Heyman joined the University of Huddersfield in September 2008 as Professor of Health Care Risk Management. He has worked in higher education since 1971, and has held the positions of Professor of Health Social Research at the University of Northumbria (1997–9) and Professor of Health Research at City University London (2000–8), where he was awarded an emeritus professorship in 2008. Whilst at City University, he led the £2,500,000 four-university Consortium for Healthcare Research, which funded twenty-one doctoral and postdoctoral fellowships in nursing, midwifery and the allied health professions. He has authored over 100 articles and books, mostly on the social science of health risk. His recent publications include *Risk, Safety and Clinical Practice: Health Care through the Lens of Risk* (Oxford University Press) and a four-edition mega-special issue of the journal *Health, Risk & Society* (2012–13), *Health Care through the 'Lens of Risk'*.

Nicky Hudson is Senior Research Fellow in the School of Applied Social Sciences at De Montfort University. She is a sociologist with an interest in medicine, reproduction, gender and ethnicity. She has worked on a number of projects on the social aspects of infertility and reproduction, funded by the Economic and Social Research Council, the Department of Health, and local NHS trusts. She co-edited *Marginalized Reproduction: Ethnicity, Infertility and Reproductive Technologies* (Earthscan, 2009), and was part of a team who completed the first published UK study on cross-border reproduction: *Transnational Reproduction: An Exploratory Study of UK Residents Who Travel Abroad for Fertility Treatment* (ESRC, RES 000-22-3390).

Carol Kingdon holds a PhD in Sociology from Lancaster University and a Masters in Sociological Research in Healthcare from the University of Warwick. She is currently Senior Research Fellow in the Faculty of Health at the University of Central Lancashire, with honorary appointments at Liverpool Women's NHS Foundation Trust and the University of Liverpool. She has undertaken research in maternity services since 2001 and led the first longitudinal study of women's choice and birth method in the United Kingdom. More recent work includes contributions to national studies of the experiences of maternity professionals and bereaved parents, following stillbirth. She regularly publishes in high-impact professional journals and contributes to books on midwifery and sociology. She is single author of *Sociology for Midwives* (Quay Books, 2009).

Mavis Kirkham is Professor of Midwifery at the University of the West of Scotland and holds honorary professorial positions at Sheffield Hallam University and the University of Technology Sydney. She has worked continuously as a midwife researcher and a clinical midwife for forty years, and still does some work as a home-birth midwife. She sees herself as a hybrid researcher, having worked in the disciplines of social anthropology, sociology, politics and history, using qualitative, observational and ethnographic methods, as well as surveys and archive work. Her abiding research interest is in people's relationship with and efforts to control their work and its setting, in terms of employment and reproductive labour. Her current research is on freebirthing. Her books include: *Informed Choice in Maternity Care*; *Birth Centres: A Social Model of Maternity Care*; *The Midwife/Mother Relationship*; *Exploring the Dirty Side of Women's Health and Tensions and Barriers in Improving Maternity Care*, with Ruth Deery and Deborah Hughes; and *Midwives Coping with Loss and Grief*, with Doreen Kenworthy.

Gayle Letherby is Professor of Sociology and Director of the Institute of Health and Community at Plymouth University. Her scholarly interests include: reproductive and non-parental identity and experience; and feminist research and epistemology. Among recent relevant publications are, with Jennifer Marchbank, *An Introduction to Gender: Social Science Perspectives* (Routledge, 2014); with John Scott and Malcolm Williams, *Objectivity and Subjectivity in Social Research* (Sage, 2013), and with Paul Bywaters, *Extending Social Research: Application, Implementation and Presentation* (Open University Press, 2007).

Jo Murphy-Lawless is a feminist sociologist and currently teaches in the School of Nursing and Midwifery in Trinity College Dublin. Since 2008, she has been a member of the Birth Project Group, a cross-national group from Trinity College Dublin, the University of Edinburgh and Edinburgh Napier University. The group facilitates workshops and support activities for birth activists, midwifery students and newly qualified midwives.

Nadine Pilley-Edwards is a long-standing committee member of the Association for Improvements in the Maternity Services (AIMS), and has run pregnancy groups since 1985. She completed a PhD on women's experiences of home births in 2002 and has researched women's experiences of being on Maternity Services Liaison Committees (MSLC), and the experiences of women who withdraw from maternity services. She was a previous co-editor of the MIDIRS *Midwifery Digest* and continues to research, write and lecture on birth issues.

Jayne Samples has been a registered midwife since 1989. She has practised in a range of settings, including community, hospital and a birth centre. She has worked as a Senior Lecturer in Midwifery at the University of Huddersfield since 2006. Her particular interests include supporting women with complex needs. She is currently a Professional Doctorate student, researching women's experiences of being labelled 'high risk'.

Edwin van Teijlingen is a medical sociologist with a long-standing interest in international health. He is Professor of Reproductive Health Research at Bournemouth University. Edwin has been involved in a range of studies in the reproductive and sexual health field, both in the UK and abroad (especially in Nepal). He has published more than 170 academic articles. Many of his studies are based on mixed-methods and/or cross-cultural approaches. He has also published a range of papers on various aspects of qualitative research methods. His edited books include *Birth by Design* (Routledge) and *Midwifery and the Medicalization of Childbirth* (Nova Science). Edwin is Honorary Professor at the University of Aberdeen (Scotland), as well as Visiting Professor at MMIHS, Tribhuvan University (Nepal); London Metropolitan University (England); and Noble College, Pokhara University (Nepal).

Acknowledgements

Ruth, Elaine and Gayle would like to thank all of the chapter authors for their hard work and commitment, and are grateful for permissions to reproduce copyright material and illustrations.

Illustration credits

Figure 1.1: © Craig Cloutier(Flickr); Figure 1.2: © Istock; Istock-photo-14764409; reproduced with permission; Figure 2.1: Wellcome Library, London. Vaginal examination in the horizontal position with the patient covered with a sheet. 'Nouvelles démonstrations d'accouchemens', Jacques Pierre Maygrier, 1822; Figure 3.1: © Istock; ©Istock-photo-20230918; reproduced with permission; Figure 4.1: © Istock; istock-photo-11966776-; reproduced with permission; Figure 4.2: © Barbara Thorpe-Tracey and the Royal College of Midwives 2009. All Rights Reserved; reproduced with permission; Figure 5.1: Photograph by Ruth Deery; Figure 5.2: Photograph by Ruth Deery; Figure 6.1: Photograph by Garry Knight(Flickr); reproduced with permission; Figure 6.2: Reproduced with permission from Laura Deery; Figure 6.3: © Istock; istock-photo-23825898_Antenatal Assessment; reproduced with permission; Figure 7.1: Photograph by Jayne Samples; Figure 7.2: ©ASTIER / BSIP / SuperStock; SuperStock_824-94803; reproduced with permission; Figure 8.1: From Deborah Davidson's Collection 5 – Memorial Tattoo Archive; reproduced with permission; Figure 9.1: Adapted from HFEA 2011; Figure 9.2: © Istock; istock-photo-15427658-subcutaneous-abdomen-injection; reproduced with permission; Figure 9.3: © Istock; istock-photo-21420591; reproduced with permission; Figure 10.1: Photograph courtesy of Salford Star/ Stephen Kingston; Figure 10.2: Photograph courtesy of Becky Reid, Albany Practice, London; Figure 11.1: Wikipedia Commons; Figure 11.2: © Istock; istock-photo-14173254-; reproduced with permission; Figure 12.1: © Istock; istock-photo-9533964-; reproduced with permission; Figure 12.2: Permission given from Warkworth Birthing Unit Managers: Feb 2014 Warkworth, New Zealand; Box 13.1: Reproduced with permission of Breathing Space/ NHS Living Life, Scotland; Figure 13.1: © Carol Kingdon; reproduced with permission; Figure 14.1: Compiled by Lorna Davies, 2012; Figure 14.2: © Istock; istock-photo-5703599-; reproduced with permission.

Introduction

Ruth Deery, Elaine Denny and Gayle Letherby

Over the years, and especially since the inception of the National Health Service (NHS), society has changed dramatically. Midwifery has also changed, becoming much more than midwives supporting women around the time of birth. The support that midwives offer now takes place within a complex set of relationships delivered in an interdisciplinary and multi-agency context. We know now that it is not useful for health-care professionals to work in isolation – another set of eyes will see something from a completely different perspective that can be enlightening and useful. For example, midwives work in collaboration and partnership with obstetricians, health visitors, social workers and general practitioners in order to plan care for women using maternity services.

Sociological theories and perspectives can help you to more fully understand the history of midwifery and the role of midwives as well as the nature of the social world that you live in. Sociology is especially useful to midwifery in terms of exploring how institutions (the NHS system in this case) are structured, the way in which power is distributed and its impact on women using our maternity services as well as on midwives. Sociology also helps in understanding the way you interact and communicate on a daily basis and make sense of social situations. As midwives you will encounter some of the most vulnerable and disadvantaged women (and their families) in society. It is crucial that you are inclusive and anti-discriminatory so that women will have a positive, fulfilling experience. A greater awareness of sociology will help you to understand both anti-discriminatory and oppressive practices.

Midwifery is about midwives being person-centred and responsive to the individual needs of women and their families/significant others in a variety of care settings. The emphasis should be on the provision of compassionate, holistic care that respects their individual needs, cultures and choices. Such principles of equity and social justice are fundamental values of midwifery, which must be addressed in all programmes of preparation for midwives (NMC 2010).

The training of midwives for the care that they provide now takes place within the context of constant tumultuous change in the NHS and Higher Education (HE). The current UK Coalition government, formed in May 2010, is continuing to introduce massive change to the NHS whilst also promoting an increasingly central role for stakeholders who balance their own interests with the well-being of society as a whole. Public-sector reforms have a dramatic impact on clinical practice, often leaving midwives (and others) ill-prepared for the increasing role of market forces, the importance of accountability, value for money and consumer choice in the provision of public services. For some time now, reconfigurations with larger, centralized obstetric units, reduced bed capacity and shorter hospital stays, compounded by midwifery shortages, alongside an ever-growing number of cases and increased workloads for midwives, have had a profound effect on the way midwives work. Sociological perspectives can help you to understand and think differently about the role of midwifery and midwives in society.

With all of this in mind, the aim of this book is to provide an accessible textbook, focusing on the significance of sociology to midwifery based on the needs of pre-registration midwifery students. It is also of relevance to post-registration students and other health-care professionals who work with pregnant women and mothers, including mental health workers, and workers in drug and alcohol misuse services, community workers and social workers.

The book is divided into three parts. Part 1 considers the contribution that sociological knowledge can make to midwifery practice. It starts by providing an overview of the sociology of, and for, midwifery, addressing the frequently raised question of why midwives need to study sociology. Then follows a consideration of the methods, methodologies and epistemologies of relevance to sociologically informed research on, and for, reproduction and reproductive experience (both the perspective of midwives and women and their significant others). The importance of the policy context to midwifery is also explored.

Part 2 looks at key issues and concerns in midwifery, exploring organizational and procedural matters relevant to midwifery, loss, risk and age, fertility and reproductive technologies, weight management, and long-term conditions and disability. These issues advantage some groups and disadvantage others, resulting in wide variations in the incidence and experience of morbidity and mortality. The role of midwives in challenging these issues as well as developing their own and women's autonomy is explored.

Part 3 explores debates and controversies within midwifery, and focuses on marginality and social exclusion from the perspectives of women's lived experiences of social exclusion and the urgent need for redefining social equality. Infant feeding is explored through the powerful influence of economic, sociocultural and relational contexts within which women feed their children. There is also critical discussion around commodification, sustainability and midwifery, and mental health issues, where the social implications of caring for women in maternity services are explored.

The chapters are designed to help you reflect on the sociological issues raised and relate them to midwifery practice, as shown in the list below.

- Each chapter begins with the key issues, giving you a signpost on what to expect.
- Learning outcomes enable you to assess whether you have understood and learned from what you have read.
- Key terms are explained in the glossary boxes to aid understanding at a glance.
- There are activities to carry out with your colleagues from midwifery or other health professions, enabling reflection and encouraging you to relate theory to practice.
- At the end of each chapter there are summary points.
- To expand your knowledge, annotated further reading and questions for discussion are included at the end of each chapter.

Once you have read this book, and engaged with the activities and discussion questions, we hope that you will feel equipped to use a sociological approach as one of your tools for planning optimum midwifery care with women and their families and other agencies. You may also feel more empowered to enter into the debates about the future of midwifery and its place in determining health policy. Most of all, we hope that you will be able to look beyond the simple explanations of everyday issues and problems in midwifery to gain a deeper, more meaningful understanding.

PART 1

MIDWIFERY AND THE IMPORTANCE OF SOCIOLOGY

Introduction

The first part of this volume sets the scene for the chapters that follow in Parts 2 and 3, by introducing you to some of the theories and concepts that inform sociology and underpin the issues of interest to midwives. Hopefully, the chapters here will provide you with a lens from which to view the rest of this book. The four chapters contained within it are theoretical, but they are written not as 'dry as dust' text, but illuminated by examples from midwifery, and the sociology of reproduction more generally. Thus, they demonstrate the value of sociology for midwives and midwifery.

Sociology has been part of the curriculum in midwifery education for over twenty years, and yet there are still some midwives and students who question its place, and find it hard to relate abstract concepts such as inequality to their work with individual mothers and their babies. Yet, as Sarah Earle and Sarah Church inform you in the first chapter, sociology is an exciting discipline, and one that has much relevance as one of the tools with which to explore and understand your practice. They show that sociology is more than just 'common sense', and provide you with illustrations of sociology applied to midwifery practice, some of which may resonate with your experience. These illustrations demonstrate how we can view things in a different way from the one we have come to accept and encourage us to challenge common assumptions that we all make about people and situations. Hopefully, after reading their chapter you will begin to develop your 'sociological imagination'.

While Earle and Church introduced you to sociology *for* midwifery, in Chapter 2 Edwin van Teijlingen explores the sociology *of* midwifery. The sociology of midwifery is concerned with sociological analyses of the occupation of midwifery. In other words, it explores questions such as the midwife's place in care, the culture of midwifery, how this influences the relationship and interactions with mothers (and other family members) and other health professions. It also explores how midwifery fits into the overall provision of health and maternity care, and its place in wider society. This raises some interesting questions about the relationship between occupation and profession, and where midwifery sits in the debates around what makes a particular area of work or care the province of professionals. This chapter also explores how sociological models such as the 'medical model' and the 'social model' help us understand concepts of pregnancy, birth, midwifery and more general concepts of 'risk' or 'need'.

Much of the material contained in this book comes from knowledge created by research. In Chapter 3, Gayle Letherby explains the research process, and introduces you to some of the debates around the relative merits of the two major research approaches – quantitative and qualitative methodology. Increasingly, research, particularly in disciplines such as sociology, is concerned with altering the balance of power within the research process, to involve the participants in the design and the outcomes of the research that they engage in. Letherby invites you to consider these wider contextual issues in conducting research, whether you intend to become involved in research yourself, to be a contributor to the research of others, or to use research findings in your own practice.

In Chapter 4, we turn to the subject of health policy, which determines how we define and provide health care, and the emphasis put on particular services such as obstetrics, and indeed to the type of services we as a nation provide to women from conception to birth and to mothers and babies postnatally. Yet, as Alistair Hewison points out, nurses and midwives are rarely involved in debates around policy, despite there being many policy initiatives that impact on their practice. Many staff working in busy clinical areas feel that policy is something that happens to them, that they have no power or influence in formulating it. Hewison explains how the policy process works, and how midwives at all levels can be involved in order to develop the services they offer, and to act as advocates for mothers and babies.

So these first four chapters may raise many issues that you had not considered before, or they may encourage you to look at familiar issues in a new way. This new way of looking at the world will help you to engage with the more substantive issues of the following parts. You may decide to read this part first in order to gain some background understanding of the issues of interest to sociologists to equip you to delve in to the chapters that follow. Conversely, you may decide to come to these chapters after you have read some of the later chapters to help you to achieve a deeper understanding of sociological ways of thinking on social phenomena.

1 Sociology

What is it Good For?

Sarah Earle and Sarah Church

Key issues:

- The nature of sociological enquiry.
- Sociology and 'common sense'.
- Developing a sociological imagination.
- Using sociology for midwifery.
- The value of developing sociological skills.
- Sociological knowledge.

By the end of this chapter you should be able to:

- Understand the role of sociology within society.
- Recognize the distinction between sociology and 'common sense'.
- Begin to develop your sociological imagination.
- Discuss why midwives should study sociology.
- Understand the value of sociological skills for midwifery practice.
- Discuss the role of sociological knowledge within midwifery.

Introduction

Sociology is an exciting discipline and can provide you with the tools to think about the world in a particular way. However, sociology isn't homogeneous; there are different types of sociology, offering distinct perspectives, and exploring a wide range of topics. Sociologists are interested in many issues, including health and illness, sex and sexuality, crime and deviance, the body, emotions, and sleep, to name just a few of the subjects that sociologists have written about!

This chapter does not try to turn you into a sociologist, nor can it; instead it seeks to show how sociology can be relevant to midwifery and to your practice as a midwife. The chapter begins by defining the discipline of sociology and its place within the social sciences. In particular, you will read about why sociology is more than 'just common sense' and will begin to understand what is meant by the term 'a sociological imagination'. The next section of the chapter focuses more specifically on the role of sociology within midwifery and the value of developing sociological skills as part of being fit to practise as a midwife. The final part of the chapter considers the place of sociological knowledge in the study of human reproduction.

So, What is Sociology?

In the broadest of terms, sociology is concerned with the study of human societies. This means that sociology is virtually limitless in scope and – in principle – it is possible to have a sociology of almost anything. Over time, sociologists have been interested in different things, and this usually reflects the concerns of the time. Early sociologists, writing in the nineteenth cen tury, were concerned by the major economic, social and political changes of that period, so their work tended to focus on the rise of **industrial capitalism**, and the role of religious belief in society (for example, see Marx 1867, Durkheim 1897, and Weber 1958). More recently, sociologists have turned their attention to other matters, including the effects of **globalization** (see Giddens 1999), the new genetics (Bunton and Peterson 2002) and the notion of the **Big Society** (for example, Jordan 2010). This book focuses specifically on sociology as applicable to midwives, midwifery practice and reproductive health, and draws very generally on other sociological work.

Sociology is one of the many social sciences which include disciplines such as anthropology, criminology, law, political science and psychology. Very generally, social science is the study of society, the way in which people behave, and how that influences the world around them. Inevitably, not all social scientists would agree with this definition since the social sciences encompass such a broad range of disciplines. There are also 'boundary disputes' between the different social science disciplines, often with as much overlap, as well as divisions, between them. For example, sociologists are generally interested in societies, whereas psychologists are usually interested in individuals. Societies are, of course, made up of individuals and are influenced by individuals, just as individuals are influenced by the societies in which they live! In practice, this means that some sociologists are more interested in society and social structures, whereas others are more interested in individuals and individual behaviour. In other words, sociology is multi-paradigmatic; that is, it consists of a variety of competing **paradigms** (Kuhn 1962) which seek to explain different phenomena.

Those who are new to sociology sometimes think that it is 'just **common sense**' and it is important to understand why this is not the case. Before reading on, complete Activity 1.1, which focuses on this very issue.

industrial capitalism
private control of the means of production

globalization
worldwide social, economic and cultural interconnectedness

Big Society
government initiative shifting responsibility to the community

paradigms
accepted ways of viewing the world

common sense
everyday interpretation of reality

📋 Activity 1.1: Is sociology just 'common sense'?

A postal questionnaire study that explored approaches to sociology within midwifery education asked lecturers to consider their approach to teaching sociology to midwives. Read some of the comments lecturers made below.

'Students find sociology a very difficult subject to study . . . Some see sociology as "just common sense", not an academic discipline.'

'Sociology . . . must be included within all midwifery programmes, but I am not sure that the students always understand its relevance to practice.'

'Maternity care takes place within a social environment, therefore the midwifery curriculum would have a gaping hole if sociology were not included . . . If midwives do not understand women's social environments they cannot provide effective care. It's as simple as that!'

(a) What do you think of the comments above?

(b) Do you believe that sociology is 'just common sense'?

(c) Do you think it is possible to provide effective care without understanding women's social environments?

(Church and Earle 2006: 342–5)

There are two important points to recognize when thinking about what is common sense. The first point is that there is often more than one 'common-sense' view and not all of these viewpoints are necessarily right or wrong. So, if we take the example of pregnancy prevention, one person might suggest that using a condom is just common sense and another might believe that taking the contraceptive pill makes more sense, whereas someone else may feel that it is common sense simply to avoid having sex altogether in order to prevent pregnancy. The second important point to acknowledge is that each of these views could be influenced by a different set of experiences guided by a range of social, political, moral or religious beliefs. Little is gained, therefore, by relying on common-sense understandings in order to make sense of the world.

The sociologist Mills (1959) coined the term 'sociological imagination'. This term refers to the way in which the personal can be influenced by social, political and economic factors. Mills explains this with reference to what he calls 'private troubles' and 'public issues'. Take the example of prenatal screening, which is a routine part of antenatal care in most modern Western countries. Sometimes prenatal screening means that difficult choices have to be made regarding further testing for fetal abnormality. Obviously, this is a personal choice for most women but such decisions are always made within a social context, influenced by the views of family and professionals, as well as by women's knowledge and understanding of disability. These decisions are also governed by a range of wider factors such as legislation, religion and medical practice.

Sociology challenges the obvious and tries to unpick what is really going on in order to make sense of society by questioning 'familiar expectations and assumptions' (Cooke 1993). Some students can find sociology difficult because it seems full of unnecessarily complex jargon. It is important to remember that every academic discipline, and every profession, has its own language, some of which is only understood by '**insiders**'. However, by engaging with sociology, and

insiders
people in a group with access to specific information

developing your sociological imagination, you gain a deeper understanding of your work as a midwife.

The Value of Sociology and Sociological Skills

The role of sociology within the health-care professions has been
widely discussed in the academic literature. For example, it has been
explored in relation to medicine (Friedson 1970), nursing (see Cooke
1993; Porter 1995; Green and Earle 2010) and speech and language
therapy (Earle 2001). Although contested by some (for example, Sharp
1994), the professions themselves seem largely in favour. Midwifery
has become embedded within a model of higher education that
emphasizes vocational training and practical competencies, alongside the study of academic subjects, particularly the social sciences.
Sociology has been included in the academic curriculum for pre-
registration midwifery since the early 1990s. Sociology is an interesting
discipline in its own right, but it also enables midwives to challenge
everyday assumptions through the development of critical thinking
skills.

There are two types of sociological knowledge of relevance to midwives: sociology for midwifery and the sociology of midwifery (see
Chapter 2). The latter refers to the application of sociology to understanding the profession of midwifery as a whole. The focus here is on
sociology *for* midwifery and this refers to the role of individual midwives and their practice, and the way in which sociology can be applied
to make sense of this. As argued by Pinikahana (2003), sociology is only
relevant to practice if it is *applied*.

A helpful way of thinking about the relevance of sociology to
midwives is to consider the distinction between 'personal education' and 'semantic conjunction', and the relationship between
academic disciplines and professional practice. Personal education
refers to the view that the study of any academic discipline – such
as sociology – is a useful preparation for practice because, as Sharp
(1994: 391) has argued, 'it inculcates in the student general intellectual and problem-solving skills, which will be transferred to the
professional setting'. In other words, sociology can help to develop
cognitive skills that can be applied within a practice situation.
Semantic conjunction refers to the fact that there might be common
themes shared between an academic discipline and a profession.
As Sharp notes, it is the 'substantive subject matter of the discipline
concerned which is of relevance to the problems faced by professionals' (p. 391). For example, in the mid-1970s, the British Sociological
Association established the Human Reproduction Study Group,
which is still in existence today (<http://www.britsoc.co.uk/study-
groups/human-reproduction.aspx>). The emergence of this group
played a significant role in establishing a sociology of childbirth, and
the work of this group continues to make an important contribution

to sociology in midwifery. So, whether adopting a personal education or semantic conjunction approach, the value of sociology is in its application to practice.

The Role of Sociological Knowledge for Midwives

Sociological knowledge can help you make sense of reproductive experiences and the nature of midwifery and midwifery practice. In particular, it can offer you ways of thinking about issues that might be different from the way you have thought about them before. Sociology offers both a broader viewpoint and a critique of the taken-for-granted aspects of reproductive experience. For sociologists, the study of human reproduction is understood within the context of societal expectations and stereotypes, as well as within the context of the **social structures** which both create and perpetuate inequalities and social exclusion. As Petchesky (1980: 81) notes, 'women make their own reproductive choices, but they do not make them just as they please; they do not make them under conditions which they themselves create but under social conditions and constraints which they, as mere individuals, are powerless to change'. For example, in the UK, the combination of poverty and social exclusion remains the single most important factor in determining reproductive health, influencing maternal and neonatal morbidity and mortality, as well as access to family planning, antenatal and maternity care, and treatment for infertility (see Box 1.1). For a fuller discussion on social exclusion, go to Chapter 10.

social structures
how society is
organized

The sociological imagination shows that individual actions and

---

Box 1.1 Poverty, social exclusion and reproductive health

- Women of lower educational status are less likely to have investigations and treatment for infertility.
- Vulnerable women are far less likely to seek antenatal care early in pregnancy.
- Young people who are in or leaving care, homeless, underachieving at school, involved in crime, or living in areas with higher social deprivation are more likely to become teenage parents.
- Women with partners who are unemployed are seven times more likely to die from causes in/directly related to pregnancy than women with partners who are employed.
- Asylum-seekers and newly arrived refugees have a maternal mortality rate nearly six times higher than Western women.
- Mothers who live in deprived areas are more likely to suffer a stillbirth or neonatal death than mothers living in less deprived areas.

(*Sources:* CEMACH 2007; CMACE 2010; FPA 2010; Morris et al. 2011)

experiences are structured by wider social factors. Some sociologists would argue that sociology can be emancipatory. Others argue that sociology should be transformative – that is, that sociological knowledge and understanding should transform into social action (Haddad and Lieberman 2002). Activity 1.2 asks you to think about the role of the midwife as an agent of social action.

🗒 Activity 1.2: Midwives, sociology and social action

Take a look at the images here and then answer the following questions.

(a) What is represented in the pictures? Make some notes on what you see and how it makes you feel.
(b) How can you influence women's health and well-being?
(c) Do you think that midwives play a role in challenging disadvantage and discrimination? If so, how can you achieve this?

The next part of this chapter explores sociological perspectives on three specific issues: diabetes, obesity, and the use of assistive reproductive technologies. The focus here is on women's experiences, their reproductive health, and the role of midwives and midwifery care.

Figure 1.1 Homelessness and pregnancy

Figure 1.2 Social deprivation and pregnancy

Women's experiences of diabetes in pregnancy

Pregnancy, childbirth and early motherhood are often experienced as natural, joyous, special and even empowering. However, when things do not go to plan, they can also be experienced as medicalized, traumatizing and disempowering. Diabetes is the most common medical complication in pregnancy and is associated with increased risks to the life and health of the mother and her baby, including obstetric complications, increased rates of Caesarean delivery, increases in congenital abnormalities and perinatal mortality and morbidity (CEMACH 2007). The rate of diabetes in pregnancy is increasing (in the UK and in other countries) and is regarded as a serious public health issue (CEMACH 2007).

Diabetes in pregnancy introduces a range of challenges for women and midwives which can have a profound effect on women's experiences of maternity care. Living with diabetes usually requires a strict regimen of self-care, including tight blood-glucose control. Some studies suggest that midwives believe that women have a moral obligation to look after themselves in pregnancy (Persson et al. 2011). However, this can create tension and may lead to problematic relationships because women might feel that they are being judged, and under constant surveillance (Watts, O'Hara and Twigg 2010). Whilst research suggests that expectations of care are usually high, women are often disappointed with their care, which often focuses too readily on their diabetes, rather than on their experiences of pregnancy (Evans and O'Brien 2005; Persson et al. 2009).

Box 1.2 Sociological approaches to diabetes in pregnancy

Drawing on a life-cycle, or 'life-course', approach can be useful to explore how diabetes in pregnancy might disrupt an individual's expectations about their own lives. A life-course approach 'encompasses social and demographic changes which affect all our lives, as well as the personal biographical events in each individual's life course' (Cotterill 1994: 112). In using this approach, it is possible to acknowledge that people's lives do not always progress as planned, or expected. Diabetes in pregnancy is one such false start which can impact on an individual's ability to plan their own lives as anticipated.

Bury's (1982) work on 'biographical disruption' is also useful in understanding how a condition such as diabetes might impact on someone's everyday life. Bury argued that a diagnosis of chronic illness could disrupt life in several ways. In the first instance, he argued that it disrupts taken-for-granted assumptions and behaviour. It also disrupts a person's explanatory system – or the way they make sense of the world. Finally, biographical disruption requires a response to this re-ordering of the world, thus necessitating a rethinking of the individual's life story and identity. The focus on diabetes, rather than on the experience of pregnancy, is often experienced as a loss of the expectation of 'normal' pregnancy and this does require change and adjustment.

Read the extract in Box 1.2, which is taken from a qualitative study of women's experiences of diabetes in pregnancy; the extract explores two sociological approaches to this issue.

Now that you have read the extract in Box 1.2, attempt the questions in Activity 1.3 before progressing to explore the issue of obesity during pregnancy and childbirth.

Activity 1.3: Reflecting on the life course

1. To what extent is the concept of 'biographical disruption' useful? Do you think that pregnancy itself can be disrupting and, if so, how? What else do you think might disrupt someone's experiences of pregnancy, childbirth and early motherhood? Do you think that men's lives can be disrupted to the same extent?
2. Spend a few minutes thinking about your own life course. What are your expectations? What are your experiences and expectations of fertility, pregnancy, childbirth and parenting?
3. How can you support a woman to make healthy lifestyle changes, whilst not judging her choices?

Obesity during pregnancy and childbirth

Obesity is widely regarded to have reached pandemic proportions, and Crossley (2004: 223) suggests that 'fat is a sociological issue', arguing that 'obesity is not defined as a bodily ideal in late modern societies. Indeed it runs contrary to the bodily ideals revealed by research, whether those be aesthetic or health related' (p. 228). For health-care professionals, the rise in obesity is a significant issue in that it poses a risk in pregnancy for both mother and baby. Indeed, the recent maternal mortality report highlights that 49 per cent of the women who died were overweight or obese. The report suggests that if obesity (a body mass index (BMI) of 30 or more) is considered on its own, it accounted for 30 per cent of mothers who died from direct causes of pregnancy (BJOG 2011).

Sociologists are interested in the way that disease becomes classified as such. Conway and Rene (2004), for example, argue that the classification of obesity is complex and influenced by a range of values, as well as by politics, economics, science and semantics. Indeed, obesity was only first referred to as a disease by the World Health Organization in 1985, but spokespersons have subsequently described it as both 'a disease in its own right' and a risk factor for non-communicable diseases (WHO 1998: 44). However, even today, its classification is disputed. Gard and Wright (2005), for instance, suggest that obesity is not actually a disease, but simply a risk factor for other diseases (such as diabetes).

Debates about the classification of obesity notwithstanding, feminist writers have also explored the issue of obesity. Drawing on the concept of patriarchal power (the oppression of women in a society that is dominated by male power), Bordo (1995) suggests that culture controls the way we understand women's bodies by defining fatness as 'bad' and thinness as 'good'. So sociologists would argue that obesity is not just a medical issue, but a social and moral one. Disability writers have also commented on the issue of obesity, drawing parallels between disability politics and fat politics. For example, Cooper argues:

> The bodies of fat and disabled people share low social status . . . Like people with mobility impairments, many fat people are disabled by a lack of access in the physical environment, for example, clothes don't fit, seats are too small, turnstiles are impossible to navigate. Fat and disabled people encounter discrimination in all areas of our lives . . . where we are constantly reminded that something is wrong with us. Most blatantly congruent are our experiences of medicalization . . . When we conceptualize fatness as a disease, we also assume that somehow it must be cured in order for our bodies to function normally. (Cooper 1997: 36–7)

Box 1.3 Feelings about obesity in pregnancy

Several themes emerged from the data, including lifestyle behaviours before pregnancy, during pregnancy and after the birth; feelings associated with childbearing when obese; the perceptions of others, including health professionals, family and friends; and factors that inhibit change of lifestyle. Most of the themes were consistent across the pregnancy and postnatal data. Data generated in pregnancy highlighted more psychological issues related to childbearing and obesity than data generated after the birth. Furthermore, in the postnatal interviews, some women reiterated some of the negative aspects of maternity care that they had already disclosed during the pregnancy interview. This paper reports on two subthemes from the 'feelings associated with childbearing when obese' theme, as these have significant implications for midwifery practice.

The humiliation of being pregnant when obese:

> She'd told me that she was finding it hard to find the baby's heartbeat because I was overweight. I come out and I was in floods of tears. You think that you're doing the baby some wrong. Where you weren't in a fit state when you started it, and you should have been. (Participant Q, 35 weeks pregnant)

> The main things are the embarrassment factor. I knew that I'd have to have consultant care again cos I'd had two previous Caesareans. You hear these stories about people being quite tactless and I was quite concerned about how embarrassed I'd feel when the issue came up. (Participant S, 33 weeks pregnant)

The medicalization of obesity when pregnant:

> I was aware that I could come into one or two problems because of the weight. I didn't realize how little they do to help you for the sake of the baby, it's like there's the baby, then there's you. In many ways, don't get me wrong, I wouldn't do anything to harm the baby at all, but it's like the baby comes first and you are like an oven. And that's how I feel. That as long as I can manage, even if I'm suffering, it's fine, because the baby's going to be fine. It all seems to be geared to that. So what they've done is denied me the right to my health, for the sake of the baby. (Participant L, 29 weeks pregnant) (Furber and McGowan 2011: 441)

Research suggests that obese pregnant women may experience stigma and negative stereotyping because of their size, and that caregivers treat women who are obese less favourably compared to other women (Nyman, Prebensen and Flensner 2010). Although not reporting research, Deery (2011) and Deery and Wray (2009) have also expressed concerns about stigmatization and negative stereotyping. Schmied et al. (2011) report that midwives actually find it quite difficult to raise the issue of obesity with women and that, when they do, there are limited resources to support women. Sociological knowledge can therefore have an impact on our understanding of the relationship between the body and society, not least in relation to obesity. This can provide us with significant insights into obese women's experiences of pregnancy and childbirth and their relationship with their caregivers. Read the extract in Box 1.3 with quotes from a published research paper by Furber and McGowan (2011) who explored the experiences related to obesity in women with a body mass index of 35 kg/m² during the childbearing process.

Now you should move on to Activity 1.4, which asks you to think about your role in supporting women who are obese in pregnancy.

📋 Activity 1.4: Supporting women who are obese in pregnancy

1. Spend a few minutes thinking about your own beliefs regarding obesity and people who are obese or overweight.
2. Now think about the feelings expressed about obesity and childbearing in Box 1.3. How might you go about supporting a woman to feel more positive about herself during pregnancy whilst not being judgemental about her weight?

Women and assisted reproductive technologies

Exploring the sociological perspectives of reproduction raises a number of issues for midwives and women. It forms a broader context for the consideration of other influences on reproduction, childbearing and motherhood, such as culture, sexuality, disability, social deprivation and age. Gaining insight into the changing nature of fertility and reproductive trends in the context of these issues can provide midwives with an awareness of fertility issues and the associated difficulties. For example, exploring assisted reproductive technologies (ART) from a sociological perspective highlights childbirth and motherhood as biological, social and genetic, presenting challenges for women and midwives in relation to the various definitions and meanings around reproduction and the role and identity of mothers. Furthermore, understanding the social meaning of motherhood, that is, what it means to be a mother, can also help midwives to support women who experience pregnancy loss following the use of assisted reproductive methods.

Feminist writers have questioned the role and influence of medicalization on reproduction, where the application of scientific knowledge has challenged the position of women's bodies within the process of reproduction (see Wray and Deery 2008). The use of such terms as 'test tube' baby reflects the absence of the woman's body and favours the medicalized approach to conception, where the emphasis lies on 'artificial' and 'assisted'. Whilst assisted reproductive technologies (ART) have enabled a number of women to become mothers, the use of assisted methods does not automatically lead to the birth of a baby; the birth rate following IVF has been reported as low as 23.7 per cent (HFEA

2010). Since pregnancy is reported in 70 per cent of women undergoing treatment, the high rate of miscarriage and discontinuation of treatment due to failure to conceive a pregnancy raises further questions in relation to the psychosocial aspects of infertility and motherhood.

Society has been described as pronatalist – that is, it encourages and supports childbearing as a predominant status for women. For this reason, women who are unable to conceive or women who decide not to become mothers may be viewed negatively. Some argue that women described as infertile are stigmatized as 'desperate' and 'suffering' (see Letherby 1994); words such as 'barren' and 'sterile' have been used, which suggest a state of hopelessness and emptiness. Whilst reproductive problems can lead to distress, research suggests that women are not 'passive victims' but that they often use or reject technologies to their own advantage (e.g., Denny 1996; Letherby 2002). A collection of work exploring women and body politics highlights this very point, showing that women contest identities, resist norms and are selectively compliant with medical authority (Lock and Kaufert 1998).

Of course, access to ART is problematic since 'choice' in the use of ART is restricted and controlled by legislation, as well as by other factors (HFEA 2010).

Whilst the NHS is guided to offer three cycles of in-vitro fertilization (IVF) (NICE 2004), women are rarely offered this level of service due to limited funding (Johnson 2011). Moreover, criteria for the funding of treatments differ from one area of the country to another, in which social factors such as age are often used. The phrase 'postcode lottery' is often quoted to reflect the disparity in policy and availability of services. As a result, a number of women seek private treatment at great cost, which results in increased stress and financial hardship for some individuals and couples. Understanding why some women may seek treatment abroad may not be difficult to understand in this context.

Box 1.4 Reasons given by women and couples for travelling abroad to seek fertility treatment

- Shortage of donor gametes in the UK
- Long UK waiting times
- Cost of treatment
- Better success rates overseas
- Dissatisfaction with care in the UK

- Treatment in a less stressful environment
- Age of treatment seeker

- Choice of donors overseas
- For multiple embryo transfer
- Convenience
- Age of UK donors
- Anonymity of donors in other countries
- Overseas clinic reputation
- As a 'last chance'
  To try something new
  Treatment not available in the UK

Source: Culley et al. 2011

Accessing different forms of treatment abroad increases opportunities for women and couples, where restrictions in the UK may prevent such possibilities. Examining the reasons why women and couples travel abroad enables us to gain a deeper understanding of their experiences. For example, Culley et al. (2011) report that women decide to travel abroad for different reasons (see Box 1.4).

Delaying childbirth has been commonly reported in the media as a reason for the increasing numbers of older women seeking assisted reproductive methods. Whilst an older mother is defined in obstetric terms as a woman over the age of thirty-five (RCOG 2010), the trend to give birth later in life is prevalent across Western countries. Live births to women over the age of forty have trebled over the last twenty years, from 9,336 in 1989 to 26,976 in 2009 (ONS 2010).

The physical and emotional aspects of becoming a mother later in life are currently under-researched. However, Cooke et al. (2011) report the views and experiences of older women who use ART. Read the extract in Box 1.5 and consider the questions that follow it.

Box 1.5 Older women and the use of ART

Cooke et al. (2011) explored women's views and experiences of delayed childbearing by conducting interviews with a purposive sample of eighteen women aged thirty-five and over. Three groups of women were the focus of this study; women with no children (n=6); women pregnant with their first child (n=6); and women who had no children who were attending a fertility clinic (n=6). The data below reflect some of the experiences of the six women who had no children and were attending a fertility clinic for treatment.

> 'I feel that I've not given [my husband] anything . . . I just feel bad about myself . . . I didn't know I had not very good eggs . . . I don't think I would have married any man.'
> (Mary, aged thirty-seven)
>
> 'You feel like you're not a woman, that is the worst thing . . . you can't do what you're put on earth to do.' (Emma, aged thirty-seven)
>
> 'There's so many hurdles isn't there? You get over one, then there's another one and another one, and another one . . .' (Lisa, aged thirty-nine)
>
> 'Going back five months ago I wasn't going to go through this again, it was too straining . . . too demanding on everything, your emotions . . . the drugs and what it does to your body physically . . . I didn't realize when I was in the process of going through the full treatment, how much it took out of me, it really did.' (Izzie, aged thirty-seven)

(a) How do these quotes reflect the way in which women view themselves in relation to reproduction?
(b) How do women describe their experiences of the process of undergoing assisted reproductive technologies?
(c) What emotions are being expressed by women in this group?

The use of ART raises a number of issues about the meaning of motherhood in society and appears to be especially significant in relation to older mothers. Sociology helps us to understand some of the challenges experienced by women around reproduction and childbirth and provides explanations for how they can be addressed.

Summary

- Sociology is more than just 'common sense' in that it challenges obvious, everyday explanations.
- The sociological imagination can enable midwives to move beyond common-sense explanations to develop a more critical, reflexive approach to midwifery practice.
- Sociology is part of a model of higher education whereby midwives gain vocational and practical competencies, as well as critical thinking skills, through the application of academic study to practice.
- Sociologists draw on different paradigms to explore the social, moral, economic and political context in which women, and others, experience reproductive health.

Questions for discussion

- How will you develop *your* sociological imagination? Reread this part of the chapter (pp. 9–10) and then think of two or three other examples of private 'troubles' and public 'issues'.
- How might sociology help you understand women's experiences of reproductive health?
- Try to identify two or three other sociological studies and reflect on how these could influence your practice as a midwife.

Further reading

Giddens, A. and Sutton, P. 2013 *Sociology*. 7th edn. Polity.
This popular book, already in its 7th edition, will provide you with a good, basic general grounding in sociological theory and method.
Earle, S. and Letherby, G. (eds) 2003 *Gender, Identity and Reproduction: Social Perspectives*. Palgrave Macmillan.
This edited book explores the sociology of human reproduction and examines a range of interesting and wide-ranging topics, including: in/fertility, infant feeding, childbirth experiences; being sterilized and childfree; and experiences of the menopause.
Stacey, M. (ed.) 1992 *Changing Human Reproduction: Social Science Perspectives*. Sage.
This book is a classic of its time and yet still very relevant. It is a

good read and has a useful introductory chapter which explains a social science perspective on the study of human reproduction. This is an edited book exploring a range of issues, including assisted reproduction, unexplained infertility, gamete donation and assisted kinship.

2 Sociology of Midwifery

Edwin van Teijlingen

Key issues:

- The occupation of midwifery.
- Theories of profession and professional development.
- The place of public health in midwifery from the perspective of sociology.
- Medical and social models of childbirth and pregnancy.
- The culture of midwifery.
- The politics of midwifery.

By the end of this chapter you should be able to:

- Discuss the reasons why sociologists study midwifery and maternity care.
- Discuss key features of midwifery as an occupation.
- Outline the two key sociological theories on the professions.
- Outline the key differences between a social and medical model of pregnancy and childbirth.
- Discuss cultural issues within midwifery.

Introduction

Following on from Chapter 1 and the focus on sociology *for* midwives, this chapter explores the sociology *of* midwifery. This is where sociologists have focused their study on midwives, the practice of midwifery or maternity services.

The chapters in Parts 2 and 3 of this book cover sociology 'for' midwifery, that is, they focus on some aspects of sociology which can be helpful for midwives' understanding of the world, including their working environment. For example, sociological teaching on inequalities and health, or stigma and discrimination, can help midwives understand the disadvantages that women and their families experience in their daily lives. In this way, sociology *for* midwifery can help midwives further develop their understanding and skills. Sociology *of* midwifery, as opposed to sociology *for* midwives, addresses midwifery in its widest sense and is the topic under examination here, where the sociological topics highlighted are: the study of midwifery as an occupation or a profession; notions of culture in the world of midwifery; midwives and public health; and the medical versus social model of pregnancy and birth.

Sociologists study people in groups (e.g., the workplace, educational institutions, communities, the family) with reference to differences between them (e.g., gender, 'race' and ethnicity, social class, dis/ability and so on), and factors related to culture and structure in society. Sociology addresses questions around the interactions between midwives and women (and their significant others, i.e., partners and/or mothers), using maternity services or the 'midwife–mother relationship', which has now been widely written about in midwifery (see Kirkham 2010a). Sociologists also study the role of gender, 'race' and ethnicity, etc., and its impact on midwifery. Activity 2.1 highlights the gender imbalance in midwifery.

Activity 2.1: Gender in midwifery and obstetrics

Throughout the world the majority of midwives are female, yet the gender imbalance is less profound in obstetrics, the branch of medicine that deals with complexities in pregnancy and childbirth. A common-sense answer to most midwives being female is often that pregnancy and childbirth are women's business. If this is true, then most of the obstetricians, if not all, would also be female.

So the question a sociologist would ask is:

What other social or cultural factors influence the gender balance in maternity care providers?

(a) What do you think of the question above?
(b) What do you think are the key explanations/factors for midwives being mostly female?

Occupation or Profession?

One of the key concepts sociologists are interested in is the study of work and particularly that of the professions. It is clear that not all occupations in society are the same. Moreover, not all occupations are equally valued within society. We all recognize that a shop assistant, a midwife and a government minister are different types of occupations. Also, we understand that some occupations do, or can, compete with each other for customers/clients: for example, bus drivers and taxi drivers or midwives and obstetricians. Some occupations are perceived to be different and 'special' and we refer to them as 'professions'. So one of the questions sociology asks is 'To what extent is midwifery a special occupation?' or 'What factors make an occupation a "profession"?' With this in mind, I now outline two different approaches to analysing occupations within sociology. The two key sociological theories of the professions that sociology offers are listed below.

(a)　trait theory, identifying key attributes of a profession
(b)　competition and conflict theory.

Table 2.1 Key attributes of a profession

1. Systematic theory.
2. Authority recognized by its clientele.
3. Broader community sanction.
4. Code of ethics.
5. Professional culture sustained by formal sanctions.

Professions: the traditional view

Starting with trait theory, nearly sixty years ago Greenwood (1957) identified the five key features listed in Table 2.1. Sociologists would argue that refuse collectors and bus drivers differ from doctors and midwives in that the latter are thought to be motivated by working for the greater good of society, rather than purely for personal or financial gain.

Midwifery in many high-income countries such as Australia, the United Kingdom (UK) and the Netherlands incorporates all the five features above. We observe that (1) midwifery has a theoretical foundation; (2) women come to midwives for advice and delivery of care, and the government seeks advice from its national association, such as the Royal College of Midwives (RCM) in the UK; (3) legally no one is allowed to assist a woman in birthing a baby, other than in an emergency, unless qualified to do so (in the UK a midwife or a doctor), but also pregnant women in the Netherlands, the UK or Australia would 'normally' expect to get maternity care from a midwife; (4) there exists a code of practice and ethics, which in the UK is governed by the Nursing & Midwifery Council (NMC); and (5) midwifery has a powerful professional organization in the RCM (van Teijlingen 2012).

Professions: a more critical view

The second theoretical view sees professions as competing for power and control over, for example, other occupations, policymakers and clients (Turner 1995; see also further reading). Medicine is often viewed as one of the archetypal professions, in that it has been successful in claiming and dominating an area of work, via state-sanctioned **monopoly power** (Freidson 1970). Indeed, making the state an ally or instrument in inter-professional rivalries is a common tactic among professions (see also Chapter 4). Doctors have also managed to exclude other health-care workers from certain areas of health work, and to define the areas of work that are available to them (Witz 1992).

This conflict approach to professional development highlights differences between occupations. For example, a key characteristic of the division of labour in maternity care is the control and influence that midwives exercise over their own work (autonomy) and that of allied occupations such as maternity care assistants and midwifery support workers. Midwifery has developed into a more autonomous profession

monopoly power control of sphere of work by one group that can prevent others gaining access

than a few decades ago, with its own education and a growth of professors of midwifery at many UK universities, its own field of practice and academic knowledge, control over its members and some power to exclude other occupations from its area of expertise. The maintenance of midwifery as a profession requires the continuing exercise of dominance over allied and competing occupations. Midwifery in the UK has an officially approved monopoly of the right to treat pregnant women and support the birth of babies (shared with doctors), as it is illegal for a layperson to assist at the birth other than in an emergency. In the UK, midwives are more often than not the most senior health-care professional attending the birth (NHS Information Centre 2010).

📋 Activity 2.2: Jobs, occupations and professions

Let us look at two very important types of work in society:

1. Work done by people who drive passengers in a bus or on a train. These are very important public-service jobs which help many people travel to their work, the hospital or the shops.
2. Work done by people who assist women to birth their babies, that is, midwives.

Fundamental questions for sociologists studying professions are:

(a) Why do we regard some occupations to be 'jobs'/'occupations' and others 'professions'?
(b) Why is driving a bus or a train seen as a 'job' and being a midwife a 'profession'?
List the key differences between (i) a job and (ii) a profession.
(c) Taking into account the differences you have listed, is there an argument for midwifery *not* to be seen as a profession?

Before we look deeper into competition between occupations, it is important to note that competition for service users (women using maternity services) does not happen in the same way that automobile companies like Volkswagen and BMW compete for customers to buy their cars. Competition can be for a range of resources and not just money; it can also be for time allocation, status and control. Analysing professions as competing bodies or organizations raises a few interesting issues. One such question would be, for example, does this mean that professions are not, or are no longer, working for the greater good? If midwives are engaged in some kind of continual professional competition this raises another question: 'Who are their competitors?' A further question to bear in mind when trying to understand inter-professional competition is the following: 'If there is inter-professional competition, is there anybody overseeing this or even acting as a "referee" between the competing occupations?' In some countries the regional hospital board, the ministry of health, or currently in the UK senior NHS officials, act as referees as they decide, for instance, how work is organized and who carries it out, or how funding is made available for postnatal home visits, or withdrawn from them.

Some sociologists regard midwifery, nursing, occupational therapy, physiotherapy and other comparable professions as not quite full-blown professions. To illustrate this 'nearly there' status, Etzioni (1969) coined the phrase 'semi-professions'. In the more traditional approach, a semi-profession is defined as an occupation in which one or some of the traits that define a profession are lacking or not fully developed. Under the more critical approach, a semi-profession is defined in terms of its power and control over its markets and competitors. Hence, van der Hulst and I defined a semi-profession as an occupation that is less powerful and enjoys less autonomy than a 'profession', but is more powerful and has more autonomy than a 'trade' (van Teijlingen and van der Hulst 1995). Central to the definition of semi-profession is gender. Etzioni described two defining features of a semi-profession as: their existence in bureaucratic organizations and the prevalence of women, both of which hinder the development of full professional status. Critiques of the semi-professions approach (for example, Witz 1992) argue that it is deterministic, as it implies a static situation with little or no opportunity for professional development.

The whole notion of 'profession' has been criticized from a gender perspective by Davies, who argues that it 'celebrates and sustains a **masculinist** vision' (Davies 1996: 669). Witz, too, argues for a 'less androcentric domain' (Witz 1992: 64). This is because the characteristics that are valued in professions and lead to the attainment of professional status, such as competition and monopoly, are traditionally associated with masculinity. More feminine qualities that are associated with the caring professions, such as cooperation and negotiation, are less highly valued and do not endow practitioners with professional status.

masculinist conforming to values associated with being masculine

The Midwifery Profession

The historical development of midwifery

Traditionally, in all parts of the world, pregnancy and childbirth were 'women's business' (at least from the perspective of care and delivery, given that men are always involved at the point of conception), and in some countries this is still the case. Yet in many Western countries we have seen a move to more (male) obstetric-led care in pregnancy and childbirth, and in some of those a move back to midwifery-led care, to a greater or lesser degree. Donnison (1977) and Witz (1992) have put forward explanations for this within the UK, based on the development of professions and the ability of some to claim and monopolize an area of work.

From the middle of the eighteenth century, men began to enter the previously female domain of childbirth, and Donnison (1977)

elucidates a number of factors that coincided to facilitate this. First, competition between medical men (and they were exclusively men) for patients was high, and to be present at the birth of a baby could give access as the provider of continuing health care to the family. Second, men had higher status, regardless of their skill, and it became fashionable to employ them rather than the local midwife. Possibly most important was the development of forceps, which enabled the successful delivery of a baby where previously mother and baby would have died. However, these were not available to midwives, their use being restricted to medical men. Midwives attempted to protect themselves and counter the expansion of men in childbirth by improving education and skill, and although the men could not get their practice established within the medical profession, the situation changed in the nineteenth century to their advantage. A new type of doctor had emerged, the general practitioner (GP) who wanted to offer midwifery as a package of general family care. In addition, there were obstetricians, by now a recognized specialism within medicine, who saw most forms of intervention during labour as their domain. The first group wanted to exclude midwives from independent practice altogether and to absorb midwifery into their own sphere of work, with female workers providing a monthly nursing service. The latter group wanted midwives registered and working independently with their own group of clients, but in highly prescribed and deskilled circumstances (Donnison 1977; Witz 1992). Both groups wanted to control the work of female attendants during labour and the postnatal period, and to restrict their area of competence. The 1886 Medical Act included midwifery as a requisite for medical registration, so that doctors had an educational advantage over midwives, and this was reinforced by the educational requirements for midwives contained within the Midwives Act 1902. The Act did provide for registration of midwives and independent practice, albeit within strict boundaries, which is in contrast to the USA where similar struggles resulted in the practice of midwifery being proscribed and childbirth being completely incorporated into medical practice.

A global perspective

We can look at the bigger picture of midwifery by taking a global perspective. Midwives have slightly different roles, and their salaries, as well as their legal and social status, differ greatly in countries across the world. Internationally, *The State of the World's Midwifery 2011: Delivering Health, Saving Lives* (UNFPA 2011: v) called for the protection of the title of 'midwife'; to 'establish its scope of practice'; 'establish criteria for entry into the profession'; and 'license and relicense midwives, maintain codes of ethics and codes of conduct, and manage sanctioning'. All these actions suggest to a sociologist an occupation that is trying to claim its ground by attempting to control who can, and cannot be, 'a recognized midwife'. The report also calls for governments to 'recognize midwifery as a distinct profession, core to the provision of maternal and newborn health services, and promote it as a career . . . invest in human resource management to develop and maintain competencies, manage entries and exits, and improve data on the practising midwifery workforce' (UNFPA 2011: v).

One of the countries where midwifery has not made much of a political inroad is Nepal. In Nepal, midwifery is regulated under nursing, which is not conducive for the development of the profession (Bogren et al. 2013). The Midwifery Society of Nepal (MIDSON), supported by the RCM and other sister midwifery organizations abroad, is urging the government of Nepal to establish proper midwifery education and recognize midwifery as an autonomous profession.

📋 Activity 2.3: Sociology of the professions

In your opinion, with reference to your own experience, which two types of sociological theory of the professions are more applicable to midwifery?

Considering the more competition-focused theories, which occupations (other than obstetrics) are in competition with midwifery and why?

Can you name some initiatives the midwifery profession has undertaken recently as a group to make the profession stronger? You may need to look at some of the professional journals to answer this.

Midwives and 'burn-out'

You may be aware of some of the recent publications on 'burn-out' in midwives. You might have come across newspaper headlines such as *Midwives are overworked and underpaid*. A combination of various social and political issues such as the increasing number of tasks allocated to midwives (see 'Public Health and Midwifery' below), a shortage of midwives internationally, the need to care for women with a wide range of social and health problems and, in the UK, a growing birth rate have increased the pressure of work for practising midwives. As several studies have highlighted, one of the results appears to be burn-out (Sandall 1997; Ball et al. 2002; Hunter 2004; Deery 2005; Hunter and Deery 2009).

Burn-out has its theoretical foundation in the discipline of psychology. Burn-out comprises three elements: (a) emotional exhaustion; (b) depersonalization; and (c) reduced personal accomplishment (Maslach et al. 2001). For a sociologist, one interesting question would be: 'Why do certain professions appear to suffer more from burn-out than others?' If all professions were roughly the same in status and in the level of control that its members share over their work, then burn-out levels need not be too different between midwives and obstetricians working in the same hospital or geographical region of the country. The fact is that midwives are much more likely to experience burn-out, and we can consider those factors in the occupational **hierarchy** or

hierarchy
members of an organization are ranked or categorized according to ability or status, from highest to lowest, or vice versa

inter-professional competition that may help us explain this phenomenon. Kirkham (2010c), for example, points to the tension for midwives between meeting the needs of the individual and the efficient running of the organization, as resulting in conflicting loyalties. Warwick (2011) adds that a historically high birth rate, increasingly complex pregnancies and births, and staff shortages add to the pressure on midwives, often leading to compromises in safety and burn-out. The relentless demands of the labour ward mean that midwives cannot always offer the continuing care to birthing women that they consider good practice (see also Chapter 10). Midwives now also have responsibility for the actions of support staff, such as maternity support workers, which adds to stress.

Public health and midwifery

One source of stress is that midwives are increasingly expected to take on additional roles, especially within the NHS. Over the past few decades, the government has added more and more public-health tasks to the midwives' workload. Decisions to increase the public-health role of midwives have been largely political rather than based on clinical evidence. In their care provision to women in pregnancy and childbirth, they are expected to deal with a wide range of problems, including the misuse of alcohol, drugs and/or tobacco; increasing rates of obesity; domestic violence; poverty and inequality (see also Chapter 10); and mental health (see also Chapter 14) (Warwick 2011). Midwifery is an interesting health-care discipline for sociologists, sitting somewhere in the middle of the spectrum of health service providers because it includes large elements of both prevention and clinical care. This position is shared with very few other disciplines. Midwives offer a range of care and cure to women and babies, similar to many doctors and nurses, but they are also expected to offer a wide range of health promotion and prevention advice and intervention, similar to many health educators/promoters. Some have argued that at a time when there is a great shortage of midwives, increasing their public-health responsibilities may challenge midwives' more 'traditional' roles in providing midwifery and maternity care. Others have argued that some public-health roles may compromise the clinical care aspects of the midwifery role (Prowse and Prowse 2008).

Sociological Models of (Maternity) Care

Sociologists analyse approaches to health and health care in terms of a 'medical' versus a 'social' model or, in this field, a midwifery model. As pregnancy and birth are 'biological and physiological events which are very much embedded in a social and cultural setting' (van Teijlingen 2003: 120), these are good examples to highlight the use and misuse of the medical and social model. Making the distinction between a medical and a social model of a social phenomenon is not exclusive to midwifery (see also Chapter 6). Over the past decades, researchers have pointed to the existence of a medical and social model in alcohol misuse, obesity, sex and eating disorders, to name but a few phenomena.

Modern Western society has a slightly paradoxical view of pregnancy. On the one hand, the average woman in childbirth is not ill because pregnancy is not an illness. On the other hand, pregnant women are deemed to need a lot of health care throughout pregnancy and childbirth. Table 2.2 highlights how the medical and social model can help explain our collective attitudes towards pregnancy and childbirth, which are biological and physiological events, occurring in most women's lives, and which have been taken into the medical domain. Those who support the idea of a medical model often claim something like 'birth is only safe in retrospect', while those more in line with the social model would make the counterclaim that 'every pregnancy is normal unless there are indications that something is wrong' or 'childbirth is in principle a normal physiological event'. The definition aligned with the medical model suggests a pregnant woman needs medical backup and a hospital birth 'just in case something goes wrong'. The social model suggests that pregnancy happens in most women's lives, it might need some 'checking-up' and advice giving, but for most it will go well without medical intervention.

The notion that pregnancy and childbirth are an 'illness' also influences the accompanying perception of inherent risk (see Chapter 7). It is worthwhile considering how women from different ethnic groups and/or other cultures may regard pregnancy, childbirth or even babies. People's concern about risk in childbirth reflects the link between parenthood and social identity, as well as deriving from awareness of the possibility of death or injury to mother or baby (van Teijlingen 2005). To highlight some of the bullet points in Table 2.2, those adhering to a medical model would state that since pregnancy is only safe in retrospect, risk selection is not possible. If you believe that you cannot predict which pregnancy is going to be 'normal' and which may need some obstetric intervention, you cannot allocate pregnant women into a low-risk and a high-risk group, that is, every woman is potentially at risk. Basically, what proponents of a medical model are saying is that everybody is 'at risk'. You will learn more about this in Chapter 7.

A second example would be the difference in attitude as to who is in control, that is, is the provision of care centred around the needs of the maternity care provider ('doctor-centred' or 'midwife-centred'), or around the needs of the pregnant woman and her family ('women-centred')? The choices available to a pregnant woman regarding, for example, place of birth or birthing position would vary according to who is considered to be at the centre of the care. Thus, choices can be

Table 2.2 Overview of medical and social model of birth and midwifery

Medical model	Social/midwifery model
• Doctor centred • Objective • Male • Body-mind dualism • Pregnancy: only normal in retrospect • Risk selection is not possible • Statistical/biological approach • Biomedical focus • Medical knowledge is exclusionary • Intervention • Public • Outcome: aims at live, healthy mother and baby.	• Women/patient centred • Subjective • Female • Holistic • Birth: normal physiological process • Risk selection is possible • Psychosocial focus • Knowledge is not exclusionary • Observation • Private • Outcome: aims at live, healthy mother, baby and satisfaction of individual needs of mother/couple.

Source: van Teijlingen 2005

restricted in hospital because the care provision is centred too much around issues related to the institution: for example, the midwives' rota, NHS health-and-safety rules, labour ward policies and guidelines, and statistical notions of risk (see Kirkham 2010b; Fahy et al. 2008).

One important aspect of the social versus medical model of pregnancy is that the situation is not static. Over time, or in a different situation, the social model may become more dominant than the medical model, and vice versa. The move from adhering to a more social model towards a more medical model, where medical diagnosis and treatment are 'taking over', is referred to as 'medicalization', while the reverse is known as 'demedicalization'. Conrad (2005: 3) refers to medicalization as a process which defines 'a problem in medical terms, usually as an illness or disorder, or using a medical intervention to treat it'. A classic text in sociology is Ann Oakley's (1980) study of childbirth, in which she describes how the medicalization of childbirth contributed to the **alienation** of women from their bodies during pregnancy and labour.

alienation
distancing of an individual from self or others

The way we see or define the issue or problem also determines the way we try to solve it. That is, if we view childbirth as low risk, from the perspective of a social model we will attempt to treat raised blood pressure in a pregnant woman slightly differently than if we view childbirth from the perspective of a medical model. For example, the model that

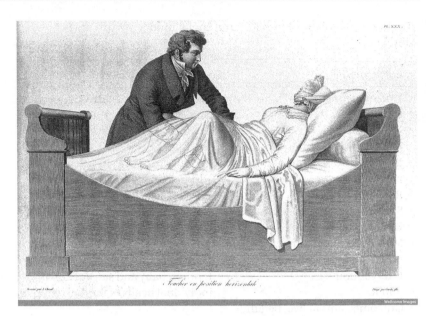

Figure 2.1 Nineteenth century sketch of a male doctor with patient. In the nineteenth century the midwifery profession came under threat as the delivery of babies became a male-centred profession

is employed has bearing on the notion of risk, or the way risk is perceived by the midwife and by the pregnant woman and/or her partner. The way we define risk in childbirth determines how society organizes maternity care: for example, what is generally seen as the safest/best place of birth and the most appropriate maternity care provider (see Edwards 2005). What we see as 'risky' also changes over time. These changes take place not only individually when a midwife or a new mother gains more experience and skill, but also collectively over time (see MacKenzie Bryers and van Teijlingen 2010; see also Chapter 7).

📋 Activity 2.4: Case study

Jane McIver, a community midwife in a very rural part of the Scottish Highlands, has just received a call from Ayesha Kamal, a thirty-four-year-old married woman who has just moved into the area from the USA. Ayesha is pregnant for the second time; she lives with her husband, a computer specialist, and their small toddler in a little town north of Inverness. She had her first baby in the USA in a highly technologized hospital under the care of an obstetrician in Dallas, Texas. The small town where she now lives has its own small midwife-led maternity unit, and Jane is affiliated with this community-based maternity unit. Jane likes working in the women-friendly low-tech environment and she is quite proud of this maternity unit.

At her booking appointment at Ayesha's own home, Ayesha praises the Texan obstetric hospital highly, even though she did not get the Caesarean Section she had asked for. She appears to be somehow dissatisfied with

Jane (whom she has never met before) as she had really wanted to see an obstetrician for her booking to make her plans for the birth known. During the booking visit Jane begins to feel increasingly uneasy, but then she remembers something she had learnt during her training from sociology. She recalls the social-medical model of pregnancy and childbirth, then she remembers how the theoretical model one holds can affect one's explanations of the issue as well as one's expectations of most likely/best solutions. Jane tries to pick up snippets of information from Ayesha, to establish to what extent Ayesha's fits a more medical model.

What kind of questions would it be helpful for Jane to ask:

- To help understand Ayesha's perspective on childbirth?
- To tailor her maternity and midwifery care for Ayesha?

Having presented the medical and social models as **dualistic** models, it is important to acknowledge that working practices are not fixed. We know that people can change, and that individual midwives or whole maternity units can change their working practices over a period of time, or in different situations. Nor do most people adhere completely to the pure form of any particular model, hence all working practice is somewhere in between two extremes of a continuum, that is, between a complete social model and a total medical one. Finally, not all professionals within a profession sit on the same part of the continuum. In other words, not all doctors adhere to the medical model and not all midwives fit neatly into the social model. Figure 2.2 highlights a few hypothetical examples of where maternity care providers could be placed along the continuum. There will be midwives whom you have met on your placements who had quite different views of midwifery and childbirth from each other. Each of them may have aligned themselves

dualistic
two inconsistent but coexisting belief systems

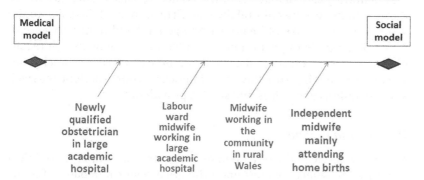

A continuum of practice from medical to social model

| Medical model | | | | Social model |

Newly qualified obstetrician in large academic hospital — Labour ward midwife working in large academic hospital — Midwife working in the community in rural Wales — Independent midwife mainly attending home births

Figure 2.2 Maternity care providers placed on a continuum of medical/social model

and their practice slightly more towards either the social or the medical model. It might be useful for you to think where you would put yourself in your thinking about the various characteristics of the medical and social models. Ask yourself if you are leaning more towards the notion of a medical model or a social model of maternity care.

Culture and Society

Culture, to a sociologist, refers to 'a complex and constantly changing mix of attitudes and beliefs, uses of language and accent, and cultural practices relating to dress, food, marriage, birth, health, illness and death' (Taylor and Field (eds) 2007: 70). Thus, culture is not the common-sense notion of art, in the form of, for example, seventeenth-century paintings, sculptures, opera, choirs and Shakespearean theatre. Nor is culture something that is just associated with other people, for example, from other countries. Understanding culture is important since it can help explain the attitudes and behaviour of some people. For instance, cultural expectations prescribe what some newly birthed women cannot do or what the woman should eat or drink. Understanding these taboos would help the midwife to give culturally appropriate advice to the new mother.

Culture is, of course, part of our everyday life, thus we might identify a culture of bullying among community midwives or in hospital (see Kirkham 1999), or a culture of racial discrimination on a ward, or a culture of home births in the Netherlands. Organizations or parts of it can develop a culture that limits health-care providers' ability to deliver good-quality patient care. For example, the Francis Report, investigating the Mid-Staffordshire NHS Foundation Trust, found a 'closed culture' with a lack of information-sharing and a focus on processes rather than quality of care (Francis 2013). The same report speaks of a 'culture of fear' and a 'culture of secrecy' as factors which resulted in poor care and, in turn, unnecessary deaths at that hospital.

While we all live in a particular national culture, it must be noted that maternity care in many countries is taking place in societies where there is an increasing cultural diversity. The impact of diversity on the provision and uptake of health care in general and maternity care in particular, and its impact on health outcomes, have been well recognized. Your own culture is likely to be influenced by your ethnicity and social class, which in turn have an influence on your experiences as well as expectations of services and service providers.

Politics and policies

Maternity services do not operate in an organizational or political vacuum. Midwifery touches upon the great political debates of abortion, euthanasia of severely compromised babies, women's rights over their bodies vis-à-vis the rights of the unborn child, and many other ones. At the more mundane political level, health is a political play-ball, and so is maternity care. If policymakers decide to spend more money on IVF (in-vitro fertilization), there will be fewer resources available for other services, including maternity care (see Chapter 9). This is known as health-care rationing. If it occurs differentially across different areas of the country, it is commonly called 'a postcode lottery', in that where you live determines the services available to you. Similar political decisions have to be made at a national level; thus, if the UK government decides to spend more money on education or defence, there will be less available for the NHS and other state services such as border control and social work. This is true unless the government also decides to raise money in another way, such as through increased taxation. In 2011, the NHS was the third-largest employer in the world. Therefore, if the UK government decides to offer an increase in salaries for midwives, nurses, ambulance drivers or hospital porters lower than the national average, it may save a large sum of money overall (see also Chapter 4).

Politics is also part of our wider culture. Professional organizations such as the RCM make their own policies that govern their members, while at the same time lobbying in an attempt to influence the government to improve policies and increase funding to strengthen maternity services and the position of midwifery as a profession. At the same time, the RCM is also trade-union representing its members when arguing with the government and relevant NHS bodies about increasing midwives' pay, pensions and working conditions.

Last, but not least, politics is also part of the daily work of a midwife. Decisions whether or not a pregnant woman 'can' have a home birth, or is 'allowed' a water birth, are part of the power politics surrounding childbirth (see also Chapter 7). Whether a midwife is blamed for a drug mistake or treated as someone who needs support is not simply a clinical decision based on guidelines and evidence. Furthermore, there can be decisions based on policies that lack evidence, managers who are afraid to take any risk, or organizational cultures that fear change. Edwards and colleagues (2011) highlighted two very different gaps in policy. First, there is the major gap between government policies that promise women choice in childbirth, and the failure to fund appropriate midwifery services at national level to fulfil those choices. Second, there is the gap between government policies that promise women choice in childbirth, and local and regional policies that make the lives of midwives who work hard to fulfil the wishes of the women they care for very difficult. Edwards and colleagues (2011) refer to midwives being bullied into offering maternity care that fits the local hospital system rather than offering women the choices they would like to make.

From this discussion, we have seen how sociology of midwifery offers sociological insights into the working of the midwifery profession, and the work of the midwife in relation to other health- and social-care professionals as well as the women and families in her care. Sociology helps to use a wider perspective that takes into consideration culture and politics, be it at the international, national, local or personal level.

Summary

- This chapter was concerned with the sociology of midwifery.
- Midwifery is a specific occupation, which has certain characteristics of a profession.
- The history of midwifery shaped the current occupation.
- The medical and social models of midwifery exist on a continuum.
- Politics is an integral part of any health-care profession, not just at national political levels but also locally on the ward or in the community.

Questions for discussion

- Do midwives perpetuate or challenge the medical model of midwifery?
- Do you think that midwives have control of their working environment? Discuss how you think midwives may be constrained by (a) obstetricians and (b) managers.
- Can you recall one or two decisions regarding midwifery care which you have witnessed, and which might have been partly driven by political considerations or financial considerations rather than clinical ones?
- How do you think that an influx of men into midwifery might change the occupation?

Further reading

Mander, R. and Murphy-Lawless, J. 2013 *The Politics of Maternity*. Routledge.
  Midwifery practice takes place within a social and political context, and this book explores the complexity of childbirth for both mothers and midwives in contemporary societies. It examines political issues such as power at the level of the individual and the state, and philosophical positions of relevance to midwifery practice.
Kitzinger, S. 2012 Rediscovering the Social Model of Childbirth, *Birth* 39/4: 301–4.
  Sheila Kitzinger reminds us that an assumption is often made that women in a traditional birth culture are bound to benefit by its replacement with a medical system. In a technocratic system, birth usually takes place in an alien environment among strangers, with routine use of interventions. Some women feel traumatized after such experiences. In this paper, Kitzinger urges us to rediscover woman-to-woman support, celebrate birth as a social process, and acknowledge that it is a political issue.

MacKenzie Bryers, H. and van Teijlingen, E. 2010 Risk, theory, social and medical models: a critical analysis of the concept of risk in maternity care. *Midwifery* 26/5: 488–96.

This paper explores the way maternity services changed from a social to a medical model over the twentieth century and suggests that the risk agenda was part of this process. The paper concludes that current UK maternity services policy to promote normality results in effective risk management screening women suitable for birth in community maternity units or home birth: however, although current policy advocates a return to this more social model, policy implementation is slow in practice.

3 Method, Methodology and Epistemology

Gayle Letherby

Key issues:

- The relationship between the research process and its product.
- Starting the process (of research) – including identifying topics and questions, choosing a method, generating questions and obtaining ethical approval.
- Doing research – including issues of power, emotion, involvement and detachment.
- Data analysis and re/presentation.
- Impact, or 'making research count'.

By the end of this chapter you should be able to:

- Understand the significance of the relationship between the research process and the research product.
- Identify the things that need to be done before the beginning of a research project and reflect on some of the dilemmas that might occur during a project.
- Discuss issues of re/presentation of data with reference to the possible impact of research.
- Plan a research project of your own.

Introduction

method(s)
tools we use for data gathering

methodology
reflection on methods used to collect data

epistemology
the theory of knowledge produced through research

If sociological research is to be of any significance – that is, useful to midwives and to the women (and men) and babies they care for – it is important to pay careful attention to the way in which data are collected, analysed and presented. Sociological research about reproduction and reproductive experience, from pre-conception through to early parenthood, may focus on the perspective and experience of the mother, her baby(ies) and significant others (for example, her partner and/or her mother); alternatively, the focus may be on the perspective and experience of the midwife and other health-care professionals, or with reference to various or all of these groups. When planning, undertaking and reporting on research, the **method(s)**, **methodology** and **epistemology** are all important. Thus, it is essential to consider both 'doing research' and the philosophy of research practice, as well as the relationship between the

research process and the **research product**. In other words, we need to recognize that the knowing/doing relationship is intimately connected because what we do during the research process affects the product that we get (Letherby 2003, 2004; Letherby et al. 2013). Researching reproduction and reproductive experience may suggest particular methods and militate against the use of others. Our methodological approach to research and experience of the research process may also be tempered by the respondent group. Issues of power, emotion, sensitivity, involvement and detachment are relevant here, as in all research; so too is the acknowledgement of difference and diversity and of research impact.

research process
step-by-step
process of
undertaking
research

research product
data, findings,
results

I begin the main body of this chapter with a consideration of a sociological discussion of the process/product relationship within research, before turning to a discussion of the main issues to consider when preparing for and doing research and analysing data. Then I turn to a consideration of whether or not research can and should 'make a difference'. Debate about method, methodology and epistemology in the last fifty years or so has highlighted both the 'messiness' of the research process and the potential value of the research product for understanding social experiences. Telling the story of the research process along with the presentation of research findings and results adds to both the accountability and status of the knowledge that researchers produce (Stanley and Wise 1993; Letherby 2003; Letherby et al. 2013).

The Relationship between the Research Process and Product

Until relatively recently, in both sociology and health care, quantitative methods were strongly believed to be the best, indeed only, methods to use. It was argued that taking a quantitative approach was the only way to ensure objective and value-free data collection and analysis. From this perspective, the researcher was viewed as a neutral observer so that different researchers exposed to the same data could replicate results, meaning that generalization from research to wider social and natural populations was possible. In other words, this 'scientific' approach was linear and orderly (Stanley and Wise 1993; Kelly et al. 1994) and enabled the 'objective' collection of facts by a value-neutral researcher (Stanley and Wise 1993; Letherby 2003). Historically, this form of research was known as positivism (although it is important to remember that not all quantitative researchers are aiming for positivism/a 'scientific' approach (see Oakley 1998 for further discussion). There has been, and is, much criticism of the use of numbers to 'prove facts' in social life, and qualitative methods are often seen as a response/critique to the so-called 'scientific' approach. Qualitative methods focus on the 'experiential' in the belief that the best way to find out about people is to let them 'speak for themselves' (Stanley and Wise 1993). The use of qualitative research is also seen by some as a way of giving respondents more control over the research process. Qualitative researchers, then, are concerned to generate data grounded in the experience of respondents. Members of the medical community were slower than sociologists to embrace the use of qualitative methods, yet, despite some continuing debate as to their value, qualitative methods are now frequently used in nursing and midwifery, and are acknowledged as providing quality outcomes directly applicable to practice activity (Thorne et al. 1997; Annells 2007).

However, it is important not to rule out *any* methods and approaches, and not to view quantitative and qualitative approaches as 'mutually exclusive ideal types' (Oakley 1998: 709). Cautioning against the choice of favourite methods without proper consideration of the research aims and objectives, Liz Kelly et al. (1994) argue that appropriate methods should be selected to suit research programmes, rather than research programmes being chosen to 'fit' favourite techniques. Ann Oakley (2004) agrees and suggests that the most important criterion for choosing a particular research method is its fit with the research question or questions, and not its relationship to academic arguments about methods. Jaqueline Scott (2010) details ways in which a mixed method approach can add to our understanding. She suggests that qualitative research enables us, for example, to explore how policy contexts influence the opportunities and constraints that shape people's lives and assist us in understanding people's experiences in particular settings. On the other hand, quantitative research enables us to identify the patterns and processes by which inequalities – related to gender, 'race' and ethnicity and other social differences – are passed on and/or modified generationally.

objectivity
research that is unaffected by researchers' opinion(s)

As noted above, previous support for quantitative approaches related not least to supposed **objectivity**. There has been much debate amongst sociologists and others about both the possibility and desirability of objectivity. For example, Max Weber, Georg Simmel, Karl Mannheim, Michel Foucault and Howard Becker (see Scott in Letherby et al. 2013 for discussion here) have all considered the significance and impact of **subjectivity** within research. Recently, in challenging the possibility of an objective, value-free approach, a number of authors have attempted to redefine objectivity. Arguing for *situated objectivity*, Malcolm Williams (2005, 2013) claims that objectivity is socially situated and value laden. Richard Jenkins (2002) argues for *good enough objectivity* and insists that researchers need to keep their hard-won critical distance in order to do good research, whereas Tim May and Beth Perry (2011) urge us to undertake multi/interdisciplinary research and engage in *corroborative objectivity*. Since the 1980s, feminist researchers have been particularly influential in this debate. Sandra Harding (1993) suggests that knowledge and truth are partial and situated and influenced by power relations, Dorothy Smith (1999) insists that social science should abandon the 'pretence' of detached, objective knowledge, and Donna Haraway (1991) provides a critique of, and challenge to, gendered binaries that position masculinity as

subjectivity
researcher involvement and influence within research

objective and femininity as subjective. In my work, I have argued for a position I call **theorized subjectivity** (see Letherby 2003, 2013) – which requires the constant, critical interrogation of our personhood (all aspects of our intellectual, professional and personal identity) within the production of knowledge (from research). Rather than attempting to redefine objectivity, I have instead been concerned (and have concerns) with 'the pursuit for objectivity' as the starting point of any discussion of objectivity and subjectivity. I have argued that if, instead, we start by accepting our subjective position – the significance of our personhood within the research process – and try to understand the complexities of 'our influence', this 'super-sensitivity' to the relevance of the personhood of the researcher could 'feasibly lead to the conclusion that our work is closer to objectivity, in that our work, if not value-free, is value-explicit' (Letherby 2003: 71).

> **theorized subjectivity** argues for researcher vigilance regarding subjectivity

Beginning the Process

Starting with a consideration of the relationship between the process and the product of research demonstrates the political nature of the whole of the research process – how what we do affects what we get. The topics we choose to research, the methods used, the identity of respondents and the composition of the research team all affect the data collected and the meanings given to it. Many groups have an influence in determining what research is done in the area of reproduction and reproductive experience, including government-funding bodies, academics, health-care professionals and, increasingly, service users. This area of study is a popular one for sociologists, and other social scientists, such as psychologists and anthropologists, as well as an increasing number of midwives and other health-care professionals, are adopting sociological approaches and/or working in teams with sociologists and other social scientists.

📋 Activity 3.1: Identifying research priorities and building research capacity

Reporting on a scoping study commissioned by the UK National Coordinating Centre Service Delivery and Organization (NCCSDO) Research and Development (R&D), Fiona Ross and colleagues (2004) undertook focus groups with service-user representatives; semi-structured interviews with representatives from nursing, midwifery, medical, social care and allied health professionals, research commissioners, policymakers, educators, managers and researchers; and an analysis of relevant literature. From this, they identified five priority areas for research in nursing and midwifery service delivery and organization, as listed below.

- Appropriate, timely and effective interventions.
- Individualized services.

- Continuity of care.
- Staff capacity and quality.
- User involvement and participation.

Jennifer Fenwick et al. (2006) conducted research with midwives in five maternity hospitals in Perth, Australia, in an attempt to identify priorities for midwifery research. Fenwick and colleagues concluded that Western Australian midwives, like their national and international colleagues, are concerned about the delivery and organization of maternity services, the invisibility of the postnatal experience and how to operationalize evidence-based care in the clinical area.

With reference to research capacity-building, rather than research priorities, Tanya V. McCance et al. (2007: accessed online) begin by highlighting variability in definitions:

Research capacity has been defined very specifically in the literature as that which relates to the ability to conduct research. Finch (2003) defined research capacity-building as 'enhancing the ability within a discipline or professional group to undertake high-quality research' (p. 427). A European scoping report also adopts a similar definition referring to research capacity, capability and culture as activity which 'typically involves training nurses as researchers' (Moreno-Casbas 2005: 9). Capacity-building, however, has been defined in much broader terms within some strategy documents as that which encompasses a range of research-related activities. McKenna and Mason (1998: 112) discuss research capacity in terms of becoming 'informed and critical consumers of research' at one level. They suggest, however, that it will only be a small percentage of individuals in any given profession who will actually carry out research. Similarly, the Scottish Executive (2002) discusses levels of involvement ranging from developing research awareness to acting as research collaborators, but highlights the existence of barriers to individuals attaining these competencies. This is reiterated by Newell (2002), from a nurse education perspective, who argues that nursing is currently in a weak position if a workforce is to be created that has the capacity to understand, undertake, disseminate and utilize research.

(a) Do you agree with the research priorities and problems related to research capacity-building identified above?
(b) Make a list of your own research priorities and research barriers.

Having identified an issue that needs researching and acquired the conditions and resources to undertake the study (e.g., the funding, the permission of the organization that employs the researcher(s)), those involved in the research then need to consider how to do the study. Keith Punch (1998, in Earle and Letherby 2008: 54) identifies good research questions as:

Clear They can be easily understood and are unambiguous.
Specific Their concepts are at a specific enough level to connect to data indicators.

Answerable We can see what data are required to answer them, and how the data will be obtained.

Interconnected They are related to each other in some meaningful way, rather than being unconnected.

Substantially relevant They are interesting and worthwhile questions for the investment of research effort.

The issue and the related questions may suggest quantitative methods (those that involve the collection and analysis of numbers), qualitative methods (involving collection, observation and analysis of words and actions), or a mixture of both. Both quantitative and qualitative researchers collect and analyse primary data (data collected for the current research project) and secondary data (already existing documents and artefacts). Examples of quantitative data collection involving primary methods are surveys (which include self-completed questionnaires) and structured interviews (which provide respondents with a limited range of questions and responses). Quantitative secondary data might include hospital or public records and previously administered and analysed questionnaires, which can all be (re)analysed by the researcher(s). Using quantitative research methods, we can measure the frequency of particular conditions and attitudes towards them – such as pregnancy loss or diabetes in pregnancy. Quantitative research methods also allow us to measure the amount of interaction between mothers and midwives. Following this, we can make comparisons between the experiences of individuals with reference to differences between them, such as the age, ethnicity or class position of the mother, or those with pregnancies defined as 'normal' or 'high risk'.

Qualitative primary methods include single, dyad (e.g., a pregnant woman and her partner) and focus group interviews, participant and non-participant observation (in person or online), exchange of letters or emails and respondent diary-keeping. Documents and artefacts, such as diaries and written autobiographies (not written for the purpose of the research), photographs, medical notes and texts, are all subject to secondary analysis. Qualitative methods focus on experience rather than measurement; for instance, instead of focusing on the amount of interaction between the midwife and mother, the qualitative researcher would be interested in the meanings of the interactions (Sharp 2005).

Mixed-method research, multi-method research, methodological pluralism or, as it is sometimes called, triangulation (which can include not only a combination of different methods but also/or a combination of methodological positions or theoretical viewpoints) is often the most desirable way to undertake research. This can include a mixture of the quantitative (such as a study using a questionnaire focusing on experience of Caesarean sections, and a review of hospital records recording the same data) and the qualitative (as in an

Figure 3.1 Qualitative research methods could include undertaking interviews with women at various stages of their pregnancy

ethnographic study of an antenatal or infertility clinic, involving non-participant observation, interviews and analysis of patient notes), or some combination of quantitative and qualitative methods (Miller and Brewer 2003).

Gaining ethical approval

Before the research can begin, the research project needs to be granted ethical approval. Depending on both the institutional base of the researcher(s) and the research site and population, this may be a multi-tiered process. Thus, for a sociologically informed project on mothers' and midwives' experience of new NICE guidelines, it may be necessary for a researcher to obtain ethical approval from their university ethics committee, from a locally based external ethics board that vets all projects involving health-care professionals, patients or patient records, and from the research and development committee of the hospital(s) concerned. In addition, most discipline areas have their own research ethics guidelines that influence research design and research process. (The British Sociological Association (BSA) Statement of Ethical Practice can be found at <http://www.britsoc.co.uk/>.) Ethics committees ensure that research projects protect the identity of respondents and that respondents are aware of what they are consenting to when they take part in research. This may be particularly difficult with individuals who are considered to be especially vulnerable (Wiles et al. 2005). The physical and emotional safety of respondents and researchers is also of concern. Increasingly, grant funders and ethics committees encourage or insist on the involvement of service users in project planning and execution (as members of project-steering groups, for example). There are some concerns as to the value of the current ethics procedure, not least because ethics committees may be 'not able to respond in a timely or constructive way to genuine ethical concerns which unfold during the course of a study' (Rossiter, cited by Truman 2003: 3.25).

As part of the ethical approval process, researchers need to indicate the characteristics of their proposed respondent group and how they will access them. Research involving gatekeepers and/or translators (i.e., people other than respondents) may discourage respondents who feel that these others may then have access to what they have divulged through the course of the research. This may be particularly relevant when respondents are asked to comment on the support, care or treatment they are receiving, as they may worry that what they say will affect their future support, care or treatment (Cannon 1989; Afshar 1994). Similarly, midwives and other health-care workers may feel uncomfortable disagreeing with hospital or community protocols or national practices. Similarly, when researching people in the private sphere, and when researching personal and family issues, individuals may not want other family members to know all the specifics of their experience or the emotions surrounding it (Exley and Letherby 2001). Researching reproduction and reproductive experiences may take place in a health-care setting or in a respondent's home, and respondents may be 'targeted' (i.e., approached because of their experience of administering or receiving a particular treatment, or working in or attending at a particular clinic) or self-selecting (e.g., answering an advert in a GP surgery, in a newspaper or professional publication, or online), and all of these different scenarios will likely affect both whom researchers are able to recruit and what respondents have to say.

Doing Research

Having designed the project, obtained ethical approval, accessed respondents and, if appropriate, held an initial meeting with the research steering group (which will likely be made up of experts and stakeholders (e.g., midwives and women)), the research can begin. Yet the need for flexibility and sensitivity is far from over. Problems and dilemmas are endemic to the whole research process, not least with reference to the presence of the researcher(s):

> When we enter a field we make footprints on the land and are likely to disturb the environment. When we leave we may have mud on our shoes, pollen on our clothes. If we leave the gate open this may have serious implications for the farmers and their animals. All of this is also relevant to what we find out about the field and its inhabitants. Thus, when doing research (fieldwork) we need to be sensitive to respondents and to the relevance of our own presence in their lives and in the research process. (Letherby 2003: 6)

It has become commonplace for the researcher to locate her/himself within the research process and produce 'first-person' accounts acknowledging that our research activities tell us things about ourselves, as well as about those we are researching, and that all texts are to some extent personal statements (e.g., Morgan 1998). Some researchers go further and draw on their own autobiography throughout the research and presentation process, including them*selves* when analysing the data and writing up, which may involve inclusion of their own experience as data. Researchers do not have to draw on their own life experiences to do *good* work, but our life experiences/identity are present at some level in all that we do and it is important to acknowledge this (Cotterill and Letherby 1993; Letherby 2003; Katz-Rothman 2007):

> ... we take ... [respondents'] autobiographies and become their biographers, while recognizing that the autobiographies we are given are influenced by the research relationship. In other words respondents have their own view of what the researcher might like to hear. Moreover, we draw on our own experiences to help us to understand those of our respondents. Thus, their lives are filtered through us and the filtered stories of our lives are present (whether we admit it or not) in our written accounts. (Cotterill and Letherby 1993: 74)

These auto/biographical concerns (the use of the / highlighting the relationship between the self and other, not least with reference to researchers and respondents *and* midwives and women) are particularly significant in research on reproduction and reproductive experiences. Not only do sociologists sometimes do research on issues that they themselves or others close to them have experienced, but midwives and other health-care researchers do research involving their peers. Researchers need to reflect on differences as well as similarities within research relationships, and again this is significant in an area which is often perceived to be 'women's business' (Earle and Letherby 2003) but which includes men as (potential) fathers, midwives, consultants, etc.

Many sociologists and other social researchers *insist* that the choice of method of data collection should meet participatory and emancipatory criteria as well as epistemological ones. Thus, the concern here is to do research *for* people, rather than to do research *on* them. Sociological researchers are increasingly concerned to shift the balance of power within research in favour of the researched (e.g., Stringer 1996; O'Neill 2008). Some insist on methods also meeting participatory and emancipatory criteria so that involvement in research is beneficial in its own right (e.g., Homfray 2008). However, it is important to remember that despite the long-held assumption that the balance of power is always held by the researcher, in reality it is often more complicated and respondents are not always the most vulnerable within research relationships. We sometimes research 'up' (e.g., consultants) rather than 'down' (patients), and anyway respondents do not always feel disempowered by either their life experience or by the research relationship. Thus, it may be inaccurate, even patronizing, to assume that the respondent needs to be empowered by the process (Letherby 2003, 2004). In addition, there is no script for respondents (despite 'Participant Information Sheets' and 'Consent Forms'), and respondents have the right to be uncooperative (Davis et al. 2000).

📋 Activity 3.2: Why get involved?

> Well quite honestly, I said I hope this research is worth it. I said to my mum, I've got this lady coming to see me this morning. She said 'What about?' I said, I hope it's not a load of old rubbish. Because there's been so much research on such rubbishy things I feel money's been wasted. So she said 'Oh it probably is . . .' Well, it's a bit indulgent isn't it, really, just talking about yourself all the time? (Oakley 1979, cited by Roberts 1992: 176).

The National Institute for Health Research (<http://www.crncc.nihr.ac.uk/ppi/ppi_how>) stresses the value of being involved as a participant in a clinical trial or in wider clinical research activities (e.g., acting as a research advisory group member, helping develop 'Participant Information Sheets', etc):

Patients and the public may benefit from being actively involved by having a say in research:

- Through sharing their experience.
- By getting research started that is important to them.
- By learning more about research activities.
- Through meeting new people – researchers, members of the public and other people from different networks.
- By gaining confidence and new skills.
- By having the chance to make a contribution (<http://www.crncc.nihr.ac.uk/ppi/ppi_how>).

(a) Before you started reading this chapter, which of the above views of research corresponded most closely with your opinion?
(b) Find a sociologically informed article that reports on research that

interests you. List what you think were the advantages and disadvantages of involvement for the respondents.

Box 3.1 A difference of opinion

In a project I undertook with a midwife colleague, focusing on mother and daughter relationships during pregnancy and early motherhood when the daughter has pre-existing diabetes, a key issue that arose from the data was that of the importance of formal and informal relationships with reference to infant feeding choices. Some daughter respondents felt they did receive enough support to successfully breastfeed, whereas others felt anxious and defensive about their infant feeding choices. For example:

> I've heard a few friends of mine who started breastfeeding and then wanted to stop but were put under tremendous amounts of pressure by their midwife, they had like bleeding nipples and in absolute agony, but they were told to carry on, keep doing it, and you know, these poor women crying their eyes out in pain and stuff, and not being able to leave the baby for even an hour because they'd have to breastfeed it. And I know that when I speak to Jan [midwife] I'm gonna have to tell her at some point because she was talking to me, going on to some latch-on classes somewhere, and I thought, 'I don't want to go to one', and then I thought 'I'm gonna have to tell her eventually', but I'm absolutely dreading it . . . and I wanna be able to say to the midwife 'I've made a decision, I don't want to breastfeed' and I don't want to have an argument with her about it, or debate. I would like her to say 'are you sure?' and I'd say 'yes' and that's the end of it. But I'm expecting more than that. (Soebia)

In discussing this as a research team we focused on the implications both for practice and for further research. It soon became clear that we (Liz and I) had different views:

> LIZ: As a midwife and an advocate for breastfeeding, exploring why women with pre-existing diabetes did not breastfeed was of great interest. Anecdotal evidence, clinical experience and a recent clinical audit showed that very few women with pre-existing diabetes exclusively breastfed their infants, with only a small number breastfeeding beyond the recommended six months . . . Thus, in supporting breastfeeding as a choice and experience for women with pre-existing diabetes, within our mother and daughter study midwives were clearly using their previous knowledge, not least from the literature suggesting supplementary feeds with formula milk can affect short- and long-term health of the infant and the mother/infants' success in breastfeeding . . .
>
> Having the professional knowledge of the benefits of breastfeeding for women with pre-existing diabetes means the clinical diabetes team, consisting of a diabetologist, obstetrician, diabetes nurse

specialist, dietician and midwife (myself), passionately promotes breastfeeding and feel disappointment when women decide in pregnancy to formula feed their infant. Therefore, reflecting professional knowledge/experience and ideological stance, we wanted to undertake research designed to explore women's choices surrounding breastfeeding and the significance of pre-existing diabetes to these choices. However, this caused a great deal of professional discussion within the research team as Gayle challenged our assumptions that the study should emphasize only breastfeeding.

GAYLE: Committed to a research agenda that attempts to make a difference to people's lives, I have always tried to approach research with an 'open mind', although I appreciate that I, like all other researchers, do not enter the field 'empty-headed'. Thus, in my research on infertility and involuntary childlessness, I aimed to highlight the misunderstandings of experience that to me appeared to characterize these issues, and in my studies of young motherhood (and fatherhood) I wanted to challenge the stereotypical view of 'teenage mums' (and 'feckless dads'). For me, then, when respondents in our mother and daughter study spoke of their anxiety surrounding their infant feeding choices, I felt angry on their behalf. So when Liz spoke of the medical importance of breastfeeding and the possibility of a project specifically on breastfeeding issues, I could only see problems. For me, this focus would only add to the negative sense of self-worth those who choose not to breastfeed feel, and support rather than challenge an unthought-through political agenda: surely those who chose to formula feed need support too, maybe even more if their infants are already 'at risk'?

It was clear to both of us that our different ideological positions could threaten our current and future working relationship. The lowest point was one afternoon when we argued about the meanings of the data and the implications for practice. We decided that the way forward was to examine and evaluate our opinions and approach. This led to an exploration of the literature related to midwives' attitudes to bottle/formula and breastfeeding, as well as that relating to women's feeding choices and experiences. We then spent a lot of time talking about our reading and how it made us feel. We continue to work together on various research, supervision and writing projects. We continue to talk and to support each other professionally and personally. In the formal presentations we give, and the reports and papers, we write as 'we', which sometimes hides the emotion work, negotiation and compromise we undertake. (Adapted from Letherby and Stenhouse 2013)

Although research might be beneficial, therapeutic even, it should not be confused with therapy or counselling, and we need always to be clear about who benefits the most (as illustrated in Box 3.1).

> The ethical or moral base of the relationship between researcher and researched cannot be adequately captured by the language of contractual consent or of care. In other contexts, when we contract or ask someone for help or assistance, we think in terms of gratitude and obligation rather than informed consent. Roberts and Sanders (2005) see the willingness of participants to be researched as a gift, one of immense value for the studies and subsequent careers of researchers; there may be little direct or immediate benefit for the subjects nor financial or material gain. (Pérez-y-Pérez and Stanley 2011: 4.3)

Like power, emotion is integral to the research process. Displays of emotion with research can be dangerous for both researcher and respondent, and provide another example of the need to be concerned with researchers' (as well as respondents') safety and well-being. Several writers have argued that emotion work is an inevitable part of fieldwork (e.g., Ramsay 1996; Sampson et al. 2008; see also Chapter 5 for a discussion of emotion work and midwifery). As Karen Ramsay argues:

> Attending to *emotional responses* to experiences in the field is a method of finding out where the researcher stands in relation to those being studied . . . and exploration of the level of *emotional management* required in the relationship between researcher and respondent places the researcher clearly within the research process . . . viewing qualitative research . . . as *emotional labour* locates the process clearly within a discussion of the academic mode of production. (Ramsay 1996: 19)

Emotion work is also evident within research teams, perhaps especially when working in multidisciplinary teams. Collaboration of any kind involves people with different experiences and will likely include collaboration and compromise (e.g., Letherby and Stenhouse 2013).

🗒 Activity 3.3: Silences in research accounts

> . . . despite what could be called the 'reflexive turn' in research reporting, the realities of doing empirical research are generally glossed over in methods textbooks, research reports and journal articles, which still provide fairly sanitized accounts of the research process. (Hallowell 2005: 2)

This chapter highlights many of the dilemmas that are an inevitable part of research.

(a) Think back to the research accounts that you are already aware of. Can you remember much detail about the methodological experience of the researchers?

(b) Pick up/access online a sociological and a midwifery journal at random.

Look at all the research-based articles. Do these articles tell you enough about the research process? If not, what else do you think the researcher should be reporting in order to make the relationship between the process and the product clear?

Data Analysis, Re/Presentation and 'Making Research Count'

Data analysis should be ongoing and not something that happens only when all of the data are collected. For this reason, the 'scientific' approach to social research has been criticized not only for its unrealistic and limited view of data collected (as neutral and value-free), but also for its focus on theory-testing, or deductivism. One response was the development of grounded theory. Grounded theory is theory developed from data (rather than informing the data collection) and which aims to be faithful to the reality of situations (Strauss and Corbin 1990). Yet no study can be completely inductive in the way that this approach suggests as researchers begin research with their own political and theoretical assumptions. So all research accounts are partial and constructed by the researcher. This does not mean that research reports are merely constructions, but they are influenced by the ideological position of the researcher(s) and their social and material location. As Liz Stanley and Sue Wise (1990: 22) argue, 'researchers cannot have "empty heads" in the way that inductivism proposes', so one must acknowledge the aspects of the intellectual and physical presence of the researcher that are gendered, classed, racial and so on. Thus, the personhood of the researcher is relevant to theoretical analysis just as it is to research design and fieldwork. Despite the dynamic nature of the research process in terms of power and emotion, involvement and detachment, and even though respondents as well as researchers are thinking, reflexive beings, researchers are in a privileged position. This is not only in terms of access to resources and access to multiple accounts, but also in terms of discipline training which enables engagement in 'second order theorizing' (Giddens 1984). Analysis involves 'interpretation', not just 'description' of respondents' and researchers' analytical processes, and making our interpretations clear is fundamental to the production of responsible, accountable knowledge and integral to an approach that acknowledges *theorized subjectivity* (Letherby 2003, 2013).

Some researchers argue that in order to avoid, or at least minimize, the exploitative aspects of research, researchers should think carefully about attempting to represent 'others': people who are not like them. However, speaking only for *ourselves* could also lead to much more research on already privileged groups and implies that those who come from unrepresented and/or minority groups have a 'duty' to represent 'others' like them. It also denies criticisms of the more powerful and privileged (Wilkinson and Kitzinger 1996; Letherby 2003).

Can research make an impact? Should it?

> The idea that social research might influence public policy pro-
> vides an inspiration for many young social scientists. In most
> English-speaking countries the sad truth is that things have never
> worked in this way. (Silverman 1999: 273)

> To the extent that such developments amount to redefining the goal
> of enquiry as the promotion of some practical or political cause, we
> see them as sources of motivated bias, and believe that they must be
> resisted by social researchers. They threaten to destroy the operation
> of the research communities on which the pursuit of scientific knowl-
> edge necessarily depends. (Hammersley and Gomm 1997: 3.3–3.4)

impact
making a difference
to people's lives

Despite some continuing suggestions that social research has little potential for **impact** and should be concerned with knowledge creation rather than impact, there is increasing agreement amongst researchers, research funders and commissioners that one goal of research should be to make a difference. Norman Denzin (1994: 501) suggests that '[i]ncreasingly the criteria of evaluation [of research] will turn ... on moral, practical, aesthetic, political and personal issues – the production, that is, of texts that articulate an emancipatory, participative perspective on the human condition and its betterment'. Others argue for (not least) community-based research, participatory research, collaborative research and action research, all of which aim for democratization of the knowledge process, and for social change (Stoeker 1996). Michael Huberman (1987) calls for 'sustained inter-activity' throughout the research process, from the definition of the problem to application of the findings, and Paul Bywaters and myself (Letherby and Bywaters 2007) for 'extending social research', with good, continued working relationships with funders and stakeholders beyond the traditional end of a project. Similarly, Sandra Nutley (2003: 12) argues that researchers who want their work to be used must pay attention to the gap between research and policy or practice worlds that have: 'different priorities, use different languages, operate to different time scales and are subjected to very different reward systems'.

Recently, sociologists (and other social scientists) in the North Americas, Australia and Britain have become focused on what we do with the presentation of academic work beyond the academy. Michael Burawoy, in his 2004 Presidential Address to the American Sociological Association (and subsequent publication in 2005), argued for 'public sociology'. Burawoy (2005) suggests that whilst professional sociology has an academic audience, public sociology has an extra-academic audience and is reflexive. Thus:

> The bulk of public sociology is indeed of an organic kind – sociologists
> working with a labor movement, neighborhood associations, commu-
> nities of faith, immigrant rights groups, human rights organizations.

Box 3.2 Practice-based evidence

In an article in the journal *Sociology*, Nick J. Fox argues that practitioners are sometimes criticized for failing to base actions on research evidence, while academic research is also sometimes criticized as irrelevant to practice. Fox argues that this conflict derives in part from an academic model of research constructed in opposition to practice. He suggests an alternative to 'evidence-based' practice and attempts to re-privilege the role of the practitioner whilst not rejecting the skills of the academic researcher. His 'practice-based' evidence model necessitates the acknowledgement of research findings as local and contingent; a sensitivity to and respect for difference; and the acceptance that theory-building should be an adjunct to practical activity. Fox argues for a praxis (theory and action) model of social research – an explicitly political approach to studying the social world. He insists that adopting a 'practice-based' evidence approach leads to the breakdown of the unequal researcher/researched and research/practice positions found in traditional research approaches and, as such, is an ethically, as well as politically engaged, research approach. (Fox 2003, reproduced and summarized in Earle and Letherby 2008)

> Between the organic public sociologist and a public is a dialogue, a process of mutual education. The recognition of public sociology must extend to the organic kind which often remains invisible, private and is often considered to be apart from our professional lives. The project of such public sociologies is to make visible the invisible, to make the private public, to validate these organic connections as part of our sociological life. (Burawoy 2005: 8–9)

This implies the need for sociologists and others conducting sociological research to operate as 'public intellectuals' working beyond the academy, and to present our work – including reference to our methods and approaches as well as our findings, policy recommendations and theoretical conclusions – to lay as well as professional audiences.

Some of the problems arising from a concern with impact and presentation beyond the academy include a lack of funding and research training for such activities. Furthermore, there are other demands on researchers (e.g., publishing in academic publications, applying for the next grant and so on), all of which can mitigate against 'making research count'/'extending social research' – yet more evidence of the significance of the politics of the (complete) research process.

🗒 Activity 3.4: Designing a research project

Focusing on any issue that interests you, write a short (two-page) research proposal. Make sure that you pay attention to gender and other aspects of difference issues in relation to:

the topic of research
the respondent group
access
fieldwork
analysis

Remember that your identity as well as those of your respondents is significant.

Summary

- This chapter has focused on the sociological research process and product.
- What we do (the process) affects what we get (the product), and this is relevant in terms of choice of research issue/topic, through to presentation of findings/results.
- Issues of power, emotion, involvement and detachment, and difference and diversity are integral aspects of the research process.
- Highlighting the relationship between the process and the product makes our research both more accountable and more useful.

Questions for discussion

- Look at the BSA Statement of Ethical Practice (2002) at <http://www.britsoc.co.uk/>. In what ways is this relevant for the research project you planned for Activity 3.4?
- What is the difference between research *of* and research *for* women (and men) and babies and the midwives and others who care for them?
- After you have read all of the chapters in this book, make a list of the things you have learnt from sociological research.

Further reading

McCance, T. V., Fitzsimons, D., Keeney, S., Hasson, F. and McKenna, H. P. 2007 Capacity building in nursing and midwifery research and development: an old priority and a new perspective. *Journal of Advanced Nursing* 59/1: 57–67.

Tanya McCance and colleagues review previous definitions of capacity-building and report on their own research which aims to identify the main strategic priorities for nursing and midwifery research and development. Capacity-building was highlighted as a central concern with three key areas identified: (1) the importance of strong and visible leadership; (2) developing research expertise that will enable the profession to deliver programmes of research; and (3) increasing the capacity of individuals and organizations to engage in development activity.

Letherby, G., Scott, J. and Williams, M. 2013 *Objectivity and Subjectivity in Social Research*. Sage.

In this text John Scott, Malcolm Williams and I reflect on the history of debates on objectivity and subjectivity, and in addition we add our own voices to the debate. The book is written as a 'trialogue' in that we each state our own positions, which is followed by responses from the others. The book as a whole highlights the importance of the process/product relationship (especially Chapters 5 and 7).

There are lots of sociological journals with relevant methods-focused articles. For example, look for *Sociological Research Online*; *Sociology*; *Sociology of Health and Illness*; *Work, Employment and Society*.

Sage Methodspace at <http://www.methodspace.com/profiles/blog/list>

An interesting and valuable resource with methods book reviews, a methods blog, a discussion space and much more.

4 Why Policy Matters

Alistair Hewison

Key issues:

- Definitions of the term 'policy'.
- The need for midwives to be aware of the nature of the policy process.
- The complexity of the policy process and its implications for midwifery.
- The impact of policy on midwifery practice and the care of women.
- The potential for midwives to influence policy.

At the end of this chapter you should be able to:

- Define the term 'policy'.
- Discuss the policy process critically.
- Summarize the main strands of health policy which have shaped midwifery practice in recent years.
- Recognize the continuing influence of policy on practice.
- Consider your involvement in the policy process as a midwife.

Introduction

Midwifery plays a vital role in improving health service delivery (WHO 2011a); however, midwives are not often identified as key stakeholders at the health policy table (WHO 2011b). In order to address this deficit, the Department of Human Resources for Health, at the World Health Organization, has identified five Key Results Areas (KRAs) as part of its strategy for 2011–15. These are health system and service strengthening; policy and practice; education, training and career development; workforce management; and partnership. With respect to midwifery policy and practice (KRA 2), the target is that nurses and midwives will play a proactive part in ensuring that the health policies, plans and decisions affecting their professions are country-specific and in keeping with the principles of inclusive leadership, effective governance and regulated practice (WHO 2011b). This indicates that policy matters at an international level because it determines whether or not clients experience the maximum benefit from midwifery services. It is also a central feature of the UK health-care system and shapes the services provided, influences the way the midwifery profession practises and, most importantly, affects the experiences of clients. Supportive and high-quality maternity care can help ensure a healthy start in life for

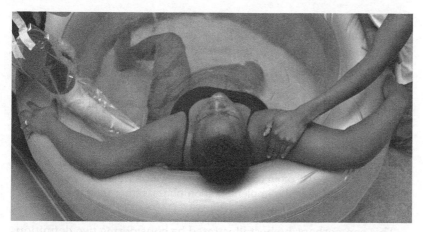

Figure 4.1 A water birth

babies and can also equip mothers and fathers with the skills to be confident and caring parents (Department of Health 2004a; DfES 2004). Indeed, it has been found that midwife-led care for low-risk women improves maternal outcomes (Caird et al. 2010). Furthermore, the majority of women will benefit from midwife-led models of care, and it has been recommended that such models of care should be available for all childbearing women (Devane et al. 2010). However, this is dependent on the quality and coherence of policy. For example, if the policy vision outlined in *Delivering High-quality Midwife Care: The Priorities, Opportunities and Challenges for Midwives* is to be realized, ensuring that in the future all pregnant women will be cared for in or near their home, by a midwife they can get to know and trust (Department of Health 2009), then organizational structures, midwifery education, provision of an adequate workforce, and changes to the role itself will all be required. These matters are all driven by policy. Consequently, it is important to examine how the policy process works, how it affects health care, and how this relates to the role of the midwife.

With this in mind, the purpose of this chapter is to discuss a number of key areas. First, the policy process will be summarized to provide a context for the next section, which focuses on current policy relating to midwifery in England. This will demonstrate the complexity of service provision in this area and identify key issues which have been highlighted as crucial to the continuing development of midwifery. In the final section, a framework is presented which may be useful in helping midwives to reflect on their role and level of involvement in the policy process.

The Policy Process

Although it is necessary to explore the nature of policy to establish the context for what follows, it is beyond the scope of this chapter to engage in a detailed discussion of the policy process, as it is a distinct area of scholarship in and of itself (see, for example, Crinson 2008; Spicker 2006; Ham 2009; Hudson and Lowe 2009; Hill and Bramley 1986). Yet attempting to present a simple definition is also fraught with difficulty. This dilemma is usefully summarized by Hill:

> The definition problems posed by the concept of policy suggest that it is difficult to treat it as a very specific and concrete phenomenon. Policy may sometimes be identifiable in terms of a decision, but very often it involves either groups of decisions or what may be seen as little more than an orientation. The attempts at definition also imply that it is hard to identify particular occasions when policy is made. Policy will often continue to evolve within what is conventionally described as the implementation phase, rather than the policy making phase of the process. (Hill 1997: 7)

This can perhaps be best illustrated by considering two definitions. In seeking to clarify what policy means, Cox suggests:

> Health policy refers to the laws and directions from governments that seek to affect and to regulate or to supply state-run health care services. In industrial countries health policy is a major area of political interest and public debate. (Cox 2010: 294)

However, in the pursuit of brevity, some other elements are not mentioned. The policy process is extremely complicated and involves not only government statements about what should occur in relation to health, but also the involvement of interest groups, professionals and consumers of health care, including women (Allsop 2000). By way of contrast, Earle (2007) presents a more detailed description:

> Policy making is complex; it is a political activity which crosses national borders. Policies can be made by individuals and organizations, as well as by governments and other agencies, and they can be made at a local level, as well as at regional, national and international levels. Policies at local and national levels often emerge from other policies that have been determined at a global level; however, local policy and practice can also influence global policy making. (Earle 2007: 5)

Although comprehensive, and useful in itemizing more of the areas that need to be considered when examining policy, it emphasizes further the scope of the term, and in seeking to include a longer list of its elements there is a risk it becomes too unwieldy to be helpful. This is not to criticize either of these attempts at definition; rather, it is to demonstrate the challenges involved in making sense of this important yet elusive concept.

🖹 Activity 4.1 Researching midwifery policy

Visit the policy section of the Department of Health website (<http://www.dh.gov.uk/health/policy/>) and enter the term 'midwifery' in the search box.

Have a look at the first ten items listed in the search results.

1. Try and determine which are policy documents, press releases, guidance notes, clinical alerts and letters.
2. Which of these is the most important in terms of your practice?
3. How would you find out about current midwifery policy at a national level?

In an effort to overcome this lack of clarity, analysts have resorted to characterizing policy as a series of 'stages'. This imposes an order on the process and is intended to serve as a means of explanation of how it operates. Dunn (2003), for example, outlines eight stages or phases, which are:

1 Agenda setting.
2 Policy formulation.
3 Policy adoption.
4 Policy implementation.
5 Policy assessment.
6 Policy adaptation.
7 Policy succession.
8 Policy termination.

Dorey (2005), on the other hand, identifies six:

1 Agenda setting.
2 Recognition of problem.
3 Consideration of options.
4 Agreement on most suitable option.
5 Legislation or introduction of new policy.
6 Implementation.

When applied, this type of model can be used to identify how a policy has been developed and perhaps why it was or was not successfully implemented. Whilst acknowledging the criticisms of the 'stagist' model, that it oversimplifies the process and does not take adequate account of why some issues are addressed and others are not, Dorey (2005) maintains it can help develop understanding of policy. It provides a useful conceptual description of the complex policy process in manageable parts (Thurber 2003). In this sense, it is a **heuristic device** that can be used as a basis for analysis (Hupe and Hill 2006; Dorey 2005; Thurber 2003). It can inform efforts to make sense of what is going on in policy terms. Policy analysis is concerned with understanding and explaining the substance of policy content, policy decisions and the way those decisions are made (Barrett and Fudge 1981). In the context of health, it is possible to identify a number of recurring and often overlapping themes and issues that present enduring policy challenges in the UK (Hunter 2008):

heuristic device
speculative idea developed to stimulate discussion

- Public versus private approaches to the provision of care.
- The challenging relationship between clinicians and managers.
- The oscillation from centralization to decentralization.
- Command and control versus markets.
- Attempts to strengthen the public and patient voice.
- The tension between a focus on downstream acute health care and upstream public health and prevention.

These also relate to midwifery and influence how services are constituted and delivered. A key aspect of health policy, and the policy process more generally, is how matters find their way on to the 'policy agenda'. Ham suggests that for an issue to appear on the agenda it must:

- Attract attention.
- Claim legitimacy.
- Invoke action.

(Ham 2009 [after Solesbury 1976])

📋 Activity 4.2: The influence of the media on the political agenda

Conduct a 'media watch' on health and midwifery issues, ideally during the week you read this chapter.

1. Select a week and try to listen/watch as many news broadcasts as possible. In addition, have a look at national and local newspapers, and the BBC News website.
2. Identify the health issues that are reported/discussed and list the categories of items, for example, new discoveries, reports of failures, changes in services, lack of resources.
3. How are the issues presented? What evidence is presented to substantiate the claims made in the stories?
4. How effective are the items in 'commanding attention' (for example, for how many days are they discussed? Does a senior politician respond/comment?)

The policy issue must be sufficiently important to attract the attention of politicians, or a particular vocal section of society, which results in people being aware of it. If it is then regarded as legitimate, in the sense that it is important enough to warrant a response, it will be followed by action. This agenda is a list of subjects or problems to which government officials, and people outside of government closely associated with those officials, are paying some serious attention at any given time (Kingdon 2003). The identification of something as a policy problem can originate from a range of sources.

ideology
beliefs influencing
how people
interpret the world

In health policy, for instance, ideas and **ideology** have been very influential. Changes in the way the health service is organized and managed have, in part, been the outcome of ideas, including market-based models of organization (Department of Health 1989) introduced by a Conservative government, and the 'third way' of 'New Labour' (Department of Health 2000) which sought to combine notions of market discipline and social democracy (Giddens 1998). The importance of such policy changes should not be underestimated, and putting them into practice is challenging (McCourt et al. 2006).

The impact of these policy-driven organizational changes directly affects the care provided for mothers. For example, Kirkham has observed that 'the pressures towards centralization make small midwifery units and birth centres vulnerable. Their running costs are obvious areas for potential savings in times of financial stringency' (Kirkham 2010: 4). This illustrates how policy decisions shape the context and provision of maternity services. Similarly, the introduction of Payment by Results (PBR), which is the rules-based payment system in England under which commissioners pay health-care providers for each patient (or in this case mother) seen or treated, taking into account the complexity of the woman's health-care needs (Department of Health 2012), has had a profound effect on practice. The focus of midwifery is on the promotion of normal birth; however, under PBR, care involving technical interventions attracts a higher tariff. This serves as a perverse economic incentive because the more 'medical' and technological the birth, the greater the income for the organization providing the service (Kirkham 2010).

Pressure groups can also identify policy problems and influence the agenda. The National Childbirth Trust, for example, has undertaken a **lobbying** function throughout its history, and in the 1960s it called on the government to reduce the use of unnecessary interventionist techniques. In later years, it was influential in informing the development of the Changing Childbirth (Department of Health 1993) policy (Newburn 2006). Another important 'voice' which can affect the issues that are addressed in the policy process is that of professionals. For instance, in the run-up to the last general election in 2010, the Royal College of Midwives (RCM) was in regular contact with the health policy teams of all the main political parties and was committed to holding whichever government was elected to account with regard to its actions in the area of maternity services (RCM 2010). Moreover, in pursuit of its mission to promote and advance the art and science of midwifery, and to promote the effectiveness and interests of midwives (RCM 2010), it is currently calling for the government to set a target of 5,000 more NHS midwives to be employed in England, using an e-petition and providing advice for RCM members on lobbying (<http://www.rcm.org.uk/>). This demonstrates how different groups seek to set the policy agenda and influence policy (see also Chapter 10).

> lobbying
> applying pressure to influence a political decision-maker

Figure 4.2 Midwives lobbying the Houses of Parliament

📋 Activity 4.3: Lobbying activities by midwives

Watch this short film from the Royal College of Midwives website (<http://protect.rcm.org.uk/news/entry/call-the-student-midwives>).

1. How effective do you think this is as a way of raising concerns about the number of midwives employed?
2. Is the imagery of midwives on bicycles a positive portrayal of the role of the midwife?
3. What sort of lobbying activity do you think is needed?
4. What other activities, other than direct lobbying, would identify the need for more midwives?

This begins to shed light on the ways in which the development of health policy is a complex political process which involves many participants, including politicians, pressure groups, civil servants, professionals and those who may see themselves as the passive recipients of policy (Hill 2009). In addition, these participants are members of groups, organizations and political parties that all have different amounts of power. This is an important determinant of whose

Table 4.1 Four main approaches to understanding the policy process

	Power structured	Power fragmented
Power distributed relatively evenly	1. Representative government with a unified executive responsive to popular will.	2. Pluralist government which operates through competition between groups.
Power distributed unevenly	3. Government by an unrepresentative elite.	4. Unpredictable and chaotic government, subject to multiple pressures.

Source: Adapted from Hill 2009

voice is heard and what gets addressed, in policy terms, following its appearance on the agenda. In essence, the different stages of the policy process take place within a broader social context and there is a range of theoretical explanations of how power is distributed. Table 4.1 summarizes the main approaches to understanding the policy process, which draws on particular theories. For example, point 1 represents 'classic' democratic government, point 2 is a variation of this whereby the reality of government in Western democracies is represented, in that power is distributed throughout society (Smith 1977), whereas in point 3 **structuralist theories** such as Marxism argue that power resides in the hands of a relatively small group in society (Collins 1994). Although **Marxism** as a theoretical approach has less influence than in the past (Hill 2009), it is indicative of a way of thinking about policy and the state. Finally, point 4 refers to societies with less developed democracies. Each of the subsequent stages of the policy process takes place within this broader context, and the outcome, in terms of the type of policy that is developed, is dependent on how this process plays out. An awareness that policymaking is not a rational, objective, neutral activity, devoid of values or the play of power (Hunter 2003), is important for midwives in making sense of their practice. Individuals and groups within health-care organizations have multiple and conflicting objectives and interests, and their desire to defend these is an important determinant of policy outcomes (Hunter 2003).

In summary, it is important to approach health policy in midwifery and health care with the following cautionary comments in mind.

1 The institutions of government are important, but must be regarded with scepticism. The discourses and ideologies that surround them may be more important than their formal characteristics.
2 There is extensive competition between groups to influence government, and this is likely to be organized in networks in which the

structuralist theory
sociological theory that an underlying set of social structures influences social phenomena

Marxism
theory of society as constituted of different classes in state of conflict

interests of all those inside government will be involved, as well as those outside.

3   Power is distributed unequally both inside and outside government, having an impact as much upon what is on the agenda and the context in which decisions are taken, as on the decision process itself. (Hill 2009: 107)

📋 Activity 4.4: Infant mortality rates

Read this extract from the *Statistical Bulletin of the Office for National Statistics for Births and Deaths in England and Wales, 2010* (<www.ons.gov.uk/. . ./birth. . ./births-and-deaths-in-england-and-wales>).

Infant mortality by health area of usual residence
Infant mortality rates vary by health area, and rates for each health area can fluctuate over time. In 2010 the West Midlands had the highest infant mortality rate among the strategic health authorities (SHAs) in England, with 5.5 deaths per thousand live births. The South West had the lowest, with 3.2 deaths per thousand live births. The highest infant mortality rate among the local health boards (LHBs) in Wales was 5.3 deaths per thousand live births in Betsi Cadwaladr University. Aneurin Bevan had the lowest, with 2.3 deaths per thousand live births. Infant mortality rates for LHBs in Wales are based on a much smaller number of live births and are therefore less robust than rates for regions within England. The substantial variation between different health areas reflects underlying differences in maternal factors such as the mother's country of birth, social class and age.

1. Is such a variation in infant mortality acceptable?
2. What wider policy changes need to be made to address this situation, particularly with regard to the factors identified in the final sentence?
3. What is the role of the midwife in addressing these concerns?

Midwives as Implementers of Policy

A further strand in the justification of the importance of policy for midwifery is the role of midwives as implementers of policy because 'although government may look dominant in the reforms, it is the professionals who hold the greatest real power to improve quality by optimizing the care they provide to each patient with whom they have contact' (Leatherman and Sutherland 2008: 67). Midwives work on the 'front line' and can be the crucial factor in whether or not a policy is implemented as intended. Getting results from a policy depends to some degree on the manner in which professionals interpret the policy and incorporate it into their day-to-day work (Barton 2008: 264). Or, to put it another way, from the perspective and experience of the health service user, the activity of autonomous nurses – and this also applies to midwives – is, in essence, health policy in action. Consequently, they are 'de facto' makers of policy at the level of everyday practice (Hannigan and Burnard 2000). Policy may thus be regarded as both a statement of intent by those seeking to change or control behaviour, and a negotiated output emerging from the implementation process (Barrett 2004). This suggests that midwives cannot avoid engaging with the policy process. So, even though a discussion of policy and mid-wifery may appear, on first examination, to be somewhat distant from the reality of practice, in practical terms it is integral to it. The work of Lipsky (1980) is helpful here. He developed the notion of 'street level bureaucrats' to explain how a policy, however well designed and well intentioned, can be circumvented by the actions of people working at the point of delivery. In the case of midwifery, the people organizing and delivering the care are the 'street level bureaucrats' and they can exert a great deal of influence on whether or not a policy works. At the level of practice and care there is a good deal of latitude for midwives and other health-care workers to adapt policy as it is implemented. For example, in a study investigating how staff caring for people who had suffered a stroke managed their roles, responsibilities and work-ing relationships, Allen et al. (2004) found that staff sought ingenious ways to work around the restrictions of the system, such as categoriz-ing patients as being in need of health care to secure funds because the social services budget was exhausted. Similarly, Exworthy (1994) found that community nurse managers significantly shaped the policy process through submission of policy alternatives. This occurred when a general manager wanted to introduce a system for organizing ser-vices based on 'locality managers' having authority over local service delivery. Over the course of a series of meetings, the nurse managers changed the approach to one based on local teams, rather than man-agers. As Exworthy observed, 'Whilst they could not be certain that they would succeed in shelving the policy, they wanted to make sure they achieved the best possible deal in the discussions that took place' (Exworthy 1994: 25). This demonstrates how practitioners are involved in policy at the level of its **implementation**.

> **implementation** execution of a decision or plan

This aspect of the midwife's role has received greater attention in recent policy. For example, the Darzi Review (Department of Health 2008a 2008b, 2008c) of the health service involved 2,000 clinicians (midwives, nurses, doctors, physiotherapists and so on) and was car-ried out in consultation with a total of 60,000 people across England, with the aim of developing a vision of an NHS fit for the twenty-first century. It resulted in a wide range of commitments, particularly in relation to leadership of the service, and concluded that in the past, 'the clinician's role within the team has often been confined to a practitioner, an expert in their clinical discipline'. Yet frontline staff 'have the talent to look beyond their individual clinical practice and act as partners and leaders' (Department of Health 2008a: 9). Indeed, in a subsequent document, it was noted that the midwifery profes-sion expects midwives to be confident at exercising a high degree of influence within organizations and across networks that provide maternity services (Department of Health 2008b: 10) – in other words: engage in policy activity.

The requirement is for a 'new professionalism' (Department of Health 2008a, 2008b), which involves clinicians working as a practitioner, partner and leader to improve quality for individuals and throughout the NHS. Although the extent to which these elements of professional activity are 'new' could be questioned, what emerges very clearly is that a management and leadership focus is evident in this vision of how professionals will work in the future. This recent reappraisal of the role of health professionals follows earlier measures which have located policy activity firmly in the remit of health professionals.

Agenda for Change (Department of Health 1999) was introduced in order to modernize the NHS pay system. The aim of the *Agenda for Change* proposals was to create a single job evaluation scheme covering all roles in the health service, in order to support a review of pay and all other terms and conditions. Although in the event three pay spines were the eventual outcome, the spine which incorporates midwifery has a series of pay bands with a number of progression points. Staff move up the scale, provided their performance is satisfactory and they demonstrate the agreed knowledge and skills appropriate to that part of the pay band or range (Department of Health 2004b).

One of the elements identified in the *Agenda for Change* bandings is: responsibilities for policy and service development implementation. One of the criteria for determining the nature and level of responsibility of people working in health care is now their involvement in policy development and implementation. The list below includes the statements for levels 5 and 6, which go some way in explaining what this means in practice. (A newly qualified midwife would normally be placed in band 5, progressing to band 6 with promotion if applicable.)

   Level 5: Responsible for a range of policy implementation and policy or service development for a directorate or equivalent.
   Level 6: Corporate responsibility for major policy implementation and policy or service development, which impacts across or beyond the organization (Department of Health 2004c).

This all serves to confirm that if midwives in the UK are to develop in their roles, and/or progress in their careers, then an understanding of and involvement in policy is vital. With this in mind, the next two sections address the two major considerations necessary to achieve this. First, the current policy landscape of midwifery is examined to highlight some of the key issues for the organization of midwifery services. Second, a policy involvement continuum, first developed in a nursing context (Hewison 2008), is presented as a framework for thinking about and planning professional development in this area of practice.

Current Policy

There has been a huge amount of policy relating to midwifery over the years (see Midwifery 2020 [2010a], for example), and a simple keyword search of the Department of Health website identifies in excess of 200 documents that have implications for midwifery. It is not possible to examine this vast array of policy which could have an impact on midwifery; consequently, a selection has been made here to focus on some key areas that have emerged recently and map out the current policy landscape. This is followed by consideration of a framework that may be useful to individual midwives when thinking about how to respond to the challenge this presents.

In 2009, in the wake of *High Quality Care for All* (Department of Health 2008a) (the Darzi Review) – one of the last major policy initiatives launched by the incumbent Labour government – the prime minister at the time, Gordon Brown, established a commission on the future of nursing and midwifery in England. The purpose of the commission was to advise on how the professions could implement and accelerate the change agenda set out in the review. The commission worked to the following terms of reference:

- Identify the competencies, skills and support that frontline nurses and midwives need to take a central role in the design and delivery of twenty-first-century services for those that are sick and to promote health and well-being. In particular, identify any barriers that impede the pivotal role that ward sisters/charge nurses/ community team leaders provide.
- Identify the potential and benefits for nurses and midwives, particularly in primary and community care, of leading and managing their own services.
- Engage with the professions, patients and the public in an interactive and robust dialogue which will identify challenges and opportunities for nurses and midwives. (Prime Minister's Commission on the Future of Nursing and Midwifery in England (PMCFNME) 2010)

This document contained twenty recommendations clustered into seven themes, and in 2011 the new coalition government issued its response to the findings of the commission. With regard to the implications for midwifery and midwifery services, the following responses to particular recommendations indicate the changes likely to arise from this policy initiative. For example, recommendation 2 concerned: 'Senior nurses and midwives' responsibility for care. It was stated that all directors of nursing, heads of midwifery and other nurses and midwives in senior management roles must accept full individual managerial and professional accountability for the quality of nursing and midwifery care, and champion care from the point of care to the board. Directors of nursing must maintain clinical credibility and act with authority to ensure that their organizations enable high-quality care. In response, the government proposed the introduction of a new contractual right for staff to raise their concerns about the quality of care direct to the Care Quality Commission (the independent regulator of all health and social care services in England) (Department of Health 2011a). This means the contracts of senior staff will be changed and the nature of the role may also need to change to reflect this.

Recommendation 4 was that the role of the ward sister and equivalent team leaders in midwifery be strengthened. This was deemed to be necessary because the strength of this leadership has an 'unambiguous link to the quality of care and reputation of the profession' (PMCFNME 2010). One specific proposal that is being 'considered' to address this issue is a pilot programme in which a junior midwife could sit on the trust board on a rotational basis in order to give junior staff an opportunity to express new ideas to decision-makers and gain an understanding of the wider operation of an NHS organization (Department of Health 2011a). No further details or timescales are included, so it is not entirely clear how this will be introduced. However, it does indicate that opportunities for direct involvement in higher-level decision-making may become available to junior midwives.

It was stated in recommendation 12 that there should be a named midwife for every woman. This arose from a recognition that the contribution of midwifery to delivering health and well-being and reducing health inequalities must be enhanced, by organizing services so that every woman has a named midwife responsible for ensuring coordination of her care and providing support and guidance (PMCFNME 2010). The government's response was: 'we expect heads of midwifery, maternity services and **commissioning** consortia to implement this locally' (Department of Health 2011a: 12). In addition, it was stated: 'we have made sure Strategic Health Authorities will not be reducing midwifery training places during 2011/12 and that since May 2010 the number of midwives had increased by 296' (p. 12). It was also stated that the numbers were being monitored (Department of Health 2011a). In policy terms, the expectation that this will be implemented at local level does not automatically guarantee it will happen, as noted in the section on policy implementation earlier. Success will depend in part on how closely the achievement of this target is scrutinized, and indeed if failure to achieve it leads to any form of sanction. Similarly, although it is stated that 'we are firmly committed to getting the number of midwives right' (Department of Health 2011a: 13), no clear indication is given of what the 'right' number might be. Indeed, as noted earlier, the Royal College of Midwives is currently campaigning for the recruitment of an extra 5,000 midwives, by lobbying the government in the form of an e-petition (RCM 2011). This illustrates how the view of what is the 'right' number of midwives can vary, depending on whose it is.

commissioning the process of ensuring that health-care services are provided for the population; the core role of commissioners is to buy services for their populations

In a comprehensive review of UK policy since the 1990s, compiled to inform the Midwifery 2020 programme (see below), Masterson (2010) distilled the following priorities from twenty-eight key policy documents:

- Choice.
- More midwife-led care.
- Continuity of carer.
- Midwives as first contact.
- Public health and health promotion, especially smoking cessation.
- Access to community and midwife-led services.
- Encouraging normal birth.
- Increasing breastfeeding rates.
- Safe services.

This summary of the policy challenges facing midwifery informed the development of the programme as a whole. The Midwifery 2020 project was a UK-wide programme involving the four UK Chief Nursing Officers in England, Northern Ireland, Scotland and Wales, conducted in partnership with the Royal Colleges, the Nursing and Midwifery Council (NMC), stakeholders in maternity care, professional bodies, higher education, user organizations, employers and commissioners of service and education across all four countries. Midwifery 2020 was commissioned by the Chief Nurses of the Health Departments of England, Northern Ireland, Scotland and Wales to set the direction for midwifery and identify the changes needed to the way midwives work, and to their roles, responsibilities and training and development requirements. It was based on the work carried out by four 'work-streams', made up of between seventeen and twenty-eight members drawn from practice, management, the university sector, professional bodies and other interest groups, and focused on:

- The core role of the midwife.
- Workforce and workload.
- Education and career progression.
- Measuring quality.
- Public health.

When the work of these groups was brought together it resulted in the production of twenty-six key messages organized under nine broad headings. Similarly, thirty-one expectations were arranged under eight headings. It is beyond the scope of this chapter to address all of these, so the section relating to midwives specifically is considered here. It was noted that midwives are key to achieving the vision of midwifery in 2020, and that their commitment to women, babies and their families is clear and their role is vitally important to the future of the maternity services. Based on this assessment, if the 'expectations' outlined in the documents are to be realized, then midwives need to:

- Build on effective communication and teamwork with colleagues in the maternity services team to continuously improve the delivery of quality services for women, babies and their families.
- Review and agree their clinical guidelines and indicators of quality.
- Promote their profession and contribute to a fresh, positive professional image.
- Review and develop their inherent contribution to public health, addressing inequalities and meeting the complex needs of women and their families.
- Develop their role as advocates for all women, particularly those with complex needs.

(Midwifery 2020, 2010b)

These requirements have implications for the practice of individual midwives and may require some professional development activity. Moreover, action in these areas needs to be coordinated with that taken by the wide range of stakeholders identified in the report, who are also exhorted to review and change their approach. Table 4.2 provides a list of all the groups that need to take action. From this, it can be seen that the wide range of people involved – from parents and service providers to regulatory and professional bodies – underlines the seemingly overwhelmingly complex nature of the policy process. If the needs of mothers and their families are to be met, how can all of these disparate interests be focused to provide the service envisioned in Midwifery 2020? This is the enduring challenge of developing and implementing policy. However, there are ways individual practitioners can make their contribution to shaping practice.

Home Birth: A Framework for Policy Involvement

In the final pages of *Midwifery 2020 – Delivering Expectations* (Midwifery 2020, 2010b), a broad range of groups is listed and exhorted to take action to support the implementation of the recommendations made in the document (see Table 4.2 for a list of the groups). However, it is acknowledged in the introduction that 'how you use the report and its key messages will depend on your role and we urge you to consider what you can do to ensure that midwives can maximize their contribution to delivering quality services for women, babies and families' (Midwifery 2020, 2010b: 4). In what follows, a framework is presented that may be useful for student midwives and those at an early stage of their professional career, in stimulating thought and reflection about policy as part of the role of the midwife (Table 4.3).

It has been demonstrated that the policy process is complex and involves many 'players', and practitioners may view it as something that affects their work but that they have little power to influence or direct. However, if it is considered that policy can function at a number

Table 4.2 Groups encouraged to take action as part of Midwifery 2020

- Midwives.
- Mothers, fathers, partners, families and consumer groups.
- The maternity care team.
- Commissioners of maternity services.
- Service providers at local, regional and national levels.
- Educationalists.
- Researchers.
- Government leads, regulatory bodies and professional bodies.

Source: Midwifery 2020, 2010b

of levels, this provides some insights on how midwives can increase their involvement in policy. A policy involvement continuum was used to develop a framework designed to assist nurses in reviewing their involvement in the policy process (Hewison 2008; see Table 4.3). The rationale for this approach is rehearsed briefly below and it is argued that a similar approach may be helpful in the discipline of midwifery.

Table 4.3 Policy involvement continuum

Type of development	Stage of career
Policy literacy	
Midwife	Student/recently qualified
Policy acumen	
Ward/department manager	Mid-career midwife
Policy competence	
Hospital manager	Senior midwife
Policy influence	
National leader	National level post

Source: Adapted from Hewison 2008

Nurses find it difficult to access the policymaking process; the study of health policy does not feature heavily in nurse education (Antrobus et al. 2004), and few nurses working in clinical settings engage in policy debates or regard health policy as a 'nursing issue' (Toofany 2005: 26). This has resulted in nurses being absent from policy debates (Hughes 2005; Robinson 1992). This is not a recent problem, as nurses were urged to become a powerhouse for change in the area of health politics and policy twenty-five years ago (Clay 1987). Later, in 1998, it was still being lamented that UK public policy persistently neglected nursing issues, with concern expressed that nursing practice was shaped by other dominant groups, including doctors and managers (Maslin-Prothero and Masterson 1998). The issue has been acknowledged as a global challenge, with the International Council of Nurses (ICN 2001) advocating that action is needed to enable nurses to influence and shape decisions. It concluded: 'It is essential that they clearly understand how policy is made and implemented, and its wider context. Without this understanding of policy development, nursing will not be included in the process' (ICN 2001: 5). Although midwifery is distinct from nursing, many of the same challenges apply. For example, when commenting on the current government's health reforms, Warwick (2011) bemoans the absence of midwives on the new **commissioning boards**, and the neglect of maternity services in the government's pronouncements. This indicates that nursing and midwifery share considerable common ground with regard to their engagement with the policy process. With this in mind, a four-level framework is proposed that may be helpful to midwives in thinking about their development needs in this area.

commissioning boards
boards that commission services

This draws on work conducted in the US and the UK, and indicates that nurses, and for the purposes of this chapter midwives, can be involved in different levels of the policy process, which are broadly consistent with the stages of a career many practitioners may reach. The framework outlines parallel levels of policy involvement. Previously presented as a series of ascending steps, that is, the more senior the post the greater the degree of policy involvement (Hewison 2008), the framework is perhaps best used to convey the range of activities possible to inform individual decisions made by practitioners about their own development. In this sense, it is not prescriptive; rather, it sets out what is possible. However, as noted earlier in the chapter, midwives cannot really avoid being involved at some level, and all need to be 'policy literate'.

Policy literacy

Policy literacy involves having some understanding of the ways in which policy issues have been shaped by larger social forces and how they have been addressed in the past (Malone 2005: 138). One way midwives in training and those who are newly qualified can develop such an understanding is by accessing relevant policy documents. It has been suggested that to understand how and why policy is formed for the provision of health services, it is often necessary to go to original sources of information such as transcripts of parliamentary speeches and debates, minutes of official meetings, official reports and government papers (Palfrey 2000). Such material is in the public domain (Abbott et al. 2004) and increasingly available on the Internet, and useful insights can be generated through the critical analysis of policy documents (Giacomini et al. 2004; Humphrey et al. 2003; Neil 2005). Clearly, formal study of the policy process as part of an education programme would also be beneficial; however, simply by reading policy documents, greater knowledge of the wider practice environment can be generated. Such documents are a crucial part of the policy process and so are worthy of consideration (Freeman and Maybin 2011; Freeman 2006). If this reading is enhanced by the application of a critical framework which can be used to interrogate the documents (see, for example, Collins 2005), then further understanding can be accrued. Finally, midwives have the advantage of front-line experience in how health policy decisions play out at the level of women and families, and if this information is effectively recorded and presented, it can generate insights on the reality of the policy process and be hard to ignore (Malone 2005: 141).

Policy acumen

At the mid-stage of their careers, or at least when they have moved on from being new practitioners, midwives, and ultimately their clients, are likely to benefit if they can develop 'policy acumen'. This term was first coined by Gough et al. in 1994 and refers to an awareness and understanding distilled from a policy analysis concerned with the nature of nursing, and in this case midwifery, which in turn helps practitioners as managers to grasp the nettle of power within the health arena. It also involves informing the public about major health problems, concerns and issues for which nurses/midwives can be advocates and caregivers (p. 265). This is particularly applicable to midwives in their role as advocates for the women in their care (Department of Health 2009). In order to achieve this level of engagement with the policy process, reflective practice, leadership and continuing education are required (Gough et al. 1994). This provides an opportunity for midwives to develop a level of understanding and influence necessary to develop policy acumen, which in turn enables them to shape the way care is organized and delivered. This can build on policy literacy, or be developed concurrently.

Policy competence

The notion of 'policy competence' has been proposed by Longest (2004) in the context of health-care management. He argued that because of the substantial and continuing impact of government policies on health-care organizations, their effective management requires that managers be cognizant of the policy context their organizations are operating in. Specifically, they must understand the policies that affect the organization, the process through which such policies are made, and all the forces that can affect the process and its outcomes (Longest 2004). If managers are to be 'policy competent', they need the ability to lead their organization's response to the challenges and opportunities emanating from the policy environment and to persuade policymakers to take decisions that favour their organizations. This indicates that an awareness and understanding of policy can operate at different levels and in different ways for those involved in health care. This level of activity is increasingly expected of midwives, particularly as they take on more senior roles. For example, 'Heads of Midwifery' should position themselves to be highly visible and persuasive in the commissioning process so that they can: influence the commissioning process at an appropriate level; use evidence to improve services; and act as advocates for women to make sure the commissioning cycle reflects their needs (Department of Health 2009: 17). In terms of the framework (Table 4.3), policy competence indicates a higher level of involvement at an organizational level to inform more effective management of midwifery services, which in turn relies on being visible and persuasive to ensure the needs of mothers, babies and families are met.

Policy influence

The policy process in health is inescapably political (Hunter 2008), and as well as exerting influence at a local level, midwifery as a profession is one of the 'voices' at the levels of national and international policy-making. For example, the role of the Chief Nurse in England, who is a senior civil servant and a Director in the Department of Health, is to provide expert advice on nursing, midwifery and health visiting to government and help to develop, implement and evaluate government health policy. This involves leading on nursing, midwifery and health-visiting policy and strategy in support of the government's objective (Department of Health 2011b). In addition, the Chief Nurse ensures an effective UK contribution is made to midwifery and health policy in international fora, including the World Health Organization, the Commonwealth and Europe (Department of Health 2011b). Clearly, to fulfil such a role requires extensive understanding of the policy process and the ability to set the policy agenda. This is in addition to getting the message heard, and selecting the right issues to pursue as central to this process (Hennessy 2000). This relies on midwives attaining a level of seniority, from which such influence can be exerted at a national level.

📋 Activity 4.5: Developing policy literacy

1. Thinking about your development as a midwifery professional, list three activities you could undertake to develop policy literacy.
2. Obtain a policy document (this could be one identified in Activity 4.1) and summarize its implications for your practice as a midwife.
3. Identify five ways you could influence policy in your future career.

Conclusion

> As an inherently political profession, nursing needs to position itself to inform, guide and lead much-needed development and change in health systems. The current disproportionate focus and investment on illness and hospital-based care is not sustainable for health systems around the world. (Webber 2011: 145)

This statement applies equally to the discipline of midwifery and, as noted in the introduction, there is a pressing need for midwives to play a proactive part in ensuring that the health policies, plans and decisions affecting their profession are country-specific and in keeping with the principles of inclusive leadership, effective governance and regulated practice (WHO 2011b). The discussion of the framework for policy involvement presented here indicates the steps midwives can take to increase their level of involvement in order to better shape services to meet mothers' needs. This requires that midwives take a broader view of practice, recognize that policy is important, and consider how they can learn more about the process and engage with it as part of their professional activity. It is hoped that the material in this chapter has both provided some helpful insights on how to manage this process and demonstrated why policy matters.

Summary

- Health policy is a key concern in the British political system and sets the context for the provision of midwifery services.
- The policy process is complex and a number of accounts have been developed to provide a way of understanding how it works.
- Midwives play a key role in the translation of policy into practice. They serve as implementers and shapers of policy where services are delivered.
- There are different ways that midwives can get involved in the policy process. This is important because it is a means of ensuring services are designed to meet the needs of women.

Questions for discussion

- Why is it important for midwives to have an understanding of how policy is developed?
- What are the advantages and disadvantages of midwives engaging in lobbying?
- Is involvement in policy part of professional activity?
- How does the involvement of midwives in shaping policy help women and their families?

Further reading

Bharj, K. and Phillips, M. 2013 *The Policy Context of Midwifery and Maternity Services*. Routledge.

Provides a discussion of the social context of midwifery and policy, addressing areas including the changing demographic profile of the UK, rising fertility rates, health inequalities, new technologies and service models and structures.

Fatchett, A. 2012 *Social Policy for Nurses*. Polity.

Although written for nurses, it includes a lot of useful material about the policy process and contemporary health policy issues, which is also relevant for midwifery. Emphasis is given to the importance of practitioners involving themselves in the policy process.

Ham, C. 2009 *Health Policy in Britain*, 6th edn. Palgrave-Macmillan.

Recognized as a 'standard' health policy text, it introduces the key factors in the policy process and relates them to health care in the UK.

Klein, R. 2010 *The New Politics of the NHS – From Creation to Reinvention*, 6th edn. Radcliffe Publishing.

A good source of information about the development of the National Health Service, which includes a useful analysis of the role of politics in the policy process.

PART 2

KEY ISSUES AND CONCERNS IN MIDWIFERY

Introduction

The second part of this volume looks at key issues and concerns in midwifery exploring emotion work, long-term conditions, risk, perinatal loss and infertility. These chapters all highlight the significance of individual women's experiences with reference to social patterns and societal expectations. Drawing on sociological theories and concepts, including some already outlined and explored in Part 1, and reporting from a wide range of sociological research, the authors of the five chapters in this Part again demonstrate how thinking sociologically is invaluable for midwives and midwifery. Each of the chapters highlights concerns of significance to midwifery practice and shows how sociological explanations can assist midwives in their work 'with women'.

In Chapter 5, Ruth Deery and Pamela Fisher outline how emotion work assists in developing fulfilling and reciprocal relationships between midwives and women, and contributes to good clinical outcomes for both mother and baby. They offer a challenge to evidence-based guidelines, arguing that whilst these are important they need to be balanced alongside a woman's right to determine her own health-care needs. They conclude that 'one size fits all' practices do not facilitate the development of meaningful relationships, and when systems and their management become all-important (economies of performance), midwives' relationships with women and each other become fragmented or, at worst, non-existent.

The next four chapters all focus on experiences that very clearly demonstrate the value of emotion work. Elaine Denny, in Chapter 6, considers the particular challenges of long-term conditions for pregnant women and mothers, their babies and families. She details the ongoing sociological critique of traditional definitions of and medical approaches to disability that focus on the individual, and considers how midwives can support women with long-term conditions to feel in control of their pregnancy, birth and postnatal experience. In

Chapter 7, Jayne Samples and Bob Heyman focus on issues of risk with specific regard to pregnancy. They remind us that definitions of risk are culturally specific and that an increased consideration of risk can lead to pregnancy being perceived as a problematic condition which needs to be medically managed. Samples and Heyman conclude that identifying and minimizing risks of harm are integral to the role of a midwife, but respecting women's autonomy is equally important. Deborah Davidson's chapter (Chapter 8) is concerned with the experience of perinatal loss, whether through the death of a fetus or baby through miscarriage, stillbirth, neonatal death, or loss through termination of a pregnancy, adoption, or the apprehension of a baby by social services of the state. Davidson focuses on grief as a normal response to such losses and considers how midwives can provide the compassionate care needed to set women and their families on the course to 'good grief'. Chapter 9, the final chapter in this Part, is written by Nicky Hudson and Lorraine Culley, the focus here being the relatively common experience of infertility and the choice that some women and couples take for (medically) assisted conception. Hudson and Culley highlight the significance of cultural differences and cultural norms to how individuals experience infertility and involuntary childlessness, and consider sociological critiques of some medical responses to infertility as well as women's (and men's) satisfaction or not with the treatment they receive.

A common thread in the chapters in this Part is that of challenges to the 'taken for granted'. Building on Part 1, the authors consider how the experience of the midwife and those s/he supports may be different from the expected norm. Thus, this part of the book should help you to develop new ways to support those you care for who are, through whatever reason, experiencing some difficulties either physically, or 'emotionally', or both. It should also provide you with an improved understanding of your own professional experience and identity.

5 Emotion Work and Midwifery

Ruth Deery and Pamela Fisher

Key issues:

- Sociological theories and emotion.
- The nature of emotion work.
- Emotions and relationships in midwifery.
- Stressful and personally satisfying experiences for midwives.
- Emotional intelligence.

By the end of this chapter you should be able to:

- Discuss the application of the sociological concept of emotion work for midwifery.
- Further develop your understanding of the nature of emotion work.
- Understand the value of developing your emotional intelligence to benefit the process of relationship.
- Recognize the effect of satisfying and devitalizing emotion work in midwifery.

Introduction

Sociology is concerned with the study of human societies, and sociological knowledge can help us to make sense of the nature and practice of midwifery (see Chapter 1). However, it was not until the 1970s that sociologists began to study emotions and emotional processes (see, especially, Hochschild 1979, 1983). This is remarkable given that emotions 'pervade virtually every aspect of human experience and social relations' (Turner and Stets 2005: 1).

Emotions are powerful motivating forces. There is compelling clinical evidence that, without emotions, people lose their desire to act (Hunter and Deery 2009; Fineman 1993, 2003). When the part of the brain associated with emotional responses is damaged, this results in a clinical condition, akinetic mutism, which entails the loss of emotion and the loss of motivation (Damsio 2006). On regaining consciousness, individuals are able to retain the ability to do specific rational tasks, including intelligence tests, but are indifferent to their own well-being and are no longer able to sustain relationships or act ethically as they used to (Damsio 2006). Thus, emotion has a significant role in telling us what is important.

In addition, whereas traditionally in Western culture reason and emotion were viewed as separate from each other and mainly incompatible, there is now a growing body of evidence that suggests a considerable overlap between them. Philosophers, neuroscientists, psychotherapists and social scientists are arguing that emotions underpin our values and evaluative judgements – in other words, our emotions tell us what we care about (Nussbaum 2001; Freshwater and Robertson 2002; Damsio 2006; Fisher and Byrne 2012). As Sherman (quoted in Oakley 1992: 82) writes: 'To see dispassionately without engaging the emotions is often to be at peril of missing what is relevant.'

Nursing and midwifery were traditionally associated with a rationalist–instrumentalist mindset, where personal feelings and emotion were associated with relationships in the private sphere and deemed 'out of place' in organizations managed according to the principles of calculation and **rationalism**. Organizations were conceptualized as composed of rational mechanisms to achieve certain business, technical and administrative ends. The 'professional self' in nursing and midwifery was therefore encouraged to reinforce professional distance and boundaries. While this emphasis on rational detachment may have facilitated the practical work of caring in nursing (see Menzies Lyth 1988), the same emphasis in midwifery may have resulted in a neglect of women's psychological and emotional needs (see Kirkham 2010). Much has been written over the last ten years in midwifery, especially in relation to a sociological interpretation of the midwife–mother relationship, as discussed throughout this chapter.

rationalism
accepting reason as the supreme authority of beliefs or conduct

The **neuroscience** of belonging is a new and exciting area of research highlighting and unravelling what midwives have long known – that belonging and feeling cared for are critical to good health (Lipton 2005; Eisenberger and Cole 2012). Imagine, for example, what might happen if a pregnant woman fears telephoning hospital midwives to say she wants to come to the hospital because she is in labour. Notwithstanding the biological and hormonal disruption to the woman's body, her fears would clearly be reduced if she were able to communicate with a compassionate and caring midwife. The research review undertaken by Eisenberger and Cole (2012) shows that those who experience satisfying social relationships live longer than those who feel socially isolated or disconnected. Feeling socially connected is also protective against a range of conditions (e.g., heart disease and mental ill health). Therefore, there is no reason not to believe that fulfilling, reciprocal relationships between midwives and women contribute to good clinical outcomes for both mother and baby. Indeed, Verny and Kelly (1981) have drawn our attention to the fact that from the moment of conception the experience in the womb helps shape and develop the brain, paving the way for personality, temperament and higher-level thinking.

neuroscience
scientific study of the nervous system

Midwives in the UK have been slow to explore the emotional aspects of their work, and it was not until 2009 that Billie Hunter and Ruth Deery co-edited the first book addressing emotions in midwifery (Hunter and

Deery 2009). Since then an increasing body of knowledge has been developed around the place of emotions in midwifery, clarifying how these can potentially shape and direct practice. Midwives often have to make themselves emotionally available to women and their families, as well as to other midwives and colleagues. Likewise, we sometimes have to adapt our emotional responses to meet organizational requirements. This demands considerable emotional effort, as midwives often deal with life-and-death situations and with the increased emotional responses of joy, pain, fear, relief, anxiety and anticipation (Deery and Fisher 2010). Such responses shape our thoughts and decision-making processes, as well as influencing the extent to which we involve our 'selves' as midwives. We have to be the 'multi-skilled emotion manager' (Bolton 2000: 156) to survive in today's midwifery.

Being multi-skilled means that we have to manage our own emotions, as well as our relationships with pregnant women and colleagues, whilst negotiating the pressures of a continuously scrutinized, market-driven maternity services arena. Those midwives who work outside the NHS system or in birth centres still have to engage in emotion management but usually within a social model of birth. Emotion work is therefore grounded in and carried out through our relationships with women, their significant others and our colleagues. This chapter, written by a midwife and a sociologist, explores how emotion work can enhance midwifery practice.

Context and Culture

Since the 1970s, there have been calls from women, midwives and some obstetricians to rethink and reform birth. As Edwin van Teijlingen highlights in Chapter 2, major reconfiguration of maternity services and moves to large, centralized hospitals have produced organizations that have been described as offering women a professionally controlled and overly bureaucratic and interventionist experience of giving birth (see also Chapter 12). As a result, the relationship between the woman and the midwife becomes sidelined. In contrast, birth centres have been described as places where women are cared for by a midwife whom they will get to know and trust and who will provide most of their care (see Page (2008) for a comparison of services), so that women can enjoy normal, physiological births. Many midwives and birthrights activists have written about and researched the detrimental effects of industrialized approaches to birth (e.g., Walsh 2007; Edwards 2008; Deery et al. 2010; Mander and Murphy-Lawless 2013).

Since the 1980s, market-led reforms, the management of risk (see Chapter 7), restricted spending and cost-saving measures in the National Health Service (NHS) in the UK have meant constant change and upheaval for midwives. An increased emphasis on quantifiable targets, efficiency savings and the rationalization of service delivery, along with processes of reorganization and centralization, has produced a culture that crushes and directly conflicts with the often intangible and unquantifiable processes needed for provision of compassionate care. Overwork and workplace practices leave midwives swamped by immediate demands, and unable to find the time to stand back and reflect on how they work (Deery 2005; Bryson and Deery 2009). Increasingly, we are hearing in the news and from midwives themselves that organizational pressures take midwives further away from their real work, leaving them stressed and even 'burnt out'.

Sadly, compassionate care, and its absence as a core NHS value, has become prominent in recent high-profile media situations (e.g., Francis 2013). Such reports highlight many reasons why the provision of care is sometimes not as it should be. Yet compassion as a concept, and how it is conceptualized by midwives in everyday practice, is not clear, especially in terms of how we assess whether our care to women and babies and their families is improving.

Figure 5.1 A midwife at her desk. Midwives often feel that they have to spend too much time filling out paperwork during the birth and not enough time assisting the expectant mother

📋 Activity 5.1: Compassionate care – what does it mean?

Read and consider the following papers:

Bryson, V. and Deery, R. 2009 Public policy, 'men's time' and power: the work of community midwives in the British National Health Service. *Women's Studies International Forum*, doi:org/10.1016/j.wsif.2009.11.004

Hall, J. 2013 Developing a culture of compassionate care – the midwife's voice. *Midwifery* 29: 269–71.

Dewar, B. and Nolan, M. 2013 Caring about caring: developing a model to implement compassionate relationship-centred care in an older-people care setting. *International Journal of Nursing Studies* 50: 1247–58. (The principles considered here can be applied across settings).

(a) Is compassion innate within human beings at birth or does it develop (or not) over the lifespan?
(b) If a student midwife demonstrates strong compassion traits at interview, what can happen during the course of training to make compassion less evident?
(c) Likewise, what can affect a midwife's approach to relationship when working in a busy maternity service?

As described above and in Chapter 2, in some parts of the UK labour and birth are increasingly centralized into larger maternity units as part of cost-saving measures. This situation contributes to an emotionally draining working (and birthing) environment, especially as maternity services described as 'woman-centred' are often run according to an industrialized conveyor-belt model, with no continuity of relationship between woman and midwife. Midwives have become interchangeable workers who must prioritize keeping the system running (Deery and Kirkham 2006). Task-based approaches and technical skills have become valued over and above the midwife–mother relationship (Hewitt and Coffey 2005; Kirkham 2010). Writing about the 'power of flow', Kirkham (2011) argues that when midwives go with the flow (see also Chapter 12) of the organization there is a tendency to practise guideline-centred care (Kotaska 2011) rather than woman-centred, compassionate care:

> The many moves to standardize services through guidelines, policies, procedures and pathways have made the organizational flow more powerful . . . the pressure to go with the flow of the organization had a divisive effect on relationships . . . controlling the flow enables organizations to run smoothly . . . the flow necessitates the development of a whole series of coping habits. (Kirkham 2011: 88)

Guideline-centred care takes place in hospitals that are professionally controlled, bureaucratic and interventionist. Whilst evidence-based guidelines are important, these need to be balanced alongside a woman's right to determine her own health-care needs. However, as Kotaska (2011) points out, person-centredness (or woman-centredness) is an end in itself and guideline-centred care is simply a means to an end. In the 1990s, there was an expectation that the advent of woman-centred care would lead to far-reaching changes in the organizational culture of midwifery, enabling midwives to manage their own emotions and to respond appropriately to others (Department of Health 1993). In other words, the aspiration was that emotionally intelligent midwives would be able to engage with women responsively and sensitively through an embodied approach that incorporates feelings, thoughts and behaviour. Unfortunately, what we now sometimes see in midwifery are organizations describing themselves as woman-centred without the necessary cultural shift taking place to make this a reality. Improving women's experiences of maternity services and supporting midwives to deliver woman-centred and compassionate care is now a high priority on the policy agenda in the UK (Flynn and Mercer 2013; NES 2013; Francis Report 2013).

📋 Activity 5.2: Reflections on a clinical shift

[A] shift that was, as usual, busy and relentless and where I cared for two women for most of the time. During this particular shift I could not be 'with woman' because I was spending most of my time running from room to room, completing paper and computer records, answering the doorbell to visitors, answering the telephone and other women's buzzers – I was 'absently present' (Berg et al. 1996: 13). For some reason, on this shift I felt ground down as the reality hit me that, for most of the time, to be a midwife in the British National Health Service meant that I could rarely be 'with woman'. During the course of the shift, I had also been reminded of my mandatory training requirements, most of them now computer based, as well as two study days to attend. My technical competence as a midwife seemed much more important than engaging with women in the birth process. I was becoming increasingly aware of how difficult it was for me to just 'be a midwife' – I felt worn out and in need of a recharge (see also Deery and Kirkham 2007). How could I possibly engage in a meaningful relationship with a woman when I had no quality time to spend with her? We were both being denied the development of a personally energizing, reciprocal relationship (see Deery 2008; Hunter 2006). On reflection, I feel sure that my 'busyness' and lack of engagement prevented the women from asking me any questions. Similarly, Bone (2002) found that nurses often presented a detached demeanour to prevent clients from making requests that they did not have time to complete. The constant stream of paperwork, form filling, lack of resources and shortage of midwives only served to reiterate that the system was more committed to the outcome of childbirth and industrialized obstetrics than the dynamics within the midwife–mother relationship. I knew I was 'going with the flow' of obstetric and managerial opinion because it made my life easier.

In studies of nursing, Bone (2002) and Lewis (2005) have also reported that nurses experience constant tensions between being the nurse they want to be and the requirements of the system. I looked around me at the way we were working and wondered how much longer we could sustain this way of working without going into emotional meltdown.

(a) What are your initial thoughts about this reflection?
(b) How might the situation have been managed differently?
(c) Was there potential to change the status quo?

(Adapted from Deery and Hunter 2010)

Having considered some of the emotional challenges associated with midwifery, we now turn to take a closer look at some sociological theories relating to emotion and consider their usefulness in making sense of the working lives of midwives.

The Sociology of Emotions

Erving Goffman is one of the major proponents of **symbolic interactionism**, which has arguably been one of the most influential theories in the sociology of health and illness (see Chapter 13 for application to mental health). Although symbolic interactionism is concerned with the way people organize face-to-face interactions (rather than emotion work), we consider how Goffman's (1959) work on symbolic interactionism is relevant to understanding emotional work in midwifery.

> **symbolic interactionism** people acting towards things based on the meaning those things have for them

Symbolic interactionism means that individual identity is formed during interaction with others. In other words, while people possess their own individuality, this individuality is only achieved in their interactions with others. For example, if people are pleasant to us, it is easier for us to form a positive self-image. If, on the other hand, people constantly disrespect us or treat us with contempt, this tends to undermine our self-confidence. In midwifery, then, social connectedness and a sense of belonging need to be key attributes of woman-centred care (Newburn and Singh 2005; Lipton 2005; Eisenberger and Cole 2012).

In *The Presentation of the Self in Everyday Life* (1959), Goffman argued that individuals often put on a theatrical performance in their interactions with others in order to give the 'right' impression. For example, midwives might wish to project an image of being 'in control' and competent, even though they may feel quite differently. Goffman explained that identity is very much connected with social roles and that a person's sense of self can be divided into two; the official self and the unsociable self. The official self is the one associated with an appropriate public performance and is based on 'certain attributes, capacities and information which, taken together, fit together in a self that is at once coherently unified and appropriate for the occasion' (Goffman

1959: 263). In other words, the official self is essentially concerned with impression management, that is, with ensuring that midwives give women and their families and work colleagues the right impression (see Hunter and Deery 2009 for further application to midwifery).

Goffman (1959) viewed the unsocialized self as being the 'real person' behind the official self. Sometimes he refers to the unsocialized self as the 'offstage self'. This reveals itself when the individual is no longer performing a social identity, and it tends to emerge when the performance of the official self is disrupted in some way. When this happens, the individual who performs the character will be seen for what he largely is, a solitary player involved in a harried concern for his production. 'Behind many characters each performer tends to wear a single look, a naked unsocialized look, a look of concentration, a look of one who is privately engaged in a different treacherous task' (Goffman 1959: 235). This view of the self as divided brings to mind a scene from the television series *Gordon Ramsay's Hell's Kitchen*: the calm 'front' presented conceals the extent of the chaos in the kitchen from blissfully unaware diners.

This notion of the divided self is important in midwifery when dealing with situations which are emotionally highly charged, in particular, life-and-death situations (Deery and Fisher 2010; Kenworthy and Kirkham 2011; see also Chapter 13). Deery's (2005) research with community midwives highlighted midwives' ability to 'psych themselves up' and use this as a coping strategy. One of the midwives described having to calibrate her emotions in order to deal with different workplace situations, stating that she had 'to psych [herself] up' when visiting some women, particularly 'if their circumstances were sensitive'. Another midwife had learned to cope by ensuring that she always put on a steeled performance for her colleagues so that they were unable to detect her stress: 'people think that you cope and think that you are all right . . . this is something you often perpetuate because you wouldn't have them know anything else . . . I think there are times inside when I've thought "God, if my colleagues knew how I was feeling right now" . . . You've got this image, haven't you . . . you've got to keep going . . .'

This midwife is using 'impression management' to mask the personal and professional challenges she is experiencing, so that her colleagues perceive her as 'coping'. Fineman (2003) describes how those who let their masks slip, or show signs of any cracks, risk leaking their feelings, and this is how 'professional image and mystique' are maintained (Fineman 2003: 37).

📋 Activity 5.3: Maintaining professional image and mystique

Consider the concepts of 'official self' and 'unsocialized self'.

(a) Do they apply to you? Have you seen these performances played out by midwives you have observed or worked with?

(b) Do midwives behave differently when supporting women or talking with their work colleagues?

(c) Have you ever observed or used 'impression management' in a midwifery setting?

Emotional Labour

We have previously written about 'emotion work' which is a generic term to describe different types of emotion engagement (Deery and Fisher 2010); here, we consider the term 'emotional labour'. Although the terms 'emotion work' and 'emotional labour' are often used interchangeably, there is a key difference. The term 'emotional labour', which is more explicitly associated with exploitation, was first coined by Arlie R. Hochschild (1983) to describe the often unacknowledged effort that employees make in ensuring that they display appropriate emotions in the interests of their *employers*. Emotional labour can therefore be regarded as a form of emotion work which is conducted in the interests of profit. For example, airline stewards have to be courteous and polite to airline passengers at all times, even when the latter are rude and aggressive. Similarly, Hochschild described how debt collectors, who are often obliged to adopt a 'hard' demeanour, were also obliged to perform emotional labour in their work (Hochschild 1983). Bolton (2005: 49) refers to emotional labour as 'capitalism's appropriation of that skill'.

Despite its association with capital, the concept of emotional labour can be equally relevant to public-sector organizations, particularly as these are now managed according to a market-based ideology (see Mander and Murphy-Lawless 2013). Midwives can be regarded as performing emotional labour when they are focusing on organizational interests (what we have previously termed 'guideline-based practice'), which might include efficiency and cost-saving measures. For Hochschild (1983), emotional labour was largely undervalued and associated with stresses among employees that had health-related repercussions. Mental health problems such as stress and 'burn-out' have been the subject of numerous research studies in midwifery (see Sandall 1998; Kirkham 1999; Ball et al. 2002; Deery 2005; see also Chapter 13). While air stewardesses are obliged to remain calm and pleasant in response to their passengers' sometimes unreasonable demands and anxieties, midwives may similarly have to conceal a range of negative emotions in order to present an acceptable face to colleagues and women and their families. This can lead to emotional dissonance, which must be concealed in the interests of the organization (maternity services, in this case).

There is little suggestion in Goffman's (1959) analysis that presenting the publicly acceptable face requires any particular emotional effort. It is to Hochschild's (1983) credit that she was the first to point out that managing one's own and others' emotions is in fact hard work. In addition, Hochschild (1983) extended Goffman's notion of the 'official self' by introducing the concepts of surface and deep acting. Though both surface and deep acting are internally inauthentic for the individual, there is a fundamental difference of intention between the two. In the case of surface acting, the individual is faking their performance by displaying emotions that they do not feel; with deep acting, they have succeeded in evoking in themselves the emotions associated with their organizational role. This can be regarded as a form of colonization of a person's emotional world, whereby authentic emotions have been replaced by organizationally determined emotions. Irrespective, however, of whether a person is performing surface or deep acting, the emotions involved are fake in the sense that they have been evoked through serving organizational requirements.

What should be noted is that Hochschild's analysis does not associate emotional labour with a person's personal attachments or values; emotional labour is about displaying or internalizing emotions that serve organizational purposes:

> As it is for people observed by Erving Goffman, the action is in the body language, the put-on-sneer, the posed shrug, the controlled sigh. This is surface acting. The other way is deep acting. Here display is a natural result of working on feeling; the actor does not try to seem happy or sad but rather expresses spontaneously a real feeling that has been self induced. (Hochshild 1983: 33)

Emotional Intelligence

The concept of emotional intelligence (EI) seems to have become the mantra of so-called effective organizations. While Hochschild's interpretation of emotional labour was mainly negative, in the sense that she viewed it as largely unacknowledged and commodified labour with

Box 5.1 Techniques of emotion work

Turner and Stets (2005: 38) have highlighted four techniques of emotion work that individuals may use for feeling and displaying the appropriate face.

Body work: whereby a person might try to alter their physiological reaction to a situation, for example, through deep breathing. This might be during a difficult conversation with another midwife or a manager.
Surface acting: whereby people might manipulate themselves to externally express (or act) the emotion from which these gestures are supposed to emanate, for example, putting on the appropriate face (happy or sad).
Deep acting: whereby a person is able to evoke within themselves emotions that serve organizational aims.
Cognitive work: whereby a person invokes thoughts and ideas associated with an emotion in order to generate the feelings.

potentially serious repercussions for mental health, the allied concept of emotional intelligence has gained ascendancy in lay, corporate and academic circles. *Emotional Intelligence: Why It Can Matter More Than IQ*, published in 1996, established Daniel Goleman as the leading authority on EI which he defined as consisting of 'the intrapersonal competencies of knowing one's emotions, managing emotions, motivating oneself; and the interpersonal competencies of recognizing emotion in others and handling relationships' (Goleman 1996: 42, see Box 5.2). The adoption of the concept of EI marks a significant shift in the way competence in the workplace is assessed. Customer care and 'patient' care are now seen as relying on emotional rapport and friendly smiles as much as on professional competence and expertise.

According to Fineman (2003), emotional intelligence makes the connection as to how emotions can be used intelligently in both our personal lives and work settings. Others claim that it is EI and not IQ that underpins satisfying and successful lives (Goleman 1988, 1996). The importance of midwifery self-awareness on the woman's maternity service experience and the drive towards evidence-based practice are crucial aspects of this approach. It has therefore been argued that EI can give midwives a greater understanding of themselves, whilst also helping them to manage their relationships with colleagues and women as well as negotiating other social complexities of midwifery (Hunter 2004b). From this perspective, if a midwife is not emotionally intelligent then she runs the risk of generating negative emotion work, followed by possible stress and burn-out.

The picture, however, is not as simple as that. Goleman's optimistic view of the potential offered by EI conflicts with some literature that suggests that (similar to emotional labour) EI is a form of organizational control. Hatcher (2008) refers to this as a situation where workers 'must become active in fashioning themselves in particular ways because their culture proposes, suggests, and imposes models of what appropriate ways to act are, in their circumstances.'

Hughes (2005) has suggested that EI's primary aim is the surveillance and control of people's emotions and values so that these are consistent with organizational agendas. This can arguably result in people performing emotions that may undermine trust. Individual interests are subsumed into those of the organization, namely, performance

Box 5.2 The five domains of emotional intelligence

Goleman (1996) claims that emotionally intelligent people have abilities in the following five domains:

- They know their emotions.
- They manage their emotions.
- They motivate themselves.
- They recognize emotions in others.
- They can handle relationships.

targets, and professionals are valued according to their contribution to the overall performance. As a result, the flexible range of emotional responses that are called for in all 'people' professions atrophies into limited and codified forms of 'emotional labour'. Edwards (2005) found in research with women choosing home birth that there was a tendency for midwives to provide formulaic, rather than emotionally intelligent, responses when communicating with women. Deery (2005) undertook research that found midwives feared hurting each other through clumsy communication. In their efforts to spare each other from emotional discomfort, midwives reported dealing with work-related issues superficially, sometimes manipulatively, often destructively, and in a manner that often sabotaged their good intentions. One participant described this as behaviour akin to a 'ladylike saboteur'. A recommendation from this research was that further interpersonal skill training be facilitated for registered midwives and incorporated into the curriculum for student midwives.

At the same time, people who are emotionally intelligent may be seen as cynical actors who are able to further their own personal goals at the cost of neglecting others' needs. Kirkham (1999) also describes how midwives 'engineer changes by a process of subtle manipulation'. Hunter (2004b) has highlighted that developing emotional intelligence in the midwifery workforce is imperative to further develop the profession. Increasingly, we are seeing organizations such as the NHS encouraging emotionally responsive leadership styles to help them achieve their goals and vision. However, we need to be aware that EI needs to be aligned with a sense of integrity or it can result in emotional hypocrisy and manipulation.

🗒 Activity 5.4: Using emotional intelligence

Having a high emotional intelligence is especially important in a health-care setting, and even more so in midwifery, where women are experiencing profound, life-changing birth events.

(a) What are some ways in which midwives can keep emotional intelligence in mind as they carry out their day-to-day work, sometimes experiencing and encountering different stressors?
(b) What are the possible risks associated with emotional intelligence?
(c) When thinking about these risks, consider feeling out of control, stressed, having anger directed at you, feeling vulnerable, being empathetic and protecting yourself from stress, either in the workplace or your personal life.

Authentic Emotional Engagement

More recent thinking of public-service work and emotions has led to the development of Hochschild's work on emotional labour (for example, see James 1989, 1992; Smith 1992; Wharton 1993; Bolton 2000, 2005; Deery and Hunter 2010; Deery and Fisher 2010; Fisher and Byrne 2012). As a result, more nuanced perspectives on emotion work have emerged that point to a more complex understanding. In midwifery, it has been suggested that midwives who interact with different women on a continuous basis have to contend with different types of emotion work (Hunter 2004a), which may vary over time. When midwives engage with women in longer interactions the consequence is longer emotional composure, which requires greater attention to performance and emotional stamina on the part of the midwife (Deery 2005).

Longer, more intense interactions also mean that women will often disclose further information about themselves, thus making it harder for the midwife to avoid showing her own personal feelings (Smith 1992). Prolonged interactions may therefore contribute to more authentic forms of engagement and relationships. Bolton (2005: 93) has produced a useful typology of workplace emotion, highlighting that there are several motivations linked to an individual's emotional responses in an organization. These motivations are also constantly emerging and changing, according to different workplace situations. A midwife therefore uses her 'emotional armour' (Hochschild 1998: 10) in a variety of ways.

Bolton's (2005) typology of the different types of emotional engagement called for a form of emotion work that she terms 'philanthropic' emotion work. This is not carried out as an obligation but is related to an authentically felt desire to help people. Philanthropic emotion work is therefore not connected with organizational imperatives but is willingly expended as a 'gift'. Philanthropic emotion work can be highly energizing and is often associated with higher levels of professional engagement and personal well-being, even in challenging situations. In a study relating to support staff working with people with learning disabilities, it was found that philanthropic emotional engagement can potentially make even the most challenging work rewarding (Fisher and Byrne 2012). What is particularly interesting about philanthropic emotion work from a sociological point of view is that it demonstrates how emotions are not merely attached to individuals, but arise *within* relationships (Deery and Fisher 2010; Fisher and Byrne 2012). For a discussion on the potential benefits of philanthropic emotion work to midwifery, see Deery and Fisher (2010).

Relationships

By now you will appreciate that emotion work in midwifery is bound up with, and cannot be separated from, relationships. Relationships with midwives matter to women, professionals and policymakers, not just in terms of physical healthy outcomes but also because of the potential to optimize a positive start to parenting (Verny and Kelly 1981; Lipton 2005; Eisenberger and Cole 2012; Kirkham 2010). Women also need an

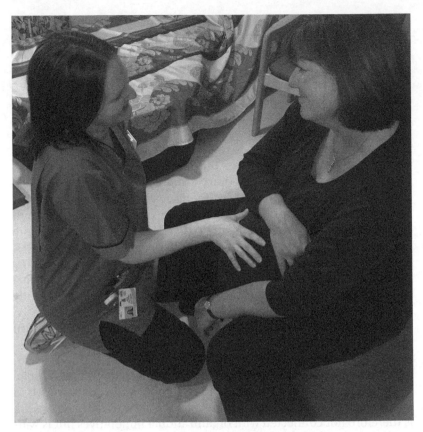

Figure 5.2 Women need an emotionally supportive midwife

emotionally present midwife who, according to Berg et al. (1996), 'sees, supports and inspires self confidence' through a trusting relationship.

Women in poverty and disadvantage especially need to be listened to and feel supported and respected, just as women with complex pregnancies need to be seen and affirmed in the same way as women with 'normal pregnancies' (see Davies and Deery 2014, for a saluto-genic, asset-based approach). As midwives, we need to be careful of stereotyping where women can feel ignored, rejected or stigmatized. Woman-centred, connected and compassionate care is paramount to such women, and as midwives we have the potential to influence their futures. As Pembroke and Pembroke (2008: 325) note, if midwives 'fill their internal spaces with their own commitments and preferences, there is no place for the woman to make contact'.

Murray Enkin et al. (2006: 268) write, 'it is not simply the woman or the setting, the attendant or the policies that influence the outcome. Rather, it is the complex interrelationships among these separate ele-ments.' This lovely quotation highlights the importance and complexity of relationship. Murray Enkin and colleagues bring to our attention that it is not just the relationship with women that is important, but also the relationship with all elements of the pregnancy, birth and postnatal journey. There is a large and growing body of knowledge in midwifery providing evidence that relationship between women and midwives matters (see Pembroke and Pembroke 2008; Kirkham 2010; Hastie 2011), and that meaningful relationships can be fulfilling. Women taking part in research have described feeling safe when midwives are actively present (Berg et al. 1996), and feeling cared for when midwives are 'always there' (Berg et al. 1996). Women have also described midwives as anchored companions (Lundgren 2004). When the opportunity to work 'with women' is available, there is congruence with midwifery values and work is experienced as emotionally rewarding and satisfying (Hunter and Deery 2009).

'Ecologies of practice' (Stronach et al. 2002) develop when midwives are able to draw on a wealth of diverse knowledge, experience and influences, including emotional, relational and experiential knowledge developed in their private lives and in the communities in which they live (Deery and Fisher 2010; Deery and Hunter 2010). Birth centres provide a good example here as a gauge, indicating social changes in progress which are revaluing human relationships relative to technology and medicine (Hunter et al. 2008). Economies of performance, however, are shaped by bureaucratic structures and imperatives and where potentially 'practice is poor, too urgent to be planned optimally or too poorly resourced to be effective' (Stronach et al. 2002: 131). When the system (the NHS in this case) takes preference, economies of performance become the preferred way of working, limiting the midwife's capacity to be visionary and make changes to practice. We are reminded here of the very poor care highlighted at Mid Staffordshire Hospital; it could be argued that this demonstrates what happens when 'economies of performance' are prioritized over 'ecologies of practice'.

Restrictions and Coping Strategies

Frank (2005) argues that when health-care practitioners seek refuge in codes, organizational rules and procedures (or economies of performance), they become what he terms 'artificial persons' – individuals who are outwardly compliant with organizational requirements but who no longer act as engaged and autonomous professionals *in their own right*. Artificial persons detach their professional behaviour from their sense of self. The professional self becomes compartmentalized away from an authentic sense of self and, as a consequence, loses the capacity to engage with sincerity in relationships with patients (women and families in the case of midwifery).

Deery and Kirkham (2007) report how positive emotional energy was experienced by a group of community midwives as a finite resource. Competing organizational and service-user demands led them to regulate and control their professional behaviour. Being an artificial person also requires considerable emotional energy. The midwives reported reaching the limit of their capacity to deal with women emotionally, and relationships with women were depicted as a one-way draining of emotional energy, leaving the midwives feeling 'empty'. Walsh (2007), on the other hand, refers to hospitality in his research at a free-standing birth centre and an emphasis on 'being' rather than 'doing'. Midwives in this long-established birth centre had developed a way of assisting birth that was flexible, trusting, respectful, democratic and sustainable (Walsh 2009). There was a network of reciprocal relationships with midwives holding the same values, which enhanced **social capital** for the local community and the individuals concerned; these midwives were authentic, not artificial.

social capital
connections within
and between social
networks

Negative or low emotional energy can lead to a form of 'splitting'. It is manifest, for example, when policy statements and guidelines are interpreted literally rather than applied with appropriate professional discretion. This evokes the earlier work of Menzies-Lyth (1988), who influentially pointed out that routine practices serve the latent function of defending nurses psychologically from the anxiety associated with their work. In contemporary midwifery, seeking refuge behind protocols and guidelines, without reflecting on these in an evidence-based way, can provide a justificatory mechanism for avoiding the emotion work associated with building relationships with women.

Deery (2005) found that midwives appeared to engage with women at different levels, in order to cope with organizational pressures and the emotion work that was demanded. The midwives seemed to have the ability to switch and swap their faces, as if this operated as a safety valve for them, helping them to 'make conscious choices based on their emotional needs and on their understanding of what they can handle at a particular time' (Carmack 1997: 141). Task-based performances became the favoured way of working for most of the midwives because this meant that they could distance themselves from women, making it easier to complete their work within the constraints of the organization. Such emotional detachment limited and fragmented the development of relationships as the midwives tried to fit women into the bureaucracy of maternity services. Indeed, they appeared to reach a point at which their increasing workloads precluded women's needs being met and emotion work became either impossible, could not be entered into, or became a stressor and not a source of energy. The midwives who appeared energized by their work were sensitive to their own personal emotional needs, and they chose their level of engagement according to the situation they were presented with at a particular time. They were also able to constantly rebalance their work situation and, rather than experiencing emotion work negatively, they found work to be a personally enhancing experience. However, midwives can lose the ability to manage and express their feelings effectively when they experience fear or stressful situations. This is sometimes to the point that they are no longer able to empathize with women and their colleagues, and work becomes routine, ritualized and depersonalized.

Being a midwife in a large centralized unit can mean becoming an obedient technician in order to cope (Deery and Hunter 2010). Crafting efficient, 'one size fits all' organizations does not facilitate the development of meaningful relationships (Sennett 2008), and when systems and their management become all-important (economies of performance) our relationships with women and each other become fragmented or, at worst, non-existent. A culture focused on doing the system's business is created, rather than a culture of women using the maternity service to their advantage. Deery (2010, 2012) has written of 'obedient technicians' and 'steeled midwives' who have no control over their working conditions; they have to be seen to cope with everything. They also engage in production-line work as a coping mechanism and a way of avoiding emotional connections. Women who experience production-line work also have no control over their childbirth experience because being obedient means having to stick to the rules. As Edwards (2009) has pointed out, sticking to the rules prevents meaningful relationships developing with women who want to challenge the rules.

In the 1950s, Menzies carried out a classic study of hospital nursing that provided an extraordinary picture of traditional ways of working within hospitals (Menzies 1979). The system Menzies sees functions as an organizational defence against stress and anxiety. Work that was task-orientated seemed to protect nurses from close contact with their patients, and depersonalization and categorization of patients meant that relationships were kept unemotional and distant. The strict routines and standard procedures that seemed to pervade the whole of nursing practice also minimized responsibility and decision-making for nurses, thus protecting them from associated stresses (Menzies 1979).

Raphael-Leff (1991) draws on the work of Menzies, stating that the strategies that have been developed by nurses to help minimize the stressful effects of emotional relationships between women and staff can also be applied to midwifery work. She specifically addresses three defensive techniques used by midwives and the organization in which they work: splitting up of the nurse–patient relationship; denial and detachment of feelings; and redistribution of responsibility. The splitting of the mother–midwife relationship is illustrated by using an example from the antenatal clinic 'where a woman may be seen by as many as 30 "interchangeable" hospital professionals in the course of one pregnancy and little attempt is made to acknowledge her as a special individual either before, during or after birth' (Raphael-Leff 1991: 225).

Raphael-Leff (1991) describes how task-orientated care and no continuity of carer are used to protect midwives from anxiety-provoking situations that might involve them building relationships with women. Thus, protection from anxiety is achieved through breaking a woman's care down into tasks, minimizing contact for the woman with a midwife and reinforcing the myth that all midwives are the same with interchangeable skills. The use of fetal monitors, ultrasound scanning machines and computerized record-keeping also seemed to minimize contact with women (see commodification around birth in Chapter 12).

Raphael-Leff (1991) believes that a certain amount of detachment and denial of feelings was necessary within the midwife–mother relationship in order that personal feelings could be controlled and over-involvement in the developing relationship was avoided. This is reinforced by Carmack (1997) in a study investigating how care-givers balance engagement with detachment to cope with cumulative demands and losses, and where it was identified, that practitioners need 'a certain amount of numbing if they are to function effectively' (Carmack 1997: 140). This mechanistic approach to work is reminis-cent of 'technical administrative rationality' where midwives work with women through time-bound, predetermined clear-cut routines and specific behaviours (Deery 2008).

Rayment (2011) undertook ethnographic research to examine the extent to which working in a midwife-led rather than a consultant-led service might help or hinder midwives' capacity to manage the emo-tional and ideological demands of their practice. Rayment's research found that in order to cope with the emotional distress experienced by the midwives, they used coping strategies to organize the people and spaces around them. Similar to Deery's (2005) research, the mid-wives often did not know that they were using such strategies because these ways of working had become part of their everyday practice. The midwives in both the above studies explained these coping strategies as necessary so that they could deal with the institutional constraints and regulations of the NHS, which were out of their control and often destructive for midwifery.

Interestingly, the coping strategies of the midwives in Rayment's study were very similar in the consultant unit and the midwifery unit. A midwife-led service provided the midwives with a space within which to nurture their philosophy of practice (see also Hughes and Deery 2002; Hughes et al. 2002; Deery et al. 2010). Whilst this provided clear benefits for their emotional well-being, it also set them against the neighbouring delivery suite. Poor working relationships severely affected their capacity to provide a service that matched their pro-fessional ideals. Rayment (2011) concluded that, whilst midwife-led units attempt to promote a midwifery model of care and a conducive working environment for midwives, their closeness to consultant-led services compounds the ideological conflict the midwives experience. The strength of their philosophy may have the unintended conse-quence of silencing open discussion about the negative influence on women of the strategies the midwives use to compensate for ideologi-cal conflict and a lack of institutional and professional support.

What this chapter underlines is that, even if midwives are unaware of it, the management of emotions and the strategies employed for dealing with emotions take up significant amounts of energy in the provision of maternity services. A more ideal situation would be one in which midwives have more opportunities for authentic emotional engagement with the women they attend. The available evidence suggests that authentic other-orientated engagement can be professionally empowering. However, it appears that current structural and cultural constraints mean that the emotion expended in maternity care is more often directed, either wittingly or unwittingly, towards strategies for professional survival. This poses questions which cannot be overlooked if the provision of compassionate care is seen as a guiding principle in service delivery.

Summary

- This chapter has focused on the place of emotions in midwifery.
- The work of Hochschild and others has captured the sociological imagination, and different disciplines and occupations have progressed her theory highlighting emotions as an area of study with important and far-reaching implications for leadership, management and practice (Smith 2008).
- Healthy relationships and social connectedness between midwives and mothers and their families can improve health and thus antenatal, intrapartum and postnatal outcomes for women, their babies and families.
- An understanding of emotion work and emotional literacy is essential for the development of an emotionally, intellectually and economically sustaining maternity workforce. The potential for midwives' personal growth is immense as well as the positive impact on the woman's well-being.

Questions for discussion

- How will you develop *your* emotion work in midwifery? Read the section on emotion work in this chapter again and then think of some examples of different situations at work that could be stressful or energizing for you.
- How can sociology help you to understand women's and midwives' emotional experiences of maternity services?
- Look through the sociological literature and try to identify some other sociological studies that could potentially influence/change your clinical practice.

Further reading

Best, S. 2003 *A Beginner's Guide to Social Theory*. Sage Publications. This book provides a useful introduction to the concepts and arguments used by leading classical and contemporary social theorists.
Fineman, S. 2008 *The Emotional Organization*. Blackwell.

This book demonstrates what is understood today about power and structural effects on emotion and identity in organizations. Many of the essays in the book will have resonance for the maternity services in terms of workplace cultures, power and institutional expectations.

Goleman, D. 2007 *Social Intelligence: The New Science of Human Relationships*. Arrow Books.

This book is a synthesis of the latest findings in biology and brain science, making links to their impact on building meaningful relationships. Goleman argues for a new model of social intelligence drawn from the emerging field of social neuroscience.

Hunter, B. and Deery, R. 2009 *Emotions in Midwifery and Reproduction*. Palgrave Macmillan.

This book uses examples of maternity care and infertility settings to explore subjects of emotional well-being, relationships, infertility, loss, breastfeeding and motherhood. There is sociological interpretation in a number of the chapters.

Hargreaves, J. and Page, L. 2013 *Reflective Practice*. Polity.

This book uses stories, exercises and a reflective timeline to enable you to develop your skills. Its emphasis is on the practical, from how to construct a reflective essay to the ethical ambiguities of whistleblowing and constructing a professional persona. The book will increase your application and understanding of some of the exercises and further reading suggested in this chapter and the overall book.

6 Long-term Conditions and Disability

Elaine Denny

> **Key issues:**
>
> - A sociological approach to long-term conditions.
> - Long-term conditions in pregnancy and the postnatal period.
> - The biomedical model of disability.
> - The social model of disability.
> - Sexuality and reproduction of disabled people.
> - Prenatal surveillance.

> **By the end of this chapter you should be able to:**
>
> - Understand some of the sociological approaches to long-term conditions.
> - Discuss how long-term conditions may be affected by pregnancy, and how pregnancy may be affected by a long-term condition.
> - Distinguish between a biomedical and a sociological perspective on disability.
> - Discuss some of the problems faced by women with a disability during pregnancy and the postnatal period.
> - Understand some of the social implications of prenatal surveillance.

Introduction

Although the aim of midwives is to achieve a healthy mother and baby, the reality is sometimes different. More adults with long-term illness or disability are becoming parents, and although the number of babies being born with disability has not radically altered over time, more babies are surviving life-threatening problems around birth. Moreover, the availability of new technologies means that parents are sometimes aware before the birth that their child has some physical or developmental problem.

Around 15.4 million people in the UK have some form of long-term illness (King's Fund 2009), and many more are thought to have an undiagnosed condition. While many people develop long-term illness late in life, some conditions, such as multiple sclerosis, endometriosis and epilepsy, are associated with the reproductive years. A long-term condition is often associated with some degree of disability, which may also have implications for pregnancy. Yet maternity services are usually organized around the needs of non-disabled women, and those with long-term illness or disability frequently feel that they are perceived as 'a problem' and automatically labelled as 'high risk' (Thomas 1997).

We are familiar with the biomedical view of disability, which dominates welfare policy and provision in the UK. In this model, it is argued that disability is a 'personal tragedy', that is, it is something that affects an individual and their family, but in the majority of cases there are no wider societal issues to consider (Oliver and Barnes 2012). The role of the medical profession is to help the disabled person to adapt and to live as normal a life as possible. Similarly, a psychological approach to disability looks at how disability impacts on the individual in areas such as self-esteem, body image and coping in an able-bodied world. Less familiar to people are sociological perspectives on long-term illness and disability.

This chapter provides an overview of sociological perspectives on long-term illness and disability and applies them to midwifery practice by considering both pregnant women and mothers who have a long-term illness or disability, and women with a fetus diagnosed with a malformation that will give rise to a severe illness or a disability. Although these issues are being addressed separately, it has to be acknowledged that much disability is caused by a long-term illness, so there is a strong association between the two and distinctions may be blurred. For example, within the chapter you will notice that epilepsy is featured in research on long-term illness, and also in research on disability.

Before we consider sociological perspectives on long-term conditions and disability, we need to think about the terminology in general usage and within sociology. The previously used term of 'chronic disease' has over time given way to 'long-term' as it did not reflect very well people who were subject to acute flare-ups in their condition or who were well for part of the time. 'Disease' has also been replaced, first by 'illness' which incorporates the subjective experience of the person, and then by 'condition' to reflect the wider non-medical aspects of ill health. 'Long-term conditions' is currently the term most government documents are employing. So the language we use tends to reflect current thinking on an issue. Similarly, the language used to portray disabled people has changed over time. Words such as 'spastic', 'imbecile' or 'retarded', which reflect both inadequate descriptions of people with disability and the low value placed on such people, have been replaced by intellectual and physical disability. However, as we shall discuss later, even though distinctions are now made between terms that were once used interchangeably, this in itself may raise problems.

The Sociology of Long-term Conditions

The sociology of long-term conditions has quite a long history, and in the 1950s and 1960s sociologists tended to adopt the term in common usage, 'chronic' illness or disease, meaning something that could not

Box 6.1 The rights and responsibilities of the sick role

Patients' rights
To be exempted from normal roles and responsibilities.
As they are not responsible for their sickness they can expect to be taken care of.

Patients' responsibilities
The obligation to want to get well.
The obligation to seek competent help and comply with treatment.

Doctors' rights
Access to the body.
Access to privileged information about the patient.

Doctors' responsibilities
To act solely in the interests of the patient.
To work to the highest standards of clinical competence.
(Parsons 1951b)

be cured and may eventually kill the sufferer, although this was not always inevitable. In Chapter 1, you were introduced to sociological concepts that are very useful in the development of a sociology of long-term conditions. Here we will briefly revisit these and also discuss some additional perspectives.

One of the earliest and best-known examinations of the sick person within society was Talcott Parsons' (1951b) work on 'the sick role'. Parsons studied sickness not only in terms of biological malfunctioning, but also in the way it is organized in order to maintain order within society. Unless it is controlled in some way, sickness may become a social deviance, causing breakdown within society. In Western societies, Parsons argued, the conditions under which people are allowed to be classified as sick are controlled by medical practitioners who can sanction and legitimize them. This control is maintained by certain rights and responsibilities being ascribed.

The concept of the sick role has been criticized for failing to account for long-term illness, where the person cannot get well and return to a pre-illness state, although Parsons himself argued that the goal of recovery is an approximation rather than an accomplishment (Parsons 1951b). The importance of Parsons' work is in identifying illness as a social phenomenon, an idea that has been developed by sociologists in more recent times.

Parsons was a sociologist from the structural functionalist tradition, but in the 1960s sociological examination of chronic illness became more focused on individual accounts, and the sense people made of it within their lives. A perspective that has been influential and enduring is Goffman's work on stigma (Goffman 1968). Goffman defines stigma as an attribute that is perceived as deviant and therefore marks a person out as different or not 'normal'. He categorizes three distinct types of stigma: first, that which arises from physical deformity; second, that which can be attributed to blemishes of character; and, third, the tribal stigma of race, nation and religion. However, the reaction to all stigmatizing conditions is not the same, since some attributes can be hidden from other people and others not. Goffman thus makes the distinction between discrediting (easily visible) attributes such as physical deformity, and discreditable (less visible) attributes such as epilepsy (Goffman 1968). Discrediting attributes are immediately stigmatizing, whereas the potential stigma of a discreditable attribute depends upon both the nature of that attribute and the extent to which knowledge of it is disclosed. So someone who is HIV positive may choose not to tell their employer or colleagues, and therefore remain discreditable, but if something occurs that requires disclosure, say time off work for treatments, then the person becomes discredited. They will then be perceived differently by others, as a person with HIV, and this perception may colour the way in which the person is treated. A woman in Sarah Wilson's study of the lives of women with HIV commented on the attitudes of midwives towards her when she gave birth: 'Staff make it very clear that they have an opinion towards you [. . .] basically scum, [. . .] handing the baby over to me in gloves, in open ward' (Wilson 2007: 616; parentheses in original). Other sociologists began to explore the experience of illness, and much of this work considered specific conditions, such as arthritis or cancer. Some studies derived from personal experience, such as that of Jobling who in 1988 studied the differences between lay and professional perspectives on treatments for psoriasis, an incurable skin condition. He described the problems for the patient and their family caused by the treatments, mainly bathing routines and the strict application of greasy ointments, which were not very effective. This added to the stigma of the condition caused by the scaly appearance of the skin (Jobling 1988). Dermatologists, however, are often unaware of the implications of their treatment decisions or the amount of work involved in adhering to them.

As you saw in Chapter 1, at the end of the 1980s Michael Bury moved beyond the study of individual illnesses and developed the concept of biographical disruption (Bury 1982, 1991, 1997). This showed how a diagnosis of a chronic illness disrupted a person's life in a number of ways, and how s/he must rethink their life story and identity. More recently, in a study with mothers diagnosed with breast cancer, Fisher and O'Connor describe how the diagnosis constituted a major disruption to women's lives and argued that their pre-diagnosis identity of 'mother' was incorporated into new identities as cancer patients, and later as survivors (Fisher and O'Connor 2012). Furthermore, from work on chronic pain, the need to add an individual's perceptions of life stage and life expectancy to the concept of biographical disruption has been suggested, as these concepts may colour experience (Richardson et al. 2006). So pregnancy and the postnatal period, as a life stage, may alter how a woman views and makes sense of her long-term condition, and influence the decisions she makes about its management.

Long-term Conditions in Pregnancy and the Postnatal Period

While all women hope for a healthy baby, the chances of this outcome for a woman with a long-term condition may be affected either by the type and severity of her illness, or by complications that arise during pregnancy (Corbin 1987). Surprisingly little research has considered the additional concerns encountered by women with long-term illness who are pregnant. A longitudinal study from the USA interviewed twenty women with a range of long-term illnesses, during pregnancy and after the birth, to elicit the strategies that they employed to manage the medical risk factors associated with their pregnancy in order to increase their chances of a healthy baby. The author uses the term 'protective governing' (Corbin 1987: 320) to capture the three elements of assessing, balancing and controlling risk adopted by women in order to manage their pregnancy. However, shared management of the pregnancy between the woman and health professionals was often complicated by the lack of shared definitions of 'risk', and the degree to which the woman or her fetus were at risk of morbidity and/or mortality. Further, biographical factors of the woman were not always taken into account by health professionals. For example, some women had competing priorities to consider, such as other children or a job, which influenced how they were able to manage risk, whereas health professionals did not have to contend with these competing risks when making treatment decisions. Women often felt torn between the conflicting needs of the pregnancy and other areas of their lives, including managing their long-term condition. A wider discussion on risk and midwifery practice can be found in Chapter 7.

Corbin's study was primarily concerned with managing risk to the baby, but in an interview study with fifteen women Hilary Thomas (2003) focused on the experience of pregnancy for women who either had a pre-existing illness before becoming pregnant, or who developed serious illness during pregnancy. Presenting her findings using a case study approach, Thomas describes two parallel or coexisting **career paths**. Women with pre-existing illnesses such as multiple sclerosis, diabetes or epilepsy already possessed the status of 'patient' before becoming pregnant. Thomas argues that pregnancy may transform that status, if more medical control over the pregnancy and/or the illness is required, and any medical threat to the fetus may take precedence over the needs of the woman. She may find that the control she possesses over the illness and its management is undermined, particularly during the birth itself. However, for women who become ill during pregnancy, for example, with gestational diabetes, a different trajectory emerges. The status of patient may be imposed, or it may be sought in

career path
progress or course through life

order to gain access to medical attention, but in either event the statuses of pregnancy and patienthood become confused. For both groups of women antenatal education, which provides a source of information for pregnant women, did not address their circumstances as pregnant women and as patients, and they did not get to know others in their situation. The women in this study were followed up after birth to provide a rare example of the postnatal experience of women whose pregnancy was medically complicated (Thomas 2004). For four of the five women who had developed hyperemesis during pregnancy, the birth provided almost instant relief, although one woman who experienced hyperemesis during two pregnancies took longer to recover. It also took longer for the women whose conditions pre-dated their pregnancy to achieve what they perceived as normality following the birth. Following the physiological disruption of pregnancy, these women also found that breastfeeding, tiredness and other medical problems affected their ability to regain their previous management and control of symptoms. Many of the women reported feeling abandoned following birth, with staff seemingly unable to help with their non-obstetric, illness-related issues. In addition, they felt controlled by hospital routines and rules that seemed to work against their best interests. For example, one woman in the study suffered with multiple sclerosis, a symptom of which is fatigue. She was determined to breastfeed, but wished to supplement with a bottle when she became overtired. The hospital in which she gave birth had a 'no top up' policy, and no allowance was made for her individual circumstances (Thomas 2004). For a wider perspective on infant feeding policy and experience, see Chapter 11.

What can we learn from these studies on the experience of women with long-term conditions during pregnancy? Taken together, they point to a situation in which women with long-term conditions feel that they can lose control over their illness when they are pregnant and during the postnatal period, particularly when their normal life is affected. Many also report that their own expert knowledge is not utilized. Conversely, women may simultaneously feel unsupported, particularly following the birth. Being aware of this, midwives can use the booking and birth planning meetings with women in order to incorporate their specific needs and choices into the pre- and postnatal period.

📋 Activity 6.1: Sarah's story

Sarah (not her real name) is a wheelchair user who gave birth last year. During her second trimester she developed pelvic girdle pain. This is how she described her experience to me:

> I found pelvic girdle pain was not taken seriously by midwives and the doctors ignored my wheelchair altogether. When I eventually managed to see a consultant to discuss birthing options, he was

dismissive of the advice given by my physiotherapist regarding safe birthing positions. The acting head of midwives also told me not to pay attention to the advice I had been given, as at the end of the day, they would do what they had to do to get the baby out.

I found that midwives behaved like bad-tempered prefects and any deviations from the 'ideal' scenario they have in their minds (healthy mother, minimal interventions, breastfed baby) were met with harassed irritation. Pelvic girdle pain is very common and seems to be a source of irritation and conflict between midwives, consultants and physiotherapists. All that matters seems to be a healthy baby.

After the birth I was in great pain and could barely walk. I wasn't shown that my bed could be raised and lowered. I was unable to reach and care for my baby. My inability to do so was taken as a sign that I might not be bonding or making enough effort. I felt victimized and completely unsupported.

A year later she is still in severe pain.

(a) Why may health professionals have not taken Sarah's pain seriously?
(b) What can midwives do to make women in a similar position feel supported?
(c) How can professionals learn from accounts of personal experience?

The Sociology of Disability

Although biographical disruption has been influential in a sociological analysis of long-term illness, it has been criticized as focusing on the individual, and ignoring wider social issues that impact on the lives of disabled people. In addition, the assumption of a previous 'undisrupted' life which was unexpectedly disrupted does not hold true for those born with a disability.

In Chapter 2, Edwin van Teijlingen discussed the medical (sometimes called the biomedical) and social models of midwifery, and the ideas of 'medicalization' and 'demedicalization'. This division has also been widely used by sociologists to examine disability. The traditional way of viewing disability has been as a medical problem for which there was no 'cure' (indeed, in the past, many disabled people were housed in large institutions called 'Homes for Incurables'). Disability was seen as being the result of bodily impairment, for example, spina bifida, and the result was a tragedy for the person and their family. This individualistic approach to disability is the basis of much medical intervention, which is aimed at adapting and rehabilitating the disabled person to the environment in which they live. The biomedical model of disability puts the emphasis on a diagnostic label and rehabilitation, with medical 'experts' defining an individual's needs, how these needs may be met, and how to minimize the consequences of impairment. The disabled person in this model has little autonomy over their life, including

Box 6.2 The distinction between impairment and disability

Impairment: functional limitation caused by lacking all or part of a limb, or having a defective limb, organ or mechanism of the body.

Disability: limitation of opportunities to take part in normal life caused by social organization of society in which the needs of disabled people are not taken into account, thus excluding them from engagement with mainstream activity. (UPIAS 1976)

their sexual and reproductive rights. This approach saw disabled children segregated in special schools where many did not reach their potential in educational achievement. Employment opportunities for many were restricted to sheltered workshops with low levels of payment. The result of poor life chances and discrimination is such that in 2009 only 50 per cent of disabled adults were in work compared with 80 per cent of non-disabled people, and 23 per cent had no qualifications (compared to 9 per cent). The average hourly wage was over £1 lower (Shaw Trust 2012). More women than men are disabled, so women can find themselves doubly disadvantaged by disablism and sexism (Sheldon 2004).

It was during the 1970s that disabled activists began to challenge the individualistic medical model by questioning official definitions and attempting to demedicalize disability. They credited their disability not to an impairment, but to the discrimination they faced within society. Very important to this shift were organizations of disabled people around the world, such as the Union of the Physically Impaired Against Segregation (UPIAS) in the UK, who pointed to the barriers within society that were crucial in denying people access to economic and social activities. It is argued that these barriers rather than a physical or intellectual impairment are responsible for disability. Within a social model of disability, a distinction is made between impairment and disability, as the definitions adapted from UPIAS show in Box 6.2.

Within sociology, the work of disabled activists such as Michael Oliver and Colin Barnes was crucial in highlighting barriers to disabled people's involvement in society and in breaking the link between impairment and disability. The social model of disability, unlike the medical model, focuses on the barriers faced by disabled people caused by the economic, social and structural organization of society (Oliver and Barnes 2012). Disabled people face discrimination in employment, as illustrated above, and in the provision of suitable housing and transport, as well as in welfare policy.

Although debates around the place of impairment within a social theory of disability continue to be had, some recent writers reject the **binary divide** of concepts such as normal/abnormal, individual/society, health/disease, arguing that it only holds meaning because of

binary divide
division into two
opposite parts

the assumption of an 'other' side (Thomas 2007). For example, 'disease' has no meaning without 'health' and vice versa. In developing an alternative approach to disability, Tom Shakespeare (2006) – who himself has a disability and is the father and son of people with disabilities – provides the following critique of the social model of disability. He points out that it was developed in the 1970s and has now become outdated for three reasons. First, the distinction between impairment and disability which is central to the social model is a **false dualism**, as impairment is also social, and disability is usually bound up with the effects of impairment. For instance, poverty or malnutrition may be a causative factor in impairment, or social arrangements may exacerbate impairment, so that impairment as with disability always takes place within a social context. Similarly, for someone suffering chronic pain, the disability they experience may be affected by what is happening within their body as much as by barriers within society. The implication of the social model is that if disabling barriers were dismantled, then disabled people would live lives free of discrimination and disadvantage, which Shakespeare disputes. Shakespeare's second argument is that even without barriers disabled people would still be disadvantaged by their impairment, because they would still experience physical limitations. This leads to the third argument that impairment is downplayed in the lives of disabled people. Others have made the case for impairment to be included in any model of disability (Crow 1996; Hughes and Paterson 1997), as they recognize the impact of physical symptoms or restrictions on people's ability to engage in ordinary activities. Liz Crow (1996) points out that disability and impairment work together as the external and internal constituents of experience, and one cannot fully be understood without attention to the other. It is also argued that differences in impairment highlight different experience, and demonstrate that 'the disabled' are not a homogeneous group. So, for example, the impact of oppression on a woman who uses a wheelchair will be different from a man with visual limitations, as will the disability experiences of a white middle-class male and a black, lesbian woman living in poverty (Hughes 2004).

> **false dualism**
> acknowledging the categorization of phenomena as mutually exclusive to be false

Building on these critiques of the social model, Shakespeare proposes an approach to disability that is interactional, by which he means 'The experience of a disabled person results from the relationship between factors intrinsic to the individual, and extrinsic factors arising from the wider context in which she finds herself' (Shakespeare 2006: 55). So it is the relationship between the impairment, the person's attitude towards it, personality, ability (intrinsic factors), and contextual (extrinsic) factors such as the attitudes of others, enabling or disabling environments, and wider cultural, social and economic issues that form the experience of disabled people. Ending discrimination will not solve all of the problems of disabled people; some will still require personal assistance or care, incur extra costs such as heating or diet, or be unable to work (Shakespeare 2006).

In a recent volume, Oliver and Barnes (2012: 181) argue that this position sidesteps 'the material reality of the social production of culture, the reality of impairment, and provide[s] little or no insight into how the problem of disablism may be resolved in terms of politics, policy or practice'.

Disabled People, Sexuality and Reproduction

Historically, it was considered that disabled people, particularly those with intellectual disability, should be discouraged from reproducing, both in order that they did not pass on their disability (**eugenic** arguments) and because it was considered that they would not make fit parents. This was fairly easy to achieve when disabled people were housed in large institutions and special schools, as the sexes could be segregated and any meetings between males and females carefully managed. Forced sterilization was also used and continued well in to the twentieth century in many countries. including Sweden and the USA (Hubbard 2006; Barnes and Mercer 2010). Within the UK and the Netherlands, a more 'voluntary' (but still coercive) approach to sterilization was taken for women classed as 'handicapped' or 'mentally subnormal and sexually vulnerable', a position supported by both politicians and the general public (Oliver and Barnes 2012: 96).

> **eugenic**
> control of reproduction to improve society

Today, disabled people are still often thought to be asexual, to not have sexual feelings, or to be incapable of performing sexual acts, a view that is perpetuated by media images and representations. There is also an attitude within society that it is repulsive for disabled people with their deformed bodies to engage in sexual acts, particularly **facilitated sex** (Bonnie 2003). As sexual relationships are seen as part of adulthood, and as disabled people are frequently infantilized and prevented from growing up, it is easy to see how they are also prevented from expressing their sexuality. Selina Bonnie informs us that when she had her first serious relationship, aged nineteen, her parents believed that she was vulnerable and being led astray, an attitude they did not take with her non-disabled siblings (Bonnie 2004). Similarly, in a focus group study conducted with thirty-two people with intellectual disability, it was found that participants were aware of their sexual rights, but felt that there were barriers which prevented them achieving these. A lack of privacy was frequently cited, with family members or carers entering bedrooms without knocking, as well as a general reluctance to acknowledge the sexuality of people with an intellectual disability (Healy et al. 2009).

> **facilitated sex**
> sexual encounter made possible by help of third party

🗒 Activity 6.2: The media and disability

Keep a diary for a week when watching the TV, going to the cinema or accessing social networking sites.
Make a note of:

- The number of people with disabilities of any type.
- How they are portrayed.
- Whether they are in sexual relationships or expecting a baby or are parents.

Discuss your findings with a colleague.

(a) How many instances did you observe of people with physical or intellectual disability?
(b) What impression do the media images on your list portray?
(c) What can midwives do to ensure that stereotypes of disabled people and sexuality do not influence the care they receive in pregnancy and childbirth?

When a woman with a physical or intellectual disability becomes pregnant questions are raised about whether she can 'cope' with a child, whether the child will suffer from having a disabled parent and whether the disability will be passed on. She becomes 'public property' in a way that other pregnant women do not. These ideas reflect a 'common-sense' approach that views the 'problem' as the woman's impairment (Thomas and Curtis 1997). When the artist Alison Lapper became pregnant, her GP presumed that she would request a termination of the pregnancy (Lapper and Feldman 2005). She told the BBC: 'When a woman gets pregnant, people usually ask things like "boy or girl?" With me, it was "is he going to be disabled like you?" What's wrong with people?' (Lane 2004).

A qualitative study with twelve women with mobility-limiting physical disabilities in the USA found that there was an assumption that they would need high-risk pregnancy care, and technological intervention for the birth because of their physical problems (Lipson and Rogers 2000). In a study from Ireland, Walsh-Gallagher et al. (2012) found that women with disabilities felt the same joy and celebration at becoming mothers as other women, but that these feelings were tempered by the negative reactions of others. Four out of the seventeen women interviewed were offered a termination, and one woman commented, 'the doctor told me about abortion, fostering and adoption like I was some sort of creature not able to manage' (p. 159). Doctors also told women that they had an increased risk of having a baby with disabilities. Both pre- and postnatally, the women had their ability to care for a child questioned, and some feared that their child would be taken from them. This study reflects the professional dominance over the lives of disabled people that authors such as Carol Thomas describe (Thomas 2007). The main professional group who exercise control, she argues, are doctors, but other occupations, such as physical therapists, health workers, social workers and teachers, all assess and define the needs of disabled people and prescribe the means of meeting them. In her earlier work, Thomas (with Penny Curtis) report how disabled mothers found that some staff were very good, but that others had 'taken over'

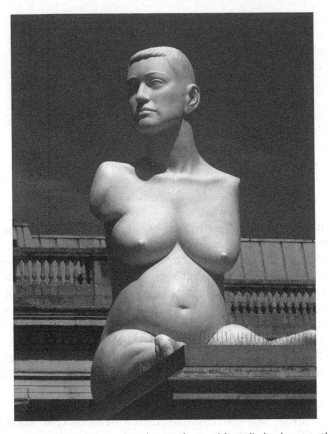

Figure 6.1 Alison Lapper, an artist who was born without limbs, became the subject of a sculpture displayed here in Trafalgar Square

and without consultation had arranged care that was either inappropriate or not needed (Thomas and Curtis 1997). Some women in this and other studies went to strenuous lengths to present themselves as 'coping', as they did not want to appear to professionals as unable to manage in case their children were taken into care (Thomas and Curtis 1997; Thomas 2006; Walsh-Gallagher et al. 2012). In a similar vein, mothers worried about being seen as 'not good enough' by both health professionals and family members, and felt vulnerable in trying to fulfil socially defined obligations of motherhood (Thomas 1997).

As we saw with women with long-term conditions, Thomas has also pointed to the extent to which the idea of risk is present in the discourses between pregnant disabled women and medical personnel. Risk was discussed in terms of both mother and baby – would the fetus be at risk because of the mother's condition, would the mother's condition be put at risk by the pregnancy? Women worried about the effect of medication on their baby, but also the risk of their condition worsening if medication was reduced. This was particularly acute in a woman with epilepsy, whose medication was not increased during pregnancy and who subsequently experienced a seizure, which could potentially have had greater impact on her baby (Thomas 1997). Two mothers in Thomas's study who gave birth to children with impairments caused by hereditary conditions experienced feelings of guilt; other mothers spoke of not taking the risk of having a child with an inherited condition. Of interest here is the adoption by the mothers of a medicalized notion of 'risk' (as was discussed in Chapter 2), with impairment seen as something to be avoided, an issue that is taken up in the next section.

Activity 6.3 Anti-epileptic drugs in pregnancy

Read the following two comments by women who have epilepsy regarding their medication.

> MELANIE: When I thought I was probably pregnant I stopped taking my medication until after my twelve-week scan. I didn't discuss it with anyone other than my husband, as I know how to manage my medication. I know the chances of an abnormality are low, just cleft lip I think, but I didn't want to take a chance. I never lose consciousness with my epilepsy so I knew the baby wouldn't be starved of oxygen if I did have a fit, and I felt that I was giving my baby the best chance.

> KATHY: I really thought that I should increase my medication when I became pregnant. The drugs are very safe now and I am on one that is suitable for pregnant women. I worry about having a fit because it could damage the baby, and I know that the hormones can cause the drug to be less effective, but the doctor says that I don't need to increase them unless the level goes down in my blood, and he will monitor that. I do worry what is best for my baby, though.

(a) How do Melanie and Kathy differ in controlling their epilepsy in pregnancy?
(b) How do they make sense of taking medication?
(c) How can midwives support pregnant women in maintaining control over their disability during pregnancy?

Prenatal Surveillance and Diagnosis

Now we turn away from considering disabled parents, and move to sociological accounts of prenatal screening and the implications for parents whose unborn child is discovered by ultrasound screening to (possibly) have a disability, or a condition that is likely to be long term. First, let us think about the definitions of some common terms used in the research on prenatal surveillance. Ultrasound scanning (or scans) uses high-frequency sound waves in order to 'see' inside the body.

soft markers
variations seen on
an ultrasound scan
that may or may not
be significant

Prenatal scanning creates an image of the developing fetus. Prenatal screening looks for signs or takes measurements which may be indicative of an abnormality (**soft markers**). For example, fluid in the clear space at the back of the neck *may* indicate Down's syndrome but it would require further prenatal diagnostic testing to ascertain whether this was indeed the case. It is the anxiety and uncertainty that this process causes parents that has been the impetus for much research and critique of prenatal surveillance.

Increasing surveillance and technological screening has opened up the pregnant body for scrutiny of the fetus unknown to previous generations. The decision to undertake or proceed with some pregnancies is constructed as a moral one, and the technological imperative to access routine screening or genetic testing and to act on its results is now accepted as a moral obligation in many countries, including the UK. However, it should be noted that not all health systems routinely screen women for fetal abnormalities, and some countries limit prenatal tests to those perceived to be at higher risk, such as older women and those with a family history of genetic disease. It is argued that the use of technology 'relies on mobilising optimistic claims about [its] future therapeutic benefits while concurrently failing to draw attention to possible uncertainties' (Williams 2006: 2). For example, some tests can point to a deviation from what is defined as 'normal' within a fetus, but health professionals cannot translate that into a definitive answer to the question 'Will my child be all right?' The meaning of an abnormal result is often highly uncertain.

So ubiquitous and 'taken for granted' has ultrasound scanning become that it has now been expanded to commercially available four-dimensional 'bonding scans', the purpose of which is for parents to see the baby and obtain 3D pictures (Roberts 2012). To visualize a fetus and to share the image with family and friends has become part of the social fabric of pregnancy.

Advocates of prenatal screening argue that reducing the number of children born with genetic disease or impairment improves human health and eliminates suffering, while opponents state that it undermines the value of human and genetic diversity (Barnes and Mercer 2010). Interviews with fifty-nine women in the Netherlands who were being offered prenatal testing found that they almost universally felt that the 'perfect' child was an unacceptable ideal. They also worried about the obsession with physical perfection within society. They expressed concern that prenatal testing would be used for eugenic means, leading to the commodification of children (Garcia et al. 2008). Similarly, Hubbard argues that prenatal screening shows an excessive preoccupation with inherited and congenital diseases, while ignoring health and safety issues in the workplace, the home or the environment that cause a far greater incidence of ill health and disability (Hubbard 2006).

These issues raise questions about ownership of the pregnant body, in the ever more reductionist attempts to create the perfect child.

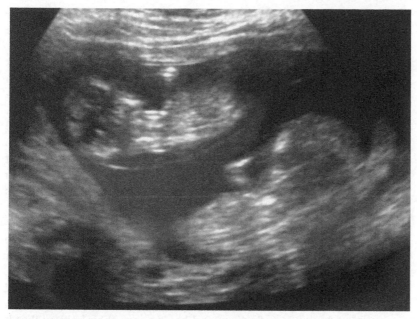

Figure 6.2 Ultrasound image of twin girls; prenatal screening looks for signs or takes measurements which may be indicative of an abnormality

Modern Western societies are in a dichotomous position whereby medical technology has increased the survival of people with long-term illness and disability, while at the same time it is developing the means to control and prevent it. This tension is highlighted in a question posed by Disabled People's International (cited in Barnes and Mercer 2010: 218): 'How can we live with dignity in societies that spend millions on genetic research to eradicate disease and impairment but refuse to meet our needs to live dignified and independent lives?'

Clare Williams points to interrelated factors that make decisions around prenatal testing unprecedented, including:

- The uniqueness of the maternal–fetal relationship.
- Decision-making on risk and probability information.
- The option of obtaining a definitive diagnosis which may itself result in miscarriage.
- Influence of enhanced visual information, a highly charged moral area where both partners may hold different views. (Williams 2006)

Some of these issues are highlighted in a study with eleven pregnant Swedish women in whom a soft marker for Down's syndrome had been found. The authors reported that most of the women expected the scan to confirm a normal pregnancy (Ahman et al. 2010). This is consistent with other research findings that the expectation of screening is confirmation both of a 'well' baby and that the pregnancy is 'real' (Georgsson Ohman and Waldenström 2008). Only two women in Ahman's study were unequivocal about wanting the information that the soft marker gave them; five were more equivocal, and four would rather not have known (Ahman et al. 2010).

Shakespeare does not believe that it is necessarily wrong to prevent impairment or that the termination of impaired fetuses will harm disabled people, but he does see problems in the way that screening is offered, and choices communicated (Shakespeare 2006). First, he argues that at a 'patient' level information is restricted to clinical descriptions of the test or the condition which it is designed to diagnose or assess risk for, rather than quality information about the lives of people who have the condition. This argument is reinforced by women in a study by Rapp (1999), few of whom knew anything about the effects of neural tube defects or chromosomal abnormalities being tested for, apart from Down's syndrome. Second, the attitudes of health professionals who, as argued above, present screening as the responsible choice, undermine the choice of parents, and make it difficult for them to dissent. Third, prenatal screening has become routinized, with scanning in particular not being viewed as something that could have serious consequences for the mother and fetus. Women are often unprepared for adverse findings and having seen their baby makes it harder to cope with its loss from termination or fetal death (Garcia et al. 2002). At a broader cultural level, Shakespeare points out that many people may not know anyone with a disability, or be aware of their lives or the opportunities and rights that are available to them. The idea of a disabled child may be unacceptable to them and these ideas may be reinforced by negative cultural stereotypes, and by messages about the advantages of genetic research and prenatal screening. All of these

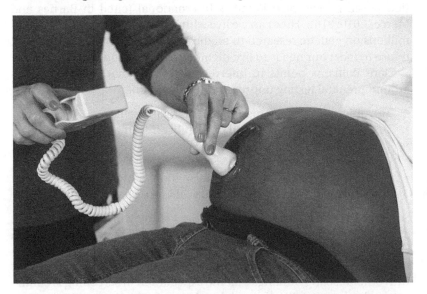

Figure 6.3 Prenatal screening to highlight possible abnormalities has been said to cause an unnecessary moral dilemma for future parents

factors may preclude prospective parents from exercising a free choice (Shakespeare 2006).

📋 Activity 6.4: The 'routine' scan

Read the following extract from Josephine Green on women's experience of prenatal scanning:

> [The] distinction between 'checking that everything is OK' and 'looking for abnormalities' is probably one of the keys to women's enthusiasm for scans: they do not view them as a threat that might give them bad news (like amniocentesis), but as a benign procedure which allows them to see their baby, and confirm that it is healthy. Their assumption that the procedure is benign is, of course, encouraged by the fact that scans are routine and given to everyone. (Green 2003: 63)

(a) Do you agree with the view expressed by Green?
(b) Do midwives have a role in advising women about the possible consequences of routing scanning?

Summary

- More people are reaching reproductive age with disability or long-term ill health of varying degrees.
- Historically, great efforts were made to ensure that they did not become sexually active, such as segregation of the sexes within institutional care, and there may still be coercion not to reproduce, particularly towards the intellectually disabled.
- Women with long-term conditions may find that they have control over their condition taken from them during pregnancy, birth and the postnatal period, but may also feel unsupported.
- Disabled women, in particular those with intellectual disability, are often perceived as not being able to adequately care for a child, or to be putting the child at risk.
- Prenatal screening has increased surveillance of pregnant women and is portrayed as the responsible choice for parents.

Questions for discussion

- Think of a pregnant woman or new mother with a long-term condition (e.g., epilepsy, multiple sclerosis or diabetes) whom you have cared for. How far did health professionals utilize the woman's expert knowledge of her condition in care planning? Did the woman retain control of her illness management?
- Consider the biomedical model, the social model and the relation model of disability. Which model do you think is most useful for applying to midwifery practice, and why?

- Should people with intellectual disabilities be dissuaded from having children? What are the implications of this (i) for the couple, and (ii) for society?

Further reading

Oliver, M. and Barnes, C. 2012 *The New Politics of Disablement.* Palgrave Macmillan.

This book, written by two sociologists with disabilities, sets out the continuing debates around the nature of disability and reasserts the political nature of disability studies in the context of changing economic and social structures.

Aune, I. and Moller, A. 2012 'I want a choice, but I don't want to decide' – a qualitative study of pregnant women's experiences regarding early ultrasound risk assessment for chromosomal anomalies. *Midwifery* 28: 14–23.

This Swedish study highlights the tensions between wanting prenatal information, but finding it difficult to make decisions in the light of that information. It provides an insight into the complex nature of the 'routine' scan.

Thomas, H. 2004 Women's postnatal experience following a medically complicated pregnancy. *Health Care for Women International* 25/1: 76–87.

This is one of the very few articles that considers the experience of women with long-term illness after they have had their baby. It provides midwives with a knowledge of the continuing lives of women once obstetric care has finished.

7 Meanings and Experiences of Risk in Midwifery

Jayne Samples and Bob Heyman

Key issues:

- Defining risk in relation to health care.
- The use of epidemiological data within maternity care.
- Risk communication and perceptions.
- The effects of high-risk labelling.

By the end of this chapter you should be able to:

- Demonstrate an understanding of the meaning of risk.
- Discuss the concept of risk with regard to midwifery practice.
- Understand the importance of accurately interpreting and communicating statistical information to women and their partners and other members of the multi-professional team.
- Demonstrate an awareness of the factors that influence perceptions of risk.

Introduction

Within midwifery practice many of the women you care for will have an uncomplicated pregnancy, birth and postnatal recovery. For others, the journey will be less straightforward, with the risk of potential complications affecting their experience in varying degrees. In this chapter, we introduce the concept of risk in relation to health care in general, and more specifically with regard to pregnancy.

Numerous definitions of 'risk' have been proposed over recent years. The majority feature two main elements: a probabilistic aspect and a negative/hazardous aspect. Some also include a temporal ingredient, pointing to considerations about *when* an unwanted outcome might occur. The Royal Society (1992: 2) defined the concept of risk as 'the probability that a particular adverse event occurs during a stated period of time, or results from a particular challenge'. They develop this further, stating that risk is 'the chance, in **quantitative terms**, of a defined hazard occurring' (p. 4). Risk therefore combines a probabilistic measure of a particular event occurring within a given timeframe, such as during pregnancy, with consideration of the potential consequences of that event. Heyman et al. (2010) offer a reframing of this definition in which each of the key terms (events, adversity, probability

quantitative terms
statistical measure of an event occurring

117

and time periods) are viewed as subject to interpretation from different perspectives: events as categories; adversity as value; probability as expectation; and time periods as timeframes. For example, pregnant women may or may not view the birth of a child with disabilities as 'adverse', and may adopt timeframes which vary from the immediate experience of pregnancy to the adult life of their unborn child.

Mohanna and Chambers (2001: 3) suggested that 'risk is the probability that a hazard will give rise to harm'. Thus, it is not certain that the event will occur (the probabilistic aspect) but, if it does occur, the event will lead to negative rather than positive consequences (the hazardous aspect) (Berry 2004). Everything we do or experience carries some element of risk (Beck 2009). However, risk is a concept that has different meanings, depending on who is using the term (Lupton 1993). Understandings about normality and deviations from these are determined socially and culturally and may change over time (Kringeland and Möller 2006). Perspectives on childbirth are shaped by complex and diverse cultural norms. As a result, providing a definition of 'normal birth' has proved challenging over recent years (e.g., Oakley 1983; Page 2000; Downe and McCourt 2008; see also Chapters 2 and 10). Pregnancies can be labelled 'high risk' for many different reasons, it is a social, culturally defined process by which risks are 'deemed to be hazardous to a population', and it is considered that sharing assumptions about which risks should be of concern contributes to maintaining social solidarity. Culture therefore plays a huge part in influencing what risks are and are not tolerated in a particular society or social group. This analysis is consistent with Foucault's (1991) concept of **'governmentality'**, which concerns the ways in which risk-oriented societies aim to control the behaviour of individuals through defining responsible risk-taking (Holmes and Gastaldo 2002).

governmentality
regulation of society using disciplinary methods

Beck (1992) explores social responses to risks arising from technology, an issue particularly relevant to medicalized births. Adequate consideration of risk relating to pregnancy and childbearing must incorporate a complex set of considerations involving the chance of an adverse event occurring in many different sets of circumstances. Whilst culture and statistics are both significant determinants of what constitutes risk, it is important to consider the needs of individuals as well as groups of women, their experiences and the responsibilities of health professionals with respect to meeting their diverse needs.

Risk in Pregnancy and Childbirth

Following the publication of *The New NHS: Modern, Dependable* (Department of Health 1997), which aimed to introduce high-standard clinical risk reduction programmes, managing risk has assumed an escalating role within health care, including maternity care. Health professionals have become increasingly orientated to risk assessment and management (Skolbekken 1995) through numerous strategies and guidelines. (This shift towards risk orientation has occurred to varying degrees and in different forms throughout the developed world. The discussion which follows will be concerned with what has happened in the UK.) Strategies such as the Clinical Negligence Scheme for Trusts (CNST), developed through the National Health Service Litigation Authority (NHSLA), aim to include reflection on risk exposure, supposedly empowering health-care providers to effectively manage risks and reduce adverse incidents. The King's Fund (2008) suggested that such measures indicate whether strategies to promote safety have been followed, but do not provide a full picture of safety since they do not take into account women's views about this, or consider the specific details of individual cases. In addition, Jokinen and Silverton (2009) questioned the value of such standards in improving safety and care, proposing that the fear of potential litigation may distort the intentions of risk reduction strategies. Rather than responding to the individual needs of women and their families, policies and guidelines may be developed to reduce vulnerability to litigation. Absolute avoidance of all adverse outcomes is not possible. However, for midwives to remain accountable, it is essential to learn from these through the use of audit and crises reporting, for example, using **root cause analysis**. Risk-retrospection may identify signs that, at the time, seemed trivial, but with hindsight were early warning signs. Interventions may or may not have resulted in avoidance or mitigation of the incident (Heyman 2010b). There is the potential for hindsight bias when reviewing an incident after it has occurred and when the consequences of previous actions or inactions have become evident. The effects of hindsight on human judgements are powerful, and easily underestimated. Midwives, doctors and managers may be more likely to express hindsight bias where this reinforces their beliefs, increasing the potential for defensive practice and fear of litigation (Heyman 2010b). For example, if a woman has chosen to birth her baby at home but develops complications that require transfer to an obstetric unit and medical interventions, this may reinforce the beliefs of some midwives and obstetricians, who view hospitals as the safer place for birth. Data extracted from reports such as root cause analyses can be useful for learning and development on an individual, organizational, local and national level. However, this apparently non-blaming approach also has the potential to become regulatory, instilling resistance and fear of reprisal or litigation (Hutter 2008). Unreflectively equating adverse events such as neonatal death with professional failings may also generate defensive practices and an increased propensity to interventions, such as Caesarean births (Shaw 2010). Providers of maternity care are less likely to face litigation for giving unnecessary procedures than for failing to intervene. Hutter (2008) also suggests that audit and analysis may result in treatment being driven by performance indicators rather than clinical need.

> **root cause analysis**
> uncovering the
> underlying causes
> of a patient safety
> incident

Maternal and child health varies globally with much lower maternal mortality rates in developed nations than in developing countries (World

Health Organization 2012). Similarly, variations exist throughout the United Kingdom with women from disadvantaged backgrounds or those with complex social needs generally experiencing poorer pregnancy outcomes. Over recent years, the number of women with complex pregnancies has increased (King's Fund 2008), which may have contributed to sustained maternal mortality and morbidity rates since the mid-1980s, despite improved management resulting in significant falls in deaths from specific conditions such as thromboembolism. Although the numbers of deaths attributed to substandard care has not risen, the Centre for Maternal and Child Enquiries (CMACE) (2011) concluded that some doctors and midwives have inadequate knowledge and skills with respect to recognizing and responding appropriately to potentially life-threatening conditions and communicating well within and between teams. Sandall et al. (2010) argue that **discourse** around risk and safety often fails to address the potentially harmful activities of health professionals, giving undue emphasis to the characteristics and behaviours of women.

discourse
communication or discussion

Whilst pregnancy and birth are normal physiological processes, leading to mainly positive outcomes for mother and baby, there is inevitably an irreducible element of risk for both (King's Fund 2008). Maternity care 'is, therefore, based on managing risk within a normal physiological process' (King's Fund 2008: 20). Some problems may be detected and managed during pregnancy, whereas others may arise suddenly or unexpectedly. Managing deviations from normal may include interventions which may themselves increase the risk of **iatrogenic** problems (King's Fund 2008). For example, cardiotocography (which records changes in the fetal heart) is used to identify suspected fetal hypoxia (lack of oxygen) during labour in women who are identified as having an increased risk of this occurring. Outcomes comparing cardiotocography use with intermittent auscultation demonstrate that cardiotocography is associated with a reduced risk of neonatal seizures. However, other outcomes such as cerebral palsy and infant mortality are not improved with its use and women are more likely to have an instrumental or Caesarean section birth (Alfirevic et al. 2006), increasing their risk of associated problems such as postpartum haemorrhage or infection. Where interventions are to be tolerated by women, any consequences of these 'should not impose a greater risk than these already tolerated by society' (Royal Society 1992: 92) and risks should be minimized to 'as low as is reasonably practical' (p. 93).

iatrogenic
condition caused by treatment for another illness

🗒 Activity 7.1: Risk and interventions

What do you think that the Royal Society (1992) mean when they say that interventions 'should not impose a greater risk than those already tolerated by society?'

(a) Make a list of interventions that may be used during labour and birth. Identify the potential consequences of each and consider whether these consequences pose a lesser or greater risk than the condition they are being used to manage.

(b) Why does the Royal Society state that risks should be minimized to 'as low as is reasonably practical'? How do you think this can be achieved in relation to pregnancy and the birth process?

Risk management programmes aim to ensure that risks are assessed appropriately, and that the potential for harm as a result of errors is minimized through strategies such as openly investigating and applying learning from any adverse incidents and identifying poor performance early so that health professionals are fit to practise. Managing risk is a core function of health professionals, and professional practice is likely to be judged on how risk is prioritized and managed (Alaszewski 1998).

Risk reduction is fundamental to antenatal care (Jordan and Aikins Murphy 2009), beginning prior to conception in some cases, for example, where genetic risks have been identified; or at the initial booking appointment where detailed history taking aims to gain insight into women's needs, identifying actual or potential risk factors. Women may then be referred to another appropriate professional for support and management that exceeds the midwife's own scope of practice (Nursing and Midwifery Council (NMC) 2012; National Institute for Health and Clinical Excellence (NICE) 2008). The booking appointment may be one of the most important events in the woman's maternity care in terms of risk assessment (Oates et al. 2011), although identifying and managing actual or potential conditions that could give rise to harm for the woman, baby or both is a continuous process throughout the **childbearing continuum**. The most recent Centre for Maternal and Child Enquiries Report (2011) highlighted a failure to refer significant numbers of potentially high-risk women. Attention was drawn to the evolving complexities associated with some women's pregnancies and the need for these women to have their problems identified and managed appropriately (de Swiet et al. 2011: 130).

> **childbearing continuum**
> process from preconception through to postnatal

Although midwives have a duty to search for strategies to limit risk and increase safety (Angelini and Kriebs 2005), they are also responsible for listening to what women want, supporting women's autonomy and respecting their choices (Kirkham 2004; NMC 2004). When providing information and supporting women's choices regarding potential outcomes, it is important to differentiate between **outcome-independent** and **outcome-contingent risks**. Outcome-independent risks should be avoidable if appropriate precautions are taken. The National Patient Safety Agency (NPSA) (2009b: 5) identified a list of eight 'Never Events' such as in-hospital maternal death from postpartum haemorrhage following elective Caesarean section. Each of these events, which carry a significant risk of severe harm or death, can be identified and managed using existing guidance to prevent their occurrence, such as ensuring the availability of blood products and appropriately skilled staff at elective Caesarean. Outcome-contingent

> **outcome-independent risks** involve no gains and should be avoided, e.g., medical errors

> **outcome-contingent risks** informed choice with trade-offs made to achieve other benefits

risk thinking incorporates consideration of values and the potential benefits of taking risks. For example, an older woman may choose to become pregnant despite knowing that statistically she is more susceptible to complications, but weighing the chance and severity of these against becoming a mother. Having a sound and critical knowledge of the evidence base and considering the individual context of a particular woman at a particular time strengthens a defendable and woman-centred approach.

Epidemiology and Risk

Epidemiology is the study of patterns of disease occurring in human populations and the factors that influence these patterns (Moon et al. 2000). It concerns describing and comparing groups of people who vary significantly in their genetic and environmental backgrounds. Being able to identify causative or contributory factors can enable preventative measures to be put into place (Webb and Bain 2011). However, this is only possible where causal factors can be modified. From an epidemiological perspective, health risks may be viewed as something to be objectively assessed, the costs and benefits carefully weighed and attempts made to eliminate or reduce undesirable consequences. However, epidemiological statistics relating to risk in health are not objective values but are measures of uncertainty, reflecting historical data, and therefore should be used critically with regard to future considerations and decision-making (Heyman 1998; Kringeland and Möller 2006). Similarly, epidemiology is based on findings relating to populations rather than individuals and is therefore relevant as a general consideration rather than to individuals. Since there is wide variation between individual circumstances, epidemiologists have to rely on statistical techniques to draw out causal relationships. For example, maternal smoking in pregnancy is strongly associated with sudden infant death even where other factors such as socioeconomic status, maternal age, sleeping position and breastfeeding are allowed for (Foundation for the Study of Infant Deaths 2011). Although terminology around epidemiology may be intimidating, midwives have a responsibility to develop a critical approach to reviewing, interpreting and applying such evidence carefully in order to facilitate the best outcome in any particular given circumstance (Shapiro 2009).

Since it is uncertain whether women are likely to be personally affected by a particular risk, epidemiological data are not always helpful in enabling them to make choices, although such data may provide the impression of scientific legitimacy when encouraging people to make the right choices (Nettleton 1997a). This ambiguity may lead women to perceive they are not at risk and subsequently disregard information that does not readily conform to their social context or behaviour. For example, women who smoke and who have a child that is healthy may perceive that they are not at risk of having a baby die from sudden infant death and consequently choose to ignore statistical information to the contrary. Whilst quantitative research findings can demonstrate how lifestyle changes can potentially improve pregnancy outcomes, from a sociological perspective understanding the ways that people manage potential and actual risks and the consequences of their approach to risk are of great significance (Beck 1992). Using statistical data to understand associations between adverse outcomes and other factors can enable the development of management strategies to address these, alongside ways of explaining risks to women.

In 2010, the **stillbirth** rate in England and Wales fell slightly from 5.2 to 5.1 per 1,000 live and stillbirths – the lowest recorded rate over the last decade (one in 200 births). The key identified risk factors for stillbirths are maternal obesity, smoking during pregnancy and multiple pregnancies (ONS 2011). Around 25 per cent of stillbirths remain unexplained, with others being attributed to conditions such as intrauterine growth restriction, congenital abnormality or infection (Sands, no date, a). Current risk-management strategies to reduce the risk of stillbirth include a measure to reduce the number of multiple pregnancies resulting from infertility treatment by introducing a selective single embryo transfer limit (Human Fertilization and Embryology Authority (HFEA) 2009). On an individual basis, risk assessment during pregnancy can help to identify women that are statistically at increased risk of stillbirth so that appropriate care and guidance can be provided. Monitoring strategies relating to fetal movements, fetal growth and placental function testing can help to identify pregnancies that have the potential to result in the birth of a stillborn baby (Sands, no date, b).

stillbirth
born after twenty-four weeks' completed gestation without signs of life

Socioeconomic factors have an important role to play in pregnancy-related outcomes. Perinatal (stillbirths and early neonatal deaths) mortality rates for 2010 in England and Wales were 7.4 per 1,000 live and stillbirths (ONS 2011). Statistics categorized by social and biological factors highlight particular groups of women who are more likely to experience a perinatal death. (A statistic above 7.4 per 1,000 births indicates an increased risk relative to the general population.) These women include younger mothers (under twenty years: 8.3), older mothers (forty years and over: 10.2), women born in western Africa (14.5), or central Asia (16.7) (ONS 2011). Conversely, women within higher socioeconomic groups have significantly lower rates of perinatal and infant deaths (deaths under one year) than women in the lowest socioeconomic groups (ONS 2011). Confidential Enquiry Reports have repeatedly drawn attention to the vulnerability of poorer socioeconomic groups and women born outside the UK. Awareness of these statistics can enable maternity care providers to develop a service within which women in higher-risk categories can access appropriate care and support.

When providing statistical information regarding individual risks, it is important to differentiate between absolute and relative risk to reduce the potential for misunderstandings and inappropriate responses, as illustrated here. In 1995, the Committee on Safety of Medicines (CSM) warned that using third-generation oral contraception approximately doubled the risk of thrombosis compared with previous preparations. This resulted in substantially decreased oral contraceptive use and a subsequent rise in pregnancies and terminations. Media reports failed to differentiate between the **absolute risk** of thrombosis as a result of taking this oral contraception, which was low (25 per 100,000 users) (Berry 2004), and the five times higher risk of pregnancy-related thrombosis (13 per 10,000 pregnancies) (Lindqvist et al. 1999). The **relative risk** of taking the oral contraceptive pill was therefore lower than the risk which faced women who became pregnant as a result of not taking the pill.

When providing information to women to enable them to make decisions, it is vital to clarify the difference between absolute and relative risk. High relative risk can be accompanied by a very small increase in absolute risk if the overall rate is low. For example, in order to make an informed choice about their birth, women considering a vaginal birth after a previous Caesarean section (VBAC) birth require information regarding potential risks, including the risk of uterine rupture. The absolute risk of uterine rupture in labour is 0.2–0.7 per cent for women having a planned VBAC. The relative risk of uterine rupture when compared with someone who has given birth previously but not by Caesarean (0.005–0.02 per cent) is thirty-seven times higher (Royal College of Obstetricians and Gynaecologists (RCOG) 2007). The way that this information is presented can significantly influence the woman's perception of this. Although the actual risk remains low at less than 1 per cent, the relative risk of being thirty-seven times more likely to have a uterine rupture may seem very high and potentially unacceptable, depending on the perspective of the individual woman. Other factors which affect these figures, such as induced labour and previous birth dystocia, must be taken into consideration when discussing VBAC.

Absolute and relative risks are relatively clear. However, 'real risk' is a problematic notion. Risks encode predictions and may be well or less well grounded in evidence. Probabilities and predictions based on epidemiological evidence *always* require additional understanding to be applied to individuals within any given category to facilitate decision-making (Shapiro 2009). Even where risk factors are strongly associated with poor outcomes in population-based studies, they do not provide certain knowledge about individual outcomes (Aikins Murphy 1994). Population statistics can be misleading when attempting to consider and determine one person's risk of an outcome and could potentially predispose women to increased interventions with a medicalized approach to pregnancy and birth (MacKenzie Bryers and van Teijlingen 2010). It is vital, therefore, that epidemiological evidence is interpreted through an individual's personal, social and cultural context (Heyman 1998). This is where clinical expertise is required,

absolute risk
the chance of developing a condition

relative risk
comparison of differences in risk between two or more categories

listening to women and combining evidence from epidemiological, historical, economic, psychological and social studies to strengthen their ability to understand and subsequently make risk-related judgements (Shapiro 2009).

Risk Communication and Perceptions of Risk

Society places great expectations on being able to control health. This is largely directed towards individuals who are expected to act responsibly for managing their own lifestyle based on scientific information. Governmentality discourse highlights the emphasis on risk factors that are within an individual's control, for example, diet, exercise and smoking, contributing to the notion of responsible citizens who can and ought to be in control of their behaviours (Nettleton 1997a). This way of thinking makes individuals morally accountable for managing their own risk factors. It can lead to stigmatization, for example, of obese pregnant women who may be considered blameworthy for voluntarily putting themselves into a higher-risk category regardless of the causes (O'Malley 2008).

Health-care professionals are encouraged to identify risk factors so that appropriate care pathways may be developed and followed to minimize or manage the perceived risk (NICE 2008). Holmes and Gastaldo (2002) argue that health care is a component of governmentality since it involves managing the population for economic and social purposes. Risk assessments provide information regarding particular risks so that individuals may then participate in risk-reduction strategies (Lupton 1993). However, risk arises from either external or internal factors, or sometimes from both, and awareness of a specific risk does not guarantee that it can be avoided or reduced (Lupton 1993). Absolute safety does not exist (Mohanna and Chambers 2001). Beck (2009: 13) suggests that 'the reality of risk is shown by its controversial character'. The concept of risk is deeply subjective, embedded in a person's lived experience (e.g., Lupton 1993; Alaszewski 2005; Zinn 2005). Situations considered dangerous or frightening to some people may be viewed as having negligible risk to others (Beck 2009).

Whilst regulation and policies may be used to address risk, health-care risks require the clinical expertise of experienced practitioners to interpret information and facilitate decision-making. Responsibility for this is significant within contemporary midwifery practice (NMC 2004), requiring a range of knowledge and skills. Midwives are expected to communicate effectively all the relevant information, and to facilitate women's decision-making, offering a realistic picture of the risks and benefits associated with each available option (Kitzinger 2006). It is important to remember that women have 'the right not to be continually informed of the risks they might be taking when engaging in certain actions, or that they should have the right not to act upon warnings if they so preferred' (Lupton 1993: 433). Therefore, discussions would benefit from including the risks and benefits of no treatment. By providing comprehensive information, midwives can enable women to base decisions on the whole truth rather than a partial truth (Edwards and Elwyn 2001) and help them to feel adequately prepared for a range of outcomes. Women who feel well informed will likely feel more positive about trusting the judgements of their caregivers during labour and birth (Fenwick et al. 2007).

Heyman (2010c: 67) identifies 'consequence selection' as essential to making risk-related choices. It is important for women to be able to identify and balance the consequences that are significant for them. Titterton (2005) recommends a person-centred approach whereby midwives and doctors enable women to identify any potential benefits and harms for themselves, their family, friends and others. Rather than considering only medical or health-related issues, this social model of risk assessment attempts to incorporate the potential effects of adverse events on wider aspects of a woman's life.

🗒 Activity 7.2: Choices and decision-making

Think about an example from your practice (e.g., home birth, vaginal birth after Caesarean, antenatal screening), and try to identify as many risks and benefits relating to this as you can. Consider:

- Health or medical-related issues.
- Titterton's person-centred approach.

(a) How can you support women to consider both personal and medical-related issues in their decision-making?
(b) What factors might influence your ability to support women's choices?

Midwives have a duty to ensure that a woman understands what information might mean for her at any particular time (NMC 2008). This is challenging, not least because some women may lack the **cognitive** or emotional ability to contextualize potentially complex information, particularly when such information relates to conditions that pose risk or uncertainty to themselves or those dependent on them (Berry 2004), or where information has been provided in an unclear or unnecessarily complicated way. Midwives and doctors may themselves have limited understanding about complex statistical issues and how they relate to probabilistic reasoning.

Individual women and midwives may vary in the ways in which they understand information best. Different methods of communicating risk can produce varying interpretations of the same event. For instance, the use of pictograms may reduce the perception of risk (Keller and Siegrist 2009). However, risk is often communicated numerically, posing barriers and increasing anxiety for people with weaker numeracy skills (Keller and Siegrist 2009; Gillespie 2012). Numerical figures based on epidemiological data may bear little relation to

cognitive
related to thinking

women's perception of their risk (Searle 1996). Additionally, women cannot know precisely how they may feel about an outcome until that experience becomes a reality for them (Heyman 2010c). Risk severity incorporates both probability and the perceived degree of adversity, which is itself subjective. Likewise, temporal issues are significant, with adverse outcomes in the distant future often perceived as less worrying than more immediate ones. Women's perception of whether their risk has increased or decreased, rather than a numerical figure, may affect their decision-making (Jordan and Aikins Murphy 2009). Results from screening and diagnostic testing are likely to affect the woman's perspective and their opinion may change as a result of their new risk status (Schwennesen and Koch 2012). Information should be framed in a way that women can relate to; this may be using everyday terms or colloquial equivalents. The Royal College of Obstetricians and Gynaecologists (RCOG) (2008) offer suggestions for clarifying the meaning of risk-related values. For example, the terms 'very common' or 'like one person in the family' may be used to illustrate a probability of one in one (1:1 – absolute certainty) to one in ten (1:10). Reframing risk in a positive way may enable women to perceive risk differently; a forty-year-old woman may perceive having a 99 per cent chance of her baby being unaffected by Down's syndrome differently from knowing she has a one in 100 risk for the same condition (UK National Screening Committee 2004).

Medical and lay perceptions of risk may vary considerably and risk statistics can be misunderstood. Enabling women to make sense of risk involves more than simply providing technical information and mathematical probabilities. To make informed choices, women must be able to contextualize risk to their personal situation (Lupton 1993). The measures that women use to understand risks are largely determined by the values embedded within their lives, their personal philosophies, family and other significant influences (Carolan 2008). Therefore, other factors such as feelings about choice and control should be incorporated into risk communication in addition to statistical outcomes (Royal Society 1992; Lane 1995). Acknowledging these social and subjective factors is vital. Attempting to respond rationally to risks is challenging within a culture where increasing numbers of risks are being identified. This pressure may increase feelings of anxiety or inadequacy (Lupton 1993; Stahl and Hundley 2003), making responses difficult to predict.

Individual perceptions of risk relate directly to decision-making; social context and prior experiences affect factors such as confidence when dealing with uncertainty (Stapleton 1997). Women may want investigations for insurance against uncertainty and perceive that more screening provides greater security, although many women fear that tests will reveal abnormalities (Searle 1996). Whilst investigations are useful for screening and identifying increased risks, they create new risks of anxiety and harmful effects of diagnostic testing. For example, chromosomal screening may lead to a woman accepting amniocentesis and an increased risk of miscarriage.

Investigations reinforce a medicalized model of care with dependence on technology for a healthy pregnancy and baby. Women may deal with any uncertainty by relying on others with appropriate knowledge to act as their advocate, thus relieving the pressure of decision-making and the responsibility for subsequent consequences (Alaszewski 2003). Given the degree of uncertainty within health care and the significance of not addressing complex risk issues appropriately, trust is very important. The woman and her partner must feel confident that they are being supported by professionals with the right knowledge and skills to manage their needs appropriately (Zinn 2008; Alasewski 2010). They need to feel that advisers have their best interests at heart, that they share the same values; or that, if not, they are willing to respect value differences, for example, regarding termination of pregnancy or bringing up a child with disabilities.

Trust is important in ensuring effective risk-knowledge communication and influencing any subsequent outcomes. This trust may be particularly important when time or information is limited or when the issues are complex or perceived as being dangerous; developing and maintaining this trust requires an honest, individualized approach and excellent communication skills (Alaszewski 2003) (see Chapter 6 for a related discussion of emotional labour in midwifery).

Where women feel unsure, they may be more receptive to clinical direction, thereby increasing the potential for informed com-

Figure 7.1 Listening to what matters to women

pliance rather than informed choice (Jordan and Aikins Murphy 2009). Communicating risk is challenging, and health professionals may fail to be non-directive, resulting in the limitation of perceived choice, for example, with antenatal screening counselling (Petersen 1999; Williams et al. 2002; Schwennesen and Koch 2012). This potential for steering women's decision-making may be influenced by midwives' and doctors' own perceptions of the risk, or by national or local agendas for health. Assumptions about individual women, for instance, regarding their cultural background, may lead to variation in the content of advice and language used (Mohanna and Chambers 2001; Pilnick and Zayts 2012). For example, it may be assumed that where a woman's religion forbids her from terminating a pregnancy, she may need minimal or no information regarding screening for fetal anomalies. Midwives must remain sensitive to cultural and personal differences within the constraints of what is acceptable and legal.

In managing risk, health professionals may face dilemmas concerned with balancing organizational and personal needs. The former include policies and guidelines which potentially restrict decision-making, and professional accountability (Deery 2005; Deery and Fisher 2010). There is a danger that if women appear to be making irrational decisions or not using risk information 'properly', health professionals may attempt to strengthen their message (Alaszewski 2005). Where women are predominantly given information that attempts to persuade by emphasizing a particular viewpoint, rather than including all considerations to aid balanced decision-making, this facade of choice is coercive and disempowering for women. Coercive power may be reinforced through verbal and non-verbal messages, socializing women into accepting pathways through fear of rejection or condemnation (Thompson 2000). Rather than making informed choices, women are thus vulnerable to informed compliance (Stapleton 1997; Kirkham 2004; Jordan and Aikins Murphy 2009). By engaging feelings and anxieties, risk communication has the potential to increase women's perceptions of their risk, psychologically steering decision-making in a way that controls the power structure in favour of the health professional (Lupton 1993; Mohanna and Chambers 2001). The Birthplace in England Collaborative Group (2011) found that women are most likely to labour and birth normally in their own home. However, health professionals who lack confidence in this setting may frame their discussions to address their personal rather than the woman's concerns, advising women to consider the baby's safety (suggesting, not necessarily correctly, that home births are more risky). Enkin (1994) warned against adopting such a beneficence approach to risk management. Pressuring women into informed compliance can undermine their self-confidence, confidence in individual practitioners and the health-care system (Alaszewski 2010), resulting in the confusion of medical with value issues. This conflicts with women's right to autonomy and the midwife's fundamental functions of advocacy and being 'with-woman'.

Vulnerability to particular risks may be misconceived (Berry 2004). Increased awareness of an adverse event may result in an increased perception of this happening and therefore healthy people may worry about health problems that do not and may never affect them (Kringeland and Möller 2006). For example, the relatively rare death or severe abnormality of a baby is viewed by society as a tragedy, thus exaggerating the reality and creating irrational fears. This can lead to confusion and emotional turmoil (Mohanna and Chambers 2001; Leichtentritt et al. 2005; MacKinnon 2006). Fear of death or harm to a baby affects not only women and their families' decision-making, but also that of health professionals. Midwives and obstetricians can become emotionally scarred by negative experiences, fearing litigation and blame (Kenworthy and Kirkham 2011), resulting in an 'action bias' (Dahlen 2011: 19) which can predispose those involved into overreacting. Dahlen warns that 'shroud-waving' (p. 19), focusing on reducing 'death and damage', may overshadow consideration of potentially long-term and frequently unnoticed emotional, spiritual and psychosocial morbidity associated with other outcomes. Failure to adopt a holistic approach to the needs and values of women can, as a consequence, generate feelings of mistrust in maternity care (Dahlen 2011).

📋 Activity 7.3: Dahlen's 'shroud-waving'

(a) Can you think of other examples of what Dahlen refers to as 'shroud-waving'?
(b) Why do you think that Dahlen has used this term?
(c) What do you think Dahlen is referring to when she talks about other long-term and frequently invisible morbidity?
(d) Why might 'shroud-waving' lead to a mistrust of maternity care?

The significance of women's social and psychological needs must not be overlooked; 10 per cent of new mothers are likely to develop some degree of depressive illness and, although uncommon, suicide is one of the leading causes of maternal death in the United Kingdom (CMACE 2011).

The Effects of Being Labelled High Risk

In spite of drivers for reduced interventions (Royal College of Midwives, no date; NHS Institute for Innovation and Improvement 2006), pregnancy and birth may be viewed as highly uncertain (Jordan and Aikins Murphy 2009). Continual technological advances increase the number of identifiable risks, generating additional scope for women's pregnancies to be considered high risk. Women may be labelled 'high risk' during pregnancy for a range of reasons, including pre-existing conditions such as diabetes, developing new complications such as pre-eclampsia, being an older or younger mother or having a disadvantaged background (NICE 2008). Although health professionals consider that they have the best interests of women and their babies at heart, the effect of labelling women, or their pregnancies, as high risk may negatively affect their psychosocial state (Stahl and Hundley 2003) and increase the potential for iatrogenic risks. Risk is often associated with danger, and a high risk indicates a lot of danger (Lupton 1993). Stressors and the responses to these are not universal (Lazarus and Folkman 1984), although many women experience negative emotions associated with being labelled high risk; this status may affect their behaviour, including their attitudes towards information and other people. Having a high-risk label in pregnancy, coupled with social factors and an uncertainty about the health of the baby, can impact on the woman's mental health, increasing the risk of anxiety and postpartum depression (Zadeh et al. 2012). Emotional problems can, in turn, affect the mother–infant and other relationships (Price et al. 2007; Lilja et al. 2011). High-risk status not only impacts on the woman concerned, but on her family's relationships and functions (Sittner et al. 2005). In addition, there is some evidence from animal studies that maternal stress during pregnancy can affect the physical health of the newborn (Newnham and Moss 2001). Enkin (1994) suggested that high-risk labelling is only beneficial where interventions can eliminate or reduce the problem; for some women this may not be possible or even desirable, although support can impact on the way that a woman copes with being viewed as high risk. Risk assessments carried out throughout pregnancy may move women from a low- to a high-risk status. However, once a woman is given a high-risk label,

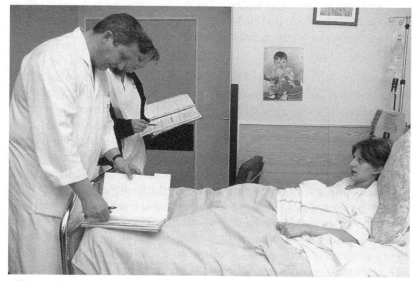

Figure 7.2 A high-risk pregnancy. Once a woman is given a high-risk label during pregnancy it is rarely removed and this can be said to add emotional strain to the pregnancy

this is rarely removed (Handwerker 1994). Carefully explaining the difference between absolute and relative risk, as discussed above, can help women to take a proportionate view. Bearing in mind the associated potential psychological consequences, a high-risk label should only be used with due consideration.

Perception that a perceived risk is reducing may positively affect women's emotions. Hatmaker and Kemp (1998) found that women with threatened preterm birth felt increasingly positive as pregnancy progressed and risk diminished. For some women, reduced perceived threat facilitates a greater appreciation of normality (Georgsson Őhman et al. 2006), although exiting high-risk status is complex for others because they feel unable to switch off 'the associated emotions' (Heyman et al. 2006: 2369). These findings have implications for ongoing support. Once the high-risk episode has ended, not all women will exit this status easily, and some may need support that extends beyond their pregnancy and early postnatal period (Heyman et al. 2006).

📋 Activity 7.4: Screening

In a study of pregnant women's responses to being at increased risk for carrying a baby with Down's syndrome, Georgsson Őhman et al. (2006) identified women who, despite receiving negative results for diagnostic tests such as amniocentesis, continued to express anxiety about their babies up to two months after their babies were born healthy.

(a) Can you think why these women still felt anxious, even though the condition for which they had received a positive screening result was excluded by diagnostic testing?

(b) How do you think that midwives could help women to avoid or overcome such long-term negative effects?

According to Thompson (2000), when medical experts have identified complications through knowledge and tests, the person concerned can adopt a socially recognized sick role (see Chapter 6), incorporating certain privileges; exempting them from normal function and the responsibility for their own condition. However, in return, certain behaviours and attitudes which reinforce a prevailing power hierarchy may be expected: demonstrating motivation to get well, seeking technical help in doing so; and cooperating with the person providing the treatment.

The traditional sick role has to some extent at least been transformed through the increasing influence of risk-thinking. Risk may be viewed as a consequence of a particular lifestyle, resulting in that person being perceived as deviant or 'voluntarily risk-inducing' (Lane 1995: 61). Generally, people are socialized into abiding by the expectations prevailing in their society. Such norms may vary over time and differ between groups. They are always subject to interpretation. Within social groups, those who do not adhere to the 'rules' because they are unaware of, do not understand or ignore them, may be classed as deviant. In relation to health care, people may be considered deviant or 'bad patients' (Thompson 2000: 279) if they fail to adopt a healthy lifestyle or make the choices preferred by health professionals. They may be considered to have failed in their responsibility and may therefore be stigmatized as deviant for failing to understand or not wanting to know (Kirkham et al. 2002). Gatrell (2004) described women experiencing hostility and feeling bullied because they had opted to deviate from health professional advice regarding antenatal diagnostic testing.

Being labelled a 'bad patient' through being 'high risk' can lead to further deviance or attempts to right this perception (Thomas 2004: 71). In a study of women's experiences of gestational diabetes, Evans and O'Brien (2005) reported women feeling that they were 'under relentless scrutiny' and reprimanded for not adhering to their recommended diet. These women responded in different ways. Some women cheated on their diet in defiance, whereas, for others, their high-risk status acted as a catalyst for lifestyle changes, leading to them feeling physically and emotionally empowered.

The location of care provision can impact on the perception of hierarchy. A hospital-based approach to childbirth has become the social norm for most families living in developed countries. This shift has contributed to birth being redefined as a medical process to be managed by doctors (Kingdon 2009). Associated with sickness, care provision within a hospital setting can reinforce a power hierarchy (Kingdon 2009). Frequent routine clinic visits, tests and interventions can strengthen women's perceptions that they are vulnerable and have limited control (Evans and O'Brien 2005; Stainton et al. 2005). Recent government initiatives (Department of Health 2004, 2007b; Midwifery 2020, 2010b) support a shift in power, so that women have greater choice and control around their pregnancy and birth and the places where they can access care. Although this is a positive step, for some women who feel uncertain about self-monitoring or decision-making, or where there is inadequate support, the notion of autonomy can actually be disempowering (MacKinnon 2006). Empowerment involves people gaining control over their own lives and taking responsibility for their own health by being enabled to develop a critical understanding of the fundamental causes of their problems and a willingness to act on this insight (Gibson 1991). For example, women who have experienced one traumatic pregnancy or birth may feel better prepared in subsequent pregnancies, having developed greater understanding of the issues and resolved to act differently to avoid coercion (Kitzinger 2006).

Thompson (2000) warns that empowerment could lead to a failure of the previously discussed legitimized sick role since the person is no longer reliant on technical help and as a consequence no longer exempt from normal functions. This weakening of the sick role may therefore be counterproductive for some people. Whilst facilitating autonomy for women is ethically sound, it can never absolve the midwife from their responsibility regarding woman's decision-making processes and choices. Midwives need support in managing this sometimes difficult dilemma.

Summary

- This chapter has focused on risk related to pregnancy and child-birth, a complex concept, which involves the probability of adverse events occurring over varying timeframes and circumstances.
- Risk-thinking can lead to pregnancy being perceived as a problematic condition which needs to be medically managed.
- Epidemiological evidence derived from population studies can be helpful in identifying categories of women who may be most likely to develop complications. However, predictions based on probabilities are less helpful for individual women as they cannot be used to forecast what will happen in single cases.
- Identifying and minimizing risks of harm are integral to the role of a midwife, but respecting women's autonomy is equally important.

Questions for discussion

- Identify two aspects of midwifery practice where effective information sharing about risk-related issues is vital. Reflect on the strategies that can be used to share this information, identifying positive and negative considerations for each.
- How can you balance your duty to identify and minimize the potential for harm whilst respecting women's autonomy in making informed choices?
- Perceptions of risk are personal and subjective. Consider and discuss the factors that can influence a woman's perceptions of risk.

Further reading

Armstrong, N. and Eborall, H. 2012 The sociology of medical screening: past, present and future. *Sociology of Health and Illness* 34/2: 161–76.
An interesting opening paper for a special edition of this journal which focuses on the sociology of screening for medical conditions.
Goodall, K. E., McVittie, C. and Magill, M. 2009 Birth choice following primary Caesarean section: mothers' perceptions of the influence of health professionals on decision-making. *Journal of Reproductive and Infant Psychology* 27/1: 4–14.
An exploration of how health professionals can influence women's choices about the mode of birth.
Stapleton, H., Kirkham, M., Thomas, G. and Curtis, P. 2002 Midwives in the middle: balance and vulnerability. *British Journal of Midwifery* 10/10: 607–11.

This article explores some of the ways that midwives manage competing responsibilities.

Walsh, D., El-Nemer, A. M. R. and Downe, S. 2008 Rethinking risk and safety in maternity care. In S. Downe (ed.), *Normal Childbirth: Evidence and Debate*, 2nd edn. Churchill Livingstone.

A thought-provoking chapter about discourses relating to risk and childbirth.

Web-based resources include:

Down's Syndrome Association: At <http://www.downs-syndrome.org.uk/>.

An excellent resource providing information about Down's syndrome for people who have Down's syndrome, their families and carers and professionals.

UK National Screening Committee: UK Screening Portal for Professionals. At <http://www.screening.nhs.uk/professionals>.

A valuable information and development resource about screening for professionals.

8 Midwives and Loss

Deborah Davidson

Key issues:

- The value of sociological knowledge in caring for women who have experienced perinatal loss.
- Using sociology to appreciate the historicity and social construction of birth and death practices.
- Interventions midwives can use to provide social support to grieving women.
- The importance of 'validation' – to recognize the women's experience of pregnancy and loss, and to provide support.

By the end of this chapter you should be able to:

- Demonstrate an understanding of perinatal loss using a symbolic interactionist perspective.
- Describe shifts in birth and death practices through a sociohistorical lens.
- Provide a sociological explanation of the complexity of grief and related concepts.
- Identify potential manifestations of grief in women who have experienced perinatal loss.
- Differentiate between positive and negative means of supporting women after a perinatal death.
- Recognize and reflect on your own experiences of loss and how they might impact on the care you provide.

Introduction

Having experienced perinatal loss twice myself, researching the topic as a sociologist has been a profound intellectual and personal journey (see Davidson 2011 for further discussion). When my losses occurred in the mid-1970s, hospitals and caregivers, in their professional roles, minimized the grief that women experienced at perinatal loss. I was told to 'go home and forget about it', to 'have another one'. What I was told was standard practice. These were unhelpful, even hurtful, comments. When I began sociological research years later, I learned that I was not alone in grief. And I learned that hospitals and caregivers had come to recognize and respond to women's grief in helpful ways. How and why this profound change occurred became the topic of my doctoral dissertation. My work continues the sociological examination of perinatal loss, grief and bereavement, and caregiver responses.

One of my earliest interviews with women who experienced perinatal loss was with Natalie, a woman whose daughter Tricia died shortly after being born at twenty-four weeks' gestation. Not long after the interview began, Natalie briefly excused herself and returned with a finely crafted wooden box, which she held out to me, saying: 'This was my baby and she was *real*.' The box contained:

- Photographs of Tricia.
- Tricia's blanket, complete with vernix.
- Tricia's booties, cap and name bracelet.
- Tricia's baptismal certificate.
- A Baby Experience Book.
- Natalie's before-and-after pregnancy journal.
- A newspaper article about a baby that survived after being born at twenty-two weeks ('Proof of a *real* live baby!' Natalie exclaimed).
- A letter from Natalie's mother, written after Tricia's death.
- A card and note from a friend.
- A Christmas card from Natalie to her recently deceased grandmother.
- A heart plaque previously given to the same beloved grandmother.

For Natalie, the box contained material evidence, tangible proof of Tricia's life and her important position in Natalie's extended family. Throughout the interview, Natalie continued to speak of her grief, and how it was not understood or responded to with compassion, even by well-meaning others.

In this chapter, I use a symbolic interactionist perspective and a **sociohistorical lens** to examine perinatal loss, and suggest helpful responses from midwives. Perinatal loss refers to the death of a fetus or baby through miscarriage, stillbirth, neonatal death, or loss through termination of a pregnancy, adoption, or the apprehension of a baby by social services of the state. While the primary focus of this chapter is on pregnant and post-pregnant women as mothers who experience perinatal loss, and these women are in the care of midwives, much of this information is relevant to partners and families as well. The terms 'women' and 'mothers' are both used to denote the same.

> **sociohistorical lens** using the intersection of social and historical factors

According to the World Health Organization (1948), 'health is a state of complete physical, mental and social well-being and not merely the absence of disease or infirmity'. We know that when social support, a key **social determinant of health**, is lacking, women's health after perinatal loss suffers. Social support can be understood as part of a healthy social environment where individuals and networks of support combine to establish and maintain caring, respectful and instrumental social interactions and relationships, buffering against adversity and improving well-being. Midwives are well positioned to play a key role in providing social support to women experiencing perinatal loss. Position statements and practice guidelines for the International

> **social determinants of health** living conditions shaped by distribution of resources

Confederation of Midwives (ICM 2011a) and the Royal College of Midwives (RCM 2012) state that midwives are expected to work *with* women. This involves hearing women's voices and involving them in decision-making about their own care.

There is usually little or no warning when a baby dies around the time of birth. So perinatal death is accompanied by shock and grief. The brevity of that lifespan diminishes our understanding of the parental experience of that life and death, and minimizes helpful responses to it (Davidson 2007, 2008). Although experiences of grief are diverse, inconsistent and change over a lifetime, and while both mothers and fathers experience grief, maternal grief at the loss of a baby is understood to be profound and persistent (Davidson 2010). A midwife's understanding of and response to perinatal loss is vital to the provision of a standard of biopsychosocial care that supports women in their loss.

This chapter is divided into four main parts. First, there is a description of the **theoretical framework** used for understanding perinatal loss sociologically, through a discussion of symbolic interactionism. Second, an understanding of beliefs and practices around birth and death is examined through a sociohistorical lens. Third, there is a discussion of grief, bereavement, mourning and memorialization as they relate to perinatal loss. And, fourth, implications for practice are suggested, following a symbolic interactionist perspective, using the sociological concept of griefwork, which is labour shared and negotiated between grieving women who have experienced perinatal loss, midwives and others (such as partners, family and friends).

> **theoretical framework**
> concepts as tools for analysis

Symbolic Interactionism: Making Meaning in Perinatal Loss

Symbolic interactionism is one of the main theoretical tools sociologists use for examination and analysis of a **phenomenon**. Although it is often misunderstood as employing only a micro level of analysis (Snow 2001), this perspective employs two levels of analysis – micro and meso – both of which involve meaning-making. Micro-level analysis examines social interactions between and among individuals, as well as how symbols are used to make meaning. Mesodomain analysis is an intermediary level of analysis between micro and macro, which is broad structural analysis. Mesodomain analysis focuses on relationships or networks, such as midwife/client and midwife/professional relationships, and on institutions, such as hospitals and other healthcare institutions (Maines and Morrione 1990). Symbolic interactionism understands that individuals interpret or define each other's actions rather than just react to them. If a woman, who has experienced her 'baby' through ideas of motherhood, pregnancy and birth – be it miscarriage, stillbirth or live birth – understands her baby's death, adoption or apprehension as a loss, she will grieve the loss. Through close and compassionate interaction, a midwife can come to recognize

> **phenomenon**
> something experienced that can be observed

her loss and provide her with some of the social support necessary to help her make meaning of the loss to begin to assuage her grief.

Recall Natalie in the scenario at the beginning of this chapter. Natalie's baby was 'real' to her despite others recognizing Natalie's pregnancy but not 'knowing' Tricia as Natalie did. For others, Natalie's baby might have been an abstract replaceable potential: replaced by a 'successful' pregnancy. But, for Natalie, this was not the case. Natalie did not lose a pregnancy; she lost a baby – her 'real' baby. When the woman who experiences perinatal death defines the death of her fetus or baby as a loss, it will be experienced as a loss eliciting grief. Women who lose their babies through adoption or apprehension by social services, as officials of the state, may also experience the loss as grief (Davidson and Letherby 2010).

Language is seen as a system of symbols through which meaning is made, shared and remade. Language has the potential to hurt or to heal (Jonas-Simpson and McMahon 2005). Natalie felt it imperative that she emphasize the reality of her baby to others. Starting soon after the death of her baby, Natalie experienced thoughtless interactions with others, even well-meaning others, both medical and lay, such as 'you can have another one [baby]', 'be glad you never got to know it', or 'it was for the best'. Such comments minimized or negated the grief Natalie felt. Instead, Natalie's experience of grief could have been recognized and assuaged by lending an ear, a hand, a heart, or simply by using Tricia's name.

Box 8.1 Definitions 1

Perinatal loss: death of a fetus or infant through miscarriage, stillbirth, neonatal death, termination of pregnancy, or adoption.

Viability: gestational age at which a fetus is expected to survive outside of the womb; in the United Kingdom viability is understood to be twenty-four weeks' gestation.

Miscarriage: spontaneous pregnancy loss prior to twenty-three weeks and six days' gestation.

Stillbirth: birth of a fetus showing no signs of life after twenty-three weeks and six days' gestation.

Neonatal death: death of a fetus within twenty-eight days after a live birth.

Termination of pregnancy: ending a pregnancy through selective, elective or therapeutic abortion prior to twenty-three weeks and six days' gestation.

Adoption: passing on the responsibilities and privileges of parenting to another.

Apprehension of a newborn: removal of a newborn from its mother by social service agencies as authorities of the state.

Understanding Birth and Death through a Sociohistorical Lens

📝 Activity 8.1: Comparing and contrasting birth practices

In *Get Me Out: A History of Childbirth from the Garden of Eden to the Sperm Bank* (2011), medical journalist Randi Hutter Epstein, MD, discusses the development and use of forceps, beginning in the late 1500s. She notes:

> Pre-forceps birth was a social and spiritual event. The midwife – the female midwife – crouched in front of the laboring woman rubbing the perineum with oils and herbs. Often, she used a birthing stool, a doughnut-shaped chair that allowed gravity to help the baby slip out. No men allowed. Post-forceps, men would gradually become a routine presence. Doctors did not like birthing stools. They preferred the patient lying in bed where they could use their tools with ease. Of course, we cannot credit the forceps with changing everything. But the forceps certainly hastened the change and opened the door for other birthing gadgets. (p. 18)

Compare and contrast this with birth practices as you know them today. Consider the role of midwives, of touch and of technology.

Understood sociologically, beliefs, expectations, behaviours, practices and rituals around birth and death are **social constructs** that vary by time and place (see also Chapter 2). The period from the late nineteenth century to the mid-twentieth century, for example, was marked by medicalization, or the process of subjecting normal bodily processes like birth and death to medical definition, scrutiny and response. Birth and death practices became controlled by professionals in institutions like hospitals and funeral homes, rather than in the private sphere by family and friends (Walter 1994). What may appear to be the private experience of perinatal death has been shaped by changes in broader **institutional arrangements** during the last half of the twentieth century. Through most of history, the death of family members of all ages was a common occurrence, and still is in some parts of the world. Poverty and poor public health led to high rates of mortality, including infant and maternal mortality. Infant mortality rates in Europe overall, for instance, were still extremely high throughout the late nineteenth century. It was not until the turn of the century that infant mortality rates began to fall. This was due primarily to **public health** measures and improved standards of living.

Understanding birth and death through a sociohistorical lens, we recognize that in times of simultaneous high fertility and high infant mortality, where poverty prevails, infant and child death is a norm in families. There are circumstances in which mothers of newborns conform to a 'lifeboat mentality', such that when babies are born weak, rather than putting scarce family resources to save the child, they

social constructs a social category created and developed by society

institutional arrangements organization of social structures

public health promotion of health through preventive action

'choose' to focus their limited family resources on their stronger children. An example of this is beautifully detailed in anthropologist Nancy Scheper-Hughes' (1992) ethnography, *Death Without Weeping: The Violence of Everyday Life in Brazil.* Scheper-Hughes looks at chronic infant and child loss in the global South shantytowns of North-eastern Brazil, where she argues that maternal grief and mourning responses were culturally and historically specific. Mothers held funerals for their babies to mark their passing, but considered the ascension of these 'angel babies' into heaven, where earthly sorrows were not present, a blessing. Remembering their babies, when asked how many children they had, a common response was to include both their deceased and living children. Wendy Simonds and Barbara Katz Rothman (1992), in *Centuries of Solace: Expressions of Maternal Grief in Popular Literature,* illustrate maternal grief in perinatal loss in the global North seen through women's writing of consolation literature – stories, poems and letters – in the nineteenth and twentieth centuries.

The concept of 'the perinatal' arose in the mid-1950s to describe rates of perinatal mortality (Weir 2006) but not maternal experience of loss. The 1960s and 1970s saw the development of obstetric and pediatric medical technologies and specialization, and subjected women to increasingly medicalized prenatal care. Perinatal loss was veiled in silence and the belief that what was unseen remained ungrieved. It was thought that to minimize or deny loss would prevent or at least ease any grief that might be experienced. Women were encouraged to 'get over it'. Their experiences of pregnancy, birth and their babies were negated, rather than their loss and respondent grief recognized and assuaged. There also occurred a broader sociohistorical shift in understanding birth and death practices. Prior to the shift, social birth was understood as occurring at the time of physical birth, while after the shift, social birth was understood as occurring before physical birth (Walter 1994). We can see this today through very early detection of pregnancy with self-diagnosis pregnancy kits and ultrasound technology that provides early images of the developing fetus. Prior to the shift, missed menses along with **quickening** declared pregnancy. Now, the fetus makes an early arrival into the **public social arena**.

quickening
early fetal movements

public social arena
group participation

▣ Activity 8.2: The public fetus, pregnancy loss and online peer support groups

Look at (for example) a Journal of a Pregnant Mother and her Unborn Child (<http://www.unbornbabyjournal.com>). Discuss the practice of expectant parents introducing their yet-to-be-born babies to others through social media such as Facebook and blogs. What consequences do you think this might have on their experience of perinatal loss?

Review the websites below. Why do you think women are drawn to these sites after perinatal loss? What strategies are used on these sites to provide social support?

Share Pregnancy & Infant Loss Support Inc. At . Healing Hearts: Baby Loss Comfort At <http://www.babylosscomfort. com/>.

Sands Forum. At <http://www.forum.sandsforum.org/>.

Persons bereaved by loss find ways to comfort themselves. The literature suggests that women are much more likely than men to both solicit and receive support, including emotional support. Pregnancy loss peer-support groups are comprised of bereaved persons, primarily women, who have experienced perinatal loss. Participation in face-to-face or online support groups provides bereaved persons a 'safe' place to discuss their experiences of loss.

maternal–child attachment early bonds between mother and child

Beginning in the 1960s, the psychological and sociological literature began to reflect an increased interest in topics of **maternal–child attachment**, including prior to birth, and in dying, death and grief. In the 1980s, a literature developed that was specific to women's experiences of perinatal loss. This work launched the construction of a new model of understanding perinatal loss by medical professionals (Davidson 2007). Also in the 1980s, pregnancy loss peer support emerged, providing women with a means of social support (Layne 2003), and laying the foundation for an improved social response to the needs of those who have experienced perinatal loss. Despite some changes to our understanding of perinatal death, dying and death are still medicalized, sanitized and hidden from public view, contributing to death remaining a **taboo subject** (Davidson 2007). This makes talking about dying and death a difficult dialogue (Davidson and Stahls 2011). While death is part of the life cycle, in the parts of the world where infant mortality rates are low, the death of a child seems like a perversion of nature, as we expect parents will predecease their children.

taboo subject not appropriate for conversation

birthmother woman who gives birth to child

The loss and grief experienced through adoption or seizure of a baby by social services, as officials of the state, is further hidden and disregarded. Adoption is generally understood as a choice made freely, and therefore not experienced as the loss of a child. **Birthmothers**, whose children are adopted by others, may experience isolation and either derision for their decision or applause based on a belief that 'they would be unfit mothers anyway'. Mothers who have their babies apprehended by social service agencies are subjected to severe social and legal scrutiny and judgement. Both scenarios create the possibility of disenfranchised grief, including complicated grief that may be left unattended and unassuaged, as discussed in the following section.

Grief, Bereavement, Mourning and Memorialization

Grief is a complex individual, multidimensional response to loss (Small 2008). Grief is also a *normal* response to loss; a response that helps the griever come to terms with the loss and, ideally, to eventually integrate

Box 8.2 Social support

Excerpt from *When Elephants Weep: The Emotional Lives of Animals*
Jeffrey Moussaieff Masson and Susan McCarthy (1995: 79)
Social animals who live in groups often behave in a friendly way toward other members of the group, even when they are not relatives. Troops of baboons and herds of zebra or elephants are not just a crowd of strangers . . . Animals have relationships with one another, some of which are affectionate.

Elephants appear to make allowances for other members of their herd. One African herd always travelled slowly because one of its members never fully recovered from a broken leg it suffered as a calf.

A park warden reported coming across a herd with a female carrying a small calf several days dead, which she placed on the ground whenever she ate or drank; she traveled very slowly and the rest of the elephants waited for her. This suggests that animals, like people, act on feelings as such, rather than solely for purposes of survival . . .

There appears to be so little survival value in the behavior of this herd that perhaps one has to believe that they behaved this way just because they loved their grieving friend who loved her baby and wanted to support her.

What grieving parents want is what this elephant received. They want others to keep to their pace. They want others to *be there for them* in their time of need, without judgment. They want compassion – meaning 'to walk with in grief'.

the loss into their life in a meaningful way. Maternal grief is a mother's highly variable emotional, physical, psychological and social response to the death of her child of any age (Davidson 2010). Maternal grief is thought to be the most persistent and profound grief; mothers themselves are surprised by its depth and intensity. While there are common maternal responses to the death of a child, experiences of maternal grief are diverse, inconsistent, and change over a lifetime. Often experienced as a deep wound, mothers say that a vital part of themselves has died along with their child. Healing after the death of a child is, for many, a lifelong process; grief changes rather than ends (Davidson 2010; Davidson and Stahls 2011).

Grief cannot be fixed, but it can be assuaged. Grief has its own timeline, which depends on the individual and their coping strategies, supportive relationships and networks, and the broader context of their life. Those who are grieving often feel that others, both professionals and friends and family, put them under a 'time gun' to 'get over it'. While grief does go through stages, phases or tasks that *ideally* culminate in some positive way, the process of grieving the death of a child is generally lifelong. These stages or tasks are not clean and clear-cut, and the grieving person often goes back and forth between and among them (Whatley 1995; Davidson 2010).

mind–body relationship
how mental and physical well-being are interrelated

Grief manifests itself in bodily, behavioural and emotional ways. Grief is a phenomenon that is experienced through the **mind–body relationship**. When maternal grief is experienced in perinatal loss, women often feel extreme tiredness and restlessness, weakened immunity and bouts of unusual pain. Common to acute grief are disorientation, anger, heightened vigilance, lack of confidence and social withdrawal. Concentration is limited and grieving people often note that they feel depressed, unusually anxious and like they are going 'crazy'. Their behaviour may change significantly; bouts of crying and anger are a common experience. It is not unusual to have feelings of guilt or blame. It is important to reiterate that these expressions are not abnormal; rather, they are a normal part of adjusting to loss (Davidson 2010; Davidson and Stahls 2011).

Levels and manifestations of grief vary by time and circumstance. Manifestations of maternal grief often sweep in like waves and tides, some of which are predictable, others not. Important dates or 'anniversaries' and the anticipation of these dates can cause grief to increase. We know that men and women often grieve differently, and that marital or partner relations often suffer given increased stress and different ways of grieving. Male parents, and male and female same-sex partners, also experience grief at the death of a baby, and their grief often goes unrecognized and unvalidated (Davidson 2010; Davidson and Stahls 2011). Disenfranchised grief (Doka 1989) is grief that is socially negated or minimized, often because of the type of loss – such as perinatal loss. Midwives are well positioned to recognize grief and have the opportunity to support women in their grief; first through recognition of grief as a normal process, and second by active and empathic listening.

In her article, 'Some questions of identity: late miscarriages, stillbirth, and perinatal loss,' Alice Lovell (1983: 760) wrote: 'She had lost her baby. When this was followed by denial of its life and death, she was even robbed of her loss . . . She was expected to forget her baby and a chunk of her life, and submit passively to having her motherhood role stripped'. Sociologically, motherhood can be understood as an institution, identity and experience, rather than as a natural part of 'normal femininity'. As an institution, motherhood is regulated in terms of social location including 'race' and ethnicity, class, ability, sexuality and age. Some mothers are considered more 'real' and worthy of the status than others. Women who choose to pass along the responsibilities for raising their babies to others through adoption, or women whose babies are apprehended by the state shortly after birth, are generally not positively sanctioned as being or having been mothers.

Although women may have grown up desiring motherhood, having expectations for their expected and unborn children, having experienced pregnancy and birth, having likely held and named their babies before or after death, and considering these babies part of their families, their motherhood is often denied (Davidson and Letherby 2010). One of the profound issues women who have experienced perinatal

Box 8.3 Definitions 2

Grief: a normal reaction to loss, which is complex and multidimensional, having somatic, behavioural and affective components (Katz, Hockey and Small 2001).

Disenfranchised grief and loss: grief and loss that are not socially acknowledged, or acknowledged inappropriately (Doka 1989).

Myth of the replacement child: the idea that a subsequent child can replace a deceased or adopted child; this is a myth (Grout and Romanoff 2000).

Bereavement: the overall experience of grief (Katz 2001).

Mourning: the social expression of grief, which is shaped by culturally accepted rituals (Katz 2001).

Cultural competence: understanding that birth and death practices vary by culture, it is important to both acquire knowledge about others' values, beliefs and practices, and to reflect on one's own in relation to midwifery care (Malott 2008).

Continuing bonds: maintaining, rather than rupturing, ties to the deceased (Bowlby 1961).

Making meaning: the process of integrating the death of a loved one into one's life in a meaningful way (Davidson 2007, 2008).

Memorialization: the practices and processes involved in continuing bonds through the making and continuation of memories of a loved one who is deceased (Davidson 2007).

loss encounter concerns their status as mother. When asked how many children they have, women may feel disloyal to their deceased babies by not including them in the number, or may be selective in when and to whom they offer information about their deceased children. A woman who says, for example, 'I have one living son and one deceased daughter', is often met with silence or unease, limiting her ability to talk about her deceased child and minimizing or denying her experience of motherhood.

Activity 8.3: Perinatal loss in the family

Women experience perinatal loss along with their family members. The following are illustrations of parents' understanding of themselves *as parents* prior to the birth of a child. Remember that siblings of the deceased baby also experience grief.

After reviewing the quotes below, consider the tension between the expressions of parenthood and family and what is meant by 'motherhood denied' (Davidson and Letherby 2010) and, more generally, by entitlements attached to being a parent. What are the implications for care of women and families who have experienced perinatal loss?

In 'Letter to my unborn baby' (pregnancy book exercise) (community. babycentre.com), 'Mama' wrote:

> From the moment I discovered you were en route to me, I loved you more than words can explain. It's a deep, unexplainable love, to love something you cannot yet see, feel, hear, or hold. Somehow though, you do, you love. You replaced the sun as the center of my universe. Every second of my life became somehow related to you. You consumed my thoughts, my dreams, my entire being . . . Mama will always be your biggest supporter, your number one fan, and your greatest admirer.

Similarly, on The Creative Mama (http://thecreativemama.com), 'Creative Mama', in a letter to her unborn baby, wrote:

> Sweet baby-to-be: In five weeks (or seven if you take after your brothers) you will arrive in this world. You are special. I know this now, and I have not even met you yet. You are our third child, but are already first in many ways.

Find the lyrics to Rapper 2Pac's song, 'Letter to My Unborn Child', and include them in your discussion.

Recall the earlier discussion of symbolic interactionism. Bereaved mothers report that their friendships change; some friends are lost and some are gained. Some friends turn away, while others, often quite unexpectedly, show support; new friendships are formed. It is sometimes difficult for others to recognize and accept that grieving parents do not 'get over it', but over time they learn to adapt. Do not expect them to return to 'normal'. As a process, bereavement involves establishing a 'new normal'.

Generally, women, as mothers of deceased children, whether their child was not yet born, stillborn or newly born, want to be acknowledged, validated and remembered. When they are not, maternal grief may be exacerbated. Inevitably, mothers want to know why their baby died and why this tragedy happened to them. Medicine can provide some, though not all, of the answers they seek. Some women find solace in their religious beliefs; some question or even renounce those beliefs. One thing women come to believe is that their lives have changed and they will never again be the same. This is not to say they will never be 'OK', or happy or fulfilled. Although it will take time, women and their families are more likely to find solace if they can make positive meaning out of their loss, which is not the same as being happy about their loss. Positive meaning can be made through affirmative and empathic interactions with midwives. Given that a midwife's responsibility is to work *with* women, and to involve women in their care, it is a midwife's responsibility to listen and to learn what women need and want.

Women should have opportunities to talk about their babies and their experience without fear of censure, silencing or judgement. Women want to make and maintain memories (Bowlby 1979; Klass et al. 1996; Uren and Wastell 2002), continuing rather than rupturing

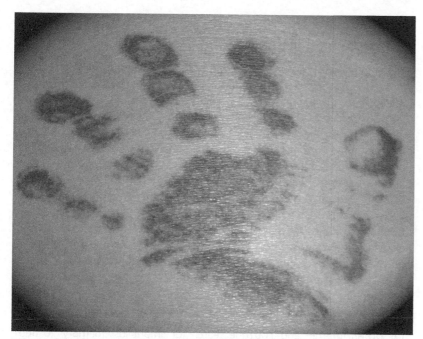

Figure 8.1 This is a tattoo in memory of Adrian. His mom Cara said, 'The tattoo is a gift to both of us, a print of Adrian's hand on my lower back. I got it on the 4th anniversary of his passing. I found it very healing, comforting, like I had him and I could never lose him, no matter where I went, I could always feel his hand.'

bonds with their babies. Such bonds may have begun in childhood in their expectations of themselves as 'mother', then deepened in pregnancy. Most women want to remember their babies with joy about their existence. This confluence of sorrow and joy is part of grieving. Some women, as a result of perinatal loss, experience empty rocking syndrome. The women sit and rock, sometimes with arms empty, sometimes with a doll, a stuffed animal or something that would have been about the weight of their baby. It is not advisable for others to put away baby clothes or furnishings after a perinatal death. Mothers should be able to decide if, when and how this will be done. Some mothers find comfort being in their baby's room; some find comfort saving clothes and furnishings for a subsequent child. It is normal for a variety of responses to be experienced, and these should not be dissuaded. 'Good grief' is accomplished when the griever is able to integrate grief and loss into their lives in meaningful ways. This is often accomplished through memorialization, or the practices and processes involved in continuing bonds through the making and continuation of memories of a loved one who is deceased (Davidson 2007, 2008, 2010). While women often find their own creative and unique ways to memorialize their children, midwives can help them begin this process shortly after the loss.

📋 Activity 8.4: Continuing bonds and making and maintaining memories

In the nineteenth century, infant and child mortality rates were still high. In 1839, a new commercial photographic process was invented that would bring photography to the middle classes. This led to memorialization of the deceased through photographs displayed in the home. These may have been the only images a family had of a deceased member. The photographed deceased, frequently babies and young children, were often posed to look as if they were alive.

Today, perinatal bereavement photography is used to create memories of dying and dead babies. As in the nineteenth century, these deceased babies are also often photographed to appear alive. Photographs are taken of the baby alone and with parents and other family members and friends. Now I Lay Me Down to Sleep (https://www.nowilaymedowntosleep.org) is a network of volunteer photographers who photograph dying or dead babies at all stages of gestation. However, midwives also do perinatal bereavement photography. In addition to photographs, parents and midwives have found many other ways to share and remember their deceased babies.

(a) Do an Internet and YouTube search for 'infant loss memory' to find examples of how parents continue bonds and memorialize their deceased babies.
(b) How might you help parents create memories?
(c) Discuss the confluence of sorrow and joy that you might experience while supporting parents by creating these memories.

A bereavement midwife is a midwife specializing in the care of women during pregnancies likely to end in the death of the baby, or who care for women who have experienced a perinatal death. This is a relatively new specialization with few practising bereavement midwives. Practising midwives are likely to be responsible for the care of women whose babies die.

Studies indicate that bereaved adults suffer from an overall lack of support and would benefit from more social support from those around them. By the late 1990s, interventions to facilitate 'good grief' for women and families who experience perinatal loss were established by passionate and compassionate caregivers who practised '**high-touch care**' (Davidson 2008). Shifting to a more biopsychosocial model of care, recognizing and attending to social and emotional needs, caregivers repositioned themselves closer to the women and their experiences of grief. Women's voices, their cries, began to be heard and responded to with social support through compassionate interaction. Rather than following practices that assumed it was best for women to 'get over it', caregivers took steps to help women and families achieve 'good grief'. They did this by recognizing and acknowledging grief, by validating the short but meaningful lives of these babies, and by helping families

high-touch care care that is very dependent on interpersonal interaction

Box 8.4 Definitions 3

Interventions: non-medical assistance, including designing and follow-ing policies and practices that recognize and respond compassionately to grief in perinatal loss. *Supportive interventions* caregiver–woman interactions to help women with their grief. *Informational interventions* connect women with post-birth information.

Facilitative interventions: help create memories making the loss real (Health Canada 2000).

Grief work: psychological concept, where grieving *individuals* attempt to break bonds with the deceased, and/or make meaning of their loss (Katz 2001).

Griefwork: social science concept, labour *shared and negotiated* between grieving parents, midwives and others to make sense of loss and reposition the deceased in their lives in a meaningful way (Davidson 2007).

Emotional labour: managing one's own and other's emotions (Hochschild 1983).

Compassion fatigue: sometimes referred to as secondary traumatic stress or vicarious traumatization, this is emotional pain or the exhaus-tion that may result from prolonged or intensive compassionate caring (Figley 1995).

create tangible memories of their babies. Whereas women had been previously left on their own to deal with and make sense of their loss – to do their individual grief work – they began to heal through the efforts of caregivers engaging them in *griefwork*, labour shared and negotiated between grieving women and others (Davidson 2007).

With every intervention, it is important to understand and respect cultural differences and know how to access further support. Griefwork begins with caregivers' compassionate interactions where women are not abandoned or ignored in their grief (Davidson 2007). It is particu-larly interesting to note that neither the Royal College of Midwifery's practice guidelines (RCM 2012) nor the International Confederation of Midwives' position statements (ICM 2011a) includes guidelines or positions for the care of women who experience perinatal death. Health Canada, however, has such guidelines for caregivers who pro-vide biopsychosocial support to women and their families in the event of perinatal loss. Supportive interventions for perinatal loss (Health Canada 2000) focus on feelings, and expressions of grief are accepted and encouraged. This involves active empathic listening – listening to understand and learn, and building respect and trust. Empathic listening and selective speaking involve validating what the woman is saying, encouraging her to talk, and providing appropriate informa-tion rather than judgement. Being with the woman – being physically and emotionally present, and comforting her even in the middle of the night, allowing or inviting her to hold and talk to and about her baby, and involving family members – are all supportive interventions. Grief cannot be fixed; a caregiver's role is to support, inform and facilitate 'good grief'.

In early grief especially, women who are experiencing perinatal loss are wrought with confusion, distress and a feeling of having little or no control over the situation. And yet it is a time when decisions are required and patterns for acknowledgement and validation of grief can begin. Informative interventions (Health Canada 2000) help women and families recognize what they can control by providing various types of information required for decision-making. Women need to know about grief, and to know they are not abnormal or 'going crazy'. They need to know about medical considerations, legal requirements and regulations, options for burial, follow-up and community services.

Perinatal death usually occurs with little or no warning. Birth and death are simultaneous or nearly so. Women experience shock, and the entire experience may feel surreal. They have spent months, even years, 'expecting' a living baby and the promise of its future. Facilitative interventions (Health Canada 2000) help women to make the loss real and to prepare for a future they had not expected. Parents may be surprised by obligations to fill out forms and dispose of remains (depending on gestational age). Compassionate care includes helping parents with these procedures. Preparing a dying or dead baby for the parents is an important facilitative intervention. Although the baby is dying or dead, it is their baby. A stillborn baby may have started decomposing *in utero*; nonetheless, there are ways to make the baby appear as aesthetically pleasing as possible. Ointment, for example, may be applied to the baby's dry lips. Blankets can be warmed so parents do not feel a cold baby. Even the tiniest babies can be dressed in attractive clothing and swaddled. Midwives can talk to the babies as they prepare them for the parents, and encourage parents to do the same. Midwives can also open dialogue about the baby, asking, for example, who in the family the baby resembles. When the parents have chosen a name for the baby, one of the simplest and most important things a midwife can do is refer to the baby by name.

Facilitative interventions also include the provision of culturally appropriate mementoes that help make the experience real and help parents remember their baby in ways that facilitate 'good grief'. Photographs, baby blankets, clothing, locks of hair, certificates, and hand and foot prints are all examples of tangible evidence of their baby's existence, while respecting cultural propriety. These mementoes may become like sacred objects to parents, who can share them with others to demonstrate a 'real' baby, when they wish, as Natalie did in the scenario that began this chapter.

The shock of perinatal death also affects midwives, who themselves may not expect or be emotionally prepared for the death of a baby in their care. They may have just come from the birth of a healthy baby, or may need to attend to the birth of a healthy baby, either of which involves agile **emotional shifts**. Like the parents, along with sorrow, midwives may experience feelings of guilt, blame and loss. Grief at a midwife's previous losses may re-emerge. A midwife's grief at the death of a baby in her care may also be disenfranchised or minimized (Kenworthy and Kirkham 2011). And yet midwives are responsible for providing compassionate care, a key element of social support. When midwives are responsive to the emotional needs of women in their care and their grief assuaged, women are then better able to manage their own emotions and the emotions of their families.

> **emotional shifts**
> swift changes between very different emotions

Participation in griefwork by caregivers demands non-medical instrumental and emotional labour (James 1989; Hunter 2005), both of which require knowledge, skill and negotiation. While instrumental labour involves 'doing', such as finding information, and making phone calls and arrangements, emotional labour requires much more *of* the caregiver. It involves not only being clinically competent and physically at hand, but also being emotionally present for the woman and her family, for her colleagues, and for herself. Compassionate care is important and demanding work. It requires empathic listening, including to body language, and careful and frequent reflection on one's own feelings and practices.

While most births will be happy and healthy, those that are not can lead midwives to compassion fatigue (Figley 1995), the emotional pain or the exhaustion that may result from prolonged or intensive compassionate caring. Compassion fatigue may be a cost of caring and participating in griefwork. Midwives also need a system of support.

Box 8.5 Validate

Responding to Grief in Perinatal Loss: Remember to VALIDATE (Whatley 1995)

V   Parents are *vulnerable*.
    Our words and actions do make a difference to their experience.
A   *Acknowledge* their experience as more painful than we know.
    Acknowledge that they will never 'get over it', but they can come to a place where they begin to integrate their experience of loss into their lives in a meaningful way.
L   *Listen. Learn* from their experience.
I   *Identify* their loved one/s by name and speak the name/s often.
D   *Do*. Provide support through supportive, informational and facilitative interventions.
A   *Allow* them anger, envy, tears and time.
    And allow them to
T   *Talk and talk and talk;* let *them* direct the conversation; focus on listening.
E   *Educate* others.

Much of this support will be provided by other midwives. Research has shown that midwives and other caregivers rely on their colleagues for support and affirmation related to this work (Hunter 2005; Davidson 2007).

Recalling Natalie and Tricia, it is crucial to validate the woman's experience of her baby and her loss.

Summary

- This chapter has focused on the experience of perinatal loss.
- It is important for midwives to recognize that the grief experienced, in many expressions, by women whose babies have died is a normal response to loss.
- Midwives are well placed to provide the compassionate care needed to set women on the course to 'good grief'.
- Midwives, themselves, may experience psychosocial consequences of caring for grieving women and should also develop a system of support.

Questions for discussion

- Thinking like a sociologist, in a symbolic interactionist perspective, what would this tell a woman grieving the loss of her child?
- Cultural competence is defined by Malott (2008: 19) as: 'a set of skills that allow individuals to increase their understanding of cultural differences and similarities within, among, and between groups . . . It involves examining one's own values and beliefs and appreciating the similarities and differences we have from others with the goal of promoting effective communication.' Along with your colleagues, reflect on how you can better provide culturally competent care to a family whose baby is dying or has died. To do so, you may need to challenge current practices.
- How can there be such a thing as 'good grief'?
- Discuss the relationship between high-touch and high-tech perinatal care.

Further reading

Cameron, J, Taylor, J. and Greene, A. 2008 Representations of rituals and care in perinatal death in British midwifery textbooks 1937–2004. *Midwifery* 24: 335–43.

This is a useful read in terms of its sociohistorical contextualization of changes in care for women who experience perinatal loss, with the most profound changes occurring over the last quarter of the twentieth century.

Spencer, L. 2011 With women in perinatal loss. *Canadian Journal of Midwifery Research and Practice* 10/1: 52–8.

This article explores women's experiences of perinatal loss and how bereaved mothers might be understood as a subculture, support from midwives, and how sociocultural issues might compound grief.

Kenworthy, D. and Kirkham, M. 2011 *Midwives Coping with Loss and Grief: Stillbirth, Professional and Personal Losses.* Radcliffe Publishing Ltd.

This book should be a required read for experienced midwives and midwives in training. Using a phenomenological approach, the authors, both researchers and midwives, interview midwives to explore the effects of perinatal loss, including possibilities for their personal growth.

SANDS 2010 *Our Major Survey of Bereavement Care Provided by UK Maternity Units to Parents whose Baby Dies.* At <http://www.uk-sands.org/>.

This survey report outlines disparities in the forms of training and resources available for bereavement care.

Simmons, H. A. and Goldberg, L. S. 2011 'High-risk' pregnancy after perinatal loss: understanding the label. *Midwifery* 27: 452–7.

While a label of 'high risk' might provoke anxiety in some women, this study found that after perinatal loss, women and health-care providers experience the label positively as it may improve antenatal care environments.

9 Infertility and Assisted Conception

What Do Midwives Need To Know?

Nicky Hudson and Lorraine Culley

Key issues:

- Definitions and causes of infertility.
- Medical treatments for infertility.
- The patient experience of infertility and its treatment.
- Sociological contributions to an understanding of infertility.

By the end of this chapter you should be able to:

- Discuss the contribution of sociology to an understanding of infertility.
- Understand key sociological and feminist critiques of assisted reproductive technologies.
- Discuss the role of midwifery in the infertility journey.

Introduction

Infertility is often experienced as a painful and unforeseen disruption to a person's expected life course. It is currently estimated that around 9 per cent of women aged between twenty-two and forty-four experience infertility (Boivin et al. 2007), which makes it very likely that at some point during your training or future career you will encounter individuals and couples who have experienced difficulty in achieving pregnancy. The aim of this chapter is to introduce you to key sociological research and debates which have contributed to our understanding of infertility and assisted conception.

While more women are accessing infertility treatment than ever before, it is not clear whether this is due to an actual increase in infertility prevalence or because of better diagnostics and greater treatment-seeking. In the UK and most Western countries, it is estimated that approximately one in six couples will experience infertility (NICE 2012). Paradoxically, infertility rates are often highest in high-fertility societies (such as many African countries) due to increased rates of pelvic infection, which is a major cause of (preventable) **infertility** (Culley et al. 2009). However, of the 9 per cent of women affected globally, only half will seek infertility care and fewer than a quarter will actually receive any specialist fertility treatment. Many

infertility
inability to conceive a child or carry a live fetus to term

women do not seek treatment for **involuntary childlessness** and many others simply have no access to **assisted conception technologies**. This may be due to inadequate public funding for such treatment or poorly developed infertility treatment services in low-resource countries. Social scientists have made a major contribution to the discussion of global inequalities in the prevalence of infertility and access to fertility treatment (Inhorn and van Balen 2002; Nachtigall 2006).

In addition to the now considerable volume of medical literature on infertility, there is a considerable literature in bio-ethics and the social sciences. Infertility and its treatment provides social scientists with a useful lens through which to study wider social relations of power and gender (for a discussion on medical and social models, see Chapter 2), and thus has been a frame for exploring a number of concerns emanating from modern and postmodern social theory. As several authors have pointed out, **assisted reproductive technologies** (ARTs) have deeply unsettled established ideas of what is 'natural' in reproduction, and have given rise to what some people regard as somewhat disturbing family forms and relationships (Strathern 1992; Franklin 1997; Thompson 2005). Children may have multiple 'parents', grandmothers may give birth to their grandchildren, people may choose the sex of their children and women well beyond the age of menopause may give birth. The ethical and moral issues which are implicated in such a uniquely intimate field are often complex, and issues such as third-party assisted conception and surrogacy in particular also raise a number of legal questions about parenting and the status of offspring. At the same time, ARTs are not without risk, both physical and social. The drugs used to stimulate the ovaries can lead to ovarian hyperstimulation syndrome (OHSS); IVF (in-vitro fertilization) is also associated with a much higher risk of multiple pregnancy, which in itself poses a risk to mothers and babies. The long-term risks to offspring, particularly following intra-cytoplasmic sperm injection (ICSI), are still unknown.

As well as raising medical concerns, ARTs bring into question *social* norms and expectations about gender relations, motherhood, family structures and childrearing. It is not surprising, therefore, that ARTs often evoke passionate public as well as academic debate, all of which should be taken into account when caring for a woman who has experienced infertility. This chapter begins with a brief review of the main causes of infertility and the ways in which infertility can be medically 'treated'. Discussion is focused on some of the key sociological research and debates which have contributed to our understanding of infertility and assisted conception. In particular, the sociopsychological consequences of involuntary childlessness and sociological and feminist debates on assisted reproductive technologies are explored.

involuntary childlessness non-parenthood due to infertility or social circumstances

assisted conception technologies/ assisted reproductive technologies medical assistance to achieve conception

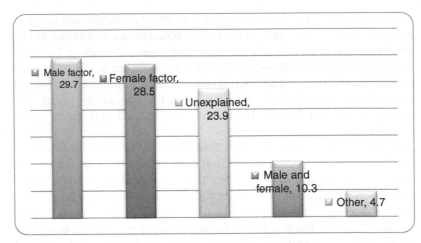

Figure 9.1 Reasons for infertility treatment (adapted from HFEA 2011)

Definitions and Causes of Infertility

As already described, infertility is very common. Primary infertility occurs where a woman has never conceived a child, and secondary infertility refers to a situation where a woman has had one or more children but is having difficulty conceiving again.

The causes of infertility are categorized according to a range of possible problems that may lie with either the male partner or the female partner, and sometimes both or neither partners. In the UK, the Human Fertilization and Embryology Authority (HFEA) collects data on these reasons for treatment (Figure 9.1) and classifies these as attributable to: male factor problems (29.7 per cent); female factors (28.5 per cent); a combination of both male and female factors (10.3 per cent); and 4.7 per cent 'other', which includes multiple diagnoses. In a large proportion of cases (23.9 per cent) there is no identifiable cause (HFEA 2011). It should be remembered that these are based on studies of couples seeking treatment, rather than community studies, and, as already discussed, up to 50 per cent of those experiencing infertility may not seek medical treatment.

There is some evidence of the impact of 'lifestyle factors' such as smoking, drug use and weight on fertility, though this is somewhat inconclusive (National Collaborating Centre for Women's and Children's Health 2012). The most important determinant of conception is female age. Fertility in women declines from the age of thirty and this is especially evident after the age of thirty-five (Maheshwari et al. 2008). There is some evidence that women are increasingly delaying childbearing, and much debate has ensued on the increasing age of first-time mothers (see below). One of the most substantial social-scientific contributions to the study of infertility concerns the psychosocial consequences of infertility and the corresponding impact on well-being.

The Sociopsychological Consequences of Involuntary Childlessness

Social scientists have drawn our attention to the fact that an inability to conceive can result in significant disruption to the expected life course. This disruption can cause distress and emotional upheaval and many people describe feeling a lack of control as a result. Numerous psychological studies suggest that feelings of grief and despair are commonly associated with infertility (e.g., Domar et al. 1992; Lukse and Vacc 1999; Newton et al. 1999; Schmidt et al. 2005), and that it can have an impact on relationships and marital functioning (Benazon et al. 1992).

In order to understand the social significance of infertility, the sociologist Arthur Greil has argued that we need to see it not just as a physiological complaint requiring treatment, but as a 'social construction' (1991: 6). By this, Greil suggests that the experience of infertility is shaped not just by the physical absence of pregnancy, but by the meaning that a lack of childbearing has in the society in which that individual or couple is located. The experience is shaped by societal expectations and **ideologies** about childbearing, the importance of children, the meaning of marriage, understandings about relatedness and family, and the existence and nature of medical 'treatments' for infertility. Thinking about infertility as socially constructed allows us to understand how societal expectations about procreation impact on childless men and women, and how this can vary in different societies and communities. For these reasons, social scientists have contested the term 'infertility' and have argued that it is a very narrowly defined, medicalized way to describe the social problem of a lack of children. The term 'involuntary childlessness' is often used in place of 'infertility' since it more effectively recognizes the socially constructed nature of this experience, and the inadequacy of the term 'infertility' in describing other forms of involuntary childlessness, such as that which has historically been experienced by single women, same-sex couples or non-treatment seekers (Letherby 2002b: 277). Language may therefore be an important consideration when speaking with clients who have sought fertility treatment for reasons other than those attributed to standard medical definitions.

> **ideologies**
> systematic body of ideas

Many authors suggest that childlessness impacts upon the life-course expectations of women in particular. Earle and Letherby (2007), for example, argue that reproduction is marked by a series of biological events which women are expected, and they themselves expect, to enter into. If these are not achieved it can lead to a breakdown in gender identity, an ambiguous status for childless individuals who have not fulfilled their status as adults, parents and, especially, as mothers. Whilst there has been much attention given to the experiences of women, until more recently there had been a notable absence of research about the impact of infertility on men (Throsby and Gill 2004; Fisher et al. 2010).

Another common experience associated with infertility is that of feeling marginalized or socially excluded on the basis of failure to fulfil the social norm of parenthood. In their study of North American women, Whiteford and Gonzalez (1995) explored the **stigma** of infertility and illustrate how this marginalization rests on the sense of having broken a group norm. Women experience 'spoiled identity' in the sense that the role which identifies them as valuable is not fulfilled. Feeling different, marginal or abnormal in some way is a common finding in social science research with women and men who experience involuntary childlessness. The work of Erving Goffman (1963) (see also Chapter 6) is used by an increasing number of authors in order to explain this social liminality (Culley and Hudson 2006; Hudson 2008; Reissman 2000; Whiteford and Gonzalez 1995; Miall 1989; Throsby 2004). The concept of stigma in this body of work is used to explore the ways in which childless individuals come to be defined as different and 'less than whole' in contexts where childbearing is considered the norm. Individuals in these studies describe a number of ways in which they attempt to conceal the fact of their infertility and its treatment from others in order to avoid the stigmatizing effects of being publicly identified as infertile.

stigma
a mark of social
disapproval

📋 Activity 9.1: Infertility and stigma

Infertility is a secret stigma, distinguished from more obvious examples of stigmatization because it is invisible. Unlike paraplegics or the blind, the infertile display no obvious stigmatizing features; only their own knowledge of their condition distinguishes them from others. (Whiteford and Gonzales 1995: 29)

(a) Why might infertility be a source of stigma?
(b) What might be the social implications of the invisibility of infertility?
(c) How might stigma operate differently in relation to ethnicity, gender and social class?

Infertility as a social concern has perhaps been most thoroughly theorized in a global perspective. Anthropological studies have demonstrated that in pro-natalist countries in particular, where children are valued symbolically, culturally and economically, childlessness often creates serious problems for women (and men) (Inhorn and van Balen 2002). Many studies draw our attention to the ways in which women tend to be blamed for the inability to conceive and produce children, sometimes with considerable consequences (Unisa 1999). For example, one study from Bangladesh found that infertile women are reported as at risk from social and familial displacement, through the process of stigmatization (Papreen et al. 2000). The experience of stigma among childless women in South India has been explored in detail by Reissman (2000), who demonstrates how the visibility and surveillance of female infertility in Indian villages is central to the stigmatizing process. Village life was a difficult context in which to hide problems with fertility, whereas more affluent, urban couples were to some extent shielded from intrusive questioning by virtue of their private, often nuclear households and were therefore better able to resist stigma. These international studies demonstrate the ways in which involuntary childlessness is experienced in different ways in varying social contexts.

Research in the UK by Culley and colleagues with British South Asian couples, highlights that couples work hard to keep their infertility 'invisible' from other family members, in order to avoid being labelled as infertile (Culley et al. 2004; Hudson 2008). This research highlights the importance of community or public perceptions of childlessness in pro-natalist communities, and the work that couples do in order to manage information about their in/fertility status. A small collection of studies has begun to explore how infertility may be experienced in a range of minority ethnic communities in Western contexts (Culley et al. 2009; Simpson et al. 2012).

These studies of the experience of infertility demonstrate that the way childless couples or individuals come to be defined, and responded to, is dependent on the way in which childlessness is constructed in any given social context. This may also have a bearing on people's experience in maternity services, where they may not wish to disclose the use of fertility treatments to health-care professionals. A number of writers have suggested that the fact that infertility has been brought under the jurisdiction of the field of medicine, particularly in the West in the last thirty years, has led to a particular understanding of the phenomenon of childlessness. The 'treatment' of infertility as a medical condition is discussed next.

Treating Infertility: Assisted Reproductive Technologies

Treatments and success rates

The development of technologies such as in-vitro fertilization (IVF) has meant that many couples can now be helped to achieve a pregnancy, and since the birth of the first 'test-tube baby', Louise Brown, in 1978, over 5 million babies have been born using assisted reproductive technologies. In some countries, a significant percentage of births are now the result of assisted conception. In the UK, it is estimated that 1.9 per cent of births are as a result of treatments such as IVF, rising to 4.6 per cent in countries like Denmark (Ferraretti et al. 2012). There are, however, extensive inequalities in the global provision of ARTs, and many women simply have no access to technological assistance with their involuntary childlessness (Bell 2010; Culley et al. 2009). The impact of socioeconomic status is also important since in many contexts access to infertility is determined by the ability to pay. Even in the UK, which is often heralded as an example of publicly funded provision, as many as 75 per cent of users will pay for their fertility treatment.

There are a number of treatment options available for infertility, not all of which involve assisted reproductive technologies such as IVF. Medicines may be given to treat women with ovulatory disorders. Surgical treatment, such as tubal surgery on blocked fallopian tubes, is much less common since the development of IVF, but may still be used if the outcome is considered good or IVF is not available. Surgery may also be used to treat endometriosis or fibroids which can inhibit pregnancy. There are few options to treat male-factor infertility, and intracytoplasmic sperm injection (ICSI) or the use of sperm donation are the most widely adopted interventions.

ARTs include the use of intrauterine insemination (IUI) (often used before resorting to more complex technologies), and IVF. Both treatments usually involve medication to stimulate the ovaries to produce more eggs than usual. In IVF, mature eggs are then retrieved, mixed with sperm in the lab and incubated for two or more days to enable fertilization. Resulting embryos are then placed in the uterus via the cervix. Surplus embryos can be cyropreserved for future use, disposed of or donated for research and/or treatment of another woman. In the case of ICSI, a single sperm is directly injected into the cytoplasm of an egg. Fertilization rates with ISCI are better than IVF alone, but once fertilization is achieved, pregnancy rates are similar. It is also important to note that not all users of ARTs are necessarily infertile. There is an apparent growth in the use of ARTs by single women, lesbian and male gay couples, women undergoing chemotherapy and couples who wish to use pre-implantation genetic diagnosis (PGD) to avoid having a child with a certain specific genetic condition.

However, while such technologies are developing apace, it is important to bear in mind that IVF is not quite the miracle technology that popular accounts often suggest. Success rates for IVF, even in high-resource countries, remain relatively low. The likelihood of achieving a live birth from IVF treatment in the UK (and elsewhere) is heavily influenced by several factors, most significant of which is the age of the female.

Table 9.1 Live birth rate, per cycle started, fresh own eggs, UK, 2009

Age of woman (years)	Live birth rate (per cent)
18–34	32.3
35–7	27.3
38–9	19.2
40–2	12.7
43–4	5.1
45+	1.5
All ages	25.2

Source: Adapted from HFEA 2011

In addition to IVF using a woman's own eggs, treatment can also be carried out using the eggs of another woman. This may be recommended for women whose own eggs are found to be unviable, either due to age or premature ovarian failure. Eggs donated from an (often younger) woman may increase success rates and therefore offer some women the opportunity to become pregnant and to give birth to a child, which has been found to be an important part of the reproductive process for women (Culley and Hudson 2009). Embryos created during the treatment of another couple can also be donated if they are no longer required. Egg sharing is a programme now run by many assisted conception centres whereby if the female partner donates a proportion of her eggs for use in another (anonymous) woman's treatment, she will receive part or all of her own treatment free of charge. There is an ongoing debate about the ethical and emotional implications of egg-sharing practice (see Rapport 2003; Gürtin et al. 2012).

Experiences and satisfaction

Despite the relative uncertainty around likely success with ARTs such as IVF, their use continues to increase. Given the experience of infertility as disruptive and distressing, this is perhaps unsurprising. Research with users of infertility treatments illustrates how this is often described as a 'roller coaster' ride in which people experience a number of highs and lows associated with the treatment cycle (Franklin 1997; Throsby 2004).

There have been a number of surveys that provide an overview of couples' experiences and levels of satisfaction with infertility treatment services. Kerr et al. (1999) report that despite experiencing a range of negative emotions related to their infertility, 84 per cent of respondents reported that they received positive help from their infertility specialist. However, 63 per cent were dissatisfied with advice offered by their GP and only 12 per cent were offered counselling on the NHS. Souter (1998) surveyed 806 women in Scotland and found that 87 per cent were satisfied or very satisfied overall with care. However, when looking at specific elements of the process, 39 per cent reported never being asked to bring their partner to appointments, 86 per cent felt they had not been given enough help with the emotional aspects of their treatment, 47 per cent felt they had not been given a clear plan for the future, and 23 per cent of those receiving drug treatment reported receiving little or no information about the treatment or side effects. Only a third had been given any written information about infertility. In questionnaire research from Finland, Malin et al. (2001) found that only 45 per cent of the 344 women in their study were satisfied with the care that they had received, which was strongly associated with an unsuccessful treatment outcome. The authors also suggest that women may feel obliged to be compliant and grateful for the care they receive, and may want to hide their anxiety and stress in order to present themselves as ideal patients. Taking a European approach, Dancet and colleagues have developed a model of 'patient-centred infertility care' (PCIC) (Dancet et al. 2012), which includes ten domains identified by people as important in assessing the quality of care they receive. The domains were: information provision; attitude of and relationship with staff; competence of clinic and staff; communication; patient involvement and privacy; emotional support; coordination and integration; continuity and transition; physical comfort; and accessibility. The authors compared the views of patients across a number of European countries and suggest that the value placed on these aspects of care is similar amongst those of differing nationalities. 'Information provision' emerged as the most important factor in patient satisfaction overall. These studies suggest that although people appear to be satisfied with treatment in general, there are specific areas which need to be improved. These include: enhanced advice from the GP; improved information (especially written) about treatment and its possible side effects; improved emotional support (including the need for a more couple-centred approach); and an increased level of clear treatment planning.

Findings from a small number of qualitative studies help to add a more nuanced, in-depth understanding of the treatment experience. Tjørnhøj-Thomsen (2005), for example, drawing on qualitative research with Danish patients, suggests that the clinician develops a familial-like relationship with prospective parents and that the clinic staff should be remembered with warmth and gratitude by those they care for. Other qualitative studies find negative feelings towards practitioners. Greil (2002) suggests that the women he interviewed (twenty-two white, middle-class women) were very critical of doctors who they felt ignored the 'human' side of their treatment (p. 110). Feeling that they have been treated as less than a person or as 'just a number' has been highlighted in both qualitative studies (Throsby 2004; Redshaw et al. 2007) and quantitative studies (Malin et al. 2001). In a rare piece of research in the UK, which explores the views of women who have been successful with ARTs, Redshaw et al. (2007) used data from a sub-sample of 230 women included in the Millennium Cohort Study, and who had reported that they had used ARTs to conceive. The study authors found that there were still critical views expressed by women, who felt that they had been 'wounded' by the process of medical treatment (p. 302). The authors suggest that women who experience higher levels of distress should be followed up at a later date, whether they are successful or not. These studies suggest that there may still be concerns amongst users of fertility services whether they are 'successful' or not and that this cannot be used as an accurate measure of their feelings about ARTs. There may be an important role for midwives in seeking to understand how women's or couples' experiences of infertility treatment impacts on their subsequent experiences of pregnancy and childbirth.

Helen Allan's work in the field of infertility demonstrates the important role that nurses have in managing the care that people receive (Allan 2001, 2002, 2007). Allan argues that, whilst they engage in 'emotionally aware' practice, they also operate in an emotionally distant role which allows them to get on with the practical business of 'nursing the clinic and the doctors' (Allen 2002: 86), a set of behaviours which can often exclude the possibility of emotional intimacy with patients. The nurse's role of physically 'being there' (ibid.) with people through the challenges of their treatment was acknowledged as significant, despite the fact that it was one in which nurses could in fact maintain emotional distance from patients.

📋 Activity 9.2: Caring for women with infertility in pregnancy

Read the case study and answer the questions below.

Jasvinder is a midwife who is caring for Marie and David. Marie is twelve weeks pregnant and they have just attended their routine dating scan. At the appointment with Jasvinder, the couple explain that pregnancy has resulted through IVF treatment, following two years of trying to conceive naturally and three cycles of IVF treatment in the last eighteen months.

(a) What considerations should Jasvinder take into account when caring for Marie and David?

(b) Might Marie and David's experiences and feelings about the treatment journey differ?

(c) How might the experience of infertility impact on their feelings about this pregnancy?

Very few of the studies mentioned above are carried out with ethnically diverse samples. In one qualitative study, British South Asian couples were asked to comment on the treatment they had received when accessing infertility services in the NHS (Culley et al. 2006). The authors found that, whilst the majority of participants were satisfied overall with the way they felt they had been treated by staff, a small minority had difficulties in relation to language needs and sensitivity of staff. There was no provision of information or resources in any South Asian language, inadequate use of interpreters, and service providers had a limited understanding of the ethnic or religious background of patients. More generally, the socioeconomic position of some communities also gives rise to particular problems. Within the UK, the Pakistani and Bangladeshi communities suffer from severe economic disadvantage (Platt 2002), and the financial burden of paying for treatment was a major issue for many couples in this study.

As well as the emotional and financial challenges of engaging with assisted conception technologies, there are physical risks attached to IVF and related treatment, both for the woman undergoing such medical intervention and for the offspring. These are areas in which sociology has made a notable contribution to our understanding of ARTs, leading feminist authors and sociologists to explore experiences of ARTs in a more critical light.

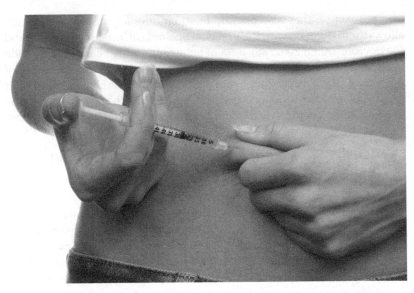

Figure 9.2 Over 5 million babies have been born using assisted reproductive technologies; self-administered hormone injections are part of the process for some

Feminist critiques

One of the earliest and perhaps most well-documented responses to the use of assisted reproductive technologies was developed by writers from within the 'radical feminist' school of thought (Crowe 1985; Corea 1985, 1987; Klein 1989; Klein and Rowland 1989). Feminists have argued that ARTs are part of the wider patriarchal project to control women and their bodies. In her critique of ARTs, Klein writes: 'technologies don't work, but we are led to believe they do; they are anti-woman; they are dangerous and dehumanizing in their theory and application' (1989: 279). Such arguments have been located within the second-wave feminist movement whose members alerted us to related concerns about the technologization of childbirth and women's reproductive bodies more generally (Thompson 2005; see also Oakley 1993; Kitzinger 1978), as well as to the ways in which these technologies valorized motherhood as the only or central role in society for women (Crowe 1985; Corea 1985). Fears about the experimental nature of ARTs, particularly in the early days of their use, were also common (Klein and Rowland 1989).

Charis Thompson (2005) has suggested that this first feminist phase of writing on ARTs eventually paved the way for a more morally ambivalent theorizing about the nature of these technologies and their implications for women, science, infertility and kinship. In particular, space for exploring the lived experiences of childless couples and their experience of using ARTs was eventually created in the research sphere. In this vein, Denny (1994) has also been critical of the early writing of radical feminists who, she argues, failed to legitimate women's experiences through their overly theoretical approach to ARTs. Denny argues that much of this work failed to examine the views of women who use ARTs, and that this is to the detriment of the radical feminist position. Later writing has tended to take better account of broader social complexities, relationships and the cultural setting in which women's experiences of reproduction and motherhood are situated (see Greil 1991, 2002; Becker 2000; Franklin 1997). This is not to say, however, that ARTs are not problematic, or that control over them has been successfully won by their users. Through these debates, feminist perspectives have been critical in drawing our attention to the ways in which infertility has become medicalized, thereby presenting involuntary childless men and women with somewhat of an obligation to seek medical treatment. More recently, feminists and bio-ethicists have drawn attention to the practice of international surrogacy, and in particular raised questions about the ethical implications of economically disadvantaged women in countries such as India acting as gestational surrogates for rich couples from the West (Gupta 2012).

Medicalization – infertility as a disease

In the Western context in particular (but increasingly also in the rest of the world), biomedical solutions to infertility such as IVF are routinely employed to offer couples a solution to the life-course disruption caused by infertility (Becker 2000; Becker and Nachtigall 1992). The promise of continuity, in the form of genetically related offspring, is one of ARTs' most attractive characteristics (Becker 2000). The ability to overcome childlessness and escape the disruption caused by infertility is an offer that few are able to resist. As Becker suggests, 'technologies embody cultural ideologies, such as the ideology of continuity, that tend to reinforce their use' (2000: 239). The technologies themselves are constituted through cultures of scientific progress and as such are imbued with promissory potential, which their users come to embody. Seeking to procreate in this way has become more culturally acceptable even when, it is argued, the knowledge that biomedicine has to offer about infertility is at best incomplete (Franklin 1997).

The marking off of the 'problem' of infertility as a medical concern has drawn considerable discussion and critique from social scientists. Not only is it criticized for valorizing biological parenthood (as highlighted by feminists), but it has also been suggested that biomedical knowledge about infertility and the means to overcome it remains, in fact, relatively limited. The experience of those who use ARTs has therefore been characterized by uncertainty, with no guarantee of any form of success (Throsby 2004; Allan 2007; Peters et al. 2007). The fact that there are no definitive medical answers to the 'problem' of infertility, with IVF having only an average 25 per cent success rate, means that possible treatment options are endless (Cussins 1998; Sandelowski 1991; Tjørnhøj-Thomsen 2005). Tjørnhøj-Thomsen (2005) suggests that the lack of a clear reason why treatment cycles fail means that there is always space for trying a new combination of drugs or a different procedure, offering endless opportunities for the hope of a pregnancy.

The treatment experience is therefore one which is often marked by failure in some respect. Many couples experience failure during the process, even if ultimately they achieve a 'take-home baby'. In a relatively rare study of the experience of IVF failure, Throsby (2004) suggests that this can be devastating, particularly for women. As Throsby notes, not only are the women to 'blame' if the treatment fails, but they are awarded no credit if the treatment is a success. She suggests that the language of IVF compounds this inequity; for example, the term 'IVF baby' effectively removes the parents from the process and instead centralizes the technology. Throsby (2004) argues that when ARTs fail they foreground the very inability to conceive that they set out to overcome, highlighting their 'un-naturalness'. This makes it more difficult for couples to re-establish a sense of normality in their lives.

Greil (1991) suggests that, in the West, there are a number of reasons why infertility has come to be defined as a medical problem.

Others have also highlighted the influence of the media in this process (Franklin 1997), and the general perception in the West that most aspects of fertility are within the control of the individual (woman) (Earle and Letherby 2007). It is therefore to some degree an inevitability that childless couples are compelled to seek a medical explanation and corresponding solution for their involuntary childlessness (Greil 1991).

Social scientists have been critical of this expansion of medical treatments for infertility, particularly in countries where childlessness has not historically been considered the jurisdiction of medical practitioners (Leonard 2002; Inhorn 2003). These criticisms are based on the perceived negative implications of medicalization for childless individuals. Given the highly invasive nature of many diagnostic tests and medical treatments, as we have seen, feminists have argued that the medical model presents an assault on women's bodies and autonomy. Another concern is that, despite its claims, medicine has only been partially successful in 'solving' infertility (Becker 2000; Sandelowski and de

Box 9.1 Infertility as a medical problem

- Medical and technical advances in the field of infertility.
- The medicalization of reproduction and women's bodies in society more generally.
- The demand for services.
- Changes in demography, such as increasing delays in childbearing (particularly amongst middle-class men and women).
- The media presentation of ARTs as a 'miracle' cure for infertility.

Lacey 2002). The HFEA statistics, which report that almost a quarter of those seeking treatment in the UK have 'unexplained' infertility, highlight the gap in knowledge about its etiology. Equally, the figure of over 75 per cent of couples who fail with IVF each year highlights the relative failure of the medical solution (HFEA 2008). It is also possible that the construction of infertility as a disease amenable to medical help implies that couples are compelled to engage with medical treatments, whose use they may otherwise not consider (Sandelowski 1991; Becker and Nachtigall 1992).

A medical definition may also conflict with childless individuals' own experiences. For example, for some couples, the recommended period of one year of trying for a baby may be considered too long. For others, the lack of children of a specific gender within the family may constitute a form of infertility which is not included in the medical definition (Pashigian 2002). Midwives should be sensitive to the fact that expectations about childbearing may differ according to ethnicity and culture. There are, of course, some advantages to a medical definition of infertility. Deploying the category of 'disease' means that involuntarily childless couples become 'patients' and are able (in theory at least) to relinquish the blame of infertility and instead make claims to treatment (Sandelowski and de Lacey 2002). This is not always successful, however. Despite the cultural hegemony of the medical model in this instance, infertility is not always perceived as a disease in the public sphere, especially in relation to rationing of treatment within the NHS.

In drawing our attention to the socially shaped nature of infertility, and the importance of cultural, political and economic factors, social scientists have highlighted the need to consider the unwanted absence of children in ways which extend beyond the physiological. Sociologists (as well as anthropologists and psychologists) have developed an understanding of infertility and its treatment which acknowledges the importance of gender, ethnic and socioeconomic inequalities, as well as the considerable authority of the biomedical model of infertility with its treatment and corresponding medicalization. Social scientists have also explored the implications of 'techno-kinship' for the new family forms that are enabled through the use of assisted reproductive technologies.

Infertility Treatment and New Family Forms

For the individuals and couples who are successful in achieving pregnancy through ARTs, the experience of medical treatment may not be the end of the story. Increasing attention has been paid in public discourse to the novel family forms that are created through the use of ARTs, and there are ongoing debates about the potential long-term risks of fertility treatment for women, and for children born through techniques such as ICSI, which permit the circumvention of specific types of male-factor infertility. Despite these concerns, ICSI is now used in 70 per cent of treatment cycles in Europe and its use is extended well beyond cases of male infertility. Throsby (2004) suggests that, although at one level ARTs appear to shore up family values, they also represent an unsettling ability to generate new structures and to fracture existing categories, such as those of mother and father; what Rosemary Gillespie refers to as a 'postmodern model of reproduction' (2001: 147). They blur the boundaries of nature and technology, presenting a hybrid form of reproduction that is not fully re-categorized in the public imagination.

ARTs offer the possibility of parenthood for those individuals who had previously been unable to consider creating a child (as opposed to adopting or fostering a child). Same-sex couples, postmenopausal women and single women are all now theoretically able to use ARTs in order to have a child. Lesbian couples can use donor sperm in order for one or both partners to become pregnant (Nordqwist 2010). They can also use sperm donation with intra-partner egg donation to allow one woman to be the genetic mother and one to be the carrying mother (Woodward and Norton 2006). Gay male couples can use egg donation and surrogacy in order to achieve pregnancy, a practice which it is suggested is becoming more common, at least in the American

Figure 9.3 A same-sex couple, recipients of ART. Same-sex couples can now use a donor egg or sperm to achieve pregnancy

context (Norton et al. 2013). A body of work has begun to explore the physical and psychosocial functioning of assisted conception families and has found that, on the whole, there are few differences when compared to 'naturally' conceived families. However, research in this field is ongoing and inconclusive, and studies have tended to be carried out with small, socioeconomically homogeneous samples (Wilson et al. 2011).

🗒 Activity 9.3: Ethics

In 2008 in India, a highly pro-natalist country, Rajo Devi Lohan became the world's oldest first-time mother at the age of seventy. Conceived using IVF with eggs from a donor and the sperm of Rajo's seventy-two-year-old husband, Naveen Lohan, the pregnancy ended over forty years of unwanted childlessness for the couple.

1. What social, technological, economic and regulatory drivers have made this situation possible?
2. What kinds of ethical questions does this example raise?

Debate continues about upper age limits for infertility treatment. In the UK there is no official maximum age limit, though treatment is rarely offered to women over the age of fifty, and not beyond the age of forty-three for NHS-funded treatment. Single women who wish to conceive using ARTs are also subject to some public scrutiny, and there is some evidence that they (as well as other patient groups) are travelling overseas in order to receive treatment with donor gametes for which there are long waiting times in the UK (Culley et al. 2011).

Summary

- The focus of this chapter has been on definitions and experiences of infertility. Sociology provides a theoretical space within which to deconstruct everyday notions of 'childlessness' and 'infertility', exposing them as socially constituted categories of meaning, as well as providing the empirical tools to explore and capture the very real implications of those categories for the lives of individuals.
- Midwives have much to gain from exploring the social context within which infertility treatment is situated.
- Understandings of infertility, and the significance given to child-bearing across the world, illustrate the importance of kinship and family continuity. However, it is the social and cultural *particularity* of infertility stories, and the social and cultural norms at play, which can offer us insights into its socially constructed nature. These theoretical and empirical insights can be used to enhance the ways in which support and care are provided to those individuals who experience infertility and unwanted childlessness, both during that experience and beyond.

Questions for discussion

- How do ideas about medicalization and the construction of infertility as a 'disease' shape individuals' experiences?
- Is infertility gendered, and, if so, in what ways?
- Discuss whether infertility treatment should be a priority for public funding?
- Discuss with your peers whether reproductive technologies should be used to allow postmenopausal women to have a child?

Further reading

Allan, H. 2002 Nursing the clinic, being there and hovering: ways of caring in a British fertility unit. *Journal of Advanced Nursing* 38/1: 86–93.

This paper describes an ethnographic study which explores the meaning of caring in a fertility treatment unit. It describes the specific care role of the nurse and the practical care work that nurses perform in relation to the unit, other staff and patients.

Becker, G. 2000 *The Elusive Embryo: How Women and Men Approach New Reproductive Technologies*. University of California Press.

Using in-depth interviews with involuntarily childless women and men, Gay Becker chronicles the quest for parenthood using reproductive technologies. She explores the ways in which technologies such as IVF have shaped our understandings of ideas about 'natural' conception, pregnancy and birth.

Becker, G. and Nachtigall, R. D. 1992 Eager for medicalization: the social production of infertility as a disease. *Sociology of Health and Illness* 14/4: 456–71.

This paper presents the case for understanding unwanted childlessness as a social phenomenon which has come to be defined as a medical problem requiring medical intervention. 'Medicalization' is a central concept in medical sociology and this paper helpfully explicates this idea in relation to infertility.

Culley L, Hudson N. and Van Rooij F. (eds) 2009 *Marginalized Reproduction: Ethnicity, Infertility and New Reproductive Technologies*. Earthscan.

This edited collection considers the significance of diverse ethnic, cultural and religious identities for understanding of technological solutions for infertility and associated treatment experiences within Western societies such as the UK, Ireland, Germany, the Netherlands, the US and Australia.

Inhorn, M. C., and van Balen, F. (eds) 2002 *Infertility around the Globe: New Thinking on Childlessness, Gender, and Reproductive Technologies*. University of California Press.

A collection of essays that explores the impact of infertility in a global context. This book brings together a number of studies that investigate the experience of women and men in a number of countries, including China, India, the nations of sub-Saharan Africa, Vietnam, Costa Rica, Egypt, Israel, the United States, and the nations of Europe.

Throsby, K. 2004 *When IVF Fails: Feminism, Infertility and the Negotiation of Normality*. Palgrave Macmillan.

This book explores the lives of women and men for whom infertility treatment does not succeed. Karen Throsby points out that in fact most IVF treatment ends in failure, and in this book she uses feminist and sociological theory to conceptualize this experience and the associated implications for identity.

PART 3

DEBATES AND CONTROVERSIES

Introduction

We now live in a highly technologized society where midwifery and maternity services would be unrecognizable to our predecessors. Whilst change is very necessary to move the profession forward and make midwifery a better world, midwives have often been overwhelmed with debates and controversies that have created anxiety-ridden contexts, not only for women using maternity services but also for midwives. It is important that you are aware of some of the debates and controversies in midwifery and the impact that these might have on women, babies and their families, and midwives themselves. Viewing debates and controversies through a sociological lens can help you to further understand and develop your approach to your clinical practice.

In Chapter 10, 'Marginality and Social Exclusion: Jeopardizing Health and Life Chances', Jo Murphy-Lawless and Nadine Pilley-Edwards emphasize the need for all women to have skilled, holistic midwifery care that incorporates women's control about the decisions relating to their care. The nature and importance of the sociological concepts of social division, inequality and social exclusion are also addressed, as is the harm that entrenched social divisions and inequalities do to people's health and life chances. The chapter takes us through the way in which social mechanisms work in our society and concludes by addressing the reasons why social exclusion impacts so severely on pregnant women and new mothers.

Chapter 11, 'Infant and Young Child Feeding: Culture and Context', is where Fiona Dykes helps midwives to apply a political economy of health perspective to illuminate political issues related to infant-feeding practices, highlighting the complex influences (economic, sociocultural and relational) upon women with regard to decisions about infant feeding. The chapter highlights a gap between international policy recommendations on infant and young child feeding and the actual practices of women with regard to infant feeding. You are encouraged to discuss why so few women actually feed their infants in accordance with the World Health Organization guidelines. The chapter concludes by encouraging you to consider the ways in which midwives can facilitate support for women with infant feeding that takes account of their own culture, context and life circumstances.

'Commodification around birth' is dealt with in Chapter 12. You will be introduced to the market model and issues of scale in maternity care, and the political implications of these. Mavis Kirkham argues that midwives endeavour to use commodities wisely and well whilst continuing to build relationships with women and their families, but clearly other models of working need urgent consideration. In Chapter 13, 'Mental Health and Illness', you will be introduced to the way in which sociology is relevant to mental health and illness during pregnancy and the transition to parenting/parenthood. Positive and negative framings of the terms 'mental health' and 'mental illness' are introduced, as well as sociological arguments relating to reproduction, women's social roles and mental health. Carol Kingdon identifies how sociology can enhance midwives' understanding of postnatal depression, and fear of childbirth and stillbirth, by locating these issues within their wider social context.

Finally, in Chapter 14, Lorna Davies challenges our thinking around sustainability and midwifery, raising awareness that it is a vast and complex territory. The social construct of sustainability has the potential to offer midwifery a new framework for long-held midwifery values and beliefs. Davies argues that ideals have become increasingly difficult to express and hold on to in contemporary health-care practice. However, if we can get individuals and communities to agree to the benefits of more sustainable ways of doing and being, then action around the other tenets may follow.

As with previous chapters in this book, you have been introduced to many sociological issues that you might not have thought about before. The purpose of the chapters has been to show that midwifery work is influenced by a range of factors that affect women and their families using maternity services, and by the conditions within which midwifery takes place.

10 Marginality and Social Exclusion

Jeopardizing Health and Life Chances

Jo Murphy-Lawless and Nadine Pilley-Edwards

Key issues:

- Social divisions, social inequalities and social exclusion.
- How power and resources are distributed unequally, contributing to social exclusion.
- Neoliberal governments and actions which reinforce social exclusion.
- The impact of social exclusion on pregnant and new mothers.

By the end of this chapter you should be able to:

- Understand the need for all women to have skilled, holistic midwifery care that incorporates women's control about the decisions relating to their care.
- Consider the nature and importance of the sociological concepts of social division, inequality and social exclusion.
- Recognize the harm that entrenched social divisions and inequalities do to people's health and life chances.
- Discuss how mechanisms of social exclusion work in our society.
- Identify why social exclusion impacts so severely on pregnant women and new mothers.
- Understand why a more equal society can help resolve the crisis of social exclusion.

Challenges for Women in Contemporary Maternity Services

The experience of childbirth is very often marred for women by deep exclusion and a lack of control over fundamental decisions about their care. This is in spite of the overwhelming research evidence on the importance of woman-centred care in achieving best outcomes. This evidence has helped to reinforce policy-framework documents in a number of countries about the central role of women's decision-making during pregnancy and birth (see Chapter 4). This process began in the UK twenty years ago with the Winterton Report that led to *Changing Childbirth* (Department of Health 1993), and has continued with documents like *Maternity Matters* (Department of Health 2007b) and *A Refreshed Framework for Maternity Care in Scotland* (Scottish Government 2011). The Winterton Report stated that:

> It is the mother who gives birth and it is she who will have the life-long commitment which motherhood brings. She is the most active participant in the birth process. Her interests are intimately bound up with those of her baby. (House of Commons, Health Committee, *Winterton Report,* 1992: v)

This was reinforced further in *Maternity Matters*:

> Healthy mothers tend to have healthy babies; a mother who has received high-quality maternity care throughout her pregnancy is well placed to provide the best possible start for her baby. (Department of Health 2007b: 8)

Early work on the sociology of childbirth by writers like Ann Oakley and Hilary Graham (Oakley 1980; Graham and Oakley 1981) presented findings on how it was routinely accepted in our maternity services that women have little voice and almost no control in this crucial period of making the transition to motherhood. Individual accounts of women's experiences published by birth activist groups such as the respected Association for Improvements in the Maternity Services (AIMS) regularly made clear how damaging this was for a new mother. Thus, in an AIMS journal article from 1975, this account appeared:

> There were three of them shouting and nagging trying to force an unwanted mask on my face, which I fought off with vigour, I'm afraid; I hadn't even groaned and was so happy until then. (Quoted in Beech 2010: 3)

There has been abundant research to contribute to reforming and improving birth care systems since that period. National policies about women's choice and continuity of midwifery care have been under-pinned by a vast array of evidence about outcomes with best midwifery care, a great number of innovative and well-evaluated community midwifery projects, and changes in midwifery training to reflect all these developments.

📋 Activity 10.1: Interpreting and acting on best evidence for maternity care

Below are two important perspectives from research findings on midwifery care:

> Throughout the women's responses, there is a clear pattern of woman-centred care being offered and of partnership with women, which may contribute to the positive evaluations of antenatal care and good clinical outcomes.
> (Sandall, Davies and Warwick 2001)

> Women who planned birth in a midwifery unit (AMU or FMU) had significantly fewer interventions, including substantially fewer intrapartum Caesarean sections, and more 'normal births' than women who planned birth in an obstetric unit. (National Perinatal Epidemiology Unit 2011)

1. How do these findings affect your thinking about the importance for women of midwife-led care as they make the transition to motherhood?
2. What is specific to midwifery care that can promote women's decision-making and result in the good outcomes cited above?
3. As a midwife, how well prepared are you to undertake this level of autonomous care for women?

However, it has proved very difficult to make best support for women a consistent part of their care on which they can rely. This observation from a recent account in an *AIMS Journal* by a woman about her three pregnancies lets us see that too little has changed: 'I struggle to understand why some go into the care profession. I have witnessed an obvious lack of humanity and empathy by not just one but several midwives' (Ellam 2010: 23).

There are complex institutional reasons as to why we have failed to secure best care for women in line with policies and evidence. The eminent midwife Mavis Kirkham (2010) observes that the industrial model of service delivery still dominates our care system. Within this model, she cites two specific factors that detract from best care. The first is the continuing push to centralize maternity services. This is usually justified by the argument that we must bring 'childbearing women to the experts', that is, the 'consultant obstetricians', rather than the midwife. This has resulted in a pattern of small units being closed, while in many cities there is often just one large maternity unit with many thousands of births each year.

A second factor Kirkham cites is the standardization of services. Here she sees two rationales at work to the detriment of women and midwives. The first is the need to shift clinical care to a basis of firm evidence. Then there is the stated need for better risk management. While both these steps seem admirable efforts towards improved services, in practice, they have resulted in the top-down application of often rigid protocols and directives which misunderstand the skill and autonomy of the midwife. They mean that each woman's individual situation and needs, and the importance of the midwife–mother relationship, are ignored as labour and birth unfold. Despite the emphasis on best-quality evidence, evidence is frequently neglected when these protocols impose decisions about risk and safety based on abstract notions rather than the specific circumstances of each woman. These complex factors continue to make maternity services unresponsive to women's broad range of needs (Kirkham 2010: 3–5).

Social Divisions in Society and How They are Created

While inflexible and unresponsive maternity services can pose problems for all women, they pose special problems for women who experience in their daily lives the effects and consequences of what sociologists term 'social divisions'. Social divisions are 'substantial differences between people' which can divide groups sharply from one another in society, leaving some groups at an advantage in respect of power and material and cultural resources compared with other groups (Payne 2006: 2–3).

We create these social divisions and sustain them in a myriad of ways without always being aware of how and why this happens, and without examining what our perceptions are about the consequences of such divisions. Education provides an excellent example. We generally believe that it is valuable for people's long-term life chances to attain as high a level of education as possible. What is less apparent is the extent to which as a society we actively constrain access to education, with some social groups least likely to gain access to higher education.

At the beginning of their young lives, children whose parents are working class, or emigrants, or who are single parents, or who come from a minority ethnic background, may have few material resources to support learning within the family home. To make up for this, poorer parents often rely on state-funded pre-school programmes and local children's centres because they understand that early learning is important for success in school later on. If those programmes themselves are cut back, or funding is diverted, or fewer staff are employed to look after greater numbers of young children, such decisions contribute over time to diminishing the life chances of these children. If they live in a geographically poorer area, the local schools they go on to attend may be less well resourced than schools in middle-class areas. Therefore, the schools are unable to help children make up for the material disadvantages at home. As children get older, parents are unable to pay for additional books, personal computers and other learning tools for them, and funds for private tutors to help children with state examinations are beyond reach. Thus, government decisions to reduce funding for schools in poorer catchment areas and for additional education resources concretely affect long-term educational attainment. As children who are worse off grow older, the disadvantages they face are cumulative and they are unable to make the same gains in educational achievements as their middle-class counterparts.

social inequalities relational processes that limit an individual's and a group's social status and opportunities

With regard to this outcome, the landmark Marmot Report on health and **social inequalities** comments: 'There is a strong relationship between the level of deprivation in a geographical area and educational attainment' (Strategic Review of Health Inequalities 2010: 64). We also know that 'rates of unemployment are highest among those with no or few qualifications and skills'. Over time this leads to 'an increased risk of one's physical and/or mental health worsening' (ibid.: 68) (see also

Chapter 7). So although in everyday conversation we may comment that children from middle-class areas have a seeming ability to work harder at school, compared with children from a much poorer area, what we are actually seeing is a structural problem arising from the social divisions of class reinforced by political decisions about policies and funding for those who are worse off.

📋 Activity 10.2: The negative consequences of poorly funded early childhood education

Review the evidence below in your peer groups and discuss how it demonstrates how poorly funded education has negative consequences for early childhood.

> Investment in early childhood education as a proportion of GDP is significantly lower in the UK than in many continental European countries, most of which have better educational outcomes than in the UK. (Joseph Rowntree Foundation 2011)

> Children from disadvantaged backgrounds are more likely to begin primary school with lower personal, social and emotional development and communication, language and literacy skills than their peers. (The Marmot Review 2010: 64)

How Social Divisions Lead to Multiple Disadvantages for Women

Social divisions, the way they are constructed and the way they are perceived lead to other substantial inequalities. In addition to social class, we can see injurious divisions reflected in such categories as gender, ethnicity, nationality and disability, amongst others (Payne 2006; Macionis and Plummer 2012: 253–4; see also Chapter 6). In relation to gender, for example, the continuing perception that women are 'natural carers' simply because they are women and give birth feeds into concrete inequalities for women of pay and professional status (Abbott 2006). In occupational terms, 'caring' work such as childcare and midwifery are seen as more appropriately staffed by women than men. These occupations consistently attract lower wages than male-associated work such as mechanics and engineering. In order to combine paid work with childcare and domestic duties, the latter being considered largely women's work, women very often work part time where wages are lower on a pro-rata basis (Office for National Statistics 2012b).

The picture becomes more complex still because of the way social divisions can reinforce multiple inequalities in people's lives to have damaging, cumulative effects. Living with a disability provides us with a salient example (see also Chapter 6). Within a medical model of disability, rather than asking the question about how society can make concrete changes to better accommodate individuals, people are seen to be inadequate by virtue of their disability. Hence people with disabilities experience considerable formal and informal discrimination and prejudice (Hyde 2006). Even though disability discrimination Acts are now part of legal frameworks nationally and internationally, societies do not take responsibility for the many ways they actively exclude people with disabilities from our social institutions, making it far harder for them to live fruitful and fulfilled lives. Instead this form of social division produces multiple layers of disadvantage.

Thus, women from a lower social-class background who have any form of impairment have an increased likelihood of a lower level of formal qualifications. With far fewer financial resources, qualifications are harder to access, and because of continuing informal discrimination, where they may be held unable to do a good job of work, there is less employment available than for an able-bodied person. Even if women with a disability can find work, they are subject to a very significant pay gap, earning considerably less when compared with a non-disabled worker (Papworth Trust 2011). Reliance on social welfare provision condemns them to economic deprivation along with a loss of personal autonomy due to the levels of bureaucratic regulation (Barnes 1991). Since 2011, deep cuts to disability allowances in Britain have severely cut access for people with disabilities to transport, housing, education and employment, making them significantly poorer.

Being poorer leads to damaging consequences for health, touching as it does on every aspect of people's lives. If women with a disability become pregnant, they may encounter still more barriers and difficulties by virtue of these cumulative inequalities, as well as having to confront entrenched prejudices about their very capacity to be mothers (Goodman 1994; Prilleltensky 2003; Begley et al. 2010; Lewiecki-Wilson and Cellio 2011). The response to Heather Kuttai's pregnancy is not uncommon: '"Oh dear" were the first words out of the mouth of the doctor I saw after I learned I was pregnant' (Kuttai 2010: 77).

Box 10.1 Experiences of disabled women who are on the margins economically

The midwifery manager wrote down on a piece of paper 'Why don't you go to the classes?' . . . I said, 'Yeah well there is a problem about me getting access. Like would you be willing to pay for an interpreter, provide the interpreter?' And she said, 'Oh gosh no, we haven't talked about that. You have to pay for an interpreter.' (Account of a hearing disabled woman from Cecily Begley et al. 2010)

All disabled parents in our borough automatically get treated as a child protection issue. (Charlie Foulkes, disabled mother, quoted in Tim Rushby-Smith 2010)

Social Exclusion as a Political Problem for Childbearing Women

Within any highly **stratified** society, that is, a society with deep social divisions, resources, privileges and status are distributed so unevenly that people in certain categories become systematically excluded from being able to participate fully in ordinary everyday life. We call this process **social exclusion**. As the examples above illustrate, social exclusion is actively created through our policies and our key institutions, with more powerful sectors of society imposing exclusion and marginalization on other weaker sectors which then become even more deeply disadvantaged. People are shut out from fundamental social, economic, political and cultural processes (Byrne 2005). The phrase 'second-class citizens' is one that reflects the extent of this exclusion and the way in which the ordinary 'social rights of citizenship' (Walker and Walker 1997: 8) are systematically denied. Those who are excluded also become subject to a much greater degree of state regulation and their poor social status is often linked to the perception that it is because of their individual failing that they are on the 'outside'.

> **stratified**
> arranged or classified

> **social exclusion**
> process blocking people from basic rights and resources

It is worth noting that successive governments since the 1990s have used the term 'social exclusion' as if it were an unproblematic matter to resolve. The implication is that, in a flourishing economy, all that needs to be done to eliminate 'social exclusion' is to assist people to move from the 'outside' to the 'inside' (Koller and Davidson 2008). However, this is by and large a move into low-paid and often temporary employment (Macionis and Plummer 2012: 514–15). These conditions, often called 'flexibility of labour', are important to the profitability of large-scale corporate enterprises like supermarkets, big retail parks and call centres. The acceptance of this rationale, that is, the need to move people from 'outside' to just 'inside', glosses over the extent to which governments have abandoned the pursuit of egalitarian social policies to genuinely support those with fewest resources to improve their life chances. This abandonment is central to the doctrine of neoliberalism, which asserts that the principal role of the state is not to support people but to support the market to function in total freedom without regulation (Harvey 2005).

Yet, when a commitment to the collective social good is abandoned by the state, society 'is no longer identified by a set of values, rights and responsibilities' (Cameron and Palen 2004: 138) which we all share; rather, the market becomes all. Letting go of such agreements has an immediate adverse effect on the provision of best-quality health and education for all, as we can see from the example of the 'postcode lottery' in health services with the poorest areas in Britain having the poorest services. Another name for this is the 'competition state', which brings with it the notion that cost-cutting, especially of people's wages and their welfare entitlements, in order for business to become globally 'competitive', is a paramount aim (Cameron and Palen 2004). The impact of these policies can be seen in Britain where what has been described as the 'low-pay, no-pay jobs market' has resulted in there now being more people in working households – 6.1 million – who are living in poverty, compared with those households where there is no work at all – 5.1 million – who also live in poverty (Aldridge et al. 2012). The working poor have become a major new social reality.

🗒 Activity 10.3: Understanding how neoliberalism works and what it does to public services which pregnant women need

Read the following two extracts explaining neoliberalism, its impact on public services and the need for state action to change the course of poverty.

> *The rule of the market* Liberating 'free' enterprise or private enterprise from any bonds imposed by the government (the state) no matter how much social damage this causes.
>
> *Cutting public expenditure for social services* like education and health care. Reducing the safety net for the poor.
>
> *Deregulation* Reduce government regulation of everything that could diminish profits, including protecting the environment and safety on the job.
>
> *Privatization* Sell state-owned enterprises, goods and services to private investors. This includes banks, key industries, railroads, toll highways, electricity, schools, hospitals and even fresh water.
>
> *Eliminating the concept of the 'public good'* or 'community' and replacing it with 'individual responsibility'. Pressuring the poorest people in a society to find solutions to their lack of health care, education and social security all by themselves, then blaming them, if they fail, as 'lazy'. (Elizabeth Martinez and Arnoldo García 2000)
>
> Recognizing how much poverty levels have changed over a longer period confounds any idea that poverty is inevitable and therefore beyond society's capacity to alter. Something has caused poverty to change; something else could cause it to change again. (Hannah Aldridge et al. 2012: 7)

Now discuss how cuts to public services affect midwifery care:

1. What do you think the impact might be on midwifery care in the community and in hospitals if NHS budgets continue to be cut?
2. What have you already noticed about midwifery care as services become more stretched?
3. How do you think this will affect disadvantaged mothers?

The withdrawal of the state from protecting the social good means that people with a low skills base cannot access good-quality training because the cost is too high for them as individuals, and so they are condemned to work and exist on the fringes of society. The commitment to neoliberal markets lies behind government schemes in a number of countries that are known as welfare-to-work schemes, or workfares (Harris et al. 2012). Possibly the worst element of these schemes is the raft of mandatory regulations and surveillance that accompany them, while at the same time they actually provide virtually no scope for entry into decently paid jobs with long-term prospects. The expectation is that individuals 'bear the burdens' of what the state will no longer carry (Harris et al. 2012: 824), even while the state presents these as necessary reforms for the economy to grow (Byrne 2005). These workfare schemes have had an 'adverse impact on people who already experience high levels of discrimination in unregulated markets' (ibid.). They are the ones who carry the personal and economic costs of 'job flexibility'.

This is very apparent in relation to single mothers, who have been left stranded between these reformed welfare payment systems, poor state childcare facilities and insecure jobs. As Melissa Benn (1998) has argued, we should recognize the urgent need to rethink how society should be supporting the work of mothers to rear their children in a loving and caring household as well as working in formal employment. As it is, there are working mothers who simply do not count because they are the unemployed or the very low paid or the mothers who are in prison (Benn 1998: 146). The extensive policy talk about 'time-poor' women trying to balance work and family life (Hinsliff 2012) concentrates on the situations of middle-class women, not the poor. Benn interviewed single mothers in Cardiff in 1997 at a point when, as a marginalized social group, they were coming under increasing attack from the government and the media about being 'welfare mothers' and having 'babies on benefits'. Single mothers were being pressured to exit from the welfare system, which itself was being cut back, and to take on paid work. Many women in these precarious circumstances did so. However, as Benn puts it, 'These women understand the market. They know exactly how the job situation has changed. Everything is fixed-term contracts. The work is there for women but it is part-time and low-paid' (Benn 1998: 162). They experience a very limited movement from the absolute margins stuck in the welfare system to just 'inside' the world of paid work, and then back to welfare again, when those temporary jobs come to an end, in line with the requirements for 'flexibility of labour'. As a result, most women experiencing social exclusion are having to manage their entire budget 'on what the well-off spend on food alone' (ibid.: 152).

The consequent strain on women suffering social exclusion spills over into other areas of their lives. Their status as disadvantaged mothers sees them potentially labelled by a health system not prepared to fully support them. We know that, compared to women with a secure social and economic position, they experience problems with the access and uptake of maternity services, they are less likely to breastfeed, more likely to experience teenage pregnancy, and more likely to have mental health problems (D'Souza and Garcia 2004; Raleigh et al. 2010). We also know that they report their experiences of care as being poorer, with less likelihood that they are treated with dignity and respect (Raleigh et al. 2010: 190).

Additionally, they are more likely to be seen as problematic for their behaviours, with scant attention being paid to the structural factors that lie behind what appear as less acceptable or healthy patterns. Smoking is a case in point. Women living in severely disadvantaged areas are more likely to smoke and are more likely to smoke in the home in front of their very young children, with implications for child health (Robinson and Kirkcaldy 2007). Amidst a raft of health-care advice, promotional material, directives and regulations, what is not taken into account is how aware women are of possible damage, how guilty they feel, and the weight of their concern for their young children while they try to limit exposure and even their reliance on smoking (Robinson and Kirkcaldy 2007; Oaks 2001: 109–10). Regulating and even criminalizing women who smoke has already happened in the United States where, in some jurisdictions, smoking in publicly owned housing is now banned (Winickoff et al. 2010). Smoking is now also banned in the United Kingdom in commercially rented accommodation. This suggests that it is easier to regulate the poor about smoking simply because so many dimensions of their lives already fall under the surveillance of the state. Oaks (2001: 171) points out that women have actually lost custody of their children, their smoking officially labelled as 'fetal abuse'. The reasons for smoking, as a coping mechanism to deal with the stress of poverty, are too often avoided by governments. They are anxious not to deal comprehensively with the consequences of social exclusion, but once more to make individual women bear the burden of their failure. Women's capacity to cope as mothers despite the odds they face is consistently questioned by the very system that has withdrawn full support.

📋 Activity 10.4: Women's experiences of social exclusion as mothers

Read these two extracts below and then discuss how social exclusion affects women as mothers.

> There are parents who need more support, but all our evidence suggests that the real practical support isolated parents need is not there. Increasingly, health visitors simply report anyone with problems to social services – who also increasingly get care orders rather than providing real support. (AIMS Press release 2004)

> One of the Whitehall cleaners who has featured in the *Observer*'s living wage campaign, in support of an hourly minimum wage of £8.55 in London, has been evicted from her home with her family, just days

before the birth of her baby. Anilsa Ramos, 36, who suffers from acute asthma, has been placed, along with her husband, mother, 12-year-old son and six-year-old niece, in bed and breakfast accommodation that is costing Newham council £1,200 a month – £300 more than its contribution to the cost of the family's privately rented house. Until earlier this month, Ramos worked 15 hours a week cleaning the Supreme Court building in Parliament Square, earning £58–£80 a week after travel costs – too little to make her eligible for maternity pay from her employer. She and her husband, Jose, who is also a cleaner, privately rented a three-bedroom house for four years. The council paid £900 a month; the family, £200. Last July, the landlord obtained a possession order because the house had been sold. (Roberts 2013)

1. In your experience, how does poverty impact on women's confidence and capacity to mother their children?
2. How can midwives help to really support pregnant women who suffer from deep poverty?
3. What do midwives need to learn in order to better support women in poverty?

The withdrawal of full support of health services by the state, reflected in too few midwives, has already had serious consequences for women in maternity services (Edwards 2008; Mander and Murphy-Lawless 2013). We urgently need to reclaim social exclusion as the fundamental challenge it is to the lives and well-being of the several hundred thousand women and their babies who are affected each year. As Rosemary Mander has written, 'It is necessary to consider where power lies in relation to these groups of childbearing women and whether and how their position is changing or can be changed' (Mander and Murphy-Lawless 2013: 30).

The Consequences of Social Exclusion on Maternity Service Users

Internationally, health authorities endeavour to compile databases on incidents of serious maternal morbidity and maternal mortality in order to understand how to improve all women's maternal health and well-being. The oldest and most respected of these surveys is the UK National Confidential Enquiry into Maternal Deaths, now in its seventh decade and recently renamed *Saving Mothers' Lives* (Mander and Smith 2008; Lewis 2012).

In line with previous reports, the most recent *Saving Mothers' Lives* (CMACE 2011) breaks down the data on the numbers of women who died in the UK between 2006 and 2008 into different categories. This approach to data analysis, with a range of clinical conditions and social factors, yields important information to health-care professionals about women who, if they share these factors, will benefit from early identification and additional support in order to have a more fulfilling and safe pregnancy, labour and birth.

The current report draws attention to, amongst others, women who were more vulnerable to poor maternal health stemming from a number of social factors, including their socioeconomic status (SES). This is what sociologists refer to as social class, which we have already encountered above. In reading Tables 1.22 and 1.23 of *Saving Mothers' Lives*, we learn that amongst those women who died in that triennial period, the vast majority were classified as unemployed (Table 1.22) or lived in the most deprived districts in England and Wales (CMACE 2011: 51–2).

This is not a new finding and it reflects the concrete effects of social exclusion. As Michael Marmot and Richard Wilkinson state, 'British statistics have shown, for as long as one has cared to look, that health follows a social gradient: the higher the social position, the better the health' (2006: 2). This holds true for maternal health as much as for perinatal and infant health. Moreover, although there has been a downward trend in the numbers of maternal deaths from women in these categories since 2000 (Lewis 2012: 23), as Rosemary Mander comments, 'the gap remains disconcertingly large' (Mander 2011: 257). Thus, even if maternal deaths are infrequent, they place a microscope on how well or badly the maternity services are functioning in relation to those women who are most in need. This has already been seen vividly in the United States where privatized medicine is the norm and where women in poverty must depend on the barest minimum of public-health care packages, with terrible outcomes for them in respect of severe morbidity and mortality (Amnesty International 2010; Bridges 2011; Lane 2008).

In Table 1.25 of the CMACE report, women who had had no antenatal care at all or missed more than three visits are listed under categories such as:

> 'Single unemployed'
> 'Partner unemployed'
> 'Most deprived quintile post code' (CMACE 2011: 54)

In other words, these were women who had been pushed to the margins of society. Thirty-five women who died received no antenatal care at all (CMACE 2011: 35), while another thirty-five were listed as 'poor attenders', leading to their receiving 'less than optimal care' (ibid.). The term itself is stigmatizing and does not help us to understand why women would decide not to seek help. We have to dig more deeply to discover an interwoven pattern of personal and social need on the part of women with multiple burdens, including why services remain far less accessible for them. One of the cases tragically illustrates this point. A woman who had a 'complex social history' refused a hospital admission while pregnant for a chest infection 'because she was concerned her children would be taken into care' (de Swiet et al. 2011: 124). To surrender her children to local social service authorities is a terrifying prospect for a woman who is marginalized. Women in this position know how difficult and challenging it is to actually be reunited with their children once they are taken into care (Robinson 2004). Although this woman was diagnosed HIV positive, her midwives were not informed, her HIV therapy was delayed and there was no protocol to deal with HIV when she went into premature labour.

This series of incidents and clinical mishaps ended in her death from sepsis and colitis, about which Rosemary Mander comments that protocols are disregarded or may not even exist (Mander 2011). Moreover, given the changes in health-care provision and the needs that existing health-care structures no longer meet, many responsibilities for their own care are being shifted on to the shoulders of women themselves (Mander 2011). If there is any degree of vulnerability or lack of resources or personal support, women may be unable to cope with any additional burden. Yet it may be very hard indeed for practitioners to comprehend why, in their view, women are not 'complying' with their instructions (Mander 2011: 256). Too few clinicians understand the intricacies of living with deep social exclusion. The 2010 NICE Guideline on Pregnancy and Complex Social Factors seeks to help clinicians identify women in need of additional support, including women who misuse substances, women under twenty years of age, women who experience domestic abuse and women who are recent migrants (National Collaborating Centre for Women's and Children's Health 2010), and proposes additional service provision, improved service organization and better delivery of care. The authors do not comment at all on where the political will is to be harnessed to promote better services for vulnerable women.

Amongst a challenging matrix of factors that may confront women is that of actually being able to access a GP. In 2010, the majority of pregnant women – many in their second or third trimester – attending the Project London Clinic (which is staffed by the Doctors of the World UK voluntary group) were asylum-seekers who had been unable to register with a GP (Ramaswami 2012). This is an especially vulnerable group of women with their very status as 'asylum-seekers' putting them at the absolute margins of society.

The term 'asylum-seeker' itself is a deliberately exclusionary one, designed to indicate they are people stripped of worth (Hyland 2001). In the last three decades, there have been mass movements of people fleeing their place of birth in sheer necessity due to countless major political, economic and environmental disasters. The scale of movement is unprecedented in the entire period of human history up to the present and has led to women giving birth in exile (Kennedy and Murphy-Lawless 2003). However, unlike the 1951 UN Convention on Refugees, the criteria for defining an 'asylum-seeker' are even more strict as governments in wealthier states seek to limit the numbers of people crossing their borders and taking up residence permanently

Figure 10.1 Young mothers at the Keep Salford Hope Maternity Unit Open protest, February 2011

(ibid.). This is in line with the dictates of neoliberalism which, within a globalized economy, wants people to move for purposes of work and living on its terms only.

Zgymunt Bauman (1998) has argued that the state designates some people 'tourists' with legitimate papers, who can travel anywhere because they spend valuable tourist dollars, while others are effectively designated 'vagabonds', who, against their best intentions for themselves and their families, become the flotsam and jetsam of an unstable world. The term 'asylum-seeker' became widespread in the EU in the 1990s as the numbers of non-European people seeking refuge swelled.

In the UK, the Asylum Act of 1999 quietly changed the terms of reference so that people whom the state designates 'asylum-seekers' have virtually no legal protection at all (Hyland 2001). Warwick et al. (2006: 129) note in their work how people so designated suffer from 'discrimination, racism, persecution and suspicion' and are effectively criminalized simply because they are trying to survive. The net effect is to leave them with the barest minimum or no access to health-care facilities, legal employment and secure legal papers. In other words, they are not even 'second-class citizens'. This lack of protection and the active measures to exclude them, including official dispersal policies around the UK, can be seen at once in the status of women who have died in childbirth.

Compared with white ethnic groups, women from black minority ethnic groups (BMEs) experienced higher numbers of direct maternal deaths, 42 per cent of the total numbers (CMACE 2011: 47), while women from black minority ethnic groups suffered 31 per cent of indirect maternal deaths (ibid.). Twenty-eight women of black African ethnicity died. Nine women in this group were UK citizens, with the remaining women being 'either recently arrived new immigrants, refugees, or asylum-seekers' (CMACE 2011: 49). While the CMACE report discusses 'poor attenders' and the fact that non-attendance for antenatal care has been a recognized risk factor for decades (CMACE 2011: 47, 49), it does not allude to the full range of social factors that contribute to non-attendance. The report does draw attention to problems of communication and the consequent threat to women's well-being if, for example, there can be no full booking history taken. The report recommends professional interpretation services for minority ethnic women, pointing out how inappropriate and even dangerous it can be to women if children or male family members speak on their behalf (CMACE 2011: 50). However, it is worth pointing out that the Danish and the Dutch governments have recently ruled that they would no longer cover the cost for professional interpretation services, which has raised concerns straight across Europe about such discriminatory practices which will hit minority ethnic groups the hardest (Phelan 2012).

These women are at the sharpest edge of government actions to maintain social exclusion. Maternity Action and the Refugee Council (Feldman 2013) point out in their research how dispersal policies critically jeopardize the health and well-being of pregnant women who are asylum-seekers. These are women who already deal with serious and chronic health conditions, including female genital mutilation or cutting (FGM/FGC). Being moved from initial accommodation to sites across the country, often with no warning, to often deeply inappropriate environments including detention, interrupts still further the possibility of stable continuity of care for them. It also breaks up the few fragile social networks that women might have begun to lay down.

Activity 10.5: Women's experiences as asylum-seekers

Read the two extracts below and then discuss what they tell us about maternity care needs of women who are registered as asylum-seekers.

> Around half of the women in this study were not so fortunate, encountering indifference, rudeness, and racism. They described health professionals acting with contemptuous disrespect for their individuality and total disregard for their feelings, apparently unable to leave their personal prejudices out of their professional practice. These experiences are far removed from the ideals of *Changing Childbirth*. (McLeish 2002)

> Dana did not have enough money before she gave birth to buy clothes and necessities for the baby. She had received an initial payment of £90 when she first claimed asylum on arrival in the

UK, but she used this money to pay for travel from outside London for her asylum interview and for fares to see her solicitor. Her next payment of £35 was due on the day she delivered, and she thought she would lose it if she did not collect it immediately. So, straight after giving birth, she left her baby in the hospital to go to the post office to collect her money to buy clothes for her baby.

'It was freezing (29 December), but if I didn't go I would lose my money. For £35 I left my baby. Two hours after I gave birth I left the hospital to go to the post office. The nurses said, "No you are not allowed to take the baby with you because you are not fine." I said, "No I have to go because she doesn't have clothes. I have to buy clothes." So when she was born for two hours she didn't have any clothes so they covered her with towels.' (Feldman 2013)

1. What do these accounts of women experiencing deep social exclusion tell you about the failure of mainstream services?

2. What are the most critical empathic skills you need to develop in order to support vulnerable women migrants in your practice?

Conclusion

In this chapter, we have explored the problems of social exclusion and marginalization with the intention of showing that these are far from straightforward or naturally occurring phenomena. They are in reality outcomes contingent on contemporary hierarchies of power, wealth and resource distribution in our societies that work actively to create inequalities. In turn, these inequalities jeopardize health and life chances. We have also argued that commonplace assumptions about people who experience social exclusion are often confused and mis-informed. Above all, it is important to bear in mind that people do not end up on the margins of society through individual 'choice'. They have had virtually no 'choice' about their circumstances, but endure what the sociologist Pierre Bourdieu describes as the work of 'a social order [which] has set up the conditions for an unprecedented development of all kinds of ordinary suffering' (2006: 4).

Michael Marmot describes the resulting serious health inequalities in the Marmot Review and also comments: 'Serious health inequalities do not arise by chance . . . Social and economic differences in health status reflect, and are caused by, social and economic inequalities in society' (Strategic Review of Health Inequalities 2010: 16). Marmot also argues that:

A fair society would give people more equal freedom to lead flourish-ing lives. . .
If the conditions in which people are born, grow, live, work, and age are favourable, and more equitably distributed, then they will have

more control over their lives in ways that will influence their own health and health behaviours, and those of their families. (ibid.)

For midwives, eager to support women as fully as possible in attaining a healthy, confident and peaceful transition to motherhood, the ultimate goal must be a flourishing and secure family life. We can see that this goal is inextricably bound up with resolving the grievous burdens of social exclusion. These must first be recognized and then responded to sensitively and effectively by midwives. Jean Davies expressed this in her work over a decade ago when she wrote that midwives need to make 'conscious efforts . . . to bridge the gap between the experiences and expectations of the midwives as professionals and those of their economically deprived clients' and this means paying attention to how women cope 'in their everyday lives and how midwifery care [can] be adapted to fit their coping mechanisms' (Davies 2001: 120).

Davies' sensitive conclusion, that the 'aim should be that women will be enabled to birth well and can see themselves as "women who can", this being "especially important for women whose experience of much around them is that they cannot"' (Davies 2001: 140), is one on which midwives need to reflect very hard. This is especially pressing in this current period of contraction, destruction and privatization of our health services, with terrible consequences for midwifery (Mander and Murphy-Lawless 2013).

Reinforcing this message, Davies speaks about how a 'midwifery service' that is 'truly community based' develops 'complex links' between 'midwives and families, which involve midwives in the lives of vulnerable women who would otherwise slip through the net' (Davies 2001: 140–1). This was the work of the Albany Practice in Peckham in south-east London, one of the poorest districts in the whole of Britain, with enduring problems of social exclusion. The Albany midwives consistently worked with women who had been abandoned by the wider society and brought them through to safe births and a remarkable understanding of what it is to be a mother. This is what one of the Albany mothers said:

> I think you grow because you grow to meet their expectations [. . .].
> They expected me to give birth well, they expected me to be a good
> parent afterwards and I grew to meet their expectations. You know?
> That's really powerful. (Quoted in Edwards 2010)

The question for midwifery and midwives is whether they can now go against the grain of dominant institutional and political discourses, as the Albany Practice did, and seek to protect vulnerable women. This will mean rejecting outright the notion that women who have been marginalized are somehow a threatening 'other' that upsets mainstream society, and instead recognizing how that same society has jeopardized a significant minority of women by seeking to exclude them.

Figure 10.2 Women and babies outside a health centre in South London

Summary

- The experience of childbirth is often marred for women by deep exclusion and a lack of control over fundamental decisions about their care despite overwhelming research evidence on the importance of woman-centred care in achieving best outcomes.
- Inflexible and unresponsive maternity services can pose problems for all women, but they pose special problems for women who experience the effects and consequences of 'social divisions'.
- Social exclusion and marginalization are far from straightforward or naturally occurring phenomena.
- For midwives, eager to support women as fully as possible in attaining a healthy, confident and peaceful transition to motherhood, the ultimate goal must be a flourishing and secure family life.

Questions for discussion

- Think of a pregnant woman you have cared for whom you consider to have been excluded. How far did health professionals make use of the woman's knowledge and her personal circumstances in care planning?
- Consider social exclusion and marginalization. How do they restrict a healthy, confident and peaceful transition to motherhood?
- How can you support and promote a secure family life for women who are marginalized?

Further reading

Gans, H. J. 2002 The uses of poverty: the poor pay all. In L. McIntyre (ed.), *The Practical Skeptic: Readings in Sociology*. McGraw Hill.
This refers to a chapter within a book. However, the whole text is worth a look. Using a conceptual framework, the book includes classic sociological research writings as well as recent pieces on fascinating topics of interest to students. There is a section on social institutions, and each of the thirty-eight readings serves to illustrate key sociological concepts and ideas.
Wilkinson, R. and Pickett, K. 2010 *The Spirit Level: Why Equality is Better for Everyone*. Penguin.
This is a meticulously researched text, which argues convincingly that inequality is the root cause of many of society's ills. It is an important and thought-provoking book that will challenge your thinking. An abundance of evidence is used to demonstrate that levels of violent crime, mental illness, drug addiction, illiteracy and obesity are almost always higher in more unequal societies. The book also highlights that even the affluent are adversely affected by inequality.
Deery, R., Hughes, D. and Kirkham, M. 2010 *Tensions and Barriers in Improving Maternity Care: The Story of a Struggling Birth Centre*. Radcliffe Publishing.
This book provides a challenging resource for all midwives, managers and policymakers. It provides a detailed analysis of the politics of a birth centre trapped in a medicalized system. It provides a vivid example of how autonomous midwifery is undermined by an organizational structure in which management focused exclusively on one model of care.
Freire, P. 1996 *Pedagogy of the Oppressed*. Penguin.
This text argues that the ignorance and lethargy of the poor are the direct result of the whole economic, social and political domination. It is suggested that in some countries the oppressors use the system to maintain a 'culture of silence'. The book encourages avoiding an authoritarian approach and fostering the right to be heard.

11 Infant and Young Child Feeding

Culture and Context

Fiona Dykes

Key issues:

- Application of a political economy of health perspective to illuminate political issues related to infant feeding practices.
- The powerful influence of economic, sociocultural and relational contexts upon infant feeding practices.
- The gap between international policy recommendations on infant and young child feeding and the actual practices of women with regard to infant feeding.
- The importance of midwives understanding the complexities inherent for women in the decision-making process with regard to infant feeding.

By the end of this chapter you should be able to:

- Understand some of the complex influences upon women with regard to their infant feeding decisions.
- Discuss some of the reasons why so few women actually feed their infants in accordance with the World Health Organization guidelines.
- Consider the ways in which midwives can facilitate support for women with infant feeding that takes account of their own culture, context and life circumstances.

Introduction

Supporting women with their infant feeding decisions and with the practical application of their choices is a key role of the midwife. The main aim of this chapter is to provide an understanding of the powerful and complex influence of political, economic, sociocultural and relational contexts upon infant feeding practices. The chapter then describes key global initiatives that aim to optimize infant and young child feeding practices and the challenges for policymakers, practitioners and women in light of the complex influences upon women and their families.

Political Economy of Health

Social scientists tend to describe, explore and research social situations through a particular **theoretical perspective** (see Chapter 1), but do not argue that this is the only way or the 'correct' way of viewing social situations; rather, it is seen as one of many ways of viewing things. The wide range of such perspectives includes that of political economy of health, with its focus upon relationships between **capitalist modes of production**, medical practice, health and illness. These are interpreted in various ways by leading authors in this field (Gough 1979; Frankenburg 1980; Doyal and Pennell 1981; Navarro 1992; Illich 1995); the perspective of Doyal and Pennell (1981) is particularly illuminating.

Doyal and Pennell (1981) illustrate the overwhelming contradictions between the goals of improving health and the imperatives of making money inherent within the capitalist mode of production. They also highlight the ways in which particular forms of medical practice have developed within societies that embrace the capitalist mode of production. They argue that the existence of any particular medical practice and its associated technology should be understood in relation to the activities of powerful groups within society whose interests are furthered by the development, maintenance and proliferation of such technologies. Medical equipment manufacturers, pharmaceutical companies and those in the food industry are among the most powerful (see Chapter 12).

Doyal and Pennell (1981) argue that many forms of medicine are potentially or actually harmful, a point strongly reiterated by Illich (1995) in his examination of the iatrogenic nature of Western medicine. Doyal and Pennell (1981) therefore challenge the continuing demands within society for *more* medicine as seriously misguided, in that *more of the same* will not tackle the social, political and economic roots of ill health within society. They also challenge public health initiatives that focus upon the individual as responsible for her/his health maintenance, therefore placing the person centre stage for blame should they become ill. This again shifts the focus away from the need for socioeconomic reform. They further argue that despite rhetoric about equal access to health care through national services, the social organization of medicine within nations employing the capitalist mode of production still reinforces socioeconomic, sexual and race divisions (see Chapter 10).

Doyal and Pennell (1981) express particular anger in relation to the ways in which we have failed to alleviate the huge burden of disease and mortality still experienced by the mass of the population in the developing world. They heavily criticize the exponential growth in the practice of exporting Western medicine to non-Western communities in which this form of medicine may be of limited value in alleviating sickness and disease in large sections of the population. In contrast, health-promoting techniques and drugs that could potentially make

theoretical perspective
a way of viewing the world

capitalist modes of production
private ownership of the means of production, distribution and exchange in a market economy

a dramatic difference may be withheld because they are non-profit-making or are sold at prices that place them out of reach of large sections of the population.

Doyal and Pennell (1981) recognize that finding solutions to the problems they describe would be highly challenging and complex. They make it clear that a socialist government would not necessarily provide a better alternative, unless it addressed all of the following:

> A socialist health service would not only have to provide equal access to medical care but would also have to address itself seriously to such problems as how to demystify medical knowledge and how to break down barriers of authority and status among health workers them-selves and also between workers and consumers. Indeed, the whole notion of 'treating patients' – of seeing them as passive recipients of medical expertise – would need to be rethought (p. 194).

Although the analysis of Doyal and Pennell (1981) took place over two decades ago it is still highly relevant today, and offers one way of making sense of the issues. James (2005) illustrates this in his writing twenty-five years later with regard to the food industry and nutrition:

> We are now in a position where the industries involved in the food chain, whether in agricultural technology, food production, process-ing, manufacturing or retailing, are all huge players. They are far more powerful than the tobacco industry and in practice have discovered the value of using the same techniques, i.e. obtaining political influ-ence through selective party funding, recruiting pliant nutritionists, scientists and doctors, and employing major public health relations companies to cope with the media. So unsurprisingly, they are able to gain access at short notice to government ministers and indeed to presidents and prime ministers. (p. 200)

The infant formula industry is one example of a powerful vested inter-est which has had a striking influence upon infant feeding practices, an issue to which we now turn.

The Infant Formula Industry

It is well known that social scientists are particularly interested in the ways in which powerful vested interests influence health behaviours. In this context, one area of particular focus is upon the activities of infant formula industries in influencing infant feeding practices.

In Western industrialized countries, during the late nineteenth and early twentieth centuries, expansion of an infant formula industry occurred concurrently with growing scientific and medical interest in breastfeeding and infant feeding generally. Palmer (2009) describes the scientific interest in the analysis of milk, human and animal, and its conversion into formula for administration via a feeding bottle; at the same time, the dairy industry was becoming more efficient with an increasing amount of low-cost cow's milk. Substantial quantities

Look Out For That First Little Tooth —

WHEN the baby begins to drool—when the saliva flows always from his little mouth—*then* the teeth are about to come, and *then*, above all—must you be careful of your baby's food. Give him the right food—and wash the little red gums and the new, tiny teeth with boric acid solution—and there will be no teething troubles for the baby or for you.

Nurse your baby if you can; but if you cannot, remember that in the last forty years, millions of babies have come to their teeth easily and naturally with the help of

Nestlé's Food

Nestlé's Food brings health and strength because it is so nearly like mother's milk. Especially in the teething time—look out for cow's milk—cow's milk meant for calves with four stomachs—cow's milk that, for all you know, comes from sick cows and unsanitary dairies—cow's milk that may bring sickness and even consumption to your child.

Nestlé's Food is made from cow's milk with all the cow dangers banished. Nestlé's is made from milk of cows that are carefully inspected. The milk is kept covered every in- stant, is purified just to make sure; all the heavy parts are modified and your baby's special needs are added. It is powdered and packed in an air-tight can. No germ can possibly touch it. You add only fresh water. But the four generations that have grown up on Nestlé's can testify better than we can.

Send coupon for a box of Nestlé's Food—enough for twelve feedings, Free, and a book about babies by specialists.

NESTLE'S FOOD COMPANY,
    241 Broadway, New York.
Please send me, **FREE**, your Book and Trial Package.

Name ....

Address ....

Figure 11.1 Early marketing presented infant formula as a safe alternative to breastfeeding

of surplus milk were becoming available and the development of milk separation and drying processes encouraged the establishment of milk laboratories during the early twentieth century for production of dried formula milk. Developing techniques such as pasteurization of milk provided further justification for the 'safe' humanization of milk (Baumslag and Michels 1995). Growth of the cheese industry generated excess whey products that became increasingly expensive to transport or dispose of, so their use for infant formula offered an economic solution (Ebrahim 1991; Palmer 2009). The industrialization and processing of milk coincided with scientific interest in infant feeding, thus creating the conditions in which the expansion of an infant formula industry could flourish.

Marketing messages were directed at women during the First World War, encouraging them into work to fill the gaps created by men at war. Infant formula was not only presented as a safe alternative to breastfeeding, but as a way of enabling women to engage in other activities. With the expansion of multinational corporations over the next few decades, they increasingly used growing media channels such as radio and television to market their products alongside the display of placards and posters in prominent public places. Breastfeeding was increasingly portrayed as unsophisticated, outmoded, primitive and prone to failure, whilst bottle-feeding was linked with Western affluence, consumerism and the liberated woman (Jelliffe and Jelliffe 1978; Sokol 1997; Palmer 2009).

Increasing hospitalization of women giving birth and the proliferation of maternity hospitals and child welfare clinics, in Western industrialized countries during the twentieth century, provided an ideal focus for the promotion of infant formula. Palmer (2009) refers to the development of a model of cooperation between formula companies and doctors, with the formula companies marketing through health-care facilities, which gave the impression that health workers were endorsing the products. This marketing channel facilitated massive expansion of sales, with companies providing gifts and financial incentives to doctors and hospitals and directing their target consumer groups through the medical system in order to obtain formula.

As the twentieth century progressed, the global influence of formula companies expanded and, in some cases, they even became involved in the design of hospitals. As Baer (1982) asserts, the design was founded on the principle of separation between mother and baby, with nurseries often situated long distances from the mothers' beds; this inevitably made breastfeeding more difficult. A key marketing strategy involved the issue of free milk samples to health centres and hospitals, with company representatives dressed as 'milk nurses' issuing free samples directly to mothers when they visited and prior to discharge from hospital. This practice contributed substantially towards the undermining of breastfeeding and the normalization of infant formula. As Sokol (1997) describes, 'informational' leaflets and posters containing company and brand names were displayed and distributed accompanied by potent messages, suggesting that when breast milk was insufficient, infant formula could be provided to optimize growth and health.

A striking relationship is evident between the growing marketing of breast-milk substitutes and a decline in breastfeeding initiation and duration rates, which took place in the UK and many other countries between the 1950s and 1970s (Stewart et al. 1991; Guilkey and Stewart 1995; Howard et al. 2000; Berry and Jones 2010; Sobel et al. 2011). By 1975, recordable breastfeeding rates had reached an all-time low in the UK (Martin 1978). This effective marketing of breast-milk substitutes continues to pose challenges for the protection, promotion and support of breastfeeding (Kaplan and Graff 2008; Rosenberg et al. 2008; do Paco et al. 2010; Sobel et al. 2011). In the UK, for example, it is now illegal to advertise infant formula that is represented as a replacement for breast milk. However, companies continue to advertise follow-on formula and toddler milk by presenting them as complementary foods. In this way the company logo can be disseminated and visualized freely, thus promoting the range of products available. This successful marketing technique is known as line extension, which involves advertising one product to promote other items (Berry and Jones 2010). Thus, companies engage in continued promotion of their brand image via the Internet, baby clubs, care lines and booklets in Bounty packs distributed to mothers while in maternity units.

📋 Activity 11.1: Marketing practices and infant feeding

List some of the marketing techniques you have seen recently with regard to infant formula and complementary foods for infants and young children.

1. How do you think these marketing techniques may influence women in your area of practice?
2. How do you feel midwives should respond to such marketing practices?

Another marketing technique is described by Berry and Jones (2010), whereby statements are made that can lead to inferences being made. They give the example of a formula brand that refers to World Health Organization (WHO) recommendations, then refers to breast milk meeting these but moves on to mention relevant constituents of breast milk and then on to some of the positive aspects of the brand of toddler milk. The reader may then make a cognitive link with the WHO as a source of authoritative knowledge and the statement about toddler milk. The use of scientific terminology also acts to reinforce the parent's sense of the legitimacy of the product. Dykes et al. (2012) illustrate that there are still ongoing challenges for health-care staff in implementing best practice with regard to infant feeding in the midst of the continuing influences of infant formula companies upon women, families and the maternity services, some of which relate to the institutionalization of infant feeding, an issue to which we now turn.

Institutionalization of Infant Feeding

In Europe and other Western countries, there was a dramatic increase in the hospitalization of women during childbirth and the postnatal period throughout the twentieth century (see Chapter 2). The ethos of the hospital, like the factory, was based on efficiency, production, control and surveillance. Alongside this development, as Millard (1990) describes, there was a growth in professional advice in family matters, centring upon regularity in maternal–infant interactions. As the twentieth century progressed, the clock became increasingly central to medical advice related to infant feeding, bringing with it regimentation similar to factory work, reducing breastfeeding to a series of measurable steps (Balsamo et al. 1992). Regimes dictated that feeds should be meticulously and rigidly controlled in terms of time spent at each breast measured to the nearest minute, for example, two minutes per breast per feed on the first day, five minutes on the second day, seven minutes on the third, ten minutes on the fourth, and from then on twenty minutes maximum on each breast (Fisher 1985). This led to the baby being deprived of mother's fat-rich hind milk, creating a hungry, dissatisfied baby, the potential to lead to a secondary milk insufficiency and a generally negative experience for the mother (Fisher 1985; Woolridge 1995).

As hospitals proliferated, there was a growing emphasis on control of infection and maintenance of hygiene and sterile conditions, with hospital staff enforcing anti-infection control measures. As Palmer (2009) highlights, the ideas around hygiene also contributed to the development of nurseries and separation of babies from mothers, for the duration of the hospital stay, with babies being looked after by masked nurses in the nurseries and brought to mothers for feeds only. Mothers were required to wear masks and cleansing of their nipples and breasts became routine. The spatial layout of postnatal wards facilitated both surveillance and the separation of mothers to avoid spread of infection. The end result for mothers was a profound loss of confidence in their ability to breastfeed, and this was potentiated by the commercialization of infant feeding (Fisher 1985; Palmer 2009). Even in the twenty-first century, care in hospitals for women may still be institutionalized, and women comment on the ways in which staff are time-pressured, rule and tick-box orientated, give prescriptive information and communicate in ways that are not person-centred (Dykes 2005b, 2006; Furber and Thomson 2006; Schmied et al. 2011a; Hoddinott et al. 2012; see also Chapter 5).

Notions of separation and measurement are still evident in the ways in which breastfeeding is described and conceptualized in the UK. Breastfeeding is commonly seen as an act of nutrition which is given more importance than the nurture of, and relationship-building with, the baby. Breasts are seen as functioning primarily to produce milk that women then deliver to the baby, based on the baby's demand. When women view breastfeeding as being all about productivity, that is, 'supply and demand', they tend to doubt their own body's ability to produce 'good enough' milk in terms of quality and quantity (Dykes 2002, 2005a, 2006). The wide reporting of 'insufficient milk' in industrialized countries around the world appears to stem, in part, from this lack of trust and confidence in breastfeeding (Dykes 1999, 2002). In other more traditional, rural communities, around the world, breastfeeding is seen as primarily relationally orientated (Maher 1992a, 1992b; Dykes 2005a). This reflects the contrast made between the Western biomedical representation of breast milk as a product important for its nutritional components, and breastfeeding seen primarily as a relational activity within more traditional communities around the world (Van Esterik 1988; Dykes 2005a; Dykes and Flacking 2010).

🗒 Activity 11.2: Institutionalization

1. What do we mean by institutionalization of infant feeding?
2. In which ways is infant feeding still institutionalized in your local maternity unit?
3. Why is perceived insufficient milk still one of the main reasons that women discontinue breastfeeding?

Complex Challenges for Women

There are many complex challenges for women in deciding how, when and where to feed their babies. It is helpful to look at recent history to help us to understand some of these. Interviews conducted by Carter (1995) with women who had babies between 1920 and 1980, in a city in the north-east of England, illuminate some of the influences upon women's infant feeding decisions at that time. Carter first makes the important point that many women breast *and* bottle fed, and each woman had her own complex, personal, socioeconomic and intergenerational context. Her research revealed that, for working-class women, there were clear conditions that precluded against prolonged and exclusive breastfeeding. These included unhealthy working conditions that were hazardous, time-consuming and exhausting. Housing was often cramped, with more than one generation living together. Breastfeeding became a symbol of poverty, associated with tough living conditions, large families, exhaustion, discomfort, embarrassment and restriction. Given the relentless demands upon women, she argues that bottlefeeding provided women with some sense of control over their lives. It also enabled them to resist medical advice to control aspects of their lives that were considered to affect their milk, for example, their diet, emotions and exercise taken. The demise of breastfeeding was compounded by reports of authoritarianism and lack of support in hospital combined with inadequate family support at home.

Throughout the same period, as Lewis (1980, 1990) reports, middle-class women and women's groups were engaged in a sociopolitical movement to demand improved rights and conditions for women. Whilst middle-class women were more likely to subscribe to medical recommendations, they also saw breastfeeding as biologically tying, with the bottle and infant formula being seen as a symbol of modernity, progress and freedom (Palmer 2009).

The twentieth century brought with it a growing sexual portrayal of women's breasts through the proliferating media channels. In line with the increasing emphasis on hygiene in hospitals, breastfeeding came to be seen as associated with bodily fluids and therefore potentially 'dirty', contaminating and representative of the body being out of control (Bramwell 2001; Bartlett 2002; Dykes 2007). The sexualization of women's breasts led to breastfeeding being increasingly seen as a private activity to be conducted away from the public gaze (Maher 1992a; Carter 1995). However, as Carter (1995) notes, even in the so-called privacy of the woman's own home breastfeeding is not a neutral activity. Wherever they were, women still had to negotiate breastfeeding with regard to time, place and space, and the presence and approval or disapproval of others. Thus, breastfeeding was becoming less visible in public settings.

The dissonance created for women by the blurring of boundaries between breastfeeding as a maternal activity and the display of sexual breasts is highlighted in the literature (Carter 1995; Stearns 1999; Mahon-Daly and Andrews 2002; Dykes 2007). This dissonance may be increased by the embodied experience of breastfeeding as intimate, sensuous and erotic (Shaw 2003). Women therefore continue to constantly negotiate the places and spaces in which they breastfeed (Pain et al. 2001; Mahon-Daly and Andrews 2002; Dykes 2007).

Running in parallel, throughout the twentieth century, was the connection made by the medical establishment, and indeed by women's groups, that breastfeeding was the natural ideal associated with good motherhood (Apple 1987; Leff et al. 1994; Carter 1995; Marshall et al. 2007). Thus, women had to 'navigate' between two discourses, breast milk as pure and life-giving but, on the other hand, potentially polluting and dirty (Shildrick 1997, 2000; Bramwell 2001; Bartlett 2002; Dykes 2007). Additionally, the 'natural ideal' was seen as prone to weakness and therefore requiring medical management with infant formula providing a 'backup' for a variety of circumstances (Dykes 2002). Given the living conditions for many women referred to above, as Carter (1995) reports, the notion of natural mothering and its associations became increasingly unappealing.

The combination of these barriers and constraints to breastfeeding, with increasing institutionalization of infant feeding and marketing of infant formula, led to a situation by the 1970s whereby within three to four generations women had turned from predominantly breastfeeding to largely formula feeding. Due to a range of global, national and local initiatives, some of which are referred to later, breastfeeding rates began to rise again from 1975 in the UK and across Europe. However,

Figure 11.2 A woman breast feeding. If a woman sees her family and friends breastfeeding she is more likely to breastfeed herself

given the powerful influences upon women, it is unsurprising that certain values, beliefs and practices have become entrenched in communities. We refer to this as **enculturation**. Therefore, if a woman sees her family and friends breastfeeding and has been breastfed herself, she is more likely to breastfeed. On the other hand, in many socially deprived communities in the UK, breastfeeding is often experienced as a marginal activity, rarely seen and barely spoken about (Hoddinott and Pill 1999; Henderson et al. 2000; Mahon-Daly and Andrews 2002). Thus, the socioeconomic circumstances within which a woman has been brought up play a major role in infant feeding decisions. A culture of bottle-feeding is very much entrenched in certain communities in the UK, with babies of parents from low-income backgrounds least likely to be breastfed. As babies who are fed on formula milk are at higher risk than breastfed babies for a wide range of illnesses, this socioeconomic variation constitutes an aspect of the cycle of nutritional deprivation (Dykes and Hall Moran 2006; Williams 2009).

> **enculturation**
> the process by which someone acquires cultural norms

This social inequity is reflected in the UK statistics collected every five years. National and regional breastfeeding statistics illustrate considerable differences relating to social group, age, educational status of the mother and the geographical area in which she resides. Preliminary results from the most recent infant feeding survey in the UK shows that 90 per cent of mothers in managerial and professional occupations commenced breastfeeding, compared with 74 per cent of mothers in routine or manual occupations (NHS Information Centre 2011).

Similar differentials are seen in other Western industrialized countries such as Australia, the USA and Canada. Grouleau and Rodriguez (2009) argue that one of the key reasons why women from lower socio-economic backgrounds are likely to discontinue breastfeeding relates to their perceived status in society. They interviewed disadvantaged French-Canadian mothers to explore their experiences of breastfeeding, and they viewed the data using a concept called symbolic capital as defined by the sociologist Bourdieu (1985); symbolic capital being a form of power that comes from one's social position in society, which affords prestige, honour and recognition. Groleau and Rodriguez (2009) reported that for mothers living in poverty, the health and rearing of their children constituted key sources of symbolic capital and therefore they quickly reverted to the cultural norm of bottle-feeding once they experienced difficulties.

Social networks have a major influence upon our values, beliefs and behaviours. This includes family, friends, neighbours and those we work with or enjoy leisure activities with. Many of the health promotion messages seem to assume that decisions are made by individuals, but in reality our choices and decisions are very much influenced by our family and friends. This is powerfully illustrated by Hoddinott et al. (2012), who explored the infant feeding experiences of women and their significant others from pregnancy until six months after birth. Family well-being was the overriding concern, held as more important than the benefits of adhering to the WHO recommendations for breastfeeding. Thus, if family well-being was considered to be in jeopardy, women would stop breastfeeding or introduce solid foods. The times at which this may occur are described as 'pivotal points'.

Global Strategies to Optimize Infant Feeding Practices

In response to concerns regarding the influences of institutionalization and commercialization of infant feeding, a number of global strategies were developed by the World Health Organization (WHO) and United Nations Children's Fund (UNICEF). See Box 11.1.

📋 Activity 11.3: Enculturation and infant feeding

1. List the ways in which your own enculturation may have influenced your values and practices related to infant feeding.
2. Think about someone you know who had a very different enculturation,

perhaps being brought up in a very different culture. How did his/her enculturation make a difference with regard to infant feeding practices?

3.   Consider the area in which you are practising. Use local authority and health services sources to find the rates of breastfeeding in different postcode areas.

Box 11.1 Global strategies to optimize infant feeding practices

International Code of Marketing of Breast Milk Substitutes (WHO 1981).
Protecting, Promoting and Supporting Breastfeeding (WHO/UNICEF 1989).
Innocenti Declaration on the Protection, Promotion and Support of Breastfeeding (WHO 1990).
Baby Friendly Hospital Initiative (WHO/UNICEF 1992).
Global Strategy for Infant and Young Child Feeding (WHO 2003).

The first key publication was the International Code of Marketing of Breast Milk Substitutes (WHO 1981). This resulted from growing international public concern during the 1970s in relation to the aggressive and unscrupulous marketing techniques used by multinational infant formula companies and their deleterious effects (Jelliffe 1972; Muller 1974). The WHO Code, as it is commonly abbreviated, was established to protect and encourage breastfeeding, and to control inappropriate marketing of artificial feeding products. It was endorsed by governments across the world; they were then expected to issue a voluntary code or to legislate to implement the code in its entirety. However, success in implementation was and still is dependent on interpretation, government priorities and commitment, public awareness and the strength of powerful vested interests (Dykes 2002; Dykes et al. 2012).

In 1989, WHO and UNICEF published a joint statement, *Protecting, Promoting and Supporting Breastfeeding* (WHO/UNICEF 1989). This statement included ten best-practice standards for maternity units, named the Ten Steps to Successful Breast Feeding, hereafter abbreviated to 'Ten Steps'. The 'Ten Steps' were constructed by the WHO/UNICEF to reflect what the two organizations saw as key actions to promote breastfeeding in maternity hospitals (WHO 1998). In 1990, WHO/UNICEF issued the *Innocenti Declaration on the Protection, Promotion and Support of Breastfeeding* (WHO 1990). This internationally endorsed declaration contained a comprehensive set of social policy targets to be reached by governments to assist a change of culture and facilitate increased breastfeeding initiation and duration rates. The declaration also contained a commitment to ensure that all maternity facilities meet the 'Ten Steps'.

In 1991, WHO/UNICEF launched its global Baby Friendly Hospital Initiative (BFHI) (WHO/UNICEF 1992). The purpose of this initiative was to support the development of an infrastructure with maternity care facilities which enabled them to implement the 'Ten Steps' (WHO/UNICEF 1989). WHO and UNICEF then set up national teams in participating countries to coordinate and monitor implementation in hospitals. BFHI accreditation is issued to those deemed to have reached a minimum externally auditable standard in relation to the 'Ten Steps'. The BFHI was developed by WHO and UNICEF to reverse the medicalization of infant feeding that occurred during the twentieth century, symbolized by rigid determination of the frequency and duration of feeds, separation of mothers and babies, and unnecessary supplementation of breastfeeding with infant formula. It aimed to restore the relational aspects of feeding between mother and baby, staff members and parents, and to provide additional support for women once they left hospital. Key aspects include: provision of professional health education; providing appropriate antenatal information; encouraging skin-to-skin contact between mother and baby; providing professional health support with lactation to include those mothers separated from their babies; avoidance of unnecessary breast milk substitutes; keeping mothers and babies together; encouraging flexible, baby-led breastfeeding; and offering mothers peer support once discharged from hospital. The actual process of implementation of such a comprehensive set of changes presents a range of challenges (Moore et al. 2007; Taylor et al. 2011; Schmied et al. 2011c; Semenic et al. 2012; Thomson et al. 2012). However, the investment in time and energy is very worthwhile as implementation of the BFHI is associated with significant increases in breastfeeding rates (Beake et al. 2011).

In 2003, the Global Strategy for Infant and Young Child Feeding was launched (WHO 2003). This was developed through a highly participatory global consultation process lasting two years. It is grounded on epidemiological and scientific evidence, while recognizing the complex political and sociocultural influences upon infant feeding practices. The Global Strategy recommends that infants should be exclusively breastfed for the first six months of life and, thereafter, infants should receive nutritionally adequate and safe complementary foods while breastfeeding continues for up to two years of age or beyond. It was envisaged that the Strategy would act as a catalyst for revitalizing international attention towards the impact of feeding practices on the well-being of infants and young children. To achieve optimal infant and young child feeding practices, the strategy calls for a renewed commitment to the *WHO International Code of Marketing of Breast-milk Substitutes* (WHO 1981), the *Innocenti Declaration on Protection, Promotion and Support of Breastfeeding* (WHO 1990) and the BFHI. The Global Strategy calls upon governments to develop, implement and evaluate a comprehensive national policy on infant and young child feeding, and thereby to enable full operationalization of its aims. This requires social, political and economic changes, and concomitant public investment to be made to remove the constraints upon women in achieving and maintaining optimum infant and young child feeding practices. The Global Strategy recognizes the social, political and economic constraints upon women and families in securing the optimum nutritional standards, as well as the growing body of research that illuminates the ways in which maternal dietary and infant feeding practices relate substantially to local cultural norms and constraints (WHO 2003; Dykes and Hall Moran 2009).

📋 Activity 11.4: Global strategies

1. Which of the above global strategies is being implemented in your area of practice?
2. What are the challenges to implementation within your local hospital setting?
3. What are the challenges to implementation in the community?

These initiatives are crucial in national policy and practice in the participating countries. However, the extent to which they are implemented across the globe relates to government commitment, prioritization, competing political agendas, the strength of powerful vested interests and a complex array of socioeconomic and cultural influences upon women and families (see Chapters 6 and 10). As midwives, we are in a situation where we are encouraged to implement these global initiatives. One of the challenges of implementing a global strategy arises from assumptions that if women are given evidence-based information this will have a direct effect on their actual practices. However, whilst everyone has the right to be informed about ways of optimizing their health and that of their children, this linear assumption ignores the complexities within people's lives. Each person we encounter in practice will have their own set of complex influences upon their life, attitudes and the ways in which they make decisions. Therefore, we need to take time with each person to listen to their story and tailor our information-giving and support accordingly (see Chapter 5). The following activity provides an opportunity for you to reflect on the different needs of three women.

📋 Activity 11.5: Three stories from the UK

Laura

Laura was brought up in a poor area in the north of England in which the majority of women feed their babies with infant formula. She is expecting her first baby; she has never seen anyone breastfeed and it is little spoken about in her community. She was bottle-fed by her mother and her older sister bottle-fed her baby. All Laura's friends bottle-fed their babies and her partner, Jack, would like to bottle-feed the baby himself sometimes. Laura is in a low-paid job and will have to return soon after the birth, and her partner is now unemployed.

Aisha

Aisha lives in England with her husband. Her mother-in-law, Safira, lives in the same street and is a strict Muslim. Safira breastfed Aisha's husband for two years according to Islamic tradition and is very keen for her grandchild to be breastfed. She offers to give support to Aisha when she breastfeeds the baby and Aisha has observed the other women in her extended family breastfeeding.

Susie

Susie was brought up in a large home by parents in a high socioeconomic occupational group, in an area where the majority of women breastfeed. Her mother breastfed her, and her partner was breastfed and is very keen for Susie to breastfeed due to the health benefits of breastfeeding. Suzie's friends and sister all breastfed, and her colleagues at work where she is a schoolteacher mostly breastfed their children. She plans to take a year's maternity leave to spend quality time with her baby.

1. What may be the key influences upon each of the women with regard to their intentions to breast or formula feed their babies?
2. What may be the key influences upon each of the women if they were to commence breastfeeding on their likelihood to continue?
3. How can the midwife best support each family?

Summary

- A political economy of health perspective is applied in this chapter to illuminate political issues related to infant feeding practices.
- There are complex influences upon women with regard to their infant feeding decisions.
- Supporting women with their infant feeding decisions and with the practical application of their choices is a key role of the midwife.
- In response to concerns regarding the influences of institutionalization and commercialization of infant feeding, a number of global strategies were developed by the World Health Organization (WHO) and United Nations Children's Fund.
- The Global Strategy recognizes the social, political and economic constraints upon women and families in securing the optimum nutritional standards.

Questions for discussion

- How will you support women with their infant feeding decisions and with the practical application of their choices?
- How might sociology help you understand women's experiences of infant feeding?
- Try to identify two or three sociological studies which address the politics of breastfeeding, and reflect on how these could influence your practice as a midwife.

Further reading

Dykes, F. 2006 *Breastfeeding in Hospital: Midwives, Mothers and the Production Line*. Routledge.
This book explores how women – particularly first-time mothers – frequently feel unsupported when they come to feed their baby. This new experience often takes place in the impersonal and medicalized surroundings of a hospital maternity ward, where women are 'seen to' by overworked midwives. This book provides a new, radical and critical perspective on the ways in which women experience breast-feeding in hospitals. It highlights that, in spite of heavy promotion of breastfeeding, there is often a lack of support for women who begin to breastfeed in hospitals, thus challenging the current system of postnatal care within a culture in which neither service-user nor provider feel satisfied. It explores practice issues while contextual-izing them within a broader social, political and economic context.
Dykes, F. and Hall Moran, V. 2009 (eds) *Infant and Young Child Feeding: Challenges to Implementing a Global Strategy*. Wiley-Blackwell.
This book explores in an integrated context the varied factors associ-ated with infant and child nutrition, including global feeding strate-gies, cultural factors, issues influencing breastfeeding, and economic and life-cycle influences.
Palmer, G. 2009 *The Politics of Breastfeeding*. Pinter & Martin.
This book explores the global and personal costs of artificial feeding. It is authoritative about the evidence for breastfeeding, while provok-ing feelings of folly regarding the social and commercial forces that stop breastfeeding as a vital function of early life and parenting from being the norm. The book exposes infant feeding as one of the most important public health issues of our time

12 Commodification around Birth

Mavis Kirkham

Key issues:

- Commodities and commodification.
- The market model in maternity care.
- Issues of scale in maternity care.
- The political implications of the above.

By the end of this chapter you should be able to:

- Understand the process of commodification within and around maternity services.
- Recognize the marketing of new commodities to childbearing women.
- Recognize the marketing of new commodities to maternity services.
- Discuss the implications of commodification for childbearing women and service providers.

Sociology and Ways of Seeing

Sociology is exciting because, as you now know, it gives us insights into things we would otherwise take for granted. Indeed, it can give us insight into the very processes by which we take things for granted (see Chapter 1). I was at a conference recently where Raymond De Vries, a medical sociologist and a strong proponent of the Dutch system of maternity care, made the profound sociological statement that 'society makes you desire the very things it limits you to' (De Vries 2012). With that thought in my mind, I approached the subsequent speakers very differently: the mother who wanted an elective Caesarean because her last birth was such an awful, disempowering experience; the obstetrician who told us how small units must be closed because they are uneconomic; the debate about the end of independent midwifery because of the need for indemnity insurance which is currently not available to independent midwives.

Birth is the entrance to society and is therefore controlled by those who hold power in that society, and birth takes place within the belief system of that society. 'It is not surprising, therefore, that – whatever the details of a given birthing system – its practitioners will see it as the best way, the right way, indeed *the* way to bring a child into the world' (Jordan 1993: 4). As was highlighted in Chapter 1, C. Wright Mills coined the term 'sociological imagination' (Mills 1959: 7) to mean the ability to see different ways of thinking and thereby not be tied to 'the best way, the right way' to see our world. This means that we increase our understanding and empathy, which must help us as midwives. It also means that we can never totally or comfortably accept 'the best way or the right way' as the only way to see our world. I think the best midwives do not completely go with the flow of received opinion and have an element of the outsider about them because they can see from many viewpoints. This also enables them to be aware of, and to analyse, the impact of changes in the context within which we practise. One of these is commodification: treating something or someone solely according to their usefulness or commercial value. As was seen in Chapter 5, Ruth Deery and Pamela Fisher address the commercial value of emotion work. This chapter addresses commodification around UK maternity services. The situation in the USA is very different, with a total market economy in health care. To understand the US situation, which sheds light on what is happening here, see Perkins (2004).

Commodities

On the first page of *Capital*, Karl Marx stated that 'A commodity is, in the first place, an object outside us, a thing that by its properties satisfies human wants of some sort or another' (1995: 13; originally published 1867). Commodities are the building blocks of our economic system: 'political economy', in Marx's terms. All economic systems incorporate political forms that are integral to the functioning of economic relations.

Commodities are sold for profit in a **market** and the profits accrued as capital are reinvested to produce more commodities in an ever-expanding market. The pressure for capital to continually expand, in order to generate profit, means that there is always a need for new markets: horizontal expansion as in globalization, and vertical expansion as in increased penetration into areas of life previously uncommodified. The spread of formula feeding for babies has created a market for formula and equipment where women previously breastfed their babies; intensive marketing has convinced mothers around the world that bottle-feeding is modern and therefore good for babies, even where communities are poor and water contaminated (see Chapter 11). To ensure economic growth and financial returns, new needs must continually be created to ensure a market for new commodities. This changes somewhat the usual meaning of the word 'needs'. Babies have a biological need to be fed, whereas parents, seeking the best and most convenient way to meet this biological need, may see their baby as needing a bottle of formula.

Commodities were originally defined as useful things produced by human labour, such as the coats and linen examples used by Marx. In modern Western societies, which are sometimes described as 'post-industrial', the industrial model has colonized new areas of

> **market**
> exchange mechanism where buyer and seller negotiate

experience. Birth has moved into increasingly large hospitals run on an **industrial model**, where women frequently state that they feel they are on a conveyor belt (Dykes 2005; Walsh 2007; see also Chapters 2 and 4). This industrial model, together with standardization of services and the introduction of an internal market into health care, has vastly extended what we see as commodities. For instance, when most midwives worked in the community and gave continuity of care to nearly all women, the need for communication through client records was limited and notes were succinct. Now that many professionals provide care to each mother, there is a need for records to be detailed, thorough and easy to access and understand. Records are also important in accounting terms as different hospital activities bring different fees. They are also seen as important in protecting the institution from potential litigation by clients. Electronic record systems and standardized models of clinical record-keeping are the commodities designed to meet these needs.

industrial model
commercial production process

📋 Activity 12.1: Midwives and commodities

1. List the commodities you use as a midwife in the course of a working day.
2. Then identify the needs which each of these commodities meets.

Commodities Associated with Birth

Occasionally, a medieval carpenter may have been paid to make a birthing stool or had given one to a midwife in gratitude or payment for her services, but such items are very durable so they would rarely have been made or sold. The widely marketed and often disposable commodities now associated with childbirth have only developed relatively recently. The proliferation of medical procedures and the large numbers of births in hospitals have created a considerable market for equipment – and this market is made even larger where equipment is disposable.

We live in a society where technology confers status and measurement is easily equated with safety (Murphy-Lawless 1998; Wagner 1994). These values create needs which open up markets for technical commodities. Electronic fetal heart monitors seem to meet an obstetric need. Though research has not shown that continuous electronic monitoring makes birth safer (Alfirevic et al. 2006), the assumption that better monitors will be safer has fuelled the development of these devices, and midwives and obstetricians have been markedly reluctant not to use them. We are therefore easily influenced by **technological imperatives** if the existence and/or development of a medical device provides a mandate for its continued use. Fuchs (1968: 8) first identified such technological consumption: 'The problem, as I see it, is that the physician's approach to medical care and health is dominated by what may be called a "technological imperative".' This worldview sees technology as the only legitimate and recognized form of knowledge (in this situation).

technological imperatives
concerted moves to adopt new technology and discard the old

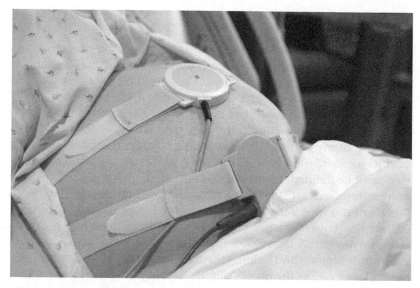

Figure 12.1 The proliferation of medical procedures and the large numbers of births in hospitals have created a considerable market for equipment

📋 Activity 12.2: The needs of a newborn baby from differing viewpoints

List the needs of a newborn baby from the viewpoint of:

(a) that baby
(b) the baby's mother
(c) a manufacturer of nursery equipment.

Manufacturers selling products around pregnancy and birth see a range of markets. In the USA, parents rejecting health care and seeking to **freebirth** can buy equipment for monitoring in pregnancy and for the birth, which is marketed to their particular needs. Breastfeeding is interesting in this respect. Until a generation ago, breastfeeding needs were met when the mother and baby were together. Now a vast range of breastfeeding accessories is marketed to fit the needs of modern lifestyles, including sophisticated electronic breast pumps with associated equipment, which fit into the sort of briefcase carried by professional women.

> **freebirth**
> birth with
> no medical
> professional in
> attendance

Advertising has created needs for many items for the new baby. As midwives, we are aware of the many commodities mothers, often those with least money, feel they must buy for their baby. They are marketed to meet a range of needs: for pretty decor, for convenience, for social status as demonstrated in products purchased, or for safety.

Occasionally, the focus on these needs exploited to sell products can prove a distraction from the few but vital needs of a new baby.

The Commodification of Services

In the distant past, midwives were paid directly for their services (Marland 1993). It was much later that midwives' services were hired out through an intermediary who made a profit on their services. The existence of the NHS, paid for out of taxation, made that a rare occurrence in this country until the introduction of a market model into the NHS in the early 1990s. In the USA, the market model has ruled in health for many years (Perkins 2004). This model reinforces the aims of efficiency and minimizing costs. To achieve this, all parts of the service must be defined, measured and costed; then every effort made to reduce these costs. Establishing what midwives are required to do, in this context, reflects the values concerned. Protocols and procedures are written, covering what midwives must do: actions which can be seen and measured. Less visible midwifery skills – those of relationship, supporting women and helping them to develop trust, confidence and networks, as well as the quiet skills of watching and waiting – are likely to be overlooked in such measurement and are usually not costed (see Kirkham 2010a; Hunter and Deery 2009). Thus, we have a situation where the commodification of the service measures what midwives do, but not what they enable mothers to achieve.

The pressures towards standardization and economy move attention away from the particularity and complexity of individual experiences. The resulting changes may highlight new needs and new market opportunities, such as doulas to give the continuity of support which midwives are no longer able to give. Doulas provide non-clinical support and care to a woman (and her partner) during childbirth and the postpartum period, but this can mean that services become further fragmented, in this example with the separation of support from clinical care.

There were always services associated with birth in addition to midwifery and later medicine. Some wealthy families employed astronomers to cast the newborn's horoscope. The obstetrician James Young Simpson kept a register of wet nurses in the 1840s for his wealthy clients who did not wish to breastfeed, but it is not known whether he charged for arranging this service (Mander 2000, 2003). Much later, services associated with birth proliferated. Now we have antenatal educators, doulas, breastfeeding counsellors, various alternative therapists and experts on early parenting, whose services parents may purchase or whose books or other products they may buy. Some of these commodities have developed as a result of changes and cutbacks in maternity services such as NHS antenatal education; some arise from the seizing of market opportunities; and some result from both these processes.

Ultrasound is fascinating in this context (for a discussion of ultrasound and disability, see also Chapters 6 and 9). Starting as a diagnostic tool, it has now developed a real social presence. The

Figure 12.2 A notice board showing the many different services now available to women before, during and after pregnancy

family album starts with a scan picture, or more likely a video, and frequent, non-medical scans are sold as meeting a need to know the baby and see its growth. 'Fetus parties' where women 'show off 3D and 4D scans' of their fetuses 'are now being used for entertainment' (*Midwives* 2012: 8). The need which this developing technology meets is in many ways one which could only develop when the technology was available. This need to know the fetus via an image on a screen is clearly a product of a society where so much knowledge is available in this way. The selling of commodities which meet this need has great potential for income generation. Embodied knowledge, the significance of quickening for dating a pregnancy and a mother's physical knowledge of her fetus, do not fit with a technological age, as well as being challenging to commodify or market, and have therefore fallen out of favour.

📋 Activity 12.3: Needs and relationships in labour

1. What are the primary needs of a labouring woman?
2. To what extent can these needs be met by products or by relationships?

Management models and training packages are now commodified. This is convenient in that they can be bought as packages and therefore enable maternity units to meet external requirements, but it also means that they are often not tailored to fit local situations.

Objects and Relationships

In Marx's original definition, a commodity is 'an object outside us, a thing' (Marx 1995: 13), produced in order to be sold for profit. Within a market-driven health service, some things which come to the health service as gifts, such as donated blood or breast milk, go on to be sold to other parts of the NHS.

With the commodification of services, relationships as well as objects are involved. In a system where a cash value has to be placed upon all that is exchanged, it is easy for what cannot be measured – relationship work and emotion work – not to be accounted for (Kirkham 2010a; Hunter and Deery 2009; see also Chapter 5). Once a management system, or a teaching package or the services of clinical midwives have been bought, it is easy to see them as things and treat them as interchangeable, and the people involved as unfeeling. Indeed, the growth of market economics and industrial models of working within the health service promotes such treatment of much that is not bought. Thus, guidelines and local practices are often accepted as things which cannot be changed. The conveyor-belt organization of large maternity units (Dykes 2006; Wagner 1994; Garcia et al. 1990) also encourages the strange assumption that it is the hospital system which produces the product of the baby, and the mother is simply a tool which has to be managed to enhance its efficient delivery. We know that birth is fundamentally about relationships, and midwifery care works best where the relationships between mothers and midwives can develop over time into mutual trust (Kirkham 2010a). Yet the industrial model of care and the tendency to see aspects of the service as objects can lead to a denial of relationship. This is perhaps most clearly demonstrated with regard to breastfeeding where the benefits of breastmillk, as a substance, are analysed and promoted (Dykes 2006; see also Chapter 11) as if separate from the complex and skilled relationship which is breastfeeding. Midwives gain job satisfaction from their relationships with mothers and with colleagues (Kirkham et al. 2006). Where relationships with mothers are highly fragmented, the service becomes commodified and economic efficiency is seen as all-important. It then becomes easy for overstretched midwives to become alienated and withdraw from relationships (Deery and Kirkham 2006). They behave like production-line workers and 'obedient technicians' (Deery and Hunter 2010). In these circumstances, midwives find it easiest to 'go with the flow' of local practice (Kirkham and Stapleton 2001), and can easily become bystanders (Clarkson 1996; Jowitt 2008), engage in 'wilful blindness' (Heffernan 2012) or bully colleagues they see as deviant (Kirkham 2007). This is very far from the committed relationship of a midwife and mother which is so successful for all concerned (McCourt and Stephens 2009; McLachlan et al. 2012).

Scale and Commodities ▮▮▮▮▮▮▮▮

The impact of a commodity depends upon the scale of its use. There are handy pieces of equipment, marketed by the midwife who originally thought of them. The stainless-steel birth mirror, created by an independent midwife, Virginia Howes, and marketed by a voluntary organization, is an example of such a commodity which helps midwives and mothers, costs little and is marketed on a small scale (see <http://www.nctshop.co.uk/>).

The use of some commodities spread as a result of marketing. The practice of pre-birth perineal shaving spread to many countries, following Gillette's successful application for patents in those countries and employment of midwives and doctors to promote this practice (Romney 1982, personal communication). Perineal shaving fell into disrepute as a result of research (Romney 1980) which was eagerly seized upon by service managers seeking to save on the cost of supplies. (Ironically, marketing to women has now made this practice common for cosmetic reasons.) The marketing of products to obstetricians and midwives has become much more sophisticated over time. As was seen earlier in this chapter, the presentation of electronic fetal heart monitoring (EFM), as meeting professionals' need for evidence which would make them feel safe in the face of litigation, has ensured a durable market even in the face of research doubting the usefulness of EFM (Alfirevic et al. 2006).

In a large centralized maternity service, many commodities are marketed as meeting the needs of the service rather than the individual mother. Sometimes the use of such commodities can limit the options of an individual mother, such as when she cannot mobilize in labour because she is attached to a monitor.

🗐 Activity 12.4: Is 'going with the flow' the answer for midwifery?

Think about some of the midwives and obstetricians you have observed to date during your midwifery training.

What observations have you made about those who 'go with the flow' and those who are not tied to 'the best way, the right way' to see our midwifery world?

How does their way of practising affect the way in which women experience maternity services?

Scale, Rights and Commodities: The Example of Insurance ▮▮▮▮▮▮▮▮

Insurance is an example of a commodity, purchased by institutions or individual professionals, which must have originally been seen as providing security in the face of possible litigation but which came, over time, to dominate maternity care. The cost of insurance is a major issue for all providers of maternity care. The Clinical Negligence Scheme for Trusts (CNST) in England, which provides insurance for NHS Trusts, has different levels of payment by these Trusts, and the level of payment is decided by how far the Trust complies with CNST guidelines (NHS Litigation Authority 2008). CNST guidelines and their interpretation have therefore become major determining factors in how health care is provided in England. This acts as a barrier against very poor care, but it can also act as a barrier against innovation and tailoring of services to meet individual needs. Ironically, despite CNST guidelines, there have been hospitals at the centre of patient-care scandals which have cost the NHS almost £300 million in damages over the past five years (Swinford 2014). Thus, such guidelines do not determine the level of health care provided.

European Economic Committee (EEC) legislation now requires all health-care professionals to carry insurance. Thus, the provision of a commodity, insurance, has become essential. Yet no insurance provider will cover the relatively small market provided by UK independent midwives. When such cover was last available, it cost more than the income of many independent midwives. At the time of writing (September 2012), it appears that the requirement to carry insurance will mean the end of UK independent midwifery in 2013. Mander and Murphy-Lawless (2013: 146–8) provide a discussion of professional indemnity insurance and independent midwifery. They highlight the Nursing & Midwifery Council's (NMC) dictatorial approach that independent midwives form a limited company and then be contracted by the NHS. However, the professional indemnity insurance issue has now been taken over by the European Union which requires member states to ensure that systems are in place for insurance (EU 2011: 4.2(d)) and, most importantly, that this is seen as a benefit to the mother 'rather than a commercial enterprise which advantages the insurance industry and constrains the organization and provision of care' (Mander and Murphy-Lawless, 2013: 148).

So the marketing of a commodity has come to determine what maternity care is available to mothers. In the several years in which UK independent midwives have not carried insurance, many mothers have knowingly chosen care from these uninsured practitioners. Women choosing such care often do so because they see themselves as damaged by previous experience of NHS care and/or because they seek home births in circumstances in which they are unable to book for home births within the NHS (Kirkham 2009). Once UK independent midwives are required to carry insurance, such women will not have the choice of care outside the NHS, which will by default become a monopoly provider of maternity services in this country. This cannot be right, for those mothers or for the NHS.

The European Court of Human Rights judgement in the case of *Ternovszky* v. *Hungary* (2010) established a woman's right to choice of place of birth. Yet the requirement for practitioners to carry insurance prevents the practice of just those midwives who have the widest experience of home birth and who can make a wider choice of place of birth available to mothers. There is something profoundly contradictory in this situation. How has a commodity, insurance, come to be seen as so essential that it prevents women from exercising their rights?

Clearly, something which was originally seen as useful has come to be seen as essential because of the power of those selling the commodity. Also, deficiencies in state provision for children with special needs have led to the parents of such children being seen as having a right to sue for money to finance their care. Yet few cases of infants with special needs are found to be due to the negligence of those who attended the birth, and all such children deserve good care. Midwives from New Zealand, where the law provides for no fault compensation in such cases, have difficulty in understanding the problems we have with insurance in this country. Clearly, the large scale of commodification in maternity care produces major political issues which need to be addressed.

The Impact upon Our Language

In recent years, with the increasing industrialization of services, we have seen the development of new concepts and a new vocabulary: the health industry, the music industry, the leisure industry, the sex industry. As you know, when the market economy increasingly penetrates our language, it frames our way of seeing things and the underpinning values of this model tend to go unchallenged. As Benner states of nursing in the USA: 'Articulating nursing knowledge into the available economic and scientific language creates conflict and incongruities with the knowledge and ethos embedded within the actual caring practices of nurses' (Benner 2000: 296). The history of midwifery and government policy (Department of Health 1993, 2004, 2007b) highlights the importance of the actual caring practices of midwives. There is a profound contradiction between the industrial model, with its drive to tightly define and control production for maximum efficiency, and the need for flexibility and responsiveness when the service is provided through a relationship. Yet the market model dominates our vocabulary, as seen in terms such as 'social capital' and 'emotional investment' (see Chapter 5).

The changing use of language reflects the industrial, conveyor-belt model where maternity care is broken down into its many constituent parts. The resulting fragmentation has led to problems being posed in such a way as to produce fragmented solutions, such as epidural anaesthesia to remove pain. Epidural anaesthesia therefore becomes an intervention leaving fear, rather than continuity of care to help women develop their resources to cope with pain and fear.

Within the market model, mothers are seen as consumers or service users, and midwives as service providers. Yet the structure of the service limits the options which midwives can provide. Choice is greatly emphasized in policy documents (Department of Health 1993, 2004, 2007b), and yet, with a limited menu from which to choose, women embarking upon life's most creative act can find themselves rendered strangely passive.

Midwives are professional consumers. A few years ago, it was proposed that NHS policy be changed to increase the number of doses of Anti-D (Rhogam) given to rhesus negative women. Full-page advertisements by the manufacturers of Anti-D were placed throughout the obstetric and midwifery press. Increasing the number of doses given was proposed as meeting the needs of those rhesus negative women who were not receiving Anti-D. This expensive and scattergun approach, for which there was no research evidence, was promoted as an answer to professional fear that some women were going untreated. That approach became policy at considerable expense, both in purchasing the additional doses of Anti-D and in midwives' time in giving it. It was not proposed that we improve the shortcoming of the previous system.

Expectations have changed over recent years, mainly reflecting what the service has to offer. The influence of technological imperatives can affect midwives' attitudes – fetal monitoring provides a good example here. Also, many women now expect a twenty-four-hour epidural service on request. A few women request Caesarean sections for social reasons. These two requests can be met, though the latter may cause a little disquiet as pre-empting medical decision-making. Requests for continuity of midwifery care or for a service without ultrasound are much more difficult to accommodate within the expectations of service providers. The use of commodities such as ultrasound and a fragmented service has become the norm. The prioritization of relationships and enhancing mothers' confidence is not seen in this way, though I know some services where a small number of women who are seen as potential troublemakers do receive continuity of care.

Time is now seen as a very valuable commodity (Bryson and Deery 2010; McCourt 2010). In the management of hospitals, efficient throughput is all-important and this has a real impact on how services are conducted. Yet this model of time itself carries risks, not least the 'risk of rushing' (Edwards 2005: 121). For mothers too, time management matters, and a Caesarean booked at a convenient date in a crowded diary can help in the management of a busy life. This assumes that time is measured in a linear fashion and can be used economically. The sense of time of a woman in labour or a breastfeeding baby is somewhat different (Dykes 2006; Kirkham 2010a).

The Impact of Commodification upon Our Values

The economic, market model has deeply influenced our values as well as, and often through, its impact upon our language. The tendency to highlight commodities which can be bought and to see maternity services in terms of measurable activities, each with a market value, adds greatly to the cost of the service and discounts those aspects of it which are not costed. The rising cost, without a parallel improvement in clinical outcomes, is worrying in a time of economic recession. The export of such a high-tech, high-cost model to poorer countries must be wrong.

Market economics is often presented as a study of incentives, considered in an ethical vacuum (e.g., Lucas 2011). Yet it is not an amoral activity. Where commodities are sold, there will be some who cannot afford to buy them and other things will be sacrificed in order to make the purchase. Since care and relationships do not count as commodities in maternity care, the pressure of measurable tasks and the service of machines are likely to be prioritized. Michael Sandel concludes:

> The question of markets is really a question about how we want to live together. Do we want a society where everything is up for sale? Or are there certain moral and civic goods that markets do not honour and money cannot buy? (Sandel 2012: 265)

Sandel's use of the word 'goods' shows the extent of the language of commodities. Surely the highest quality of care at the start of life and good relationships with trusted carers should be amongst the 'goods' which society should provide for all citizens.

Commodification as a Political Issue

Commodification in maternity care is a complex and highly political issue. There are useful, delightful and life-saving commodities sold to maternity service providers and to parents. The complexities of commodification are to do with power, and the larger the scale on which commodities are produced and used, the greater the economic and social power exercised around them. The larger the scale on which maternity services operate, the more technology is used and the larger the market for commodities and the greater the potential for profit. As all who use or work in public services know, there are other important issues besides profit and efficiency.

Shakespeare put into the mouth of one of his characters the profound words:

> That smooth-faced gentleman, tickling commodity,
> Commodity, the bias of the world;
> [...]
> Since kings break faith upon commodity,
> Gain, be my lord, for I will worship thee!

(Shakespeare, *King John*, II.i.592–3, 615–16)

Commodities can become 'the bias of the world' if the only factor under consideration is 'gain'. New technology is seductive ('that smooth-faced gentleman'), and the needs it meets are nurtured by advertising, which often plays upon our fears. But all innovations have to be paid for. In a service where a major cost is salaries, such payments mean less midwife time with clients, either because of cutbacks in staffing or because of the time the midwife must spend attending to the new innovation rather than relating to her clients (Bryson and Deery 2010). Such commodities merit careful assessment of the gains and the losses that would follow from their purchase.

Jeremy Seabrook made the rhetorical statement:

> All that is most precious and vital to survival has been transformed into inert goods and mechanistic services, into which life can be breathed only by the profane kiss of money, which long ago ceased to be a simple medium of exchange and became a semi-mystical substance. This is why it is only in the realm of the economy that miracles are now expected. (Seabrook 2012: 54)

Yet we know that economics and commodities play only a part in the achievements of childbearing women and their carers. The emphasis placed upon commodities, such as scans and new ways of organizing services, can mask the social relations within which these services are embedded. So often these relations are overstretched and impoverished.

Commodification deeply penetrates our attitudes and the pressures for efficiency change our actions. When we are pressed for time (that most precious commodity) and there are endless tasks which must be done, it is easy to process women rather than care for them. Every time we touch a woman, we convey our professional values. As professionals we exercise power; our touch is political.

Whenever a woman feels our touch she knows whether we are manoeuvring her into position for the next required procedure, or expressing our concern with a wish to nurture her and her baby. Our listening is also political: whether we take a standard history or listen to the individual's story tells a woman so much about us and the service. We therefore make real political choices every time we meet a client. We can decide to relate to her in ways which cannot be measured but which are immeasurably important for her future. To do this, we need a degree of autonomy which does not fit with the current organization of the service. At a national level political action is therefore needed.

Services do not have to be run on the market model chosen, relatively recently, for the NHS, though the values which underpin it do seem to be all-pervading in the Western world. There are other ways of looking at birth and public services: a Guardian model for public services is proposed by Jane Jacobs (1992), or simply a decision by society to support generous services around birth as an investment (to use market terminology) in the future of its citizens. Some management theorists would argue that the NHS market model is totally out of date, being rooted in an early twentieth-century Taylorist, fragmented model of production long since abandoned in industry as inflexible (e.g., Fairtlough 1994, 2005; Allan et al. 2002). David Boyle suggests that, rather than tightening up systems even more, real effectiveness can only happen when people are given whole jobs to do together with the freedom to innovate (Boyle 2011). This certainly fits with what we know of midwives' relationship with their work and their clients (Kirkham et al. 2006).

Meanwhile, midwives endeavour to use commodities wisely and well whilst continuing to build relationships with mothers. They convey the values of the service in their every contact with clients, and where they act beyond those values they do so at increasing cost to themselves. Clearly, other models of working need urgent consideration.

Summary

- Commodification is treating something or someone solely according to their usefulness or commercial value.
- We live in a society where technology confers status, and measurement is easily equated with safety. These values create needs which open up markets for technical commodities.
- The commodification of maternity services measures what midwives do, but not what they enable mothers to achieve. Less visible midwifery skills, like those of relationship and supporting women, are likely to be overlooked in such measurement.
- The pressures towards standardization and economy move attention away from the particularity and complexity of individual experiences.
- Commodification deeply penetrates our attitudes and the pressures for efficiency change our actions.

Questions for discussion

- How will an increased understanding of commodification affect your midwifery practice? Think of two or three examples that might challenge you, and how you plan to deal with this in the reality of complex practice situations.
- How can sociology help you to understand commodification and its application to relationship in midwifery?
- Identify some sociological studies which are related to commodification, for example, relationships and midwifery, and electronic fetal monitoring, and reflect on their role in commodification of maternity services.

Further reading

Perkins, B. B. 2004 *The Medical Delivery Business.* Rutgers University Press.
In this book, Barbara Bridgman Perkins discusses how twentieth-

century medical care and its reforms were not designed to meet people's health needs. Perkins documents how US medicine developed as a business, and challenges the conventional view that a dose of the market is good for medicine. She uses examples drawn from maternal and infant care, highlighting that business strategies used in a medical environment could lead to inappropriate interventions. Although written in the context of US birth, much of the content is applicable to birth in the UK. Perkins argues that the medical care system itself needs to be 're-formed', and that the reform process should stress democracy, caring and social justice over economic theory.

McCourt, C. 2010 *Childbirth, Midwifery and Concepts of Time.* Berghahn Books.

The chapter contributors in this book explore the centrality of the way time is conceptualized, marked and measured to the ways of perceiving and managing childbirth. The writers discuss how women, midwives and other birth attendants are affected by issues of power and control, but also actively attempt to change established forms of thinking and practice. The stories are critical and will help you to think differently, especially about time as a commodity.

Walby, S. 2009 *Globalization and Inequalities, Complexity and Contested Modernities.* Sage Publications.

In this book, the author analyses the tensions between the different forces shaping global futures. She critically examines the regulation and deregulation of employment and welfare, the transformation of gender regimes, path-dependent trajectories, tipping points and global political waves, which are all applicable to maternity services and midwives.

Mander, R. and Murphy-Lawless, J. 2013 *The Politics of Maternity.* Routledge.

This title critically explores the complex issues surrounding childbirth practices in today's society and in a climate that is increasingly medicalized, amidst greater insecurity at broad social and political levels. There is rigorous and thought-provoking analysis of current clinical, managerial and policymaking environments. This book will help prepare you for the transition from education to the reality of the system to which you may become socialized (or not).

13 Mental Health and Illness

Carol Kingdon

Key issues:

- Definitions of mental health and illness.
- Gender differences in reported symptomology and treatment-seeking behaviours.
- Relationship between social norms, parental roles and mental health.
- Postnatal depression: problems of definition, disclosure and treatment.
- Anxiety, fear and trauma surrounding childbirth.
- (Still)birth: acknowledging birth and parenting loss.
- Breaking the silence and stigma surrounding mental health and illness.

By the end of this chapter you should be able to:

- Discuss positive and negative framings of the terms 'mental health' and 'mental illness' in general and in maternity care in particular.
- Understand how the reporting of mental illness can differ between men and women.
- Recognize sociological arguments relating to reproduction, women's social roles and mental health.
- Identify how sociology can enhance midwives' understanding of post-natal depression, fear of childbirth and stillbirth by locating these issues within their wider social context.
- Begin to challenge negative stereotypes and stigma surrounding mental health and illness in everyday midwifery practice.

Introduction

In common with earlier chapters in this book, this chapter is concerned with the application of sociology to an aspect of midwifery care. The specific focus of the chapter is how sociology is relevant to mental health and illness during pregnancy and the transition to parenting/parenthood. Mental health is a fundamental aspect of the midwife's role. In the UK, the importance of routine assessment of the mental health of women from early pregnancy onwards is emphasized in national guidelines (NICE 2007, 2008) and the last four triennials of the Confidential Enquiry into Maternal and Child Health (CEMACH) (Lewis 2001, 2004, 2007, 2011). Sadly, suicide and mental illness remain a leading cause of maternal death in the UK. At the same time, the morbidity associated with poor mental health during pregnancy and following childbirth is known to have a significant effect on women, family relations and children's subsequent development (Rowan et al. 2010). Whilst mild depression is thought to be no more common than in the general population, research suggests that 10 per cent of new mothers are likely to develop a depressive illness, up to half of whom may suffer severe depression; and puerperal psychosis (the most extreme form of mental illness associated with pregnancy and child-birth) affects two in every thousand new mothers. The most significant predictor of mental illness during pregnancy is a previous episode of severe mental illness (Lewis 2011). What is more, since 2000 there has been increasing evidence that up to 5 per cent of postnatal women in developed countries exhibit symptoms of post-traumatic stress disorder (PTSD) directly related to their birth experience (Andersen et al. 2012). Thus, it should be part of everyday practice for midwives to engage with mental health issues and to provide care for women who may have new or recurring illness.

The purpose of this chapter is to challenge midwives to think critically about what mental health and illness is beyond medical classifications, and to locate mental (ill)health within wider culture and society. It begins by exploring the social meanings attributed to the terms, axes of inequality relevant to mental health (most notably gender), the significance of stigma, and the provision of and access to mental health services. The chapter then focuses on three topical issues for more detailed sociological critique: postnatal depression; fear of childbirth (tokophobia); and stillbirth. Neither 'tokophobia' nor 'postnatal depression' actually appears in current antenatal and postnatal mental health guidance (NICE 2007), but both have become ubiquitous in professional journals and popular media as mental health issues associated with pregnancy, childbirth and the transition to motherhood/ing. In contrast, stillbirth is currently emerging as a global health priority. This chapter ends by briefly considering the silence that has until now surrounded this sensitive but surprisingly common and unquestionably important issue. Although midwives and loss is the focus of Chapter 8, for the purposes of this chapter it is important to identify that when a baby is born dead it has implications for the mental health of everyone close to both the mother and the baby. This includes midwives.

What is Meant by the Terms 'Mental Health' and 'Mental Illness'?

According to the World Health Organization:

> Mental health is not just the absence of mental disorder. It is defined as a state of well-being in which every individual real-

izes his or her own potential, can cope with the normal stresses of life, can work productively and fruitfully, and is able to make a contribution to her or his community.
(World Health Organization 2007)

This definition epitomizes a positive framing of mental health as a component of general well-being related to the absence of biopathological symptoms and the ability of individuals to fulfil their *social roles*. Current UK guidelines for antenatal and postnatal mental health care (NICE 2007) distinguish between three main categories of mental illness:

- Depression (mild depression; moderate and severe depression; treatment resistant depression).
- Anxiety (generalized anxiety disorder and panic disorder; obsessive compulsive disorder; post traumatic stress disorder); and eating disorders (anorexia; binge-eating disorder; bulimia nervosa).
- Severe mental illness (bipolar disorder; schizophrenia).

This definition is categorical. In other words, it differentiates between type of illness (using medical classifications) and severity. There is no reference to the causation, consequences or wider social context that shape individuals' experience of mental illness. As you know, sociological theory and research can assist midwives to understand this broader social context (see also Chapter 3). For example, sociologists have shown how the popular context of health beliefs about mental health and illness may be shaped by inaccurate, negative portrayals in the media (Philo 1996; Philo et al. 2010). The latter research with UK television audiences found that whilst participants were aware of a range of portrayals of mental health issues in television drama (positive and negative), nonetheless they still perceived a link between negative portrayals and widely held public perceptions of individuals with mental illness as violent and dangerous. Whereas an Australian content analysis of media coverage relating to women and depression found that whilst health-care policy and depression literature privileges biomedical and psychological expertise in explaining depression and promoting health-seeking behaviours, women's magazines (in advice columns, celebrity and personal stories) foreground an individualizing discourse of depression (Gattuso et al. 2005). In other words, depression is portrayed less as a biomedical illness and more as a problem of self-management, interwoven with notions of feminine identity and social role expectations. As this chapter unfolds, gendered differences in the prevalence and kinds of mental illness associated more with women than men will become clearer. The relationship between social norms, feminine identity and mental health should also become apparent.

Like physical illness (see Chapter 6), anyone can experience mental illness, at any time in their lives. This includes young children, the very old and students, as illustrated in the mental health campaign poster in

Box 13.1 Mental health campaign poster

Anyone can get ill. A mental health awareness campaign poster that seeks to challenge the stereotypes and stigma surrounding mental illness.

Box 13.1. Negative perceptions of mental illness per se, and the stigma individuals may feel or suffer in relation to others, add a further layer of complexity to this experience. Before reading further, complete Activity 13.1.

📋 Activity 13.1: Lay beliefs about mental health and illness

1. What social *stereotypes* do you think of in relation to the terms 'mental', 'mental health' and 'mental illness'?
2. To what extent do you think negative perceptions of mental illness are embedded in culture and language formation?
3. How may you perpetuate or challenge these stereotypes in your practice?

The term 'stigma' is widely used in society. The ubiquity of its association with mental illness is illustrated in the UK Mental Health Charity MIND's regular bulletin entitled *The Daily Stigma* (<http://www.mind.org.uk/>). As a sociological concept, stigma originates from a classic study by Erving Goffman (1963), *Stigma: Notes on the Management of Spoiled Identity*. The enduring relevance of Goffman's writings was emphasized earlier, in Chapter 6. For the purposes of this chapter, it is important to restate that Goffman defines stigma as an attribute that is viewed as deviant and thus marks a person as different, and/or not as 'normal'. To use Goffman's words, stigma refers to the social and psychological processes whereby an individual is 'reduced in our minds from a whole and usual person to a tainted, discounted one' (Goffman 1963: 12). Goffman distinguishes between three types of stigma:

- Stigmas of the body (i.e., physical attributes considered to be deformities or disabling).
- Stigmas of character (i.e., criminal record or mental illness).
- Stigmas associated with social groups (i.e., according to 'race' or ethnicity).

As identified in Chapter 6, some of these attributes can be hidden from others, whilst others cannot. This leads Goffman to make an important distinction between *discrediting* (easily visible) attributes and *discreditable* (less visible) attributes. The former are immediately stigmatizing, whereas the degree to which the latter are stigmatizing depends on both the nature of the attribute and the extent to which knowledge of it is disclosed. Mental illness falls into this category. Individuals with a mental illness suffer both from the symptoms of their illness, and the challenges posed by public misconceptions and prejudice. The stigma experienced is twofold; first, the stigma of public reaction, and, second, the stigma individuals turn in on themselves (Corrigan and Watson 2002).

In the context of this chapter, 'stigma' is a particularly useful sociological concept for helping midwives to understand why women may try and conceal mental health problems, or, following a diagnosis, may decline active treatment. Goffman's insights on the presentation of a discreditable social *self* are particularly relevant because they highlight the disjuncture between an individual's virtual social identity and their actual social identity – in other words, the socially constructed normative role expectations of an individual (i.e., all mothers are innately child-centred and happy) that must be presented to prevent the self being discredited, as opposed to the attributes an individual actually possesses (i.e., many mothers are exhausted and unhappy), which are stigmatizing. To present oneself according to these normative role expectations during early motherhood may cause additional stress and exacerbate illness. What is more, the stigma surrounding different kinds of mental illness (i.e., anxiety and depression, severe illnesses such as schizophrenia) are commonly associated with stereotypes or perceptions that are only partially correct, rather than detailed understanding. In the context of maternity care, stigma may be both experienced by women and play a role in how health-care professionals, including midwives, perceive women and families (see also Chapter 10).

The sociology of mental health and illness is a well-established subfield in sociology. Arguably, mental health and illness as a topic is particularly suited to sociological critique because the organic basis of mental illness, and its links to behaviour, have been much harder to establish than other forms of illness and disease. Indeed, in wider society, mental illness is called into question in ways physical illness is not. Early works influential in sociology originated from the anti-psychiatry movement (i.e., Laing and Esterson 1964; Szasz 1961, 1970; Chesler 1972, 2005) and sociologists concerned with the social effects of the labelling of an individual as mentally ill (i.e., Goffman 1961; Scheff 1966). One common thread in these works involved accusations of **medicalization** as a means of social control, particularly as at the time involuntary incarceration in asylums was standard practice. The enduring relevance of these works, particularly to the UK, is debatable, as NHS care has evolved significantly since the 1960s and 1970s. What is more, a common criticism of some of these works is that they fail to acknowledge that mental illness does have a material reality outside of medical classifications (it does exist), and for some the label 'mental illness' can be a positive experience facilitating access to much-needed care and treatment. Arguably, sociological studies most relevant to this chapter include those with enduring universal relevance (i.e., Goffman 1963; Foucault 1971), contemporary work on the growth of the emotion industry (i.e., Hochschild 1983; Horwitz and Wakefield 2007; see Chapter 5), and feminist literature on the relationship between gender and mental (ill)health. Please refer to the recommendations for further reading at the end of this chapter for further detail. The purpose of the next section of this chapter is to highlight inequalities in the social distribution of mental illness.

> **medicalization**
> process of human problems being defined and treated as medical conditions

The Social Patterning of Mental Health and Illness

Globally, there is currently little difference in the overall prevalence of rates of mental illness between men and women (Kessler et al. 2005; McManus et al. 2009; WHO 2009). The British sociologist Joan Busfield (2010: 179) helpfully summarizes three main conclusions that may be drawn from these data:

1 There remains considerable gender variation in psychiatric symptomology. Women typically have higher levels of emotional problems and men typically have higher levels of behaviour and substance-use disorders.
2 The extent of overall gender disparity depends on how mental illness is defined and operationalized.

3 Women are more likely than men to be receiving treatment, and this includes **psychoactive medication**.

According to Busfield (2010), these observed gender differences can be explained by, first, consideration of the extent to which the data are an artefact of the measures used – in other words, how the boundaries were set as to what counts as mental illness. Second, greater emotionality is one aspect of cultural assumptions about femininity causing men and women to differ in their willingness to discuss emotional difficulties. Third, the life experiences, levels and types of stress faced by men and women are different in character, as are the ways they deal with them. For example, women are more likely to experience, but not necessarily disclose, sexual abuse, whilst men are more likely to externalize trauma and exhibit aggressive behaviour. However, this is not to say that all women with mental (ill)health self-identify, are identified during routine contact with health professionals, or are treated. This may be particularly true during pregnancy, childbirth and early motherhood.

In the UK, two national surveys of perinatal mental health reported deficiencies in referral pathways, insufficient staff training and a lack of specialist services (Tully et al. 2002; Oluwato and Friedman 2005). Subsequently, following the publication of policy (Department of Health 2004) and national guidance (Lewis 2004; NICE 2007; NICE 2008), many NHS Trusts providing maternity services began to introduce clinical guidelines, and a few had access to specialist perinatal psychiatrists (Rowan and Bick 2008). Nonetheless, a follow-up interview study suggests concerns remain about the ongoing identification of mental health needs and appropriate follow-up amongst pregnant and newly delivered women (Rowan et al. 2010). At the meso level, little is known about the extent of the use of mental health screening questions by midwives after the initial antenatal interview, and lines of responsibility for identification and/or referral between primary and secondary care services remain unclear. On the one hand, perinatal mental health services are arguably now a priority; on the other hand, their longstanding peripheral status and relatively underdeveloped structure(s) leave them particularly vulnerable to efficiency savings in a resource-scarce NHS. The challenges facing perinatal mental health service provision are multifaceted and extend beyond the clinic. Many women referred to mental health services do not access treatment in the form of psychological therapies or social support; pharmacological treatment options for women who are pregnant or breastfeeding are limited and compliance low, for fear of harming their baby. Much service provision rests on the assumption that women are willing to disclose mental health concerns and/or illness. This is not necessarily the case. Women may be unaware of the seriousness of the problem themselves or they may actively conceal a problem to avoid the repercussions of disclosure. Referral to safeguarding teams is known to result in avoidance of care

psychoactive medication chemical substance acting on central nervous system to affect brain function

and necessary treatment, increasing the risk of deterioration in the mother's mental health and suicide (Lewis 2011: 138).

Current recommendations for maternity care specifically highlight that over half of maternal suicides were white, married, employed, living in comfortable circumstances and aged 30 years or older (psychosis 11; severe depressive illness 6; adjustment/grief reaction 3). Clearly the risk of suicide cannot be equated with socioeconomic deprivation (Lewis 2011). At the same time, the link between mental illness and social class is well established in sociological research. It was first identified in a classic study in the USA by August Hollingshead and Frederick Redich (Hollingshead and Redich 1956). It highlighted the relationship between type and severity of illness, and nature and quality of treatment. In essence, the lower an individual's social class, the more severe their illness and the less adequate their treatment (if received at all). In the UK, the association between social class, poverty and mental illness amongst women is also long-established; of particular note are the serial studies by Brown and Harris (1978, 1989). These studies are part of a large body of sociological work documenting how the material circumstances of women's lives and social role obligations, most notably the domestic division of labour combined with mothering, may contribute to unhappiness. Before we explore the relationship between mental health and motherhood in more detail, it is also important to highlight general differences in reporting and treatment of mental illness according to ethnic group.

It is widely reported that men and women from black Caribbean communities are over-represented in UK treatment statistics for psychosis and schizophrenia, but are under-represented in primary care consultations for depression (Edge and Rogers 2005). At the same time, women from South Asian communities also have a low prevalence rate of treated depression (Burr and Chapman 2004). Box 13.2 offers further detail from these two studies. Midwives need to be culturally sensitive to how women from different ethnic groups may deal with mental illness, and be aware that screening tools (i.e., Edinburgh postnatal depression scale, Cox et al. 1987) are not validated in many non-white populations.

Mental (Ill)Health and Motherhood

> The birth of a child, especially a first child, represents a landmark event in the lives of all involved. For the mother particularly, childbirth has a profound physical, mental, emotional and social effect. No other event involves pain, emotional stress, vulnerability, possible physical injury or death, and permanent role change, and includes responsibility for a dependent helpless human being.
> (Simkin 1992: 64)

As highlighted in Chapter 1, whilst pregnancy, childbirth and early motherhood can be experienced as natural, joyous, and even

Box 13.2 Cultural context and women's experiences of depression

Surveys suggest a disparity between high rates of depression amongst women from South Asian communities and treatment rates in primary care. It has been suggested that the *low prevalence of treated depression* in this community is attributable to women somatizing their feelings of psychological or emotional distress. In other words, they present with physical symptoms. A qualitative study by Burr and Chapman (2004) shows how the South Asian women who participated in their focus groups made strategic choices in how they presented their symptoms as legitimate, which, in turn, gained them access to what they perceived to be appropriate health care. Women suggested physical symptoms were more appropriate than emotional distress to justify a visit to their GP, but this is not to suggest these women were not experiencing mental health issues, as evident in the dialogue below:

> *Participant 1:* Yeah, you go for headaches.
> *Participant 2:* You go for medical advice but not psychological.
> *Participant 1:* It has to be physical even if it is like little pains.
> *Participant 3:* Sometimes it's like you go to the doctor's and it's for everything. It's like *you've got a headache*.
> *Participant 4:* You let it build up before you go to the doctor's.
> *Participant 3:* Yeah, you've got flu and everything, you know?
> *Participant 1:* The doctor doesn't understand how you have got everything at the same time. [*laughter from group*]
> (Burr and Chapman 2004: 443)

A different kind of disparity is evident amongst women from black Caribbean communities in the UK. Edge and Rogers' (2005) mixed-method epidemiological and qualitative interview study found that black Caribbean women were *significantly more likely to report risks* for perinatal depression (i.e., socioeconomic vulnerability, deprivation, less social support, lone parenting) compared to white British women, *but significantly less likely to report symptoms*. Qualitative interview data suggests that the low rates of diagnosed depression may be rooted in black Caribbean women's identity formation as 'strong-black-women', which serves as a powerful cultural signifier of black Caribbean matriarchal culture and their link to generations of black women who have overcome adversity, slavery and racism (p. 22). These women's sense of spirituality was also considered an enabling resource.

> *Participant 12:* I think there's a big cultural difference between black and white women. I just think there's something spiritual about being able to handle the pressure and having no choice . . . there's a backbone, a spirit that somehow has been passed on from generation to generation [of black women] about being able to cope, being able to juggle.
> (Edge and Rogers 2005: 19)

empowering, they can also be experienced as medicalized, traumatizing and disempowering. Caring for a newborn baby is exhausting. This is true irrespective of maternal age, geographical location or socioeconomic circumstance (affluent or deprived; primary or contributory breadwinner). During the 1960s and 1970s, feminist authors highlighted and advanced understanding of the linkages between gender and mental health. As well as identifying changing constructions and measures of mental disorders, for the first time they identified a disjuncture between women's expectations of motherhood and their actual experiences. The American writer Betty Friedan's (1963) book, *The Feminine Mystique* was amongst the first texts concerned with the unhappiness some women experience when confined to the domestic sphere following childbirth. She drew attention to how the reproductive capabilities of the female sex to gestate and birth children are conflated with a division of labour in **patriarchal** societies, where women are primarily responsible for unwaged domestic labour and childcare. This influential book encouraged women to seek mental fulfilment in work outside the home at a time when second-wave feminism was just emerging. In the UK a study by Hannah Gavron (1968), *The Captive Wife*, is equally of note. Slightly later work by Ann Oakley (1979, 1980) extended understanding of depression following childbirth as a human response to a life event of unparalleled significance in terms of social role change.

patriarchal
system with men as primary authority figures

In 2011, Ginny Brunton and colleagues published a systematic review of cross-disciplinary research reporting women's experiences of the transition to first-time motherhood that had been published between 1975 and 2009. It identified 125 studies in total, amongst which **mental health** was the most popular topic (twenty studies), with its popularity as a topic increasing over time. Five sociological studies focusing on women's experiences of the transition to first-time motherhood, maternal identity and sense of self were selected for more in-depth review (Bailey 1999; Earle 2000; Miller 2005; Oakley 1980; Thomson and Kehily 2008). The resulting synthesis was based on the views of 183 women. Many of the themes related to mental and emotional status were similar over the decades, especially those relating to fear of pain of childbirth and feelings of being overwhelmed postnatally. However, there appeared to be greater anxiety during pregnancy about complications at the birth in the latest decade. The themes reported in Brunton et al. (2011) are reproduced in Box 13.3.

mental health
level of psychological well-being

Social support is known to be an important factor contributing to new mothers' ability to cope during the postnatal period (Oakley 1992; Bloomfield et al. 2005). In particular, two types of social support are known to impact positively on a mother's mental health and reduce the risk of depression (Manuel et al. 2012). The first is instrumental support, which may be practical (i.e., childcare and domestic tasks) or financial. The second is emotional support, which includes companionship amongst mothers and intimacy with partners (see Deery and Hunter

Box 13.3 Becoming a mother: a research synthesis of women's views on the experience of first-time motherhood

In data from five in-depth sociological studies involving 183 women in total, which were undertaken between 1975 and 2009, the following themes relating to mental health were evident:

• Anxiety about labour and birth, especially pain, lack of control and everything being OK with the baby.
• Shock as an emotional (as well as physical) response to childbirth.
• Postnatal distress on wards.
• Postnatal lack of coping – stress, worry, feeling overwhelmed, and comparisons with other mothers – 'I'm not normal'.
• Increase in identification with own femininity and with other women.
• Link between prior maternal identification and coping with motherhood postnatally.
• Lack of freedom; loss of pre-baby independence; lack of control over own life – expressed by some as bewilderment; others as depression.
• Lack of self-confidence/self-worth as a precursor of postnatal difficulties; but others viewing motherhood as a means of gaining self-worth.

(Reproduced from Brunton et al. 2011: 23)

2010; Hunter and Deery 2009). It has been suggested that mothers are increasingly isolated in (post)modern society (Drentea and Moren-Cross 2005). Yet women themselves continue to recognize the need to develop and maintain strong social support networks during the transition to motherhood (Brunton et al. 2011). This remains the same despite significant changes in women's relationship to the labour market (primary breadwinner; combining careers and motherhood) and their actual material and social support networks (children in paid childcare; fewer children in communities; increase in lone-parent households). In England, expectant and new parents can get support with parenting skills, financial matters, training and employment advice at local Children Centres (see <https://www.gov.uk/find-sure-start-childrens-centre>) that also run free-of-charge scheduled and drop-in groups for new mums and young families. The aim of these sessions is to foster new social groupings of mothers in local communities. The mums of the toddlers in Figure 13.2 met during a Children's Centre First-Time Mums' group in 2010, and continue to meet at the time of writing.

There is a growing sociological literature on parenting role expectations and experiences (i.e., Hays 1996; Miller 2005, 2010; Gattrell 2005). There is also an emerging literature from cultural and media studies, detailing the reality television sub-genre of pregnancy and parenting programmes. For example, see Tracey Jensen's (2010) critique of Channel 4's *Supernanny*, entitled 'What kind of mum are you at the moment?', and Imogen Tyler's (2011) analysis of the BBC's *Underage*

Figure 13.1 Children's centre parenting play and stay group

and Pregnant. Collectively, these works highlight the increasing visibility (and critique) of parenting practices in society, the multiple pressures and role expectations facing parents today (particularly mothers), and the opportunities for mothers and fathers to negotiate new ways of parenting and observe other parents.

The interactions between face-to-face support, virtual communities, media representations and health-care providers are increasingly complex but important considerations for midwives. The continuous developments of digital technologies (Internet and mobile) are transforming how prospective and new mothers may access information and exchange parenting experiences or anecdotal advice. One US study of 180 mothers and their online interactions during early motherhood suggests websites can create online communities that provide valuable opportunities for emotional support amongst new mothers (Drentea and Moren-Cross 2005).

📋 Activity 13.2: Digital communities

1. Access one of the many UK-based parenting websites (e.g., <http://www.babycenter.com/>; <http://www.netmums.com/>; <http://www.mumsnet.com/>) and read a selection of posts from new mothers. Make a note of the extent to which chatroom participants:

   (a) Participate (i.e., frequency and timing of posts).
   (b) Offer emotional (i.e., compassion and companionship) or instrumental support (i.e., practical responses).

(c) Are judgemental or stereotypical in responses.
(d) May be socially isolated and/or unhappy.

2. Discuss with a midwifery colleague how you can best support women with mental health issues in an age of digital communication and social media.

3. Identify appropriate national websites and social media links for your locality that can offer support to women who may be feeling socially isolated and/or unhappy. For example, the PSS Postnatal Depression Service in Liverpool has a Facebook page <https://www.facebook.com/PSSPNDservice>, detailing local groups.

Postnatal Depression: Problems of Definition, Disclosure and Treatment

This chapter has identified that support is an important factor in preventing depression during the transition to motherhood. The social significance of depression during this time is such that it has its own name – postnatal depression (PND) – whereas depression associated with other significant life events that involve loss of identity, role transition and unfamiliarity do not (i.e., divorce, unemployment). As a term, 'postnatal depression' emerged during the 1950s when medical diagnostic criteria were first established. However, in arguments reminiscent of the anti-psychiatry movement of the 1950s, sociologists continue to challenge evidence of a biological mechanism for maternal depression to the present day (Edge and Rogers 2005; Oakley 2005). Sociologists and others have highlighted the cultural specificity of PND, which is more prevalent in Western (post-)industrial societies (Halbreich and Karkun 2006). They have also shown how the experience of postnatal depression is tied up with structural factors, social support and questions of identity and self; in particular, the disjuncture between the normative role expectation of a 'good mother' and the reality of motherhood (Oakley 1980; Everingham et al. 2006).

Non-medical conceptualizations of postnatal depression, such as that theorized by Ann Oakley (1980), have received little recognition (Nicolson 1998). Oakley emphasized the nature of childbirth as a human life event, with the majority of women's accounts of depression interpreted as human responses to hospitalization, surgery, body and career change, exhaustion, overwork and social isolation (i.e., a normal human response), rather than depression as a deviation from normative notions of femininity (i.e., motherhood is joyous). Current national guidance relating to antenatal and postnatal mental health explicitly states that the term 'postnatal depression' should be avoided because this is all too 'often used inappropriately as a term for any perinatal mental disorder' (NICE 2007: 3). Whilst this statement is primarily concerned with the misattribution of symptoms and the inappropriate care that may result, it inadvertently alludes to the absence of an agreed medical definition of postnatal depression. Box 13.4 highlights a number of different ways of framing both the problem of postnatal depression and possible solutions.

📋 Activity 13.3: Postnatal depression

1. Read the study by Lloyd and Howe in Box 13.4. It was conducted in Australia over a decade ago; to what extent does each of the frames resonate with how you perceive postnatal depression?
2. Which (if any) of the solutions reflect multi-agency provision of perinatal mental health services in your area?

Box 13.4 What is postnatal depression?

Beverly Lloyd and Penelope Hawe (2003) conducted ten interviews with senior professionals involved in research, policy and services in maternal mental health for two Australian cities. The purpose of their study was to uncover the health professionals' underlying perspectives, positions and assumptions, which determined how they framed postnatal depression (PND) as a problem, and the implications for service provision. They identified seven 'frames' used by professionals to define, source, evaluate and suggest solutions.

Innate vulnerability
First, innate vulnerability refers to PND as a psychiatric category, concerned with correct diagnosis using ICD-10 or DSM-4 criteria, and appropriate management of women for whom '*it will come out whatever life stress they have*'. The problem therefore is framed as a predominantly medical one, as is the solution – improved medical services for women diagnosed with PND.

Crisis in coping
Second, crisis in coping suggests that PND is a broad condition with diagnosis being difficult. This framing emphasizes an individual woman's (in)ability to cope with the tasks of parenting. In other words, a woman might not 'fit' a diagnostic box but may not be coping as well as they think they should be. Thus, the needs of the individual are the paramount consideration in the treatment plan.

Chain of negative consequences
In the third framing, the principal problem is the chain of negative consequences that can flow from PND, affecting the mother, infant and the rest of the family – in other words, the long-term consequences of a mother's depression. In this frame, early and appropriate treatment of PND is paramount to try and avoid wider social consequences.

Parenting in a hostile world
The fourth framing prioritizes the significance of social and economic context (poverty, unemployment, single parenthood), and recognizes the potential for any woman to become ill as a result of challenging circumstances. The solution in this frame involves changing social

structures to support women and families better, and empowering women to help themselves.

Role conflict

The fifth framing suggests that PND is a response to the tension women in post-industrial societies experience, as they are expected to now combine motherhood and careers. The day-to-day pressures of 'doing it all', coupled with combining two very different roles, are viewed as the cause of PND in some women. The solutions are acceptance of the motherhood role and assistance to help women resolve conflict.

The transition to motherhood

In the sixth framing, the dominant feature was a professional's perception of an increasing tendency amongst some women to exaggerate the negative aspects of the transition to motherhood and self-identify as having PND. In this frame, PND is not viewed as a mental illness per se and the solutions centre on assisting women to negotiate the changes in their lives as they learn to live as a mother.

Undervalued motherhood

In the final framing, the root of the problem of PND is presented as the undervaluing of motherhood in society. This is different from the fourth frame in that it focuses on the isolation of women with young children in general. Thus, the solutions emphasize changing community attitudes and making the difficulties associated with parenting more visible.

At the same time as sociologists have been critical of the collapsing of a range of mothering experiences into a single medical diagnosis, postnatal depression is very real for some women. The exact number of women affected is widely reported as between 10 and 15 per cent of all postnatal women (Brown and Lumley 2000; Lewis 2011). However, the extent to which this figure includes or excludes severe depression is debatable. One study suggests that less than 50 per cent of cases are identified in routine clinical practice (Hearn et al. 1998). There is also evidence that white British women will conceal problems for fear of stigma, whilst current screening tools are not appropriate for use with women from many ethnic minorities. As the primary health professional caring for the majority of pregnant women in the UK, supporting women with postnatal depression poses many challenges for midwives, although sociological perspectives can assist midwives to see beyond medical classifications to the wider social context.

Anxiety and Fear of Childbirth

As highlighted earlier in this chapter, systematic review evidence suggests that since the year 2000 women have reported greater anxiety during pregnancy about complications at birth (Brunton et al. 2011). Since 2000, there has also been increasing evidence that up to 5 per cent of postnatal women in developed countries exhibit symptoms of post-traumatic stress directly related to their birth experience (Andersen et al. 2012). In England, in the decade since the millennium, the emergency Caesarean section rate increased from 12 per cent to 14.8 per cent. The number of instrumental births also increased from 11.1 per cent to 12.4 per cent (BirthChoice UK). These figures may account for some of the increased anxiety expressed by prospective and new mothers about birth in general and their births in particular. However, one study suggests that what has also changed is women's willingness to accept obstetric interventions (Green and Baston 2007) and much has been written in midwifery journals about women losing confidence in their abilities to birth (Garrod 2011). There has also been a cultural shift in society with birth becoming more visible. A sub-genre of reality television has emerged since the late 1990s that includes *One Born Every Minute* (Dragonfly Film and Television Productions Ltd 2010), and home movies of births now proliferate on <www.youtube.com/>. Whilst many media representations of birth may be read as anxiety-provoking, their influence on actual fear of childbirth is uncertain.

Anxiety and extreme fear of childbirth is a psychological illness, medically defined by the term 'tokophobia'. Medical classifications of tokophobia continue to evolve from a condition previously recognized as predating pregnancy (usually emerging during adolescence) to a condition now subdivided into primary tokophobia (prior to or in first pregnancy), or secondary tokophobia (as a result of previous birth experience). Fear of giving birth and so-called Caesarean delivery for maternal request are interrelated issues (Hildingsson et al. 2011). Very few women request a Caesarean section in the absence of an obstetric indication, and amongst the few that do studies show evidence of intense fear of death, fetal injury and genital tract damage (Ryding et al. 2003; Wiklund et al. 2008). Fear is an omnipresent theme even when women report Caesarean birth was their choice (Bryant et al. 2007; Kingdon et al. 2009; Fenwick et al. 2010). The psychological importance of counselling women who express fear of childbirth and/ or who may request a Caesarean delivery is recognized in the national Caesarean Section Guideline, which recommends that women should have the opportunity for discussion and support from a health-care professional with expertise in perinatal mental health to address anxiety about childbirth (NICE 2011).

(Still)birth: Acknowledging Birth and Parenting Loss

You have read about midwives and loss in Chapter 8. Thus, for the purposes of this chapter, we will only briefly consider the importance of acknowledging stillbirth for everyone involved. Studies have shown that stillbirth is associated with anxiety, depression and post-traumatic stress disorder in mothers, couples and siblings (Cacciatore et al. 2008; Cacciatore 2011; Rådestad et al. 1996; Turton et al. 2009). Emotional distress and grief are often intensified because there is little consensus of social norms when a baby is born dead. Consequently, stillbirth has until recently been little-talked-about and socially isolating event (Kenworthy and Kirkham 2010). Sociologists have been guilty of ignoring stillbirth too (Layne 2003). One insightful sociological study is Samantha Murphy's qualitative interview study of ten couples and twelve mothers. It shows how bereaved mothers are at risk of experiencing some form of stigma arising from their loss of identity as a mother after the stillbirth of a child, and their perceived loss of identity as a 'good' mother (Murphy 2011). During interviews, women tried to reclaim a moral identity as a mother by talking about how they had behaved responsibly during pregnancy and acted in the best interests of their unborn child. This identity work was performed to counter the emotional distress associated with feelings of blame and to construct themselves as a moral mother who lost a baby, rather than a discreditable and undeserving mother. Fathers made no such claims. It is crucial that midwives perpetuate neither the silence that has long surrounded stillbirth, nor the stigma that many mothers are made to feel by a society that cannot reconcile the paradoxical coalescence of birth and death (Cacciatore 2011).

Two recently published studies (undertaken by teams that include midwives and sociologists) suggest that psychological distress following stillbirth can be exacerbated by insensitive staff attitudes and uncaring behaviours during birth. Nordlund et al. (2012) undertook a web survey of 213 bereaved parents recruited via the Swedish National Infant Foundation, whilst Downe et al. (2013) interviewed twenty-two families who had previously completed a web survey via the Stillbirth and Neonatal Death Charity (Sands) website. In both these studies, acknowledging the importance of the birth itself, treating the baby as a baby (i.e., washing, dressing, cuddling) and acknowledging the significance of the parents' loss were especially important to mothers. Although both these studies identify how insensitive staff attitudes and uncaring behaviours can exacerbate parents' emotional distress, Downe et al. (2013) also report how confident and caring midwives can have a positive effect on parents' long-term psychological well-being.

We know from studies of maternity professionals that caring for families experiencing a stillbirth is a stressful aspect of their work (Chan et al. 2007; Gold et al. 2008; Downe et al. 2012; Kelley and Trinidad 2012). In one survey of more than 800 obstetricians, one in ten reported that they had considered giving up obstetric practice because of the emotional toll experienced by them personally when caring for a woman with a stillbirth (Gold et al. 2008). Doreen Kenworthy and Mavis Kirkham's (2011) book details the experiences of two groups of midwives and suggests helpful coping strategies both for midwives during births and in the weeks and months that follow.

Conclusion

This chapter concludes where it started with the hope that it has encouraged you to think more critically about how midwifery practice is shaped by wider culture and society. Mental illness, like physical illness, can affect anyone at any time, and takes many forms. This chapter has exposed the gendered 'nature' of how mental health and illness is defined and experienced. Although the most significant predictor of mental illness during pregnancy is a previous episode of severe mental illness, depression following childbirth is no more prevalent than in the general population. Whilst few sociologists would dispute that perinatal illness exists, many continue to challenge how maternal difficulties are represented and understood by medical science and society. I hope this chapter has equipped you with an introduction to mental health and illness that leads you to challenge care practices that could be otherwise and to provide the best possible care for women and their families.

Summary

- Assessment and care relating to mental health and illness is an integral part of midwifery practice.
- Sociology can help midwives understand the relationship between social role expectations, women's experiences of birth, motherhood/mothering and mental health.
- Whilst women are more likely than men to be receiving treatment for depression and anxiety, during pregnancy and early motherhood women may be more reluctant to access treatment for mental illness for fear of stigma and stereotyping as a 'bad' mother.
- Midwives' care during the birth of live and dead babies can affect women's mental health positively or negatively.

Questions for discussion

- How will you develop *your* understanding of mental health in midwifery? Think of some examples of different situations at work where a sociological understanding of mental health could help informed decision-making.
- How can sociology help you to understand the relationship between social role expectations, women's experiences of birth, motherhood/mothering and mental health?
- Look through the sociological literature and try to identify some other sociological studies that could potentially influence/change your clinical practice in relation to women's mental health.

Further reading

Rogers, A. 2010 *A sociology of mental health and illness*, 4th edn. McGraw-Hill, Open University Press.
This book explores the social and institutional constructs that systematically seek to label and then remove the rights of individuals. There is compelling evidence of the continuing ignorance that pervades society's views of the mentally ill, but also how we could all be classified with some form of mental illness, except for the protection of 'class'.

Lewis, G. 2011 Centre for Maternal and Child Enquiries (CMACE). *Saving Mothers' Lives: Reviewing Maternal Deaths to Make Motherhood Safer: 2006–08.*
The Eighth Report on Confidential Enquiries into Maternal Deaths in the United Kingdom. BJOG (2011) 118(Suppl.1): 1–203 available at <http://onlinelibrary.wiley.com/doi/10.1111/bjo.2011.118.issue-s1/issuetoc>. See pp. 132–42: 'Deaths from psychiatric causes' by Margaret Oates and Roch Cantwell.

Grabowska, C. 2003 Unhappiness after childbirth. In Squire (ed.), *The Social Context of Birth*, Radcliffe Publishing, pp. 236–48.
This chapter sits within a book that provides an essential understanding of how social issues affect midwives, the birth process and motherhood. This is often neglected in the technocratic modern culture of childbirth. Appreciating the social context surrounding women and their families enriches the understanding a midwife must have if she is to work successfully alongside a woman and her family throughout a pregnancy and birth in an insightful, intelligent and informed manner.

14 Sustainability and Midwifery Practice

Lorna Davies

Key issues:

- Defining the broad concept of sustainability.
- The need to become more sustainable in health care.
- Social sustainability and its application to midwifery practice.
- The roles and responsibilities of midwives in achieving a state of sustainability.

By the end of this chapter you should be able to:

- Describe the tenets of sustainability and their synergistic qualities.
- Discuss the relevance of social sustainability within health-care practice.
- Analyse the theory of social sustainability.
- Apply the principles both philosophically and practically to midwifery practice.
- Recognize the potential for midwives to act as agents in creating a sustainable society.

Introduction

A few years ago, as a result of having a long-held interest in environmental issues, I was invited to take the lead in the development of the materials for an undergraduate course on Sustainability and the Midwife. The course materials have been categorized into three separate modules: Sustainability, a Global Perspective; Sustainable Health Care; and Sustainability and Midwifery Practice. Whilst creating the materials, I became ever more interested in the idea of midwifery as a form of sustainable health-care practice. I firmly believed that the underlying philosophy of the midwifery profession was essentially aligned with sustainability. However, as I delved further into the field of sustainability in order to build up a repository of resources, it became evident that I may have stumbled upon 'unexplored territory'. After extensive searching, it became apparent that this was an area that had not been approached from a midwifery perspective. There was little indication of any discourse around the subject area of midwifery and sustainability and a dearth of any research evidence within the broad midwifery literature. Midwifery had a huge amount to offer and could ostensibly have a key stakehold in the area of sustainability in health care, and yet the profession was significant by its absence.

The principal aim of this chapter, therefore, is to introduce you to the concept of social sustainability within the context of midwifery practice and maternity services. The subject area of sustainability is much more wide-ranging than you may imagine and includes a host of sociological-related elements, but it is all too frequently associated with ecological 'problems'. It is easy to become overwhelmed with the magnitude of the problems often associated with sustainability, such as climate change, loss of biodiversity, population growth and so forth. These problems are real and they are without doubt likely to have a significant effect in the years ahead, but they can give us a sense of not being able to do anything significant and consequently leave us feeling disempowered.

This chapter will help you to understand that sustainability is much more than an environmental issue, encouraging you to view the subject from a sociological perspective within the context of midwifery practice. It will generate some ideas and provide you with tools to work with. It is essentially about **change agency**, about changing the way in which we view our world and perhaps about what we can do to make it a better place. Although the primary focus of the chapter is the sociological perspective, this is not necessarily a clear-cut matter because the social, environmental and economic dimensions of sustainability are synergistic components that are often difficult to critique in isolation because they are so closely interrelated. Sustainability is therefore multidisciplinary in nature.

> change agency
> creating the best
> approach to change

There is a saying that one little candle can light a dark room (Anon.), and we should never underestimate how our individual power can effect change. It has been suggested that we are far more likely to take on responsibility for the planet when we feel a sense of personal ownership (Szerszynski and Urry 2002). This may mean taking more responsibility in our personal lives by reducing, reusing and recycling, for example. However, a sense of ownership may be more effectively achieved from the strength of a collective rather than an individual position. It is becoming increasingly common for professions to take a specific slant on the broad issue of sustainability within their own sphere of practice (Stenman 2011), and there is no reason to believe this would not be true for midwives. By exploring ways of addressing some of the issues arising from our unique position within midwifery, we may be able to contribute to the wider health-care position on sustainability as well as enhancing our own sphere of practice. We will begin by exploring the general concept of sustainability, relate the principles to health care broadly and finally apply them specifically to midwifery practice.

🖹 Activity 14.1: Sustainability and midwifery

1. What does the term 'sustainability' mean to you?
2. Are there ways in which you attempt to make your own life more sustainable?
3. Can you identify what could be considered challenges to any of these attempts?
4. How do you think that the matter of sustainability relates to us in midwifery practice?
5. Are there issues that are specific to our sphere of practice that we could embrace and act upon?

The Concept of Sustainability

The concept of sustainability would certainly appear to be a central feature of our contemporary global culture. You will have realized that a newspaper cannot be opened or a television programme viewed where sustainability does not feature. This may be a story about unseasonable weather trends or a documentary about the effects of a pesticide on fertility rates in an area. The term has become commonplace with environmentalists, politicians, policymakers, economists, corporate businesses and others, each staking their individual claims and defining the concept to serve their own agenda.

As issues relating to the environment have become increasingly important, at both local and global levels (see Chapter 11), the parameters of sustainability have broadened in the last few decades to more fully include economics, politics and other social phenomena. However, the only consensus on sustainability seems to be that although there is a huge potential for interface between aspects of the concept and the areas that use it, there is no real shared universal understanding of what sustainability really means. As a consequence, it has been described as a 'dialogue of values that defies consensual definition' (Ratner 2004: 51).

The definition that seems to be most universally accepted dates back to the Brundtland Report of 1987 where 'sustainable development' is described as 'meet[ing] the needs of the present without compromising the ability of future generations to meet their own needs' (World Commission on Environment and Development (WCED), 1987: 43). Although this is a useful definition, it does primarily relate to 'development', a factor that has been described by some critics as an **oxymoron** when used in relation to sustainability, which should be about restricting rather than promoting growth (Mebratu 1998).

oxymoron
figure of speech using contradictory terms in conjunction

🖹 Activity 14.2: The concept of sustainability

It may be useful to consider the significance of the concept of 'sustainability' and to ask yourself if there is a clear understanding of what the term actually means.

- What is it that we are aiming to sustain?
- What makes some things or attributes worthy of sustaining?
- How can we judge the value of sustainability when there seem to be so many competing interests?

The three tenets of sustainability

In spite of its critics and its perceived shortcomings, the Brundtland definition was endorsed and expanded at an important summit in Rio, Brazil, where it was agreed that ecological, economic and social dimensions were the three tenets of sustainability and that they carried equal weighting in terms of their importance (UN 1993). The tenets are frequently represented as three pillars holding up the roof of sustainability. The theory suggests that if one of the pillars is missing or is even slightly shorter than the others, then the 'roof' will not be supported.

It is useful at this juncture to spend a short time exploring the broad principles of the three tenets in order to provide a background to the broad subject area.

Environmental Threats of a Changing World

Most of us are aware that during the last fifty years demands on the world's resources have been stretched beyond measure. Some critics suggest that this has resulted primarily because of the growth in consumerism and high-resource demands in the thirty-four

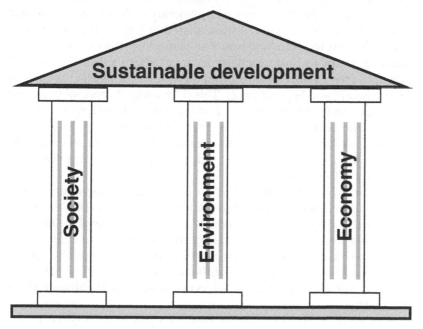

Figure 14.1 Three pillars of sustainability

Box 14.1 Environmental threats to human health resulting from climate change

1. Extreme weather events and natural disasters which are likely to lead to massive human population displacement.
2. The effects of pollutants and toxins such as radioactive leachate, which affect human health directly and via the food chain. These affect not only the current generation but equally the health of future generations.
3. A shortage of essential commodities such as food and water, resulting from increasing demand and decreasing supply.
4. An increase in vectors carrying disease, such as malarial-carrying mosquitoes.

OECD an international organization that assists governments to address the economic, social and governance challenges of a globalized economy

developing economies are said to have lower standards of living and economies in transition; many have deep and extensive poverty

anthropogenic effects that are derived from human activities, as opposed to those occurring in biophysical environments without human influence

countries of the **OECD** (Organization for Economic Co-operation and Development). The OECD was founded in 1961 to stimulate economic progress and world trade, alongside the mounting needs in the so-called **developing economies** such as China, India and some Latin American countries such as Brazil (Moore-Lappe 2011; Hawken 2007). There is a strong belief that climate change is unequivocally occurring and weather patterns appear to be noticeably changing (Moore-Lappe 2011; McKibben 2010; Hawken 2007). There is also an increasing acceptance that the change is **anthropogenic**. The threats of climate change are a serious threat to life forms on the planet. These effects are predicted to increase in the years to come (McMichael et al. 2012). The environmental threats to human health resulting from climate change on a planetary scale are significant and many (Burke 2012). Some of these (listed in Box 14.1) could almost certainly lead to security crises. For example, as those with refugee status attempt to find sanctuary in areas where subsistence is still possible (see Chapter 10), the potential for civil conflict would be great (Femia and Werrell 2012). This 'Domesday Scenario' is viewed as a real and serious threat by many international agencies and health-care workers (Goodman 2011). As key players, health-care workers are being advised to take on board the issues and urged to take action on climate change in a drive to minimize these threats to human health (Burke 2012).

The world's population has also increased exponentially in the last fifty years, placing further demands on resources (UNFPA 2011). The earth's populace has become a much more mobile force in recent decades and life expectancy has increased overall, which also impacts on resource management. The world's population has increased from 3 billion inhabitants in 1960 to 7 billion in 2011. The majority of the population growth is occurring in sub-Saharan Africa and Asia.

This increase in low-resource countries has invariably led to the need for a greater number of midwives and it is estimated that 350,000 more midwives are currently required globally. As you know from Chapter 10, more midwives would ensure access to safe maternity care for more women, which would reduce the incidence of perinatal and maternal mortality and lead to improvements in the health of women and children. A healthier population tends to have a smaller number of children, which would lead to a reduction in the overall birth rate. The public health role of midwives would also help to provide communities of birthing women with greater control over their fertility, which would reduce both the number of births and the number of perinatal and maternal mortalities.

The Economic Sustainability of Health Care

There is now an argument that in attempting to meet our perceived needs and wants in the form of material goods, we are stripping the earth of its **biotic capacity** to sustain life. This is occurring in order to sustain our existing economic status quo and has clearly had profound effects on our societal structures (Hawken 2007).

biotic capacity
capacity of organisms to increase in numbers

The concept of economic growth is bound to the idea of expansion of wealth and power (Harvey 2005). The problem with the idea of continued economic growth and progress is that there are limits to this, and therefore the idea of continuing expansion and growth can be seen as unrealistic (Jackson 2011). The current economic model only works as long as there is continued demand (Schor 2010). The unyielding petitioning for economic expansion has led to the accusation that **capitalism** is leading society to the brink of economic and ecological ruin (McGregor 2001).

capitalism
economic system maintained by private individuals or companies

As you know, over the course of the last half-century, and notably in the last few decades, many Western-style health-care systems chose to adopt a **neoliberal** ideological approach. In this paradigm, health care has been placed within a free-market business-style model built around **consumerist** principles (see Chapter 12). This has occurred even in those countries with a strong tradition of a welfare state, such as the UK. It is argued that welfare states, established to ensure the welfare of citizens, are too expensive and give the medical profession too much power under the protection of the 'nanny state' (Sandall et al. 2009). The model has used strategies from the world of commerce and industry, such as risk management; strategic planning; cost–benefit analyses and performance-based targets, and they result in market-based behaviour within the public-based facilities of health care (Jameton and McGuire 2002).

neoliberal
economic philosophy espousing free-market economics and globalized free trade

consumerist
encouragement of consumption

The World Health Organization (WHO) has expressed grave concerns about the effects of the 2008 global economic crisis on health-care systems The crisis is said to have increased social inequality and, according to a report produced by the WHO, this should lead to an appraisal of global values relating to health care (Chan 2009).

🗒 Activity 14.3: Sustainable health-care systems

It is argued that for a health-care system to be sustainable it would need to be accessible to all in order to negate social inequality, be financially viable and independent of corporate influence, and to be delivered with as little impact to the environment as possible (Naylor and Appleby 2012).

- Do you think that your current maternity-care system promotes consideration of social inequality? Revisit Chapter 10 to aid your thinking. Why do you believe this to be true or not?
- Do you think that your current maternity-care system is independent of corporate influence? Why do you believe this to be true or not?
- Do you think that your current maternity-care system is delivered with as little impact to the environment as possible? Why do you believe this to be true or not?

It seems that we are faced with health-care services at crisis point, attempting to juggle ever-increasing health-care needs with the resources available. The attempt to maintain a balance-check on these conflicting interests has led in many cases to increased waiting times for treatment, access issues and growing public concerns about the quality and safety of health-care provision. All these issues are addressed in many of the chapters within this book. The reasons for the escalating health-care costs are manifold and varied according to the setting, but can be seen to include increasing populations, longer lifespan expectancy, greater reliance on technology, increasing scope and cost of pharmacological treatments, a rising prevalence of chronic disease, and a change in expectation on the part of the users of the services (Erixon and van der Marel 2011).

Additionally, there has been wide criticism of health-care systems for engaging with an ideology that has contributed to the commodification of health (Shaffer and Brenner 2004; see also Chapter 11). There is also an argument that the free-market approach in health care has led to an increased reliance on medical technology and pharmaceutical industries, which reap financially from a market-based economy (Jameton and McGuire 2002; see also Chapter 12).

Social Sustainability

Social sustainability is less easy to measure than economic growth or environmental impact, and is seen as the weakest pillar when it comes to its analytical and theoretical underpinnings (Lehtonen 2004). A definition of social sustainability would also appear to be elusive (Colantonio 2008). Many of the definitions of sustainability relate to the environment and the economy, and social science input is perceived principally as a means of promoting the message of environmental or economic sustainability (McKenzie 2004). This subsequently impacts on the development of a socially inclusive policy approach around

Box 14.2 Features of social sustainability

- Equity of access to key services, including health, education, transport, housing and recreation.
- Equity between generations, meaning that future generations will not be disadvantaged by the activities of the current generation.
- A system of cultural relations in which the positive aspects of disparate cultures are valued.
- Widespread political participation of citizens not only in electoral procedures, but also in other areas of political activity, particularly at a local level.
- A system for transmitting awareness of social sustainability from one generation to the next.
- Mechanisms for a community to collectively identify its strengths and needs.

(McKenzie 2004: 12)

sustainability (Adebowale 2002). McKenzie (2004: 12) has suggested that a range of different approaches should be used to address the challenge of a tenuous 'working definition' for social sustainability, which he describes as 'a life-enhancing condition within communities', and that this condition presents the features listed in Box 14.2.

The concept of social sustainability also appears to be in a constant state of evolution, regularly taking on a new shape within a relatively short time span. For example, in the 1980s, basic needs and human rights, alongside poverty and equity and **social justice**, were the main foci of social sustainability. In the 1990s, the emphasis was on concepts such as social capital, city liveability strategies, demographic change, health and safety, and **social cohesion** (Wackernagel and Rees 1996; Elkington 2004). In the last decade, what have been termed 'happiness orientated policies' have been emerging (Ormerod and Johns 2007). This grouping includes areas such as empowerment, participation and access; identity, sense of place and culture; well-being, happiness and quality of life.

> **social justice**
> based on concept of human rights

> **social cohesion**
> the bonds that bring people together

Criteria are sometimes used to map the constituents of social sustainability within a given situation, and these can be used as a benchmark to monitor improvements. Some of the most useful tools can be found in public health-related documents, but town-and city-planning environmental strategies can provide a good source of useful measures. One such evaluation, developed by Christchurch City Council in New Zealand, uses criteria from a range of international town planning and public health documents. The tool is designed to assess the impact of city-planning policies and proposals on public health by using evaluation criteria built around the guiding principles of social sustainability (Billante 2008). It would be relatively easy to adapt most of these to apply to midwifery practice.

Box 14.3 Criteria with brief definitions of concepts

Criteria	Brief definition of concept
Social and community capacity	The main precept of social capacity theory is that relationships matter and that social networks are a valuable asset. By making human connections, we can create relationships and communities that can benefit people's lives.
Equity	Equity refers to fairness in matters relating to social and economic issues. An equitable approach attempts to establish the principles of social justice. Inequity exists where there is an imbalance in the distribution of resources. Particular attention is paid to the needs of minority, disenfranchised and non-mainstream groups.
Community resilience	The capability to anticipate risk, limit impact and bounce back rapidly through survival, adaptability, evolution and growth in the face of turbulent change.
Community safety	Providing local community facilities that enhance feelings of security and safety. A perception of safety has an impact on stress, mental health and feelings of social isolation for individuals in a community.
Neighbourhood amenity	A neighbourhood amenity that is aesthetically pleasing and designed with safety considerations increases feelings of security and safety.
Cultural diversity	A strong sense of cultural identity is recognized as a key factor for an individual's health. Living in an environment of acceptance and tolerance enhances mental health and promotes social cohesion between people within a multicultural community.
Resource management	Health impacts due to climate change can be mitigated through addressing the causes of climate change, such as greenhouse gas emissions and environmental contamination.
Active lifestyles	Encouraging people to incorporate exercise into their daily routines, for example, by walking or cycling to work, reduces dependency on motor vehicles as well as increasing levels of fitness and its associated benefits.
Transport accessibility	Evidence shows that accessible local facilities enhance social equity by reducing the need to own a car to get access to services.
Natural capital	Natural capital is made up of resources and ecosystem services from the natural world. Natural capital is influenced by individual and collective human action.

Sustainable Health Care: An Emergent Movement

> Health is fundamentally rooted in sociocultural and political-economic systems, and thus intertwined with the world system and anthropogenic climate change. (Baer and Singer 2008: 7)

Over the coming decades, some of the environmental changes that we have discussed are predicted to have major ramifications for health-care service and provision (McMichael, Montgomery and Costello 2012). It is therefore essential that all health-care professionals, including midwives, are aware of the potential impact on their own specific area of practice, as well as having a more generic knowledge and understanding of the meaning of sustainability.

Sustainability in health care could be seen to translate as the potential for the long-term maintenance of health and well-being of the human population (Bromley 2008). As you know, our health is dependent on the health of the environment that we inhabit, the social structures that we create and function within and the frameworks that regulate our economic models (IPCC 2001).

A sense of increasing awareness of a greater need for sustainability in health care has been gaining momentum in the last few years, which, whilst spearheaded almost exclusively by medicine and focused primarily on climate change, feels like a step in the right direction. There has been a mushrooming of sustainable health organizations within many countries and health-care systems. Organizations such as the UK-based Centre for Sustainable Healthcare and the US organization Healthcare without Harm have been launched, and prestigious journals like the *British Medical Journal* and the *Lancet* have published editions dedicated to promoting the 'climate change in health' message to their readers. In July 2012, a session titled 'Greening the Health Sector' was held at the Rio + 20 Summit in Brazil, which identified the environment as *the* major determinant of human health and well-being. Many health-care professionals are questioning the role of corporate sponsorship of conferences and professional development materials. Web-based organizations like No Free Lunch, which is operated by health-care providers who believe that pharmaceutical promotion should not guide clinical practice, are emerging alongside Facebook pages for Sustainability and Nursing. However, midwifery is significant by its near absence in most of the discussion around sustainability to date. It is essential that the issues that we have considered so far are raised and explored within a framework of midwifery practice, because it is time for the profession to recognize the contribution that midwives can make to sustainable health care.

Sustainability and Midwifery Practice

> What makes midwifery so desirable to women? Simply put, midwifery promotes well-being. It is an art of service, in that the midwife recognizes, responds to and cooperates with natural forces. In this sense,

> midwifery is ecologically attuned, involving the wise utilization of resources and respect for the balance of nature. (Davis 1997)

Midwives, by virtue of their role, could conceivably be perceived as part of an ecologically responsible profession (Davies et al. 2010: 2). In promoting physiological birth, the model essentially supports a low-resource and minimal intervention approach. However, it could be argued that midwives have an even more important role, and this hinges on social responsibility. If we look to the most recent international definition of the midwife (ICM 2005), the midwifery model would appear to support the values of equity, social justice and community capacity. As part of their role, midwives work to safeguard the health and well-being of new families with health promotion and education strategies. Therefore, the midwife can be seen to be playing an extremely important role in terms of social sustainability.

It could be said that midwifery is firmly grounded in a tradition of social sustainability. If we consider the historical credentials of midwifery as a sustainable health-care practice, an impressive track record is demonstrable. Midwifery is arguably the oldest health-care profession, which has survived as an entity in all human societies in spite of considerable persecution and oppression (Towler and Bramhall 1998). Yet midwives still contribute to the support of childbearing women, albeit within a role which has largely evolved within a medicalized model (see Chapter 2). Traditionally, in most societies, the midwife was a village woman who learned her trade by attending the births of her family and neighbours within her immediate community, with skills and knowledge being handed down through generations of women (Thomas 2000). This was the case until the beginning of the twentieth century in many Western countries, and remains so in some non-Western parts of the world today.

You may have noted the disestablishment of many communities as a result of increasing migration and urbanization; the increasing involvement of the medical profession in birth-related matters, the professionalization of midwifery in the latter years of the nineteenth and early twentieth centuries, and the rise of the nursing profession (van Teijlingen 2005a; see also Chapter 2). The factors listed above are said to have contributed to a move away from the traditional values of midwifery to a medicalized and **technocratic** model, and are sometimes criticized as militating against a woman-centred socially based approach to midwifery care (Davis-Floyd 2009). However, in recent years, a shift seems to have taken place, in some countries at least.

technocratic
form of government controlled by technical expert

In many Western health-care practices, there appears to be a reconsideration of where midwifery should be sited within a health-care system. Some countries such as New Zealand and Canada have attempted to reclaim the traditional values of midwifery, and to place them within the context of a contemporary health-care setting as part of a primary care-based service. In both of these cases, it took the effective demise of the profession in the late twentieth century to spur action on the part of both the community and the remnants of the midwifery profession, demanding a return to these values and a recognition of their value to society (e.g., Guilliland and Pairman 2010). Both systems are today able to offer women a model of 'partnership' with midwives, which provides them with care that offers relational stability between each woman and midwife in the form of continuity of midwifery carer throughout the pregnancy, birth and postnatal period.

In the UK recently, a taskforce was established to introduce a social enterprise model which promises to provide a bridge between coop-eration and competition in the National Health Service. It is claimed that such a model has the potential to provide a vehicle for midwives to challenge the traditional public-sector structures and to provide a women-centred, midwifery-led, continuity-of-carer model (Midwifery 2020, 2010b). There are currently concerns around potential fragmen-tation of the maternity services with the introduction of such a model, and there are question marks around issues such as transfer of employ-ment terms and conditions, and what happens if the social enterprises do not for whatever reason work (Addicott 2011). However, this is an interesting development and it may provide a new and exciting phase in the provision of midwifery care in the UK.

The midwife might not be part of the village any more, in the literal sense at least, but if current trends are anything to go by then they should be aiming to be a part of the childbearing woman's community in a broader sense, in order to optimize a woman-centred and socially based approach to practice, and to strengthen their skills in organizing and leading local services for women and families.

Protecting, Preserving and Promoting the 'Eco-niche'

A relationship, as referred to in analysis around social sustainability, begins with the relationship that we have with ourselves, as this will shape all other social connections in our lives (Layard 2005). Various authors have suggested that our consumer-driven society has encour-aged us to develop our identity around what we have and do, rather than who we are (see Chapter 11). It could be argued that this makes us dependent on others for our self-esteem (as Ruth Deery and Pamela Fisher suggest in Chapter 5). It has been said that personal happiness and well-being are equated with autonomy, achievement and the development of interpersonal relationships, and less with the acquisi-tion of material wealth and goods (Kahneman and Sugden 2005). By educating, encouraging, supporting and listening to women, midwives have the opportunity to assist them in building self-esteem and per-sonal resilience, which is described as the ability to take on demanding levels of change whilst maintaining personal resourcefulness.

The privileged relationship of midwives with women during the childbearing continuum offers the opportunity to observe at first hand the initiation of the most significant and profound connection, that of the mother–baby dyad. Whether you realize the huge implication of the successful establishment of that relationship is perhaps less clear.

By using good verbal and non-verbal communication skills, the midwife is in a strong position to facilitate the connection between the woman and her baby. It is well documented that solid early attachment is likely to lead to greater ability of the individual to form relationships throughout life (Verny and Kelly 1981; Grossman and Waters 2005). This is a really important consideration in terms of social sustainability because it is theorized, as you know from Chapter 5, that the ability to forge relationships is a significant factor in achieving well-being and that people who readily form relationships are generally happier, healthier and able to make a valuable and positive contribution to society (Christakis and Fowler 2009; Layard 2005). The measure of happiness as an indicator of societal well-being is an area that social scientists have been working on for some time, and it is now established that factors such as reduced rates of infant mortality correlate positively with members of societies that offer greater subjective expressions of happiness (Kahneman 2011).

In this context, the midwife's role in the facilitation and preservation of the mother–baby dyad in pregnancy, and in the early hours, days and weeks of new motherhood, is of paramount importance. This endeavour has been referred to as 'facilitating the econiche' (Davies et al. 2010). An econiche simply means that a living organism has all its needs met by another organism within a natural closed-loop system. The midwife's role of protecting, promoting and preserving this econiche could therefore be viewed as a key societal role. In the antenatal period, the midwife is in an ideal position to work at helping the mother establish a connection with her baby. This may be as simple as talking to the baby during an abdominal palpation or getting the woman to palpate her own baby. It may be getting her to sing to her baby or play music. During birth it means protecting the environment, encouraging physiological birth and prolonged mother/baby contact following birth. In the early days of new mothering, it may mean encouraging the woman and her partner to spend precious time as a new family. Thus, the 'mother–midwife relationship' would appear to bestow a very important function, stretching far beyond addressing the physical needs of the woman as defined by the medical model (Kirkham 2010a). This consideration should provide a fairly compelling argument for a continuity-of-carer model such as those discussed earlier within the chapter.

Community of Childbirth

If social sustainability hinges on relationships, then the midwife has another important role in promoting socially sustainable health care. In his book *The Tipping Point,* Gladwell (2000) speaks of a role that he describes as the 'social connector', the people who 'link us up with the world'. There are many ways in which midwives could take on the role of social connector within their practice setting. This may be achieved in the form of childbirth and parenting education, or through any other number of ventures that may promote relationships and assist women in establishing their own new network of friends and support. An example of where this has been successful is the Centering Pregnancy Scheme, where women attend their antenatal assessment within a group setting and then share experiences and discussion with the guidance and support of midwives (Carlson and Lowe 2006). A special consideration should be given for provision of service for minority groups. Such groups may particularly benefit from access to a shared source of community-based resources that midwives could coordinate.

The midwife may also act as a social connector by encouraging the active involvement of the woman's partner or her family members, so that with skilful communication and interpersonal skills, existing relationships may be strengthened.

Within their role, midwives have the potential to play an active part in achieving functionality and sustainability within a number of other communities of practice. No health profession is an island and, in addition to the role that they play as part of the community of childbearing women and their families, midwives also have a role to play in building relationships both within the midwifery profession and with associated health-care and related professionals.

Primary Care and Public Health

Maternity services could demonstrate a commitment to social sustainability by ensuring that the profession is firmly sited within a model of primary care, supported by secondary services with a strong public health emphasis. This would provide the service with a focus on health and well-being which should detract from any tendency to pathologize and medicalize pregnancy and childbirth unnecessarily (Murphy-Lawless 2010).

Within a primary-care model, the midwife can provide antenatal and postnatal care in women's homes or community settings, where the focus is on enhancing and supporting pregnancy and childbirth as a normal life process. Here, the midwife is more likely to be able to support the physical, psychosocial, cultural and spiritual well-being of the woman and her family, and this holistic approach is believed to result in more positive outcomes (Page et al. 2001; Hatem et al. 2008; Hodnett et al. 2011). The provision of birthing centres and a good home-birth service may further enhance that process. It is well established that the greater the level of intervention, the higher the carbon footprint. Therefore, it is in the interests of the employing health-care processes to support the drive to reduce intervention levels by promoting birthing environments that look at outcomes in a far more holistic manner (Tracy 2010).

📋 Activity 14.4: Midwifery in a neighbourhood centre

Imagine a service where midwifery is co-sited within a neighbourhood centre which provides access and opportunities for social contact and which supports local communities and businesses. Such a centre would meet the social sustainability indicator for safety by providing a safe space for women to meet and socialize.

Think of all the different ways in which this could be used as a 'hub' to serve the local childbearing community: for example, pregnancy yoga classes, or a nutrition-in-pregnancy cooking course. This kind of activity would promote an active lifestyle, another indicator.

- What might such a facility look like?
- How could it be run in a sustainable way?

Other Areas of Sustainability

Although the main focus of this chapter has been on social sustainability, there are other areas of sustainability that are significant in relation to midwifery practice. Self-sustainability in the form of self-compassion is important, and there is an increasing body of knowledge in the health-care sector in relation to self-compassion (see Deery 2014). In a profession where burn-out rates are far too high, we need to look after ourselves and to look after each other. How can we care for others if we do not look after ourselves?

Environmental sustainability in the form of resource management is an important consideration in both midwifery practice and maternity services. There is a strong 'greening of the health service' movement in the UK, and similar movements in other parts of the world where the efficient use of resources in institutional settings is being seriously addressed. Midwives could contribute to these efforts by looking critically at their use of transport, telecommunications and equipment, and asking themselves if they could reduce their carbon footprint by reducing, reusing and recycling. Martis (2010) proposes that the introduction of a 'green midwifery movement' might provide a useful platform to address some of these issues.

📋 Activity 14.5: Creating an eco-birthing kit

If you were asked to produce an 'eco-birthing kit' of essential equipment that would fit in a small backpack, what do you imagine you might include? Be as creative as you can.

Professional sustainability is the other area of major significance. If the profession of midwifery is to play an active and effective part in the development of sustainability strategies, both for the profession itself

Figure 14.2 Cloth nappies

and for the broader health-care agenda, it will require a framework that aligns the role of midwifery alongside the principles of sustainability. The International Congress of Midwives (ICM), has developed an internationally accepted framework for practice, which is designed to provide a sustainable foundation for the profession. Education, regulation and professional association are viewed as the key factors in ensuring the continuing development of the midwifery profession on a global platform. International standards for both midwifery education and the regulation of midwives were endorsed and ratified for the first time at the International Confederation of Midwives Council Meeting in Durban, South Africa, in June 2011 (ICM 2011b).

Conclusion

Sustainability is a vast and complex territory. The focus in this chapter has been primarily on social sustainability, and, as this is a textbook about sociology, this would seem to be appropriate. However, this also feels like a fitting starting point in terms of exploring the broader subject area of sustainability. As previously discussed, there is an argument that if we can get individuals and communities to agree to the benefits of more sustainable ways of doing and being, then action around the other tenets may follow.

The social construct of sustainability has the potential to offer midwifery a new framework for long-held midwifery values and beliefs. Such ideals have become increasingly difficult to express and hold on to in contemporary health-care practice (Davies, Daellenbach and Kensington 2010). Midwives have remonstrated that they are an atypical profession within health-care practice because they do not fit well within a high-tech and medicalized model, which is designed to diagnose and treat illness and disease. For multiple and complex reasons, over the course of the last few decades, midwifery has been driven into the sphere of this obstetrically dominated paradigm. This position does not articulate well with a holistic midwifery model, and this has effected marked dissonance and has undoubtedly contributed to spiralling levels of intervention and subsequent physical, emotional and psychological trauma for many women and their babies. From a philosophical standpoint, sustainability embraces the midwifery-driven philosophical principle of holism and should therefore be given serious consideration as a new and exciting paradigmatic advancement for midwifery.

Summary

- The concept of sustainability is increasingly featuring within our contemporary global culture.
- The scope of sustainability is a broad one that includes a host of sociological-related elements as well as ecological, economic, cultural and others.
- Sustainability in health care could be seen to translate as the potential for the long-term maintenance of health and well-being of the human population.
- The social model of midwifery supports the values of equity, social justice and community capacity.
- Maternity services could demonstrate a commitment to social sustainability, by ensuring that the profession is firmly sited within a model of primary care, supported by secondary services with a strong public health emphasis.

Questions for discussion

- How might midwifery help to address the potential threats from climate change such as changing disease patterns and disrupted food distribution?
- Are there any sustainability and health organizations operating within your local area? What might you have to offer to such a group?
- Do you think that sustainability should be more comprehensively included in midwifery undergraduate and post-registration education?

Further reading

Baer, H. and Singer, M. 2008 *Global Warming and the Political Ecology of Health: Emerging Crises and Systemic Solutions.* Left Coast Press.
An excellent and thought-provoking introduction to the political ecology of health by anthropologist Baer and research scientist Singer.

Davies, L., Daellenbach, R. and Kensington, M. 2010 *Sustainability, Midwifery and Birth*. Routledge.
Explores the challenges of creating a sustainable midwifery profession by critically reflecting on the issues at stake.
Giddens, A. 2011 *The Politics of Climate Change*, 2nd edn. Polity.
Well-known sociologist Anthony Giddens presents a measured socio-political perspective on the area of climate change.
UNFPA 2011 *The State of the World's Midwifery 2011: Delivering Health, Saving Lives*. At <http://www.unfpa.org/sowmy/report/home.html>.
This report provides the first comprehensive analysis of midwifery services and issues in countries where the needs are greatest, and gives some insight into the impact that midwives can make in difficult and challenging circumstances.

Conclusion

Ruth Deery, Elaine Denny and Gayle Letherby

Throughout this book there has been an attempt to link midwifery and sociology and to stimulate and develop your 'sociological imagination' (Mills 1959). In present Western society, midwives are constantly involved in situations where they are expected to meet the diverse needs of women and their families and at the same time maintain their own professional development. This book is not intended to provide you with answers to some of these situations; rather, its intention is to help you think outside of the box and to ask questions. As with other editions in this series, sociology is presented as multi-paradigmatic. This means that sociology can provide you with a set of theories, concepts and methodological tools, which you can apply to everyday midwifery practice. So, rather than receiving a set of answers, you are presented with and encouraged to think about different ways of knowing in a non-assuming, questioning and critical manner.

You have probably found some chapters, or parts of chapters, more helpful or applicable than others. This will depend on your life experience and knowledge, and the stage of your training. Each chapter has been written to ensure that its sociological relevance is applicable to most, but not all, aspects of midwifery. One or more of the chapters may have powerful resonance for you and some may be more interesting than others. For example, if you are interested in the medicalization of childbirth, you will find Chapters 2, 7 and 12 of relevance. Similarly, those of you interested in how contemporary society can sometimes exclude women from our maternity services will be interested in Chapters 6, 8, 9 and 10. As you reach the end of your training and progress through your career, your interests may change and you might find that all of the sociological issues raised in this book have particular importance.

The sociology of health and medicine has become a vast and growing area of study – the issues addressed in this book are not those of most importance to the editors. Rather, they are the result of our initial discussions and individual expertise when planning the book. The sociology of health deals with issues that are familiar to us all and it is this aspect that ensures the discipline can be applied so well to your clinical practice as midwives. The book is not exhaustive and, as editors, we know there are a number of omissions. Primarily, it has been our intention to outline some of the key debates within midwifery and to show how these are relevant to sociology. We hope the book has given you a good grounding and that you have been encouraged to think sociologically.

Each of the chapters has been written as a starter for study in that particular area. Further study of sociological theory will reveal to you a wider range of theoretical perspectives than those described in this book, thus stimulating your sociological imagination. Postmodernism is one such theory, suggesting that there is no one valid 'truth' or 'reality', thus challenging rationality and sometimes science itself. You now know as midwives that there are many competing discourses and forces that are part of your clinical practice. Different theories help us to examine 'the fragmentary, flawed, difficult nature of reality or realities' (Brown et al. 2008). As such, sociological theory can help you to better understand the complexities of clinical practice. A guide to classic and contemporary theories in sociology can be found in McDonnell et al. (2009). Feminist theories and methodological approaches are particularly useful and relevant for contemporary midwifery practice. Gayle Letherby has written extensively from a feminist sociological perspective and you might find Letherby (2003) particularly useful.

The role of the midwife in public health has received much greater attention in recent years. A deeper understanding of public health will increase your awareness of the effects that the environment can have on pregnant and birthing women and their families. In Chapter 14, Lorna Davies provides some challenging, forward thinking about sustainability from a sociological perspective. Sustainability is a neglected area in midwifery and you will find the book edited by Davies et al. (2010) provides a useful sociological interpretation of sustainability in midwifery.

We have not focused on all the facets of public health in this book. Some areas have been alluded to in the chapters, but not dealt with in any depth: for example, obesity, the workplace and occupational health and education. The book edited by Lorna Davies and Ruth Deery (2014) has chapters that present some critical – some might say radical – perspectives on obesity. In Chapter 7, Jayne Samples and Bob Heyman introduce you to the concept of risk in midwifery, which is a vast area. Hopefully, you will be stimulated to read more around the complexities and uncertainties of clinical practice and birth, with the realization that nothing is ever clear-cut and there are indeed many grey areas. The book written by Bob Heyman and colleagues (2010c) explores how risk is constructed, encouraging the reader to analyse risk-management issues, and to critically evaluate the claims made about existing and new technologies, in an informed way. The book covers all aspects of risk relevant to a clinical setting and is closely related to decision-making.

We hope this text has indeed stimulated your sociological imagination and begun a lifelong interest in sociology and sociological theory and research methods. As we have stated earlier, there is not always an answer to the complexities that clinical practice presents to us, but sociology can enhance our understanding and contribute to our clinical practice, helping us to make a positive difference.

Glossary

absolute risk: the chance of developing a condition

alienation: estrangement or distancing of an individual from themselves (or part of themselves) or from others

anthropogenic: effects that are derived from human activities, as opposed to those occurring in biophysical environments without human influence

assisted conception technologies/

assisted reproductive technologies: medical assistance to enable an individual or couple to conceive or carry a baby to term

Big Society: a government initiative that seeks to shift power and responsibility away from politicians to the community and community groups

binary divide: a division into two opposite parts, e.g., men/women, north/south; in sociology the notion of binary divisions is often challenged and structures within society are viewed more as being on a continuum, e.g., rather than being abled/disabled, people are viewed as variously abled

biotic capacity: the capacity of a population of organisms to increase in numbers under optimum environmental conditions

birthmother: a woman who has given birth to a child, as opposed to an adoptive mother

capitalism: an economic system in which investment in and ownership of the means of production, distribution and exchange of wealth is made and maintained by private individuals or corporations

capitalist mode of production: the production system of capitalist societies which are characterized by private ownership of the means of production, distribution and exchange within a market economy, and production for profit (Marx 1970)

career paths:	progress or course through life
change agency:	recognizing the opportunity for change, identifying the best approach, and making that change happen
childbearing continuum:	the continuous process from preconception through to postnatal
cognitive:	related to thinking
commissioning:	the process of ensuring that health-care services are provided for the population; the core role of commissioners is to buy services for their populations
commissioning boards:	the NHS Commissioning Board was established on 31 October 2011; its role was to make all the necessary preparations for the successful establishment of the NHS Commissioning Board (NHS CB) in October 2012 before it took on full statutory responsibilities in April 2013, replacing the system where strategic health authorities and primary care trusts were the commissioners
common sense:	an everyday interpretation of reality and events
consumerism:	the theory that an increasing consumption of goods is economically beneficial
developing economies:	are said to have lower standards of living and economies in transition; many have deep and extensive poverty
discourse:	communication or discussion
dualistic/dualism:	two seemingly inconsistent systems of belief or concepts that exist at the same time
emotional shifts:	swift changes between very different emotions
enculturation:	the process by which a person gradually learns the norms of the culture in the particular society in which s/he is brought up, acquiring the values and practices considered acceptable in that culture
epistemology/ epistemological:	the theory of the knowledge we produce through research
eugenic:	the idea that society can be improved by control of reproduction; only those deemed genetically 'fit' should reproduce, and others, such as those with learning disabilities, should be dissuaded

facilitated sex: a sexual encounter that is made possible by the help of a third party, for example, in helping with position

false dualism: the idea that certain phenomena can only be categorized as mutually exclusive may be false, and they are actually more complex, e.g., states of health cannot merely be described as 'ill' or 'well'

freebirth: a birth with no medical professional in attendance who is trained to facilitate the birth process

globalization: social, economic and cultural interconnectedness across the world, where an increased proportion of economic, social and cultural activity is carried out across national borders; the process of globalization has significant economic, business and social implications

governmentality theory: involves the disciplining and regulation of society using power, disciplinary and self-governing methods, which is achieved 'without direct or oppressive intervention' (Flynn 2002: 163), but by establishing norms and standards against which behaviours are measured; according to Holmes and Gastaldo (2002), nursing is a component of governmentality because it involves shaping the population for social and economic purposes by promoting health as desirable through education and alleviating suffering through care

heuristic device: an abstract concept or model useful for thinking about social and physical phenomena; e.g., sociologists use the concept 'social structure' to help them define and analyse aspects of society that create patterns and regularity in the everyday roles and activities of individuals

hierarchy: members of an organization are ranked or categorized according to ability or status, from highest to lowest, or vice versa

high-touch care: care that is very dependent on interpersonal interaction

iatrogenic: a condition or state which is caused by treatment for another disease or condition (Black 2007)

ideology: in its simplest form an ideology is a 'world

view' or the way people see and interpret the social world; more generally, it is regarded as a complete and consistent set of attitudes, moral views and empirical beliefs, and is often associated with political orientation; well-known ideologies including communism, fascism and nationalism; ideology relates to policy in that the policies put in place reflect certain underlying beliefs enshrined in the ideology of those shaping the policy

impact: an increasingly acknowledged part of research; research funders and commissioners and ethics committees often now ask for evidence that the research will make some kind of positive difference to the lives of respondents and/or others like them

implementation: the process of putting a decision or plan into effect; execution

industrial capitalism: a period characterized by the private control and ownership of the means of production and the rise of public and private social welfare

industrial model: the commercialization of production, with ever more complex production processes and waged labour

infertility: the inability to conceive a child after twelve months of trying and/or the inability to successfully carry a live fetus to term

insiders: a person within a group or organization that may have access to particular information or viewpoints

institutional arrangements: organization, policies and practices of social structures such as government, family or hospital

involuntary childlessness: non-parenthood (not by choice), which is different from chosen non-parenthood (voluntary childlessness) and might be the result of infertility or of social circumstances (e.g., not meeting the 'right' partner or having one's children taken away by social services)

lobbying: applying pressure, presenting arguments and/ or using incentives, sometimes gifts, to try and make a political decision-maker favour one position over another

market: an exchange mechanism where a buyer and a seller both try to maximize their position and realize the best deal; in a perfect market both parties have power, but in many situations power is skewed in favour of one

Marxism: a political and economic theory of society as being constituted of different classes which are in a constant state of conflict

masculinist: conforming to ideas and values associated with being masculine, e.g., assertiveness, confidence, competitiveness

maternal–child attachment: early bonds between mother and child

medicalization: a process where human conditions and problems are defined and treated as medical conditions, and then become the subject of medical study, diagnosis, prevention or treatment; it is a label that was devised by sociologists in terms of the role and power of professionals, patients and corporations, and also for its implications for ordinary people whose self-identity and life decisions may depend on the prevailing concepts of health and illness

mental health: a level of psychological well-being or an absence of a mental disorder. From a holistic perspective, mental health may include a person's ability to enjoy life, and create a balance between life activities and efforts to achieve psychological resilience; mental health can also be defined as an expression of emotions, and as signifying a successful adaptation to a range of demands

method(s): the tools we use for data gathering, e.g., questionnaires, interviews, observation

methodology: the theoretical, systematic analysis of the methods applied to a field of study; the theoretical analysis of the body of methods and principles associated with a branch of knowledge

mind–body relationship: how mental and physical well-being are interrelated

monopoly power: when an individual or group has a dominant position and control over a sphere of work and can prevent others from gaining access

neoliberalism: an economic philosophy that espouses free-market economics and globalized free trade; this set of economic policies has become widespread during the last twenty-five years or so; 'liberalism' can refer to political, economic or even religious ideas, and 'neo' means we are talking about a new kind of liberalism

neuroscience: the scientific study of the nervous system; it is an interdisciplinary science that collaborates with other fields to include different approaches used to study the molecular, cellular, developmental, structural, functional, evolutionary, computational and medical aspects of the nervous system

objectivity: the view that research can, and some would argue should, be value free, that is, unaffected by the researcher's view, opinions and so on

OECD: the Organization for Economic Co-operation and Development (OECD) is an international organization that assists governments to address the economic, social and governance challenges of a globalized economy

outcome-contingent risks: are taken in order to achieve other benefits and therefore should be assessed in relation to informed choice; the management of outcome-contingent risks always involves trade-offs, e.g., between autonomy and safety

outcome-independent risks: are not undertaken in order to achieve gains and therefore should be avoided as far as possible, e.g., medical errors

oxymoron: a figure of speech in which apparently contradictory terms appear in conjunction

paradigm: an accepted way of viewing the world

patriarchy/ patriarchal: a social system in which men are the primary authority figures central to social organization; it implies the institutions of male rule and privilege, and entails female subordination; the female equivalent is matriarchy

phenomenon: something experienced or that can be observed

policy implementation: the stage/phase in the policy process where the ideas/principles stated in the policy are put into action

psychoactive medication: a chemical substance that crosses the blood–brain barrier and acts primarily upon the central nervous system where it affects brain function, resulting in alterations in perception, mood, consciousness, cognition and behaviour; many psychoactive drugs have therapeutic utility, e.g., as anaesthetics, analgesia, or for the treatment of psychiatric disorders

public health: the promotion of health of entire populations through prevention of disease and injury

public social arena: or public sphere, related to participation by many

quantitative terms: the statistical measure of an event occurring

quickening: the feeling of early fetal movements

rationalism: the principle or habit of accepting reason as the supreme authority in matters of opinion, belief or conduct

relative risk: used to compare the differences in risk between two or more categories of people

research process: a step-by-step process of undertaking research where the researcher progresses from one step to the next; however, the steps need to be viewed as an iterative process rather than a fixed set of steps

research product: variably called data, findings, results – is the knowledge we present at the end of the project

root cause analysis: 'a technique used to uncover the underlying causes of a patient safety incident' (National Patient Safety Agency (NPSA), 2009a:16)

social capital: connections within and between social networks, meaning that social networks have value. Networks and trusting, meaningful relationships are important, as social contacts affect the productivity of individuals and groups in the maternity services, for example

social cohesion: describes the bonds that bring people together in society

social construct: a social mechanism or a category created and developed by society; a perception of an individual, group or idea that is 'constructed' through cultural or social practice

social determinants of health: living conditions shaped by distribution of resources, largely responsible for health inequities

social exclusion: refers to processes in which individuals or entire communities of people are systematically blocked from rights, opportunities and resources which are normally available to members of society and which are key to social integration

social inequalities: refers to relational processes in society that have the effect of limiting or harming a group's social status, social class and social circle; areas of social inequality, for example, access to voting rights, freedom of speech and assembly, the extent of property rights and access to education, health care and quality housing

social justice: is based on the concepts of human rights and equality

social structures: the way that society is organized and constructed

sociohistorical lens: using the intersection of social and historical factors

soft markers: variations seen on an ultrasound scan that are not usually significant but may be an indication of a serious problem in the fetus

stigma: a mark or symbol of social disapproval

stillbirth: born after twenty-four or more weeks' completed gestation without, at any time, breathing or showing signs of life

stratified: arranged or classified, for example, stratifying women into a well-defined risk group. Social stratification is not simply a reflection of individual differences; it is carried over from generation to generation and is universal but variable; a stratified society does not just have inequity but beliefs justifying social positions

structuralism/ structuralist theory: a sociological perspective of the social world which asserts there is a set of social structures which are unobservable, yet which generate observable social phenomena; often concerned with the location of power

subjectivity: researcher involvement and influence within research which was, and sometimes still is, viewed negatively

symbolic interactionism: a major sociological perspective that puts forward the idea that people act towards things based on the meaning those things have for them; and these meanings are derived from social interaction and modified through interpretation

taboo subject: not considered appropriate for conversation

technocratic: is a form of government in which scientists and technical experts are in control

technological imperative: the idea that once a technology becomes available there is a concerted move to adopt it, with whatever the technology replaces being viewed as obsolete or inferior

theoretical framework: concepts, definitions and theories as tools for analysis

theoretical perspective: a philosophical stance or way of viewing the world that acts as a 'lens' through which we can describe social situations

theorized subjectivity: acknowledges the inevitability of subjectivity and argues for researcher vigilance as to its significance

References

Abbott, P. 2006 Gender. In G. Payne (ed.), *Social Divisions*, 2nd edn. Palgrave Macmillan, pp. 65–101.

Abbott, S., Shaw, S. and Elston, J. 2004 Comparative analysis of health policy implementation – the use of documentary analysis. *Policy Studies* 25/4: 259–66.

Abramsky, L. and Chapple, J. 2003 (eds) *Prenatal Diagnosis: The Human Side*, 2nd edn. Nelson Thornes.

Adebowale, M. 2002 Towards a socially inclusive sustainable development research agenda. In Malcolm Eames and Maria Adebowale (eds), *Sustainable Development and Social Inclusion: Towards an Integrated Approach to Research.* Joseph Rowntree Foundation, pp. 4–14.

Addicott, R. 2011 *What are the Challenges and Opportunities for Social Enterprise? Social Enterprise Summit – Bridging Co-operation and Competition in the NHS?* The King's Fund.

Afshar, H. 1994 Muslim women in west Yorkshire: growing up with real and imaginary values amidst conflicting views of self and society. In H. Afshar and M. Maynard (eds), *The Dynamics of 'Race' and Gender: Some Feminist Interventions.* Taylor & Francis, pp. 127–47.

Ahman, A., Runestam, K. and Sarkadi, A. 2010 Did I really want to know this? Pregnant women's reaction to detection of a soft marker during ultrasound screening. *Patient Education and Counseling* 81: 87–93.

Aikins Murphy, P. 1994 Editorial: risk, risk assessment and risk labels. *Journal of Nurse Midwifery* 39/2: 67–9.

AIMS 2004 *Health Visitors are Now the Health Police*, press release (1 October). At <http://www.aims.org.uk>.

Alaszewski, A. 1998 Risk in modern society. In A. Alaszewski, L. Harrison and J. Manthorpe (eds), *Risk, Health and Welfare.* Open University Press, pp. 3–23.

Alaszewski, A. 2003 Risk, clinical governance and best value: restoring confidence in health and social care. In S. Pickering and J. Thompson (eds), *Clinical Governance and Best Value: Meeting the Modernisation Agenda.* Churchill Livingstone.

Alaszewski, A. 2005 Risk communication: identifying the importance of social context. *Health, Risk and Society* 7/2: 101–5.

Alaszewski, A. 2010 Information about health risks. In B. Heyman, M. Shaw, A. Alaszewski and M. Titterton (eds), *Risk, Safety and Clinical Practice: Health Care through the Lens of Risk.* Oxford University Press. pp. 123–36.

Aldridge, A., Kenway, P., MacInnes, T. and Parekh, A. 2012 *Monitoring Poverty and Social Exclusion.* Joseph Rowntree Foundation and New Policy Institute. At <http://www.jrf.org.uk/>.

Alfirevic, Z., Devane, D. and Gyte, G. M. 2006 Continuous cardiotocography (CTG) as a form of electronic fetal monitoring (EFM) for fetal assessment during labour. *Cochrane Database of Systematic Reviews* 3, Art. No.: CD006066. DOI: 10.1002/14651858.CD006066.

Allan, H. 2001 Nursing the clinic and managing emotions in a fertility unit: findings from an ethnographic study. *Human Fertility* 4/1: 18–23.

Allan, H. 2002 Nursing the clinic, being there and hovering: ways of caring in a British fertility unit. *Journal of Advanced Nursing* 38/1: 86–93.

Allan, H. 2007 Experiences of infertility: liminality and the role of the fertility clinic. *Nursing Inquiry* 14/2: 132–9.

Allan, J., Fairtlough, G. and Heinzen, B. 2002 *The Power of the Tale: Using Narratives for Organizational Success.* John Wiley.

Allen, D., Griffiths, L. and Lyne, P. 2004 Accommodating health and social care needs: routine resource allocation in stroke rehabilitation. *Sociology of Health & Illness* 26/4: 411–32.

Alliance for Natural Health 2008 *Sustainable Healthcare – Working towards the Paragdigm Shift.* ANH.

Allsop, J. 2000 *Health Policy and the NHS – towards 2000.* Longman.

Amnesty International 2010 *Deadly Delivery: The Maternal Health Care Crisis in the USA.* Amnesty International Secretariat. At <http://www.amnestyusa.org/>.

Andersen, L.B., Melvaer, L.B., Videbech, P. and Lamint, R. F. 2012 Risk factors for developing post-traumatic stress disorder following childbirth: a systematic review. *Acta Obstet Gynecol Scand.* 91/11: 1261–72; doi: 10.1111/j.1600--0412.2012.01476.x. Epub 13 August 2012.

Angelini, D. J. and Kriebs, J. 2005 Liability and risk management issues in midwifery. *Journal of Midwifery and Women's Health* 50/6: 453.

Annells, M. 2007 Guest editorial: what's common with qualitative nursing research these days? *Journal of Clinical Nursing* 16/2: 223–4.

Antrobus, S., Masterson, A. and Bailey, J. 2004 Scaling the political ladder. *Nursing Management* 11/97: 23–8.

Aphramor, L. 2005 Is a weight-centred health framework salutogenic? Some thoughts on unhinging certain dietary ideologies, *Social Theory & Health,* 3/4: 315–40.

Apple R. 1987 *Mothers and Medicine – a Social History of Infant Feeding 1890–1950.* University of Wisconsin Press.

Armstrong, N. and Eborall, H. 2012 The sociology of medical screening: past, present and future. *Sociology of Health and Illness* 34/2: 161–76.

Aune, I. and Moller, A. 2012 'I want a choice, but I don't want to decide' – a qualitative study of pregnant women's experiences regarding early ultrasound risk assessment for chromosomal anomalies. *Midwifery* 28: 14–23.

Bacon, L. and Aphramor, L. 2011 Weight science: evaluating the evidence for a paradigm shift, *Nutrition Journal,* 10/9. At <http://www.nutritionj.com/content/10/1/9>.

Baer, E. 1982 Babies means business. *New Internationalist* 110 (April): 22–3.

Baer, H. and Singer, M. 2008 *Global Warming and the Political Ecology of Health: Emerging Crises and Systemic Solutions.* Left Coast Press.

Bailey, L. 1999 Refracted selves? A study of changes in self-identity in the transition to motherhood. *Sociology* 33/2: 335–52.

Ball, L., Curtis, P. and Kirkham, M. (2002) *Why Do Midwives Leave?* Royal College of Midwives.

Balsamo, F., De Mari, G., Maher, V. and Serini, R. 1992 Production and pleasure: research on breastfeeding in Turin. In V. Maher (ed.), *The Anthropology of Breastfeeding, Natural Law or Social Construct.* Berg Publishers, pp. 59–90.

Barnes, C. 1991 *Disabled People in Britain and Discrimination: A Case for Anti-discrimination Legislation.* Hurst.

Barnes, C. and Mercer, G. 2010 *Exploring Disability,* 2nd edn. Polity.

Barrett, S. M. 2004 Implementation studies: time for a revival? Personal reflections on 20 years of implementation studies. *Public Administration* 82/2: 249–62.

Barrett, S. and Fudge, C. 1981 Examining the policy–action relationship. In S. Barrett and C. Fudge (eds), *Policy and Action: Essays on the Implementation of Public Policy*. Methuen, pp. 3–32.

Bartlett, A. 2002 Breastfeeding as headwork: corporeal feminism and meaning for breastfeeding. *Women's Studies International Forum* 885: 1–10.

Barton, A. 2008 New Labour's management, audit and 'what works' approach to controlling 'untrustworthy' professions. *Public Policy and Administration* 23: 263–77.

Bauman, Z. 1998 *Globalization: The Human Consequences*. Polity.

Baumslag, N. and Michels, D. L. 1995 *Milk, Money and Madness – The Culture and Politics of Breastfeeding*. Bergin & Garvey.

BBC (2012) Fetus parties: worries over the commercialization of pregnancy, according to CEO, Royal College of Midwives. At <http://www.bbc.co.uk/news/health-16223121>.

Beake, S., Pellowe, C., Schmied, V., Dykes, F. and Bick, D. 2011 A systematic review of structured versus non-structured programmes to support the initiation and duration of exclusive breastfeeding in acute and primary care settings. *Maternal and Child Nutrition* 8: 141–61.

Beck, U. 1992 *Risk Society: Towards a New Modernity*. Sage Publications.

Beck, U. 2009 *World at Risk*. Polity.

Becker, G. 2000 *The Elusive Embryo: How Women and Men Approach New Reproductive Technologies*. University of California Press.

Becker, G. and Nachtigall, R. D. 1992 Eager for medicalization: the social production of infertility as a disease. *Sociology of Health and Illness* 14/4: 456–71.

Beech, B. L. 2010 Midwifery – who cares what women want? *AIMS Journal* 22/1 (2010): 3–4.

Begley, C. et al. 2010 The Strengths and Weaknesses of Publicly-funded Irish Health Services Provided to Women with Disabilities in Relation to Pregnancy, Childbirth and Early Motherhood. Dublin: National Disability Authority. At <http://www.nda.ie/cntmgmtnew.nsf/0/419BBFC356BC438A80257705003FA51D/$File/NDA%20report%20final%20draft%20_full_%2018th%20May%202010.pdf>.

Bell, A. 2010 Beyond (financial) accessibility: inequalities within the medicalization of infertility. *Sociology of Health and Illness* 32/4: 631–46.

Benazon, N., Wright, J. and Sabourin, S. 1992 Stress, sexual satisfaction, and marital adjustment in infertile couples. *Journal of Sex & Marital Therapy* 18/4: 273–84.

Benn, M. 1998 *Madonna and Child: Towards a New Politics of Motherhood*. Jonathan Cape.

Benner, P. 2000 The quest for control and the possibilities of care. In M. A. Wrathall and J. Malpas (eds), *Heidegger, Coping and Cognitive Science*, vol. 2. MIT Press, pp. 293–309.

Berg, M., Lundgren, I., Hermansson, E. and Wahlberg, V. 1996 Women's experience of the encounter with the midwife during childbirth. *Midwifery* 12: 11–15.

Berry, D. 2004 *Risk Communication and Health Psychology*. Open University Press.

Berry, N. and Jones, S. 2010 It's all formula to me: women's understandings of toddler milk ads. *Breastfeeding Review* 17: 21–30.

Best, S. 2003 *A Beginner's Guide to Social Theory*. Sage Publications.

Bharj, K. and Phillips, M. 2013 *The Policy Context of Midwifery and Maternity Services*. Routledge.

Billante, V. 2008 *Health Promotion and Sustainability Through Environmental Design. A Guide for Planning*. Christchurch City Council.

BirthChoiceUK.com. 2013 Historical statistics. At <http://www.birthchoiceuk.com/>.

Birthplace in England Collaborative Group 2011 Perinatal and maternal outcomes by planned place of birth for healthy women with low risk pregnancies: the Birthplace in England national prospective cohort study. *British Medical Journal* 343. d7400.

BJOG 2011. *Saving Mothers' Lives. Reviewing Maternal Deaths to Make Motherhood Safer: 2006–2008 The Eighth Report of the Confidential Enquiries into Maternal Deaths in the United Kingdom.* Wiley-Blackwell.

Black, A. and C. 2007 *Dictionary of Nursing: Over 11,000 Terms Clearly Defined,* 2nd edn. A&C Black.

Bloomfield, L., Kendall, S., Applin, L., Attarzadeh, V., Dearnley, K., Edwards, L., Hinshelwood, L., Lloyd, P. and Newcombe, T. 2005 A qualitative study exploring the experiences and views of mothers, health visitors and family support centre workers on the challenges and difficulties of parenting. *Health & Social Care in the Community* 13: 46–55.

Bogren, M. U., Bajracharya, K., Berg, M., Erlandsson, K., Ireland, J., Simkhada, P. and van Teijlingen, E. 2013 Nepal needs midwifery, *Journal of Manmohan Memorial Institute of Health Sciences (JMMIHS)* 1/2: 41–4.

Boivin, J., Bunting, L., Collins, J. A. and Nygren, K. G. 2007 International estimates of infertility prevalence and treatment-seeking: potential need and demand for infertility medical care. *Hum Reprod.* 22: 1506–12.

Bolton, S. C. 2000 Who cares? Offering emotion work as a 'gift' in the nursing labour process. *Journal of Advanced Nursing* 32: 580–6.

Bolton, S. C. 2005 *Emotion Management in the Workplace.* Palgrave Macmillan.

Bone, D. 2002 Dilemmas of emotion work in nursing under market-driven health care, *International Journal of Public Sector Management* 15/2: 140–50.

Bonnie, S. 2003 *Disability and Sexuality: An Irish Perspective.* Keynote speech from Sexuality, Disability and Relationships Conference 2003.

Bordo, S. 1995. *Unbearable Weight: Feminism, Western Culture and the Body.* University of California Press.

Bourdieu, P. 1985 The forms of social capital. In G. Richardson (ed.), *Handbook of Theory and Research for the Sociology of Education.* Greenwood.

Bourdieu, P. et al. 2006 *The Weight of the World: Social Suffering in Contemporary Society.* Polity.

Boyle, D. 2011 *The Human Element: Ten New Rules to Kick–start Our Failing Organisations.* Routledge.

Bowlby, J. 1979. *The Making and Breaking of Affectional Bonds.* Tavistock.

Bramwell, R. 2001 Blood and milk: constructions of female bodily fluids in western society. *Women and Health* 34: 85–96.

Bridges, K. M. 2011 *Reproducing Race: An Ethnography of Pregnancy as a Site of Racialisation.* University of California Press.

Bromley, D. W. 2008 'Sustainability', *The New Palgrave Dictionary of Economics,* 2nd edn. Abstract.

Brown, B., Crawford, P. and Hicks, C. 2008 *Evidence-Based Research, Dilemmas and Debates in Health Care.* Open University Press.

Brown, G. W. and Harris, T. 1978 *The Social Origins of Depression.* Tavistock Publications.

Brown, G. W. and Harris, T. 1989 *Life Events and Illness,* Guildford Press.

Brown, S. and Lumley, J. 2000 Physical health problems after childbirth and maternal depression at six to seven months postpartum. *BJOG: An International Journal of Obstetrics and Gynaecology* 107: 1194–1201. doi: 10.1111/j.1471-0528.2000.tb11607.x.

Brunton G., Wiggins, M. and Oakley, A. 2011 Becoming a mother: a research synthesis of women's views on the experience of first-time motherhood. London, EPPI Centre, Social Science Research Unit, Institute of Education University of London.

Bryant, J. et al. 2007 Caesarean birth: Consumption, safety, order and good mothering. *Social Science and Medicine* 65: 1192–1201.

Bryson, V. and Deery, R. 2009 Public policy, 'men's time' and power: the work of community midwives in the British National Health Service, *Women's Studies International Forum*, doi:org/10.1016/j.wsif.2009.11.004.

Bryson, V. and Deery, R. 2010 Social justice and time: the impact of public sector reform on the work of midwives in the National Health Service. In Valerie Bryson and Pamela Fisher (eds), *Redefining Social Justice: New Labour Rhetoric and Reality*. Manchester University Press, pp. 99–118.

Bunton, R. and Peterson, A. 2002. *The New Genetics and the Public's Health*. Routledge.

Burawoy, M. 2005. 2004 American Sociological Association presidential address: for public sociology, *The British Journal of Sociology* 56/2: 259–94.

Burke, T. 2012 Climate change: what needs to be done. *British Medical Journal* 344: e1358. At <http://www.bmj.com/>.

Burr, J. and Chapman, T. 2004 Contextualising experiences of depression in women from South Asian communities: a discursive approach. *Sociology of Health & Illness* 26: 433–52.

Bury, M. 1982 Chronic illness as biographical disruption. *Sociology of Health & Illness* 4: 167–82.

Bury, M. 1991 The sociology of chronic illness: a review of research and prospects *Sociology of Health and Illness* 13/4: 451–68.

Bury, M. 1997 *Health and Illness in a Changing Society*. Routledge.

Busfield, J. 2010 Gender and mental health. In E. Kuhlmann and E. Annandale (eds), *The Palgrave Handbook of Gender and Healthcare*. Palgrave Macmillan, pp. 192–208.

Byrne, D. 2005 *Social Exclusion*, 2nd edn. Open University Press.

Cacciatore, J. 2011 Psychosocial care. In C. Y. Spong (ed.), *Stillbirth: Prediction, Prevention and Management*. Blackwell, pp. 203–28.

Cacciatore, J., Rådestad, I. and Frederik Frøen, J. 2008 Effects of contact with stillborn babies on maternal anxiety and depression. *Birth: Issues in Perinatal Health* 35/4: 313–20.

Caird, J., Rees, R., Kavanagh, J., Sutcliffe, K., Oliver, K., Dickson, K., Woodman, J., Barnett-Page, E. and Thomas, J. 2010 *The Socioeconomic Value of Nursing and Midwifery: A Rapid Systematic Review of Reviews*. EPPI Centre, Social Science Research Unit, Institute of Education.

Cameron, A. and Palen, R. 2004 *The Imagined Economies of Globalization*. Sage Publications.

Cameron, J, Taylor, J. and Greene, A. 2008 Representations of rituals and care in perinatal death in British midwifery textbooks 1937–2004. *Midwifery* 24: 335–43.

Cannon, S. 1989 Social research in stressful settings: difficulties for the sociologist studying the treatment of breast cancer. *Sociology of Health and Illness* 11/1: 62–77.

Carlson, N. S. and Lowe, N. 2006 Centering pregnancy: a new approach in prenatal care. *The American Journal of Maternal Child Nursing* 31/4: 218–23.

Carmack, B. J. 1997 Balancing engagement and detachment in caregiving. *Image: Journal of Nursing Scholarship* 29/2: 139–43.

Carolan, M. C. 2008 Towards understanding the concept of risk for pregnant women: some nursing and midwifery implications. *Journal of Clinical Nursing* 18: 652–8.

Carter, P. 1995 *Feminism, Breasts and Breastfeeding*. Macmillan.

CEMACH 2007 *Confidential Enquiry into Maternal and Child Health. Diabetes in Pregnancy: Are We Providing the Best Care?* CEMACH.

Centre for Maternal and Child Enquiries (CMACE) 2011 Saving mothers' lives:

reviewing maternal deaths to make motherhood safer: 2006–2008. The eighth report on confidential enquiries into maternal deaths in the United Kingdom. *BJOG* 118 (Suppl. 1): 1–203.

Chan, M. 2009 Impact of financial crisis on health: a truly global solution is needed. Statement by WHO Director-General, Dr Margaret Chan. At <http://www.who. int/ mediacentre/news/statements/2009/financial_crisis_20090401/en/index. html>.

Chan, M. F., Lou, F. L., Zang, Y. L., Chung, Y. F., Wu, L. H., and Cao, F. L. et al. 2007 Attitudes of midwives towards perinatal bereavement in Hong Kong. *Midwifery* 23/3: 309–21.

Chesler, P. 1972 *Women and Madness.* Doubleday.

Chesler, P. 2005 *Women and Madness.* Palgrave Macmillan.

Christakis, N. A. and Fowler, J. H. 2009 *Connected: The Surprising Power of Our Social Networks and How They Shape Our Lives.* Hachette Digital, Inc.

Church, S. and Earle, S. 2006 Approaches to sociology within midwifery education. *British Journal of Midwifery* 14/6: 342–5.

Clarkson, P. 1996 *The Bystander.* Whurr.

Clay, T. 1987 *Nurses, Power and Politics.* Heinemann.

CMACE 2010 *Perinatal Mortality 2008.* CMACE.

CMACE 2011 *Saving Mothers' Lives: Reviewing Maternal Deaths To Make Motherhood Safer: 2006–2008 March 2011 The Eighth Report of the Confidential Enquiries into Maternal Deaths in the United Kingdom.* BCOG 118 Supplement 1 March 2011. At <http://onlinelibrary.wiley.com/>.

Colantonio, A. 2008 Traditional and emerging prospects in social sustainability. 2008/02: *EIBURS Working Paper Series.* At <http://www.brookes.ac.uk/>.

Collins, R. 1994 *Four Sociological Traditions.* Oxford University Press.

Collins, T. 2005 Health policy analysis: a simple tool for policy makers. *Public Health* 119: 192–6.

Commission on the Future of Nursing and Midwifery in England 2010 *Frontline Care.* Department of Health.

Conrad, P. 2005 The shifting engines of medicalization. *Journal of Health & Social Behavior* 46: 3–13.

Conway, R. and Rene, A. 2004 Obesity as a disease: no lightweight matter. *Obesity Reviews* 5: 145–51.

Cooke, H. 1993 Why teach sociology? *Nurse Education Today* 13/3: 210–17.

Cooke A., Mills, T. A. and Lavender, T. 2011 Advanced maternal age: delayed childbearing is rarely a conscious choice. A qualitative study of women's views and experiences. *International Journal of Nursing Studies;* doi: 10 10 16/j. inurstu.201107013.

Cooper, C. 1997 Can a fat woman call herself disabled? *Disability & Society* 12/1: 31–41.

Corea, G. 1985 *The Mother Machine: Reproductive Technologies from Artificial Insemination to Artificial Wombs.* Harper & Row.

Corea, G. 1987 *Man-Made Women: How New Reproductive Technologies Affect Women.* Indiana University Press.

Corbin, J. M. 1987 Women's perceptions and management of a pregnancy complicated by chronic illness. *Health Care for Women International* 8: 317–37.

Corrigan, P. W. and Watson, A. C. 2002 Understanding the impact of stigma on people with mental illness. *World Psychiatry* 1/1: 16–20.

Cotterill, P. 1994 *Friendly Relations? Mothers and Their Daughters-in-law.* Taylor & Francis.

Cotterill, P. and Letherby, G. 1993 Weaving stories: personal auto/biographies in feminist research. *Sociology* 27/1: 67–80.

Cox, D. 2010 Health policy. In E. Denny and S. Earle (eds), *Sociology for Nurses*, 2nd edn. Polity, pp. 293–310.

Cox, J. L., Holden, J. M. and Sagovsky, R. 1987 Detection of postnatal depression – development of the 10-item Edinburgh postnatal depression scale. *British Journal of Psychiatry* 150: 782–6.

Crinson, I. 2008 *Health Policy: A Critical Perspective*. Sage Publications.

Crossley, N. 2004 Fat is a sociological issue: obesity roles in late modern 'Body Conscious' societies. *Social Theory and Health* 2: 222–35.

Crow, L. 1996 Including all of our lives: renewing the social model of disability. In Barnes, C. and Mercer, G. (eds), *Exploring the Divide: Illness and Disability*. Disability Press, pp. 55–73.

Crowe, C. 1985 'Women want it': In-vitro fertilization and women's motivations for participation. *Women's Studies International Forum* 8/6: 547–52.

Culley, L. and Hudson, N. 2006 Diverse bodies and disrupted reproduction: infertility and minority ethnic communities in the UK. *International Journal of Diversity in Organizations, Communities and Nations* 5/2: 117–26.

Culley L. and Hudson N. 2009 Constructing relatedness: ethnicity, gender and third party assisted conception in the UK. *Current Sociology* 57/2: 257–75.

Culley, L., Hudson, N. and Van Rooij, F. (eds) 2009 *Marginalized Reproduction: Ethnicity, Infertility and New Reproductive Technologies*. Earthscan.

Culley, L., Hudson, N., Blyth, E., Norton. W., Pacey, A. and Rapport, F. 2011 *Transnational Reproduction: An Exploratory Study of UK Residents who Travel Abroad for Fertility Treatment Summary Report*. At <http://www.transrep.co.uk/>.

Culley, L., Rapport, F., Johnson, M., Katbamna, S. and Hudson, N. 2004 *Improving Policy and Practice: A Study of the Provision of Infertility Services to South Asian Communities. Report to Dept. of Health*. De Montfort University.

Culley, L. A., Hudson, N., Rapport, F. L., Katbamna, S. and Johnson, M. R. D. 2006 British South Asian communities and infertility services. *Human Fertility* 9/1: 37–45.

Culley, L. et al. 2011 Crossing borders for fertility treatment: motivations, destinations and outcomes of UK fertility travelers. *Human Reproduction*. 26/9: 2373–81.

Cussins, C. 1998 Producing reproduction: techniques of normalization and naturalization in infertility clinics. In S. Franklin and H. Ragoné (eds), *Reproducing Reproduction: Kinship, Power, and Technological Innovation*. University of Pennsylvania Press, pp. 66–101.

Dahlen, H. 2011 Perspectives on risk, or risk in perspective? *Essentially MIDIRS* 2/7:17–21.

Damsio, A. 2006 *Decartes' Error*. Vintage.

Dancet, E.A.F. et al. 2012 Patients from across Europe have similar views on patient-centred care: an international multilingual qualitative study in infertility care. *Human Reproduction* 27/6: 1702–11.

Davidson, D. 2007 *The Emergence of Hospital Protocols for Perinatal Loss, 1950–2000*. York University (Canada). ProQuest Dissertations and Theses, n/a.

Davidson, D. 2008 A technology of care: caregiver response to perinatal loss. *Women's Studies International Forum* 31/4: 278–84.

Davidson, D. 2010 Grief, child loss. In A. O'Reilly (ed.), *Encyclopedia of Motherhood*. Sage Publications, pp. 467–70.

Davidson, D. 2011 Reflections on doing research grounded in my experience of perinatal loss: From auto/biography to autoethnography. *Sociological Research Online* 16/1. At <http://www.socresonline.org.uk>.

Davidson, D. and Letherby, G. 2010 Motherhood denied. In A. O'Reilly (ed.), *Encyclopedia of Motherhood*. Sage Publications, pp. 815–17.

Davidson, D. and Stahls, H. 2011 Maternal grief: creating an environment for dialogue. *Journal of the Motherhood Initiative for Research and Community Involvement* 1/2: 16–25.

Davies, C. 1996 The sociology of professions and the profession of gender. *Sociology* 30/4: 661–78.

Davies, J. 2001 Being with women who are economically without. In M. Kirkham (ed.), *The Midwife – Mother Relationship*, 1st edn. Macmillan, pp. 120–42.

Davies, L. and Deery, R. 2014 *Nutrition in Pregnancy and Childbirth, Food for Thought.* Routledge.

Davies, L., Daellenbach, R. and Kensington, M. (eds) 2010 *Sustainability, Midwifery and Birth.* Routledge.

Davis, E. 1997 *Heart and Hands: A Midwife's Guide to Pregnancy and Birth.* Celestial Arts.

Davis, J. Watson, N. and Cunningham-Burley, S. 2000 Learning the lives of disabled children. In P. Christensen and A. James (eds), *Research with Children: Perspectives and Practices.* Psychology Press.

Davis-Floyd, R. (ed.) 2009 *Birth Models That Work.* University of California Press.

Davis-Floyd, R. E., Bourgeault, I. L. and Benoit, C. 1994 *Reconceiving Midwifery.* McGill-Queen's University Press.

Deery, R. 2005 An action research study exploring midwives' support needs and the effect of group clinical supervision. *Midwifery* 21/2: 161–76.

Deery, R. 2008 The tyranny of time: tensions between relational and clock time in community based midwifery. *Social Theory and Health* 6/4: 342–63, doi:10.1057/sth.2008.13.

Deery, R. 2010 Transfers from midwife led to obstetric led care: some insights from midwives. *Essentially MIDIRS* 1/3: 17–22.

Deery, R. 2011 'Obesing' pregnant women: by whom, and for what reasons? *AIMS Journal* 23/4: 12–13.

Deery, R. 2012 Connection as part of soulful midwifery. *The Practising Midwife* (September) 15/8: 5.

Deery, R. 2014 Resilience, self-compassion and mindfulness in midwifery. *The Practising Midwife* 17/2: 5.

Deery, R. and Fisher, P. 2010 'Switching and swapping faces': performativity and emotion in midwifery. *International Journal of Work Organization and Emotion* 3/3: 270–86.

Deery, R. and Hunter, B. 2010 Emotion work and relationships in midwifery: enhancing or challenging? In M. Kirkham (ed.), *The Midwife–Mother Relationship*, 2nd edn. Palgrave Macmillan, chapter 3, pp. 37–54.

Deery, R. and Kirkham, M. 2006 Supporting midwives to support women. In L. Page and R. McCandlish (eds), *The New Midwifery: Science and Sensitivity in Practice*, 2nd edn. Elsevier Ltd, chapter 6, pp.125–40.

Deery, R. and Kirkham, M. 2007 Drained and dumped on: the generation and accumulation of emotional toxic waste in community midwifery. In M. Kirkham (ed.), *Exploring the Dirty Side of Women's Health.* Routledge, pp. 72–83.

Deery, R. and Wray, S. 2009 'The hardest leap': acceptance of diverse body size in midwifery. *The Practising Midwife* 12/10: 14–16.

Deery, R, Hughes, D. and Kirkham, M. 2010 *Tensions and Barriers to improving Maternity Care: The Story of a Struggling Birth Centre.* Radcliffe Publishing.

Denny, E. 1994 Liberation or oppression? Radical feminism and in-vitro fertilization. *Sociology of Health and Illness* 16/1: 62–80.

Denny, E. 1996 New reproductive technologies: the views of women undergoing treatment. In Williams and Calnan (eds), *Modern Medicine. Lay Perspectives and Experiences.* UCL Press, pp. 207–28.

Denzin, N. K. 1994 The art and politics of interpretation. In N. K. Denzin and Y. S. Lincoln (eds), *Handbook of Qualitative Research*. Sage Publications.

Department of Health 1989 *Working for Patients* (Cm555). Department of Health.

Department of Health 1993 *Changing Childbirth*, part 1 (Report of the Expert Maternity Group). HMSO.

Department of Health 1997 *The New NHS: Modern, Dependable*. The Stationery Office.

Department of Health 1999 *Agenda for Change – Modernising the NHS Pay System*. Department of Health.

Department of Health 2000 *The NHS Plan – A Plan for Investment, a Plan for Reform*. Department of Health.

Department of Health 2004 *Better Information, Better Choices, Better Health: Putting Information at the Centre of Health*. Department of Health.

Department of Health 2004a *National Services Framework for Children, Young People and Maternity Services*. Department of Health.

Department of Health 2004b *Agenda for Change – Final Agreement* (3614). Department of Health.

Department of Health 2004c *NHS Job Evaluation Handbook*, 2nd edn (3615). Department of Health.

Department of Health 2007a *National Service Framework for Children, Young People and Maternity Services Standard 11: Maternity Services*. Department of Health.

Department of Health 2007b *Maternity Matters: Choice, Access and Continuity of Care in a Safe Service*. Department of Health. At <http://www.dh.gov.uk/>.

Department of Health 2008a *High Quality Care for All: NHS Next Stage Review Final Report*. Department of Health.

Department of Health 2008b *Framing the Nursing and Midwifery Contribution: Driving Up the Quality of Care*. Department of Health.

Department of Health 2008c *A High Quality Workforce: NHS Next Stage Review*. Department of Health.

Department of Health 2009 *Delivering High-quality Midwife Care: The Priorities, Opportunities and Challenges for Midwives*. Department of Health.

Department of Health 2011a *The Government's response to the recommendations in Front Line Care: The Report of the Prime Minister's Commission on the Future of Nursing and Midwifery in England*. Department of Health.

Department of Health 2011b *About the Chief Nursing Officer*. At <http://www.dh.gov.uk/>.

Department of Health 2012 *Payment by Results*. At <http://www.dh.gov.uk/>.

de Swiet, M., Williamson, C. and Lewis, G. 2011 Other indirect deaths. In Centre for Maternal and Child Enquiries (CMACE), *Saving Mothers' Lives: Reviewing Maternal Deaths to Make Motherhood Safer: 2006–2008. The Eighth Report on Confidential Enquiries into Maternal Deaths in the United Kingdom*, BJOG 118 (Suppl. 1): 119–31.

Devane, D., Brennan, M., Begley, C., Clarke, M., Walsh, D., Sandall, J., Ryan, P., Revill, P. and Normand, C. 2010 *Socioeconomic Value of the Midwife: A Systematic Review, Meta-analysis, Meta-synthesis and Economic Analysis of Midwife-led Models of Care*. Royal College of Midwives.

De Vries, R. 2012 Keynote Speech at *Human Rights in Childbirth Conference*, The Hague, Netherlands.

Dewar, B. and Nolan, M. 2013 Caring about caring: developing a model to implement compassionate relationship-centred care in an older-people care setting. *International Journal of Nursing Studies* 50: 1247–58.

DfES 2004 *Every Child Matters: Change for Children*. Department for Education and Skills.

Doka, K. 1989 *Disenfranchised Grief: Recognizing Hidden Sorrow*. Lexington Books.

Domar A., Broome, A., Zuttermeister, P.C., Seibel, M. and Friedman, R. 1992 The prevalence and predictability of depression in infertile women. *Fertility and Sterility* 58/6: 1158–63.

Donnison, J. 1977 *Midwives and Medical Men*. Heinemann.

do Paco, A., Rodrigues, R. G., Duarte, P., Pinheiro, P. and de Oliveira J. M. 2010 The role of marketing in the promotion of breastfeeding. *Journal of Medical Marketing* 10: 199–212.

Dorey, P. 2005 *Policy Making in Britain – An Introduction*. Sage Publications.

Downe, S. and McCourt, C. 2008 From being to becoming: reconstructing childbirth knowledges. In S. Downe (ed.), *Normal Childbirth: Evidence and Debate*, 2nd edn. Churchill Livingstone, pp. 3–28.

Downe, S., Kingdon, C., Kennedy, R., Norwell, H., McLaughlin, M. J. and Heazell, A. E. 2012 Post-mortem examination after stillbirth: views of UK-based practitioners. *European Journal of Obstetric Gynecology Reproductive Biology* 162/1: 33–7.

Downe, S., Schmidt, E., Kingdon, C., Heazell, A. E. P. 2013 Bereaved parents' experiences of stillbirth in UK hospitals: qualitative interview study. *British Medical Journal* 3: e002237. Doi:10.1136/bmjopen-2012-002237.

Doyal, L. and Pennell, I. 1981 *The Political Economy of Health*. Pluto Press.

Drentea, P. and Moren-Cross, J. L. 2005 Social capital and social support on the web: the case of an internet mother site. *Sociology of Health and Illness* 27/7: 920–43.

D'Souza, L. and Garcia, J. 2004 Improving services for disadvantaged women. *Child: Care, Health and Development* 30/6: 599–611.

Dunn, W. N. 2003 *Public Policy Analysis – An Introduction*, 3rd edn. Pearson/Prentice Hall.

Durkheim, E. 2007 [1897] *On Suicide*. Penguin Classics.

Dykes, F. 1999 'Falling by the wayside': a phenomenological exploration of perceived breast milk inadequacy in lactating women. *Midwifery* 15: 232–46.

Dykes, F. 2002 Western medicine and marketing – construction of an insufficient milk syndrome. *Health Care for Women International* 23: 492–502.

Dykes, F. 2005a 'Supply' and 'Demand': Breastfeeding as Labour. *Social Science & Medicine* 60/10: 2283–93.

Dykes, F. 2005b A critical ethnographic study of encounters between midwives and breastfeeding women on postnatal wards in England. *Midwifery* 21: 241–52.

Dykes, F. 2006 *Breastfeeding in Hospital: Midwives, Mothers and the Production Line*. Routledge.

Dykes, F. 2007 'Resisting the gaze': the subversive nature of breastfeeding. In M. Kirkham (ed.), *Exploring the 'Dirty' Side of Women's Health*. Routledge, pp. 87–100.

Dykes, F. and Flacking, R. 2010 Encouraging breastfeeding: a relational perspective. *Early Human Development* 86: 733–6.

Dykes, F. and Hall Moran, V. 2006 Transmitted nutritional deprivation from mother to child: a socio-biological perspective. In V. Hall Moran and F. Dykes (eds), *Maternal and Infant Nutrition and Nurture: Controversies and Challenges*. Quay Books, pp. 6–39.

Dykes, F. and Hall Moran, V. (eds) 2009 *Infant and Young Child Feeding: Challenges to Implementing a Global Strategy*. Wiley-Blackwell.

Dykes, F., Hall Moran, V., Burt, S., Edwards, J. and Whitmore, M. 2003 Adolescent mothers and breastfeeding – experiences and support needs: an exploratory study. *Journal of Human Lactation* 19: 391–401.

Dykes, F., Richardson-Foster, H., Crossland, H., Thomson, G. 2012 'Dancing on a thin line': evaluation of an Infant Feeding Information Team to implement the

WHO Code of Marketing of Breast-milk Substitutes. *Midwifery,* doi:10.1016/j. midw.2011.08.012.

Earle, S. 2000 Pregnancy and the maintenance of self-identity: implications for *Health and Social Care in the Community* 8/4: 235–41.

Earle, S. 2001. Teaching sociology within the speech and language therapy curriculum. *Education for Health* 14/3: 383–91.

Earle, S. 2007 Promoting public health in a global context. In C. E. Lloyd, S. Handsley, J. Douglas, S. Earle and S. Spurr (eds), *Policy and Practice in Promoting Public Health,* Sage Publications, pp. 1–32.

Earle, S. and Letherby, G. (eds) 2003 *Gender, Identity and Reproduction: Social Perspectives.* Palgrave Macmillan.

Earle, S. and Letherby, G. 2007 Conceiving time? Women who do or do not conceive. *Sociology of Health & Illness* 29/2: 233–50.

Earle, S. and Letherby, G. (eds) 2008 *The Sociology of Healthcare: A Reader for Health Professionals.* Palgrave Macmillan.

Ebrahim, G. L. 1991 *Breastfeeding: The Biological Option.* Macmillan Press.

Edge, D. and Rogers, A. 2005 Dealing with it: black Caribbean women's response to adversity and psychological distress associated with pregnancy, childbirth, and early motherhood. *Social Science and Medicine* 61/1: 15–25.

Edwards, A. and Elwyn, G. 2001 Understanding risk and lessons for clinical risk communication about treatment preferences. *Quality in Health Care* 10 (Suppl. 1): 9–13.

Edwards, N. P. 2005 *Birthing Autonomy: Women's Experiences of Planning Home Births.* Routledge.

Edwards, N. 2008 Safety in birth: the contextual conundrums faced by women in a 'risk society', driven by neoliberal policies. *MIDIRS* 18/4: 463–70.

Edwards, N. P. 2009 Women's emotion work in the context of current maternity services. In B. Hunter and R. Deery, *Emotions in Midwifery and Reproduction.* Palgrave Macmillan.

Edwards, N. 2010 Why does the Albany Midwifery Model work? *AIMS Journal* 22/1. At <http://www.aims.org.uk/Journal/>.

Edwards, N., Murphy-Lawless, J., Kirkham, M. and Davies, S. 2011 Attacks on midwives, attacks on women's choices. *AIMS Journal* 23/3. At <http://www.aims. org.uk/>.

Eisenberger, N. I. and Cole, S. W. 2012 Social neuroscience and health: neurophysiological mechanisms linking social ties with physical health. *Nature Neuroscience* 15/5: 669–74.

Elkington, J. 2004 *The Triple Bottom Line: Does it all Add Up?* Earthscan.

Ellam, T. P. 2010 Home Birth Bullying. *AIMS Journal* 22/1: 22–3.

Enkin, M. 1994 Risk in pregnancy: the reality, the perception, and the concept. *BIRTH.* 21/3: 131–4.

Enkin, M., Glouberman, S., Groff, P., Jadad, A. R. and Stern, A. 2006 Beyond Evidence: The Complexity of Maternity Care. *Birth* 33/4: 265–9.

Epstein, Randi Hutter 2011 *Get Me Out: A History of Childbirth from the Garden of Eden to the Sperm Bank.* W.W.Norton & Co.

Erixon, E. and van der Marel, E. 2011 What is driving the rise in health care expenditures? An Inquiry into the Nature and Causes of the Cost Disease. ECIPE Working Paper No. 05/2011. At <http://www.ecipe.org/publications/>.

Esterik Van, P. 1988 The insufficient milk syndrome: biological epidemic or cultural construction? In P. Whelehan (ed.), *Women and Health Cross-cultural Perspectives.* Bergin & Garvey, pp. 97–108.

Etzioni, A. (ed.) 1969 *The Semi-Professions and Their Organization.* Free Press.

EU 2011 The application of patients' rights in cross-border healthcare: Directive

2011/24/ EU of the European Parliament and of the Council of 9 March 2011. *Official Journal of the European Union* 88/45.

Evans, M. K. and O'Brien, B. 2005 Gestational diabetes: the meaning of an at-risk pregnancy. *Qualitative Health Research* 15/1: 66–81.

Everingham, C.R., Heading, G. and Conor, L. 2006 Couples' experiences of postnatal depression: a framing analysis of cultural identity, gender and communication. *Social Science and Medicine* 62: 1745–56.

Exley, C. and Letherby, G. 2001 Managing a disrupted lifecourse: issues of identity and emotion work. *Health* 5/1: 112–32.

Exworthy, M. 1994 The contest for control in community health services: general managers and professionals dispute decentralization. *Policy and Politics* 22/1: 17–29.

Fahy, K., Foureur, M. and Hastie, C. 2008 *Birth Territory and Midwifery Guardianship.* Elsevier.

Fairtlough, G. 1994 *Creative Compartments: A Design for Future Organisation.* Adamantine Press.

Fairtlough, G. 2005 *The Three Ways of Getting Things Done. Hierarchy, Heterarchy and Responsible Autonomy in Organizations.* Triarchy Press.

Family Planning Association (FPA) 2010 FPA response to consultation on *Teenage Pregnancy Strategy: Beyond 2010.* At: <http://www.fpa.org.uk/>.

Fatchett, A. 2012 *Social Policy for Nurses.* Polity.

Feldman, R. 2013 *When Maternity Doesn't Matter: Dispersing Pregnant Women Seeking Asylum.* Maternity Action and Refugee Council. At <http://www.refugee-council.org.uk/>.

Femia, F. and Werrell, C. 2012 *Retired General Keys and British Rear Admiral Morisetti: Climate Change a Global Security Issue.* The Centre for Climate and Security. At <http://climateandsecurity.org>.

Fenwick, J., Butt, J., Downie, J., Monterosso, L. and Wood, J. 2006 Priorities for midwifery research in Perth, Western Australia: a Delphi Study. *International Journal of Nursing Practice* 12/2: 78–93.

Fenwick, J., Staff, L., Gamble, J., Creedy, D. K. and Bayes, S. 2010 Why do women request caesarean section in a normal, healthy first pregnancy? *Midwifery* 26/4: 394–400.

Fenwick, S., Holloway, I. and Alexander, J. 2007 Achieving normality: the key to status passage to motherhood after a caesarean section. *Midwifery* 25: 554–63.

Ferraretti, A. P et al. 2012 Assisted reproductive technology in Europe, 2008: results generated from European registers by ESHRE. *Human Reproduction.* Advance Access.

Figley, C. R. 1995 Compassion fatigue as secondary traumatic stress disorder: an overview. In C. R. Figley (ed.), *Compassion Fatigue: Coping with Secondary Traumatic Stress Disorder in Those Who Treat the Traumatized.* Brunner/Mazel, pp. 1–20.

Finch, J. 2003 Commentary: a look at the bigger picture in building research capacity. *Nursing Times Research* 8/6: 427–8.

Fineman, S. 1993 Organizations as emotional arenas. In S. Fineman (ed.), *Emotion in Organizations.* Sage Publications, pp. 9–35.

Fineman, S. 2003 *Understanding Emotion at Work.* Sage Publications.

Fineman, S. 2008 *The Emotional Organization.* Blackwell.

Fisher, C. 1985 How did we go wrong with breast feeding? *Midwifery* 1: 48–51.

Fisher, C. and O'Connor, M. 2012 'Motherhood' in the context of living with breast cancer. *Cancer Nursing* 35: 157–63.

Fisher, J., Baker, G. and Hammarberg, K. (2010) Long-term health, well-being, life satisfaction, and attitudes toward parenthood in men diagnosed as infertile: challenges to gender stereotypes and implications for practice. *Fertility and Sterility.* 94/ (2): 574–80.

Fisher, P. and Byrne, V. 2012 Identity, emotion and the internal goods of practice: a study of learning disability professionals. *Sociology of Health and Illness* 34/1: 79–94.

Flynn, R. 2002 Clinical governance and governmentality. *Health, Risk and Society* 4/2: 155–73.

Flynn, M. and Mercer, D. 2013 Is compassion possible in a market-led NHS? *Nursing Times* 109/7: 12–14.

Foucault, M. 1971 *Madness and Civilization.* Tavistock.

Foucault, M. 1991 Governmentality. In G. Burchell, C. Gordon and P. Miller (eds), *The Foucault Effect.* Harvester Wheatsheaf, pp. 87–194.

Foundation for the Study of Infant Deaths 2011 Factfile 2. *Research Background to Reduce the Risk of Cot Death Advice by the Foundation for the Study of Infant Deaths.* [online] At <http://fsid.org.uk>.

Fox, N. J. 2008 Practice-based evidence: towards collaborative and transgressive research. *Sociology* 37/1: 82–102.

Francis, R. 2013 *Report of the Mid Staffordshire NHS Foundation Trust Public Inquiry* (HC 947). The Stationery Office. At <http://www.midstaffspublicinquiry.com/report>.

Frank, A. W. 2005 *The Renewal of Generosity. Illness, Medicine and How to Live.* University of Chicago Press.

Frankenberg, R. 1980 Medical anthropology and development: a theoretical perspective. *Social Science & Medicine. Part B: Medical Anthropology* 14/4: 197–207.

Franklin, S. 1997 *Embodied Progress: A Cultural Account of Assisted Conception:* Routledge.

Freeman, R. 2006 The work the document does: research, policy, and equity in health. *Journal of Health Politics, Policy and Law* 31/1: 51–70.

Freeman, R. and Maybin, J. 2011 Documents, practices and policy. *Evidence & Policy* 7/2: 155–70.

Freidson, E. 1970 *The Profession of Medicine.* University of Chicago Press.

Freire, P. 1996 *Pedagogy of the Oppressed.* Penguin.

Freshwater, D. and Robertson, C. 2002 *Emotions and Needs.* Open University Press.

Freshwater, D. and Stickley, T. 2004 The heart of the art: emotional intelligence in nurse education. *Nursing Inquiry* 11: 91–8.

Friedan, B. 1963 *The Feminine Mystique.* Dell.

Friedson, S. 1970 *The Profession of Medicine: A Study in the Sociology of Applied Knowledge.* Dodd Mead.

Fuchs, V. R. 1968 The growing demand for medical care. *New England Journal of Medicine* 279: 192.

Furber, C. M. and Thomson, A. M. 2006 'Breaking the rules' in baby-feeding practice in the UK: deviance and good practice? *Midwifery* 22: 365–76.

Furber, C. M. and McGowan, L. 2011 A qualitative study of the experiences of women who are obese and pregnant in the UK. *Midwifery* 27/7: 437–44.

Fyfe, A., Burns, D., Butcher, G. and Deery, R. 2012 Connecting body and soul through hypnobirthing: a small-scale evaluation. *MIDIRS* 22/4: 415–18, 420–2.

Gans, H. J. 2002 The uses of poverty: the poor pay all. In L McIntyre (ed.), *The Practical Skeptic: Readings in Sociology.* McGraw Hill, pp. 304–9.

Garcia, J., Kilpatrick, R. and Richards, M. (eds) 1990 *The Politics of Maternity Care.* Clarendon Press.

Garcia, E., Timmermans, D. R. M. and Van Leeuwenc, E. 2008 The impact of ethical beliefs on decisions about prenatal screening tests: searching for justification. *Social Science and Medicine* 66: 753–64.

Garcia, J., Bricker, L., Henderson, J., Martin, M.-A., Mugford, M., Nielson, J. and

Roberts, T. 2002 Women's views of pregnancy ultrasound: a systematic review. *Birth* 29: 225–50.

Gard, M. and Wright, J. 2005 *The Obesity Epidemic: Science, Morality and Ideology.* Routledge.

Garrod, D. 2011 Rebuilding confidence in women's abilities in birth. *British Journal of Midwifery* 19/12: 830.

Gattrell, C. 2005 *Hard Labour: The Sociology of Parenthood.* Open University Press.

Gattuso, S., Fullagar, S. and Young, I. 2005 Speaking of women's 'nameless misery': the everyday construction of depression in Australian women's magazines. *Social Science and Medicine* 61: 1640–8.

Gavron, H. 1968 *The Captive Wife.* Penguin.

Georgsson Ohman, S. and Waldenström, U. 2008 Second-trimester routine ultrasound screening: expectations and experiences in a nationwide Swedish sample. *Ultrasound in Obstetrics & Gynecology: The Official Journal of the International Society Of Ultrasound in Obstetrics and Gynecology* 32: 15–22.

Georgsson Öhman, S. G., Saltvedt, S., Waldenström, U., Grunewald, C. and Olin-Lauritzen, S. 2006 Pregnant women's responses to information about an increased risk of carrying a baby with Down's Syndrome. *Birth* 33: 64–73.

Giacomini, M., Hurley, J., Gold, I., Smith P. and Abelson, J. 2004 The policy analysis of 'values talk': lessons from Canadian health reform. *Health Policy* 67: 15–24.

Gibson, C. H. 1991 A concept analysis of empowerment. *Journal of Advanced Nursing* 16/3: 354–61.

Giddens, A. 1984 *New Rules of Sociological Method.* Macmillan.

Giddens, A. 1998 *The Third Way – The Renewal of Social Democracy.* Polity.

Giddens, A. 1999 *Runaway World: How Globalization is Shaping Our Lives.* Profile Books.

Giddens, A. 2009 *Sociology,* 6th edn. Polity.

Giddens, A. 2011 *The Politics of Climate Change,* 2nd edn. Polity.

Gillespie, C. 2012 The experiences of risk as 'measured vulnerability': health screening and lay uses of numerical risk. *Sociology of Health and Illness* 34/2: 194–207.

Gillespie, R. 2001 Contextualizing voluntary childlessness within a postmodern model of reproduction: implications for health and social needs. *Critical Social Policy* 21/2: 139–59.

Gladwell, M. 2000 *The Tipping Point: How Little Things Can Make a Big Difference.* Little Brown.

Goffman, E. 1959 *The Presentation of Self in Everyday Life.* Penguin.

Goffman, E. 1963 *Stigma: Notes on the Management of Spoiled Identity.* Prentice-Hall, Inc.

Goffman, E. 1968 *Stigma: Notes on the Management of a Spoiled Identity.* Penguin.

Gold, K. J., Kuznia, A. L., Hayward, R. A. 2008 How physicians cope with stillbirth or neonatal death: a national survey of obstetricians. *Obstetrics and Gynecology* 112: 29–34.

Goleman, D. 1988 *The Meditation Mind.* Tareher Books.

Goleman, D. 1996 *Emotional Intelligence. Why It Can Matter More Than IQ.* Bantham Books.

Goleman, D. 2007 *Social Intelligence: The New Science of Human Relationships.* Arrow Books.

Goodall, K. E., McVittie, C. and Magill, M. 2009 Birth choice following primary caesarean section: mothers' perceptions of the influence of health professionals on decision-making. *Journal of Reproductive and Infant Psychology* 27/1: 4–14.

Goodman, M. 1994 *Mother's Pride and Others' Prejudice: A Survey of Disabled Mothers' Experiences of Maternity.* Maternity Alliance.

Goodman, B. 2011 The need for a 'sustainability curriculum' in nurse education. *Nurse Education Today* 31/8: 733–7.

Gough, I. 1979 *The Political Economy of the Welfare State*. Macmillan.

Gough, P., Maslin-Prothero, S. E. and Masterson, A. 1994 Policy for and of nursing. In P. Gough, S. Maslin-Prothero and A. Masterson (eds), *Nursing and Social Policy: Care in Context*. Butterworth Heinemann, pp. 264–81.

Grabowska, C. 2003 Unhappiness after childbirth. In C. Squire (ed.), *The Social Context of Birth*, Radcliffe Publishing, pp. 236–48.

Graham, H. and Oakley, A. 1981 Competing ideologies of reproduction: medical and maternal perspectives on pregnancy. In H. Roberts (ed.), *Women, Health and Reproduction*. Routledge & Kegan Paul, pp. 50–74.

Green, B. and Earle, S. 2010 Why should nurses study sociology? In E. Denny and S. Earle (eds), *Sociology for Nurses*, 2nd edn. Polity, pp. 28–49.

Green, J. M. 2003 Women's experiences of prenatal screening and diagnosis. In Healy, E., McGuire, B. E., Evans, D. S. and Carley, S. N. 2009 Sexuality and personal relationships for people with an intellectual disability. Part I: service–user perspectives. *Journal of Intellectual Disability Research* 53: 905–12.

Green, J. and Baston, H. 2007 Have women become more willing to accept obstetric interventions and does this relate to mode of birth? Data from a prospective study. *Birth* 34: 6–13.

Greenwood, E. 1957 Attributes of a profession. *Social Work* 2: 45–55.

Greil, A. L. 1991 *Not Yet Pregnant: Infertile Couples in Contemporary America*. New Rutgers University Press.

Greil, A. L. 2002 Infertile bodies: medicalization, metaphor and agency. In M. Inhorn and F. v. Balen (eds), *Infertility around the Globe: New Thinking on Childlessness, Gender and Reproductive Technologies*. University of California Press, pp. 101–18.

Grossman, K. E., Grossman, K. and Waters, E. 2005 (eds) *Attachment from Infancy to Adulthood: The Major Longitudinal Studies*. Guilford Press.

Grouleau, D. and Rodriguez, C. 2009 Breastfeeding and poverty: negotiating cultural change and symbolic capital of motherhood in Quebec, Canada. In F. Dykes and V. Hall Moran (eds), *Infant and Young Child Feeding: Challenges to Implementing a Global Strategy*. Wiley-Blackwell, pp. 80–98.

Grout, L. A. and Romanoff, B. D. 2000 The myth of the replacement child: parents' stories and practices after perinatal death. *Death Studies* 24: 93–13.

Guilkey, D. K. and Stewart, J. F. 1995 Infant feeding patterns and the marketing of infant foods in the Philippines. *Economic Development and Cultural Change* 43: 369–99.

Guilliland, K. and Pairman, S. 2010 *Women's Business: The Story of the New Zealand College of Midwives, 1986–2010*. New Zealand College of Midwives.

Gupta, J. A. 2012 Reproductive bio-crossings: Indian egg donors and surrogates in the globalized fertility market. *International Journal of Feminist Approaches to Bioethics* 5/1: 25–51.

Gürtin, Z., Ahuja, K. and Golombok, S. 2012 Emotional and relational aspects of egg-sharing: egg-share donors' and recipients' feelings about each other, each others' treatment outcome and any resulting children. *Human Reproduction* 27/6: 1690–1701.

Haddad, A. T. and Lieberman, L. 2002 From student resistance to embracing the sociological imagination: unmasking privilege, social conventions, and racism. *Teaching Sociology* 30/3: 328–41.

Halbreich, U. and Karkun, S. 2006 Cross-cultural and social diversity of prevalence of postpartum depression and depressive symptoms. *Journal of Affective Disorders* 91/2; 97-111.

Hall, J. 2013 Developing a culture of compassionate care – the midwife's voice. *Midwifery* 29: 269–71.

Hallowell, N., Lawton, J. and Gregory, S. 2005 *Reflections on Research: The Realities of Doing Research in the Social Sciences*. Open University Press.

Ham, C. 2009 *Health Policy in Britain*, 6th edn. Palgrave-Macmillan.

Hammersley, M. and Gomm, R. 1997 Bias in Social Research *Sociological Research Online* 2/4. At <www.socresonline.org.uk/>.

Hampshire, K., Blell, M. and Simpson, B. 2012 'Everybody is moving on': infertility, relationality and the aesthetics of family among British-Pakistani Muslims. *Social Science & Medicine* 74/7: 1045–52.

Handwerker, L. 1994 Medical risk: implicating poor pregnant women. *Social Science and Medicine* 38/5: 66–75.

Hannigan, B. and Burnard, P. 2000 Nursing, politics and policy: a response to Clifford. *Nurse Education Today* 20/7: 519–23.

Haraway, D. 1991 *Simians, Cyborgs and Women: The Reinvention of Nature*. Routledge.

Harding, S. 1993 Rethinking standpoint epistemology: what is 'strong objectivity'? In L. Alcoff and E. Porter (eds), *Feminist Epistemologies*. Routledge, pp. 49–82.

Hargreaves, J. and Page, L. 2013 *Reflective Practice*. Polity.

Harris, S. P., Randall, O. and Gould, R. 2012 Parity of participation in liberal welfare states: human rights, neoliberalism, disability and employment. *Disability and Society* 27/6: 823–36.

Harvey, D. 2005 *A Brief History of Neoliberalism*. Oxford University Press.

Hastie, C. 2011 The birthing environment. In L. Davies, R. Daellenbach and M. Kensington (eds), *Sustainability, Midwifery and Birth*. Routledge, Chapter 8, pp. 101–14.

Hatcher, C. 2008 Becoming a successful corporate character and the role of emotional management. In S. Fineman (ed), *The Emotional Organization*. Blackwell, Chapter 11, 153–66.

Hatem, J., Sandall, J., Devane, D., Soltani, H. and Gates, S. 2008 Midwife-led versus other models of care for childbearing women. *Cochrane Database of Systematic Reviews* 3, The Cochrane Collaboration. John Wiley & Sons Ltd.

Hatmaker, D. D. and Kemp, V. H. 1998 Perception of threat and subjective wellbeing in low-risk and high-risk pregnant women. *The Journal of Perinatal and Neonatal Nursing* 12/2: 1–10.

Hawken, P. 2007 *Blessed Unrest: How the Largest Movement in the World Came into Being and Why No One Saw It Coming*. Viking.

Hays, S. 1996 *The Cultural Contradictions of Motherhood*. Yale University Press.

Health Canada 2000 *Family-Centred Maternity and Newborn Care: National Guidelines*. Minister of Public Works and Government Services, Ottawa.

Healy, E., McGuire, B. E., Evans, D. S. and Carley, S. N. 2009 Sexuality and personal relationships for people with an intellectual disability. Part I: service–user perspectives. *Journal of Intellectual Disability Research* 53: 905–12.

Hearn, G., Iliff, A., Jones, I. et al. 1998 Postnatal depression in the community. *British Journal of General Practice* 48/428: 1064–6.

Heffernan, M, 2012 *Wilful Blindness*. Simon and Schuster.

Helman, C. 2007 *Culture, Health and Illness*, 5th edn. Hodder Arnold.

Henderson, L., Kitzinger, J. and Green, J. 2000 Representing infant feeding: content analysis of British media portrayals of bottle feeding and breast feeding. *British Medical Journal* 321: 1196–8.

Hennessy, D. 2000 The emerging themes. In D. Hennessy and P. Spurgeon (eds), *Health Policy and Nursing: Influence, Development and Impact*. Macmillan, pp. 1–38.

Hewison, A. 2008 Evidence-based policy: implications for nursing and policy involvement. *Policy, Politics & Nursing Practice* 9/4: 288–98.

Hewitt, J. and Coffey, M. 2005 Therapeutic working relationships with people with schizophrenia: literature review. *Journal of Advanced Nursing* 52/5: 561–70.

Heyman, B. (ed.) 1998 *Risk, Health and Health Care: A Qualitative Approach*. Arnold.

Heyman, B. 2010a The social construction of health risks. In B. Heyman, M. Shaw, A. Alasewski and M. Titterton (eds), *Risk, Safety and Clinical Practice: Health Care through the Lens of Risk*. Oxford University Press, pp. 37–58.

Heyman, B. 2010b Time and health risks. In B. Heyman, M. Shaw, A. Alasewski and M. Titterton (eds), *Risk, Safety and Clinical Practice: Health Care through the Lens of Risk*. Oxford University Press, pp. 107–22.

Heyman, B. 2010c Values and health risks. In B. Heyman, M. Shaw, A., Alasewski and M. Titterton (eds), *Risk, Safety and Clinical Practice: Health Care through the Lens of Risk*. Oxford University Press, pp. 59–84.

Heyman, B. and Brown, P. 2012 Perspectives on the 'lens of risk' interview series: Interview with Nick Pidgeon. *Health, Risk & Society* 14/2: 117–27.

Heyman, B., Hundt, G., Sandall, J., Spencer, K., Williams, C., Grellier, R. and Pitson, L. 2006 On being higher risk: a qualitative study of prenatal screening for chromosomal anomalies. *Social Science and Medicine* 62: 2360–72.

Heyman, B., Shaw, M., Alasewski, A. and Titterton, M. (eds) 2010 *Risk, Safety and Clinical Practice: Health Care through the Lens of Risk*. Oxford University Press.

Hildingsson, I., Nilsson, C., Karlstrom, A. et al. 2011 A longitudinal survey of childbirth related fear and associated factors. *JOGNN* 40/5: 532–43.

Hill, M. 1997 *The Policy Process in the Modern State*, 3rd edn. Prentice Hall.

Hill, M. 2009 *The Public Policy Process*. Pearson Longman.

Hill, M. and Bramley, G. 1986 *Analysing Social Policy*. Blackwell.

Hinsliff, G. 2012 *Half a Wife: The Working Family's Guide to Getting a Life Back*. Chatto & Windus.

Hochschild, A. R. 1979 Emotion work, feeling rules, and social structures. *American Journal of Sociology* 85: 551–75.

Hochschild, A. R. 1983 *The Managed Heart: Commercialization of Human Feeling*, University of California Press.

Hochschild, A. R. 1998 Sociology of emotion as a way of seeing. In G. Bendelow and S. J. Williams (eds), *Emotions in Social Life*. Routledge, pp. 3–15.

Hoddinott, P. and Pill, R. 1999 Qualitative study of decisions about infant feeding among women in the East End of London. *British Medical Journal* 318: 30–4.

Hoddinott, P., Craig, L. C., Britten, J. and McInnes, R. M. 2012 A serial qualitative interview study of infant feeding experiences: idealism meets realism. *British Medical Journal*: 1–14. At <http://bmjopen.bmj.com/>.

Hodnett, E. D., Gates, S., Hofmeyr, G. J., Sakala, C. and Weston, J. 2012 Continuous support for women during childbirth. *Cochrane Database of Systematic Reviews* 10. The Cochrane Collaboration. Published by John Wiley & Sons, Ltd.

Hollingshead, A. B. and Redich, F. C. 1956 *Social Class and Mental Illness*. Wiley.

Holmes, D. and Gastaldo, D. 2002 Nursing as a means of Governmentality. *Journal of Advanced Nursing* 38/6: 557–65.

Homfray, M. 2008 Standpoint, objectivity, and social construction: reflections from the study of gay and lesbian communities. *Sociological Research Online* 13/1. At <http://www.socresonline.org.uk>.

Horwitz, A. V. and Wakefield, J. C. 2007 *The Loss of Sadness: How Psychiatry Transformed Normal Sorrow into Depressive Disorder*. Oxford University Press.

House of Commons 1992 *Winterton Report*. Health Committee, House of Commons, p. v.

Howard, C., Howard, F., Lawrence, R., Andresen, E., deBlieck, E. and Weitzman, M. 2000 Office prenatal formula advertising and its effects on breastfeeding patterns. *Obstetrics and Gynaecology* 95: 296–303.

Hubbard, R. 2006 Abortion and disability. Who should and who should not inhabit the world. In L. J. Davis (ed.), *The Disability Studies Reader*, 2nd edn. CRC Press, pp. 93–103.

Huberman, M. 1987 Steps towards an integrated model of research utilization. *Knowledge* (June): 586–611.

Hudson, N. 2008 Infertility in British South Asian Communities. Negotiating the Community and the Clinic. Unpublished PhD thesis. De Montfort University. At <https://www.dora.dmu.ac.uk/>.

Hudson, J. and Lowe, S. 2009 *Understanding the Policy Process*, 2nd edn. The Policy Press.

Hughes, B. 2004 Disability and the body. In Swain, J., French, S., Barnes, C. and Thomas, C. (eds), *Disabling Barriers – Enabling Environments*, 2nd edn. Sage Publications, pp. 63–8.

Hughes, B. and Paterson, K. 1997 The social model of disability and the disappearing body: towards a sociology of impairment. *Disability & Society* 12: 325–40.

Hughes, D. and Deery, R. 2002 Where's the midwifery in midwife-led care? *The Practising Midwife* 5/7: 18–19.

Hughes, D., Deery, R. and Lovatt, A. 2002 A critical ethnographic approach to facilitating cultural shift in midwifery. *Midwifery* 18: 43–52.

Hughes, F. A. 2005 Policy – a practical tool for nurses and nursing. *Journal of Advanced Nursing* 49/4: 331.

Hughes, J. 2005 Bringing emotion to work: emotional intelligence, employee resistance and the reinvention of character. *Work, Employment and Society* 19/3: 603–25.

Human Fertilization and Embryology Authority (HFEA) 2008 *Facts and Figures*. At <http://www.hfea.gov.uk/>.

Human Fertilization and Embryology Authority (HFEA) 2009 *Code of Practice*, 8th edn. HFEA.

Human Fertilization and Embryology Authority (HFEA) 2010 *Fertility Facts and Figures 2010*. At <http://www.hfea.gov.uk>.

Human Fertilization and Embryology Authority (HFEA) 2011 Fertility treatment in 2010. Trends and figures. At <http://www.hfea.gov.uk/>.

Human Fertilization and Embryology Authority (HFEA) 2012 Quick facts about infertility. At <http://www.hfea.gov.uk/>.

Humphrey, C., Ehrich, K., Kelly, B., Sandall, J., Redfern, S. Morgan, M. and Guest, D. 2003 Human resources policies and continuity of care. *Journal of Health Organization and Management* 17/2: 102–21.

Hunter, B. 2004a Conflicting ideologies as a source of emotion work in midwifery. *Midwifery* 20/3: 261–72.

Hunter, B. 2004b The importance of emotional intelligence. *British Journal of Midwifery* 12/10: 604–5.

Hunter, B. 2005 Emotion work and boundary maintenance in hospital-based midwifery. *Midwifery* 21/3: 253–66.

Hunter, B. 2006 The importance of reciprocity in relationships between community-based midwives and mothers. *Midwifery* 22/4: 308–22.

Hunter, B. and Deery, R. 2009 *Emotions in Midwifery and Reproduction*. Palgrave Macmillan.

Hunter, B., Berg, M., Lundgren, I. et al. 2008 Relationships: the hidden threads in the tapestry of maternity care. *Midwifery* 24: 132–7.

Hunter, D. J. 2003 *Public Health Policy*. Polity.

Hunter, D. J. 2008 *The Health Debate*. The Policy Press.

Hupe, P. L. and Hill, M. J. 2006 The three action levels of governance: re-framing the policy process beyond the stages model. In B. G. Peters and J. Pierre (eds), *Handbook of Public Policy*. Sage Publications, pp. 13–30.

Hutter, B. M. 2008 Risk regulation and health care. *Health, Risk and Society* 10/1: 1–7.

Hyde, M. 2006 Disability. In G. Payne (ed.), *Social Divisions*, 2nd edn. Palgrave Macmillan, pp. 185–202.

Hyland, M. 2001 Refugee subjectivity: 'bare life' and the geographical division of labour. *The Physics Room Issue 13 The Revolution Issue*. At <http://www.physicsroom.org>.

Illich, I. 1995 *Limits to Medicine. Medical Nemesis: The Expropriation of Health*, 2nd edn. Marion Boyars Publishers.

Inhorn, M. C. 2003 'The worms are weak': male infertility and patriarchal paradoxes in Egypt. *Men and Masculinities* 5/3: 236–56.

Inhorn, M. C., and van Balen, F. (eds) 2002 *Infertility around the Globe: New Thinking on Childlessness, Gender, and Reproductive Technologies*. University of California Press.

International Confederation of Midwives (ICM) 2005 *Definition of a Midwife*. At <www.internationalmidwives.org>.

International Confederation of Midwives (ICM) 2011a *ICM Position Statements*. At <http://www.internationalmidwives.org/>.

International Confederation of Midwives (ICM) 2011b *Global Standards for Midwifery Education*. At <http://www.internationalmidwives.org/>.

International Council of Nurses (ICN) 2001 *Guidelines on Shaping Effective Health Policy*. ICN.

IPCC 2001 *Climate Change 2001: The Scientific Basis*. Cambridge University Press.

Jackson, T. 2011 *Prosperity without Growth: Economics for a Finite Planet*. Earthscan Ltd.

Jacobs, J. 1992 *Systems of Survival. A Dialogue on the Moral Foundations of Commerce and Politics*. Hodder and Stoughton.

James, N. 1989 Emotional labour: skill and work in the social regulation of feelings. *Sociological Review* 37/1: 15–42.

James, N. 1992 Care = organisation + physical labour + emotional labour. *Sociology of Health & Illness* 14/4: 488–509.

James, W. P. T. 2005 The policy challenge of coexisting undernutrition and nutrition-related chronic diseases. *Maternal & Child Nutrition* 1: 197–203.

Jameton, A. and McGuire, C. 2002 Toward sustainable health care services: principles, challenges, and a process. *International Journal of Sustainability in Higher Education* 3/2: 113–27.

Jelliffe, D. B. 1972 Commerciogenic malnutrition. *Nutrition Reviews* 30: 199–205.

Jelliffe, D. B. and Jelliffe, E. F. P. 1978 *Human Milk in the Modern World*. Oxford University Press.

Jenkins, R. 2002 *Foundations of Sociology: Towards a Better Understanding of the Human World*. Palgrave Macmillan.

Jensen, T. 2010 What kind of mum are you at the moment? Supernanny and the psychologizing of classed embodiment. *Subjectivity* 3/2: 170–92.

Jobling, R. 1988 The experience of psoriasis under treatment. In Anderson, R. and Bury, M. (eds), *Living with Chronic Illness: The Experience of Patients and Their Families*. Unwin Hyman, pp. 225–44.

Johnson, G. 2011 *Holding Back the British IVF Revolution? A Report into NHS IVF Provision in the UK Today*. All Party Parliamentary Group on Infertility. At <www.garethjohnsonmp.co.uk/>.

Jokinen, M. and Silverton, L. 2009 Relevance of the CNST Maternity Standards for the

Royal College of Midwives. In NHSLA/DNV *Launch Seminar for the Revised CNST Maternity Clinical Risk Management Standards.*

Jonas-Simpson, C. and McMahon, E. 2005 The language of loss when a baby dies prior to birth: cocreating human experience. *Nursing Science Quarterly* 18/2: 124–30.

Jordan, B. 1993 *Birth in Four Cultures*, 4th edn. Waveland Press.

Jordan, B. 2010 *Why the Third Way Failed: Economics, Morality and the Origins of the 'Big Society'.* The Policy Press.

Jordan, R. G. and Aikins Murphy, P. 2009 Risk assessment and risk distortion: finding the balance. *Journal of Midwifery and Women's Health* 54/3: 191–200.

Joseph Rowntree Foundation 2011 *Response to the UK Government's Tackling Child Poverty and Improving Life Chances: Consulting on a New Approach.* At <http://www.jrf.org.uk/>.

Jowitt, M. 2008 Bystanding behaviour in midwifery. *Midwifery Matters* 118: 11–16.

Kahneman, D. 2011 *Thinking, Fast and Slow.* Farrar, Straus and Giroux.

Kahneman, D. and Sugden, R. 2005 Experienced utility as a standard of policy evaluation. *Environmental and Resource Economics* 32: 161–81.

Kaplan, D. and Graff, K. 2008 Marketing breastfeeding – reversing corporate influence on infant feeding practices. *Journal of Urban Health* 85: 486–504.

Katz-Rothman, B. 2007. Writing ourselves in sociology. *Methodological Innovations.* At <http://erdt.plymouth.ac.uk/>.

Katz, J, Hockey, J. and Small, N. 2001 *Grief, Mourning and Death Ritual. Facing Death.* Open University Press.

Keller, C. and Siegrist, M. 2009 Effect of risk communication formats on risk perception depending on numeracy. *Medical Decision Making* 29/4: 483–90.

Kelley, M. C. and Trinidad, S. B. 2012 Silent loss and the clinical encounter: Parents' and physicians' experiences of stillbirth – a qualitative analysis. *BMC Pregnancy and Childbirth* 12: 137.

Kelly, L., Burton, S. and Regan, L. 1994 Researching women's lives or studying women's oppression? Reflections on what constitutes feminist research. In M. Maynard and J. Purvis (eds), *Researching Women's Lives from a Feminist Perspective.* Taylor & Francis, pp. 27–48.

Kennedy, P. and Murphy-Lawless, J. 2003 The maternity care needs of refugee and asylum-seeking women in Ireland. *Feminist Review, Special Edition: Asylum and Exile* 73: 39–53.

Kenworthy, D. and Kirkham, M. 2011 *Midwives Coping with Loss and Grief: Stillbirth, Professional and Personal Losses.* Radcliffe Publishing.

Kerr, J., Brown, C. and Balen, A. 1999 The experiences of couples who have had infertility treatment in the United Kingdom: results of a survey performed in 1997. *Human Reproduction* 14/4: 934–8.

Kessler, R. C., Chiu, W. T., Demler, O. et al. 2005 Prevalence, severity and co-morbidity of 12-month DSM-IV disorders in the national co-morbidity survey replication. *Archives of General Psychiatry* 62/6: 617–27.

Kingdon, C. 2009 *Sociology for Midwives.* Quay Books.

Kingdon, C., Neilson, J., Singleton, V., Gyte, G., Hart, A., Gabbay, M. and Lavender, T. 2009 Choice and birth method: mixed-method study of caesarean delivery for maternal request. *BJOG International Journal of Obstetrics and Gynaecology* 116: 886–95.

Kingdon, J. W. 2003 *Agendas, Alternatives and Public Policies*, 2nd edn. Longman.

King's Fund 2008 *Safer Births: Everybody's Business: An Independent Inquiry into the Safety of Maternity Services in England.* King's Fund.

King's Fund 2009 *Long-term Conditions* [Online]. At <http://www.kingsfund.org.uk/topics/>.

Kirkham, M. 1999 The culture of midwifery in the National Health Service in England. *Journal of Advanced Nursing* 30/3: 732–9.

Kirkham, M. 2004 *Informed Choice in Maternity Care*. Palgrave Macmillan.

Kirkham, M. 2007 Traumatized midwives. *AIMS Journal* 19/1: 12–13.

Kirkham, M 2009 *Review of Cases Cared for by Independent Midwives where a Stillbirth or Neonatal Death Occurred*. University of Dundee, Department of Nursing and Midwifery. At <http://www.dundee.ac.uk/>.

Kirkham, M. 2010 In fear of difference, in fear of excellence. *The Practising Midwife* 13/1: 13–15.

Kirkham, M. 2010a *The Midwife–Mother Relationship*, 2nd edn. Palgrave Macmillan.

Kirkham, M. 2010b The maternity services context. In M. Kirkham, *The Midwife–Mother Relationship*, 2nd edn. Palgrave Macmillan, pp. 1–16.

Kirkham, M. 2010c We need to relate. In M. Kirkham, *The Midwife–Mother Relationship*, 2nd edn. Palgrave Macmillan, pp. 250–71.

Kirkham, M. 2011 Sustained by joy: the potential of flow experience for midwives and mothers. In L. Davies, R. Daellenbach and M. Kensington (eds), *Sustainability, Midwifery and Birth*. Routledge, pp. 87–100.

Kirkham, M. and Stapleton, H. (eds) 2001 *Informed Choice in Maternity Care: An Evaluation of Evidence Based Leaflets*. NHS Centre for Reviews and Dissemination.

Kirkham, M., Morgan, R. M. and Davies, C. 2006 *Why Midwives Stay*. Department of Health and University of Sheffield.

Kirkham, M., Stapleton, H., Curtis, P. and Thomas, G. 2002 Stereotyping as a professional defence mechanism. *British Journal of Midwifery* 10/9: 549–52.

Kitzinger, S. 1978 *Women as Mothers*. Random House.

Kitzinger, S. 2006 *Birth Crisis*. Routledge.

Kitzinger, S. 2012 Rediscovering the Social Model of Childbirth. *Birth* 39/4: 301–4.

Klass, D., Silverman, P. R. and Nickman, S. L. 1996 *Continuing Bonds: New Understandings of Grief*. Taylor & Francis.

Klein, R. D. 1989 *Infertility: Women Speak Out about Their Experiences of Reproductive Medicine*. Pandora Press.

Klein, R. 2010 *The New Politics of the NHS – From Creation to Reinvention*, 6th edn. Radcliffe Publishing.

Klein, R. and Rowland, R. 1989 Hormonal cocktails: women as test-sites for fertility drugs. *Women's Studies International Forum* 12/3: 333–48.

Koller, V. and Davidson, P. 2008 Social exclusion as conceptual and grammatical metaphor: a cross-genre study of British policymaking. *Discourse and Society* 19/3: 307–31.

Kotaska, A. 2011 Guideline-centered care: a two-edged sword. *Birth* 38: 97–8; doi 10.1111/j.1523–536x.2011.00469.x.

Kringeland, T. and Möller, A. 2006 Risk and security in childbirth. *Journal of Psychosomatic Obstetrics and Gynecology* 27/4: 185–91.

Kuhn, T. 1962 *The Structure of Scientific Revolutions*. University of Chicago Press.

Kuttai, H. 2010 *Maternity Rolls: Pregnancy, Childbirth and Disability*. Fernwood Publishing.

Laing, R. D. and Esterson, A. 1964 *Sanity, Madness and the Family*. Penguin.

Lane, K. 1995 The medical model of the body as a site of risk: a case study of childbirth. In J. Gabe (ed.), *Medicine, Health and Risk: Sociological Approaches*. Blackwell, pp. 53–72.

Lane, M. 2004 *The Modern-Day Venus de Milo* [Online]. London: BBC. At <http://news.bbc.co.uk/>.

Lane, S. 2008 *Why Are Our Babies Dying?: Pregnancy, Birth, and Death in America*. Paradigm Publishers.

Lapper, A. and Feldman, G. 2005 *My Life in My Hands*. Simon & Schuster.

Layard, R. 2005 *Happiness: Lessons from a New Science.* Allen Lane.

Layne, L. 2003 *Motherhood Lost: A Feminist Account of Pregnancy Loss in America.* Routledge.

Lazarus, R. S. and Folkman, S. 1984 *Stress, Appraisal and Coping.* Springer.

Leatherman, S. and Sutherland, K. 2008 *The Quest for Quality: Refining the NHS Reforms – A Policy Analysis and Chartbook.* The Nuffield Trust.

Leff, E., Gagne, M. and Jefferis, S. 1994 Maternal perceptions of successful breast-feeding. *Journal of Human Lactation* 10: 99–104.

Lehtonen, M. 2004 The environmental–social interface of sustainable development: capabilities, social capital, institutions. *Ecological Economics* 4: 199–214.

Leichtentritt, R. D., Blumenthal, N., Elyassi, A. and Rotmensch, S. 2005 High-risk pregnancy and hospitalization: women's voices. *Health and Social Work* 30/1: 39–47.

Leonard, L. 2002 Problematizing fertility. 'Scientific' accounts and Chadian women's narratives. In M. Inhorn and F. Van Balen (eds), *Infertility Around the Globe: New Thinking on Childlessness, Gender and Reproductive Technologies.* University of California Press, pp. 193–214.

Letherby, G. 1994 Mother or not, mother or what? Problems of definition and identity. *Women's Studies International Forum* 17/5: 525–32.

Letherby, G. 2002a Childless and Bereft? Stereotypes and realities in relation to 'voluntary' and 'involuntary' childlessness and womanhood. *Sociological Inquiry* 72/1: 7–20.

Letherby, G. 2002b Challenging dominant discourses: identity and change and the experience of 'infertility' and 'involuntary childlessness'. *Journal of Gender Studies* 11/3: 277–88.

Letherby, G. 2003 *Feminist Research in Theory and Practice.* Open University Press.

Letherby, G. 2004 Quoting and counting: an autobiographical response to Oakley. *Sociology* 38/1: 175–89.

Letherby, G. 2013 'Theorised Subjectivity'. In G. Letherby, J. Scott and M. Williams, *Objectivity and Subjectivity in Social Research.* Sage Publications, pp. 79–101.

Letherby, G. and Bywaters, P. (eds) 2007 *Extending Social Research: Application, Implementation, Presentation.* Open University.

Letherby, G. and Stenhouse, E. (forthcoming) Researching relationships, relationships in research: reflections on multidisciplinary work on pregnancy, birth and early motherhood. In S. Wray and R. Rae (eds), *Personal and Public Lives.* Cambridge Scholars Publishing.

Letherby, G., Scott, J. and Williams, M. 2013 *Objectivity and Subjectivity in Social Research.* Sage Publications.

Lewiecki-Wilson, C. and Cellio, J. 2011 *Disability and Mothering: Liminal Spaces of Embodied Knowledge.* Syracuse University Press.

Lewis, G. 2001 Why mothers die 1997–1999: the fifth report of the confidential enquiries into maternal deaths in the United Kingdom. *The Confidential Enquiry into Maternal and Child Health (CEMACH).* RCOG.

Lewis, G. 2004 Why mothers die 2000–2002: the sixth report of the confidential enquiries into maternal deaths in the United Kingdom. *The Confidential Enquiry into Maternal and Child Health (CEMACH).* RCOG.

Lewis P. 2005 Suppression or expression: an exploration of emotion management in a special care baby unit, *Work Employment and Society* 19/3; 565–81.

Lewis, G. 2007 Saving mothers' lives: reviewing maternal deaths to make motherhood safer – 2003–2005. The seventh report of the confidential enquiries into maternal deaths in the United Kingdom. *The Confidential Enquiry into Maternal and Child Health (CEMACH).* RCOG.

Lewis, G. 2011 *Saving Mothers' Lives: Reviewing Maternal Deaths to Make Motherhood Safer: 2006–08.* Centre for Maternal and Child Enquiries (CMACE).

Lewis, G. 2012 Saving mothers' lives: the continuing benefits for maternal health. From the United Kingdom (UK) *Confidential Enquiries Into Maternal Death Seminars in Perinatology* 36/1: 19–26.

Lewis, J. 1980 *The Politics of Motherhood. Child and Maternal Welfare in England 1990–1939.* Croom Helm.

Lewis, J. 1990 Mothers and maternity policies in the twentieth century. In J. Garcia, R. Kilpatrick and M. Richards (eds), *The Politics of Maternity Care, Services for Childbearing Women in Twentieth-Century Britain.* Clarendon Press, pp. 15–29.

Lilja, G., Edhborg, M. and Nissen, E. 2011 Depressive mood in women at childbirth predicts their mood and relationship with infant and partner during the first year postpartum. *Scandinavian Journal of Caring Sciences* (July 2011). At <http:// onlinelibrary.wiley.com>.

Lindqvist, P., Dahlbäck, B. and Maršál, K. 1999 Thrombotic risk during pregnancy: a population study. *Obstetrics and Gynecology* 94: 595–9.

Lipsky, M. 1980 *Street-level Bureaucracy.* Russell Sage Foundation.

Lipson, J. G. and Rogers, J. G. 2000 Pregnancy, birth, and disability: women's health care experiences. *Health Care for Women International* 21: 11–26.

Lipton, B. 2005 *The Biology of Belief.* Hay House.

Lloyd, B. and Hawe, P. 2003 Solutions foregone? How health professionals frame the problem of postnatal depression. *Social Science and Medicine* 57: 1783–95.

Lock, M. and Kaufert, P. A. (eds) 1998 *Pragmatic Women and Body Politics.* Cambridge University Press.

Longest, B. B. 2004 An international constant: the crucial role of policy competence in the effective strategic management of health service organizations. *Health Services Management Research* 17: 71–8.

Lovell, A. 1983 Some questions of identity: late miscarriages, stillbirth, and perinatal loss. *Social Science and Medicine* 17/11: 755–61.

Lucas, A. 2011 Marketing in maternity. *RCM Midwives* 15/3: 42–3.

Lukse, M. P., and Vacc, N. A. 1999 Grief, depression, and coping in women undergoing infertility treatment. *Obstetrics & Gynecology* 93/2: 245–51.

Lundgren, I. 2004 Releasing and relieving encounters: experiences of pregnancy and childbirth. *Scandinavian Journal of Caring Sciences* 18/4: 368–75.

Lupton, D. 1993 Risk as moral danger: the social and political functions of risk discourse in public health. *International Journal of Health Services* 23/3: 425–35.

McCance, T. V., Fitzsimons, D., Keeney, S., Hasson, F. and McKenna, H. P. 2007 Capacity building in nursing and midwifery research and development: an old priority and a new perspective. *Journal of Advanced Nursing* 59/1: 57–67.

McCourt, C. 2010 *Childbirth, Midwifery and Concepts of Time.* Berghahn Books.

McCourt, C. and Stevens, T. 2009 Relationship and reciprocity in caseload midwifery. In B. Hunter and R. Deery, *Emotions in Midwifery and Reproduction.* Palgrave, pp. 17–35.

McCourt, C., Stevens, T., Sandall, J. and Brodie, P. 2006: 'Working with women: developing continuity of care in practice'. In L. Page and R. McCandlish (eds), *The New Midwifery – Science and Sensitivity in Practice*, 2nd edn. Churchill Livingston/ Elsevier, pp. 149–65.

McDonnell, O., Lohan, M., Hyde, A., and Porter, S. 2009 *Social Theory, Health and Healthcare.* Palgrave Macmillan.

McGregor, S. 2001 Neoliberalism and health care. *International Journal of Consumer Studies*, 25: 82–9.

Macionis, J. and Plummer, K. 2012 *Sociology: A Global Introduction*, 5th edn. Prentice Hall.

McKenna, H. and Mason, C. 1998 Nursing and the wider R&D agenda: influence and contribution. *Nursing Times Research* 3/2: 108–15.

McKenna, H. P., Ashton, S. and Keeney, S. 2004 Barriers to evidence-based practice in primary care. *Journal of Advanced Nursing* 45/2: 178–89.

McKenzie, S. 2004 *Social Sustainability: Towards Some Definitions.* Hawke Research Institute Working Paper Series No 27, University of South Australia.

MacKenzie Bryers, H. and, van Teijlingen, E. 2010 Risk, theory, social and medical models: a critical analysis of the concept of risk in maternity care. *Midwifery* 26: 488–96.

McKibben, B. 2010 *Earth: Making a Life on a Tough New Planet.* New York Times Books.

MacKinnon, K. 2006 Living with the threat of preterm labor: women's work of keeping the baby in. *Journal of Obstetric, Gynecologic and Neonatal Nursing.* 35/6: 700–8.

McLachlan, H. L., Forster, D. A., Davey, M. A., Farrell, T., Gold, L., Biro, M., Albers. L., Flood, M. Oats, J. and Waldenström, U. 2012 Effects of continuity of care by a primary midwife (caseload midwifery) on caesarean section rates in women of low obstetric risk: the COSMOS randomised controlled trial. *BJOG: An International Journal of Obstetrics & Gynaecology* 119/12: 1483–92.

McLeish, J. 2002 *Mothers in Exile: Maternity Experiences of Asylum Seekers in England.* At <http://www.maternityaction.org.uk/>.

McManus, S., Meltzer, H. and Brugh, P. et al. 2009 *Adult Psychiatric Morbidity in England, 2007.* The Information Centre.

McMichael, T., Montgomery, H. and Costello, T. 2012 Health risks, present and future, from global climate change. *British Medical Journal* 344: e1359. At <http://www.bmj.com/>.

Maher, V. 1992a Breast-feeding in cross-cultural perspective: paradoxes and proposals. In V. Maher (ed.), *The Anthropology of Breastfeeding, Natural Law or Social Construct.* Berg Publishers, pp. 1–36.

Maher, V. 1992b Breast-feeding and maternal depletion: natural law or cultural arrangements? In V. Maher (ed.), *Anthropology of Breastfeeding, Natural Law or Social Construct.* Berg Publishers, pp. 151–80.

Maheshwari, A. et al. 2008 Effect of female age on the diagnostic categories of infertility. *Human Reproduction* 23/3: 538–42.

Mahon-Daly, P. and Andrews, G. J. 2002 Liminality and breastfeeding: women negotiating space and two bodies. *Health and Place* 8: 61–76.

Maines, D. R. and Morrione, T. J. 1990 On the breadth and relevance of Blumer's perspective: introduction to his analysis of industrialization. In H. Blumer (ed.), *Industrialization as an Agent of Social Change.* Aldine de Gruyter, pp. xi–xxiv.

Malin, M., Hemminki, E., Räikkönen, O., Sihvo, S. and Perälä, M. L. 2001 What do women want? Women's experiences of infertility treatment. *Social Science & Medicine* 53/1: 123–33.

Malone, R. E. 2005 Assessing the policy environment. *Policy, Politics & Nursing Practice* 6/2: 135–48.

Malott, A. M. 2008 Teaching skills for cultural competence: are midwives prepared for practice? *Canadian Journal of Midwifery Research and Practice* 7/3: 19–29.

Mander, R. 2000 The wet nurse in nineteenth-century Edinburgh. *Proceedings of the Royal College of Edinburgh Physicians.* 30/3: 258–64.

Mander, R. 2003 An analysis of Simpson's notebook data on the wet nurse. *Midwifery* 19/1: 46–54.

Mander, R. 2011 Saving mothers' lives: the reality or the rhetoric? *MIDIRS* 21/2: 254–8.

Mander, R. and Murphy-Lawless, J. 2013 *The Politics of Maternity.* Routledge.

Mander, R. and Smith, G. D. 2008 Saving mothers' lives (formerly 'why mothers die'): Reviewing maternal deaths to make motherhood safer. *Midwifery* 24/1: 8–12.

Manuel, J. I., Martinson, M. L., Bledsoe-Mansori, S. E. and Bellamy, J. L. 2012 The influence of stress and social support on depressive symptoms in mothers with young children. *Social Science & Medicine* 75/11: 2013–20.

Marland, H. (ed.) 1993 *The Art of Midwifery: Early Modern Midwives in Europe.* Routledge.

Marmot, M. and Wilkinson, W. 2006 *Social Determinants of Health*, 2nd edn. Oxford University Press.

Marshall, J., Godfrey, M. and Renfrew, M. J. 2007 Being a 'good mother': managing breastfeeding and merging identities. *Social Science and Medicine* 65: 2147–59.

Martin, J. 1978 *Infant Feeding 1975: Attitudes and Practices in England and Wales.* Office of Population Censuses and Surveys, HMSO.

Martinez, E. and García, A. 2000 *What is 'Neo-Liberalism'? A Brief Definition.* At <http://www.globalexchange.org/>.

Martis, R. 2010 Good housekeeping in midwifery practice. In L. Davies, R. Daellenbach. and M. Kensington, *Sustainability, Midwifery and Birth.* Routledge, pp. 141–54.

Marx, K. 1970 *A Contribution to the Critique of Political Economy.* Moscow: Progress Publishers.

Marx, K. 1992 [1867] *Capital, Volume 1: A Critique of Political Economy.* Penguin.

Marx, K. 1995 *Capital.* Oxford University Press.

Maslach, C., Schaufeli, W. and Leiter, M. P. 2001 Job burnout. *Annual Review of Psychology* 52: 397–422.

Maslin-Prothero, S. and Masterson, A. 1998 Continuing care: developing a policy analysis for nursing. *Journal of Advanced Nursing* 28/3: 548–53.

Masson, Jeffrey Moussaieff and McCarthy, Susan 1995 *When Elephants Weep: The Emotional Lives of Animals.* Delta, p. 79.

Masterson, A. 2010 *Midwifery 2020: UK Policy Review Report.* At <http://www.midwifery2020.org/>.

May, T. and Perry, B. 2011 *Social Research and Reflexivity: Content, Consequence and Context.* Sage Publications.

Mebratu, D. 1998 Sustainability and sustainable development; historical and conceptual review. *Environmental Impact Assessment Review* 18: 493–520.

Menzies, I. E. P. 1979 *The Functioning of Social Systems as a Defence against Anxiety.* Tavistock Institute of Human Relations.

Menzies-Lyth, I. 1988 *Containing Anxiety in Institutions*, selected essays, vol 1. Free Association Books.

Miall, C. E. 1989 Reproductive technology vs. the stigma of involuntary childlessness. *Social Casework* 70: 43–50.

Midwifery 2020. 2010a *Policy Library.* At <http://www.midwifery2020.org/>.

Midwifery 2020. 2010b *Midwifery 2020 – Delivering Expectations.* [online] Jill Rogers Associates. At <http://midwifery2020.org.uk/>.

Millard, A. 1990 The place of the clock in pediatric advice: rationales, cultural themes, and impediments to breastfeeding. *Social Science and Medicine* 31: 211–21.

Miller, R. L. and Brewer, J. D. 2003 *The A–Z of Social Research: A Dictionary of Key Social Science Research Concepts.* Sage Publications.

Miller, T. 2005 *Making Sense of Motherhood: A Narrative Approach.* Cambridge University Press.

Miller, T. 2010 *Making Sense of Fatherhood: Gender, Caring and Work.* Cambridge University Press.

Mills, C. W. 1959 *The Sociological Imagination.* Penguin.

Mills, C. Wright 1970 [1959] *The Sociological Imagination.* Pelican.

Mohanna, K. and Chambers, R. 2001 *Risk Matters in Healthcare: Communicating, Explaining and Managing Risk.* Radcliffe Medical Press.

Moon, G., Gould, M., Brown, T., Duncan, C., Iggulden, P., Jones, K., Litva, A., Subramanian, Sv. and Twigg, L. 2000 *Epidemiology: An Introduction.* Open University Press.

Moore, T., Gauld, R. and Williams, S. 2007 Implementing baby friendly hospital initiative policy: the case of New Zealand public hospitals. *International Breastfeeding Journal* 2: 8.

Moore-Lappe, F. 2011 *EcoMind – Changing the Way We Think, to Create the World We Want.* Nation Books.

Moreno-Casbas, T. 2005 *Nursing Research in Europe Scoping Report.* Institute of Health 'Carlos III'.

Morgan, D. 1998 Sociological imaginations and imagining sociologies: bodies, auto/biographies and other mysteries. *Sociology* 32/4: 647–63.

Morris, M., Oakley, L., Maconochie, N. and Doyle, P. 2011 An investigation of social inequalities in help-seeking and use of health services for fertility problems in a population-based sample of UK women. *Human Fertility* 14/1: 16–22.

Muller, P. 1974 *The Baby Killer: A War on Want Investigation into the Promotion of Powdered Baby Milks in the Third World.* War on Want.

Murphy, S. 2011 Reclaiming a moral identity: stillbirth, stigma and 'moral mothers'. *Midwifery;* doi:10.1016/j.midw.2011.06.005.

Murphy-Lawless, J. 1998 *Reading Birth and Death: A History of Obstetric Thinking.* Cork University Press.

Murphy-Lawless, J. 2010 Globalization, maternity and midwifery services. Struggles in meaning and practice in states under pressure. In L. Davies, R. Daellenbach and M. Kensington, *Sustainability, Midwifery and Birth.* Routledge, pp. 11–22.

Nachtigall, R. D. 2006 International disparities in access to infertility services. *Fertil Steril* 85: 871–5.

National Collaborating Centre for Women's and Children's Health 2010 Pregnancy and complex social factors: a model for service provision for pregnant women with complex social factors. *NICE Guideline CG* 110. At <http://guidance.nice.org.uk/CG110>.

National Collaborating Centre for Women's and Children's Health 2012 *Fertility: Assessment and Treatment for People with Fertility Problems (draft).* Commissioned by NICE. Royal College of Obstetricians and Gynaecologists Press. At <http://www.nice.org.uk/>.

National Institute for Health and Clinical Excellence (NICE) 2004 Fertility: assessment and treatment for people with fertility problems. *Clinical Guidelines* 11. At <http://www.nice.org.uk/>.

National Institute for Health and Clinical Excellence (NICE) 2007 *Antenatal and Postnatal Mental Health.* NICE.

National Institute for Health and Clinical Excellence (NICE) 2008 *Antenatal Care: Routine Care for the Healthy Pregnant Woman.* NICE.

National Institute for Health and Clinical Excellence (NICE) 2011 *Caesarean Section Guideline.* NICE.

National Institute for Health and Clinical Excellence (NICE) 2012 *New NICE Guidelines for Infertility.* At: <http://www.nhs.uk/>.

National Patient Safety Agency (NPSA) 2009a *Being Open: Communicating Patient Safety Incidents with Patients, Their Families and Carers.* NPSA.

National Patient Safety Agency (NPSA) 2009b *Never Events: Framework 2009/2010.* NPSA.

National Perinatal Epidemiology Unit 2011 *Birthplace Cohort Study, Key Findings.* At <https://www.npeu.ox.ac.uk/>.

Navarro, V. 1992 Has socialism failed? An analysis of health indicators under socialism. *International Journal of Health Services* 22: 583–601.

Naylor, C. and Appleby, J. 2012 *Sustainable Health and Social Care: Connecting Environmental and Financial Performance*. The King's Fund.

Neil, W. J. 2005 Taking a closer look: using deconstruction to explore recent Department of Health policy guidelines on copying letters to patients. *Journal of Health Organization and Management* 19/1: 73–80.

Nettleton, S. 1997a Governing the risky self: How to become healthy, wealthy and wise. In A. Petersen and R. Bunton (eds), *Foucault, Health and Medicine*. Routledge, pp. 207–22.

Nettleton, S. 1997b *The Sociology of Health and Illness*. Polity.

Newburn, M. 2006 What women want from care around the time of birth. In L. Page and McCandlish (eds), *The New Midwifery – Science and Sensitivity in Practice*, 2nd edn. Churchill Livingston/Elsevier, pp. 3–20.

Newburn, M. and Singh, D. 2005 *Are Women Getting the Birth Environment They Need? Report of a National Survey of Women's Experiences*. National Childbirth Trust.

Newell, R. 2002 Research and its relationship to nurse education: focus and capacity. *Nursing Education Today* 22: 278–84.

Newnham, J. P. and Moss, T. J. 2001 Antenatal glucocorticoids and growth: single versus multiple doses in animal and human studies. *Seminars in Neonatology* 6: 285–92.

Newton, C. R., Sherrard, W. and Glavac, I. 1999 The Fertility Problem Inventory: measuring perceived infertility-related stress. *Fertility & Sterility* 72/1: 54–62.

NHS Education for Scotland (NES) 2013 *Compassionate Connections*. At <http://www.nes.scot.nhs.uk/>.

NHS Information Centre 2010 – last update *Hospital Episodes Statistics: Maternity, 2008–2009*. Web page at <www.ic.nhs.uk/>.

NHS Information Centre 2011 *Infant Feeding Survey 2010: Early Results*. At <http://www.ic.nhs.uk/>.

NHS Institute for Innovation and Improvement 2006 *Focus on Normal Birth and Reducing Caesarean Section Rates*. NHS Institute for Innovation and Improvement.

NHS Litigation Authority 2008 *Clinical Negligence Scheme for Trusts. Clinical Risk Management Standards for Maternity Care*. Willis.

Nicolson, P. 1998 *Postnatal Depression: Psychology, Science and the Transition to Motherhood*. Routledge.

NMC 2004 *Standards of Proficiency for Pre-registration Nursing Education*. NMC.

Nordlund, E., Börjesson, A., Cacciatore, J. and Radestad, I. 2012 When a baby dies: motherhood, psychosocial care and negative effect. *British Journal of Midwifery* 20/11: 780–4.

Nordqwist, P. 2010 Out of sight, out of mind: family resemblances in lesbian donor conception. *Sociology* 44/6: 1128–44.

Norton, W., Hudson, N. and Culey, L. 2013 Gay men seeking surrogacy to achieve parenthood. *Reproductive BioMedicine Online* 27: 271–9.

Nursing and Midwifery Council (NMC) 2004 Standards of proficiency for pre-registration nursing education, NMC.

Nursing and Midwifery Council (NMC) 2008 *The Code: Standards of Conduct, Performance and Ethics for Nurses and Midwives*. NMC.

Nursing and Midwifery Council (NMC) 2010 *Standards for Pre-registration Nursing Education*. NMC.

Nursing and Midwifery Council (NMC) 2012 *Midwives Rules and Standards*. NMC.

Nussbaum, M. C. 2001 *The Upheavals of Thought: The Intelligence of Emotions*. Cambridge University Press.

Nutley, S. 2003 *Bridging the Policy/Research Divide: Reflections and Lessons from the UK*. St Andrews: Research Unit for Research Utilization, University of St Andrews.

Nyman, V. M. K., Prebensen, A. K. and Flensner, G. E. M. 2010 Obese women's experiences of encounters with midwives and physicians during pregnancy and childbirth. *Midwifery* 26/4: 424–9.

Oakley, A. 1979 *Becoming a Mother.* Martin Robertson.

Oakley, A. 1980 *Women Confined. Towards a Sociology of Childbirth.* Martin Robertson.

Oakley, A. 1983 Social consequences of obstetric technology: the importance of measuring 'soft' outcomes. *BIRTH* 10/2: 99–108.

Oakley, A. 1992 *Social Support and Motherhood: The Natural History of a Research Project.* Blackwell.

Oakley, A. 1993 *Essays on Women, Medicine and Health.* Edinburgh University Press.

Oakley, A. 1998 Gender, methodology and people's ways of knowing: some problems with feminism and the paradigm debate in social science. *Sociology* 32/4: 707–32.

Oakley, A. 2004 Response to 'Quoting and counting: an autobiographical response to Oakley'. *Sociology* 38/1: 191–2.

Oakley, A. 2005 *The Ann Oakley Reader.* The Policy Press.

Oakley, J. 1993 *Morality and Emotions.* Routledge.

Oaks, L. 2001 *Smoking and Pregnancy: The Politics of Fetal Protection.* Rutgers University Press.

Oates, M., Harper, A., Shakespeare, J. and Nelson-Piercy, C. 2011 Back to basics. In Centre for Maternal and Child Enquiries (CMACE), Saving Mothers' Lives: reviewing maternal deaths to make motherhood safer: 2006–2008. The Eighth Report on Confidential Enquiries into Maternal Deaths in the United Kingdom. *BJOG:* 118 (Suppl. 1): 16–21.

Office for National Statistics (ONS) 2010 *Live Births.* At <http://www.ons.gov.uk/>.

Office for National Statistics (ONS) 2011 *Births and Deaths in England and Wales 2010.* At <http://www.ons.gov.uk/ons/>.

Office for National Statistics (ONS) 2012a *Birth Cohort Tables for England and Wales, 2009.* At <http://www.ons.gov.uk/ons/>.

Office for National Statistics (ONS) 2012b *Statistical Bulletin, Annual Survey of Hours and Earnings, 2012 Provisional Results.* At <http://www.ons.gov.uk/>.

Oliver, M. and Barnes, C. 2012 *The New Politics of Disablement.* Palgrave Macmillan.

Oluwato, O. and Friedman, T. 2005 A survey of specialist perinatal mental health services in England. *Psychiatric Bulletin* 29: 77–179.

O'Malley, P. 2008 Governmentality and risk. In J. O. Zinn (ed.), *Social Theories of Risk and Uncertainty.* Blackwell, pp. 52–75.

O'Neill, M. 2008 Sex, violence and work: transgressing binaries and the vital role of services to sex workers in public policy reform. In G. Letherby, K. Williams, P. Birch and M. Cain (eds), *Sex as Crime?* Willan Publishing, pp. 80–98.

Ormerod, P. and Johns, H. 2007 Against happiness, *Prospect* (online version): 133.

Page, L. 2000 Keeping birth normal. In L. Page, *The New Midwifery,* 1st edn. Elsevier, pp. 105–21.

Page, L. 2008 Being a midwife to midwifery: transforming midwifery services. In K. Fahy, M. Fourier and C. Hastie (eds), *Birth Territory and Midwifery Guardianship.* Books for Midwives, pp. 115–29.

Page, L., Beake, S., Vail, A., McCourt, C. and Hewison, J. 2001 Clinical outcomes of one-to-one midwifery practice. *British Journal of Midwifery* 9: 700–6.

Pain, R., Bailey, C. and Mowl, G. 2001 Infant feeding in North East England: contested spaces of reproduction. *Area* 33/3: 261–72.

Palfrey, C. 2000 *Key Concepts in Health Care Policy and Planning.* Macmillan.

Palmer, G. 2009 *The Politics of Breastfeeding.* Pinter and Martin.

Papreen, N., Sharma, A., Sabin, K., Begum, L., Ahsan, S. K. and Baqui, A. H. 2000 Living with infertility: experiences among urban slum populations in Bangladesh. *Reproductive Health Matters* 8/15: 33–44.

Papworth Trust 2011 *Disability in the United Kingdom 2011, Facts and Figures.* Papworth Trust. At <http://www.papworth.org.uk/>.

Parsons, T. 1951a *The Social System.* Routledge & Kegan Paul.

Parson, T. 1951b Illness and the role of the physician: a sociological perspective. *American Journal of Orthopsychiatry* 21/3: 452–60.

Pashigian, M. 2002 Conceiving the happy family: infertility and marital politics in Northern Vietnam. In M. Inhorn and F. Van Balen (eds), *Infertility Around the Globe: New Thinking on Childlessness, Gender and Reproductive Technologies.* University of California Press, pp. 134–51.

Payne, G. 2006 *Social Divisions,* 2nd edn. Palgrave Macmillan.

Pembroke, N. F. and Pembroke, J. J. 2008 The spirituality of presence in midwifery care. *Midwifery* 24: 321–7.

Perez-y-Perez, M. and Stanley, T. 2011 Ethnographic intimacy: thinking through the ethics of social research in sex worlds. *Sociological Research Online* 16/2. At <www.socresonline.org.uk/>.

Perkins, B. B. 2004 *The Medical Delivery Business.* Rutgers University Press.

Persson, M., Hörnsten, A., Winkvist, A. and Mogren, I. 2011 'Mission impossible?' Midwives' experiences counseling pregnant women with gestational diabetes mellitus. *Patient Education and Counseling* 84: 78–83.

Persson, M., Winkvist, A. and Mogren, I. 2009 'From stun to gradual balance' – women's experiences of living with gestational diabetes mellitus. *Scandinavian Journal of Caring Sciences* 24: 454–62.

Petchesky, R. 1980 Reproductive freedom: beyond a woman's right to choose. *Signs* 5/4: 661–85.

Peters, K., Jackson, D. and Rudge, T. 2007 Failures of reproduction: problematizing 'success' in assisted reproductive technology. *Nursing Inquiry* 14/2: 125–31.

Petersen, A. 1999 Counselling the genetically 'at risk': the poetics and politics of 'non-directiveness'. *Health, Risk and Society* 1/3: 253–65.

Pfeffer, N. 1993 *The Stork and the Syringe: A Political History of Reproductive Medicine.* Polity.

Phelan, M. 2012 Medical Interpreting and the Law in the European Union. *European Journal of Health Law* 19/4: 333–53.

Philo, G. 1996 *Media and Mental Distress.* Addison Wesley Longman.

Philo, G., Henderson, L. and McCracken, K. 2010 *Making a Drama out of a Crisis: Authentic Portrayals of Mental Illness in TV Drama.* The Glasgow Media Group. Report available at <http://www.shift.org.uk/>.

Pilnick, A. and Zayts, O. 2012 'Let's have it tested first': choice and circumstances in decision-making following positive antenatal screening in Hong Kong. *Sociology of Health and Illness* 34/2: 266–82.

Pinikahana. J. 2003 Role of sociology within the nursing enterprise: some reflections on the unfinished debate. *Nursing and Health Sciences* 5/2: 175–80.

Platt, L. 2002 *Parallel Lives?: Poverty Among Ethnic Minority Groups in Britain.* Child Poverty Action Group (CPAG).

Polese, M. and Stren, R. (eds) 2000 *The Social Sustainability of Cities: Diversity and the Management of Change.* University of Toronto Press.

Porter, S. 1995 Sociology and the nursing curriculum: a defence. *Journal of Advanced Nursing* 2/6: 1130–5.

Price, S., Lake, M., Breen, G., Carson, G., Quinn, C. and O'Connor, T. 2007 The spiritual experience of high-risk pregnancy. *Journal of Obstetric, Gynecologic and Neonatal Nursing* 36/1: 63–70.

Prilleltensky, O. 2003 A ramp to motherhood: the experiences of mothers with physical disabilities. *Sexuality and Disability* 21/1: 21–47.

Prime Minister's Commission on the Future of Nursing and Midwifery 2010 *Front Line Care: The Future of Nursing and Midwifery in England.* Report of the Prime Minister's Commission on the Future of Nursing and Midwifery in England 2010. Produced by COI for the Prime Minister's Commission on the Future of Nursing and Midwifery in England. First published March 2010. London. At <http://www.nhshistory.net/>.

Prowse, J. and Prowse, P. 2008 Role redesign in the National Health Service: the effects on midwives' work and professional boundaries. *Work, Employment & Society* 22: 695–712.

Punch, K. F 1998 *Introduction to Social Research: Quantitative and Qualitative Approaches.* London: Sage.

Rådestad, I., Nordin, C., Steineck, G. and Sjögren, B. 1996 A comparison of women's memories of care during pregnancy, labour and delivery after stillbirth or live birth. *Midwifery,* 14/2: 111–17.

Raleigh, V. S., Hussey, D., Seccombe, I. and Halit, K. 2010 Ethnic and social inequalities in women's experience of maternity care in England: results of a national survey. *Journal of the Royal Society of Medicine* 103: 188–298.

Ramaswami, R. 2012 Why migrant mothers die in childbirth in the UK. Open Democracy. At <http://www.opendemocracy.net/>.

Ramsay, K. 1996 Emotional labour and qualitative research: how I learned not to laugh or cry in the field. In E. S. Lyon and J. Busfield (eds), *Methodological Imaginations.* Macmillan, pp. 131–47.

Raphael-Leff, J. 1991 *Psychological Processes of Childbearing,* Chapman and Hall, London.

Rapp R. 1999 *Testing Women, Testing the Fetus: The Social Impact of Amniocentesis in America.* Routledge.

Rapport, F. 2003 Exploring the beliefs and experiences of potential egg share donors. *Journal of Advanced Nursing* 43: 28–42.

Ratner, B. D. 2004 Sustainability as a dialogue of values: challenges to the sociology of development. *Sociological Inquiry* 74/1: 50–69.

Rayment, J. 2011 Midwives' emotion and body work in two hospital settings: personal strategies and professional projects, PhD thesis, University of Warwick.

Redshaw, M., Hockley, C. and Davidson, L. L. 2007 A qualitative study of the experience of treatment for infertility among women who successfully became pregnant. *Human Reproduction* 22/1: 295–304.

Reissman, C. K. 2000 Stigma and everyday practices: childless women in south India. *Gender & Society* 14/1: 111–35.

Rich, A. 1995 The Blue Ghazals, in *Collected Early Poems 1950–1970.* Norton.

Richardson, J. C., Ong, B. N. and Sim, J. 2006 Is chronic widespread pain biographically disruptive? *Social Science & Medicine (1982)* 63: 1573–85.

Roberts, H. 1992 (ed.) *Women's Health Matters.* Routledge.

Roberts, J. 2012 'Wakey wakey baby': narrating four-dimensional (4D) bonding scans. *Sociology of Health and Illness* 14: 299–314.

Roberts, Y. 2013 'Living wage' Whitehall cleaner evicted days before giving birth. *Guardian,* 23 February 2013. At <http://www.guardian.co.uk/>.

Robinson, J. 1992 Introduction: beginning the study of nursing policy. In J. Robinson, A. Gray and R. Elkan (eds), *Policy Issues in Nursing.* Open University Press, pp.1–8.

Robinson, J. 2004 Health visitors or health police? *AIMS Journal* 16/3. At <http://www.aims.org.uk/>.

Robinson, J. and Kirkcaldy, A. J. 2007 Disadvantaged mothers, young children and smoking in homes: mothers' use of space within their homes. *Health and Place* 13: 894–903.

Rogers, A. 2010 A sociology of mental health and illness, 4th edn. McGraw-Hill, Open University Press.

Romney, M. L. 1980 Pre-delivery shaving: an unjustified assault? *Journal of Obstetrics and Gynaecology* 1: 33–5.

Rosenberg, K. D., Stull, J. D., Adler, M. R., Kasehagen, L. J. and Crivelli-Kovach, A. 2008 Impact of hospital policies on breastfeeding outcomes. *Breastfeeding Medicine* 3: 110–16.

Ross, F., Smith, E., Mackenzie, A. and Masterson, A. 2004 Identifying research priorities in nursing and midwifery service delivery and organization: a scoping study. *International Journal of Nursing Studies* 41/5: 547–58.

Rowan, C. and Bick, D. 2008 An evaluation of the provision of perinatal mental health services in two English strategic health authorities. *Evidence-Based Midwifery* 6/4: 76–82.

Rowan, C., McCourt, C. and Bick, D. 2010 Provision of mental health services in two English strategic health authorities: views and perspectives of the multi-disciplinary team. *Evidence Based Midwifery* 8/3: 98–106.

Royal College of Midwives (RCM) no date *Campaign for Normal Birth.* [online] At <http://www.rcmnormalbirth.org.uk/>.

Royal College of Midwives (RCM) 2010 *The Royal College of Midwives and Subsidiary Company Report and Consolidated Accounts For the Year Ended 31 August 2009.* Royal College of Midwives. At <http://www.rcm.org.uk/>.

Royal College of Midwives (RCM) 2011 *Protect Maternity Services.* At <http://www. rcm.org.uk/>.

Royal College of Midwives (RCM) 2012 *Evidence Based Guidelines.* At <http://www. rcm.org.uk>.

Royal College of Obstetricians and Gynaecologists (RCOG) 2007 *Birth After Previous Caesarean Birth: Greentop Guideline No. 45.* RCOG.

Royal College of Obstetricians and Gynaecologists (RCOG) 2008 *Obtaining Valid Consent: Clinical Governance Advice No. 6.* RCOG.

Royal College of Obstetricians and Gynaecologists (RCOG) 2009 *Reproductive Ageing.* Royal College of Obstetricians and Gynaecologists Press.

Royal College of Obstetricians and Gynaecologists (RCOG) 2010 *Guidelines.* At: <http://www.rcog.org.uk/>.

Royal Society Study Group. 1992 *Risk Analysis, Perception and Management.* Royal Society Publishing.

Rushby-Smith, T. 2010 The challenges of disability and pregnancy. *Guardian,* 23 November 2010. At <http://www.guardian.co.uk/>.

Ryding, E. L., Persson, A., Onell, C. and Kvist, L. 2003 An evaluation of midwives' counselling of pregnant women in fear of childbirth. *Acta Obstetrician et Gynecologica Scandinavica* 82: 10–17.

Sampson, H., Bloor, M. and Fincham, B. 2008 A price worth paying?: considering the 'cost' of reflexive research methods and the influence of feminist ways of 'doing'. *Sociology* 4/5: 919–34.

Sandall, J. 1997 Midwives, burnout and continuity of care. *British Journal of Midwifery* 5/2: 106–11.

Sandall, J. 1998 Occupational burnout in midwives: new ways of working and the relationship between organizational factors and psychological health and well-being. *Risk Decision and Policy* 3/3: 213–32.

Sandall, J., Davies, J. and Warwick, C. 2001 *Evaluation of the Albany Midwifery Practice.* Final Report, March 2001. King's College. At <http://openaccess.city. ac.uk/>.

Sandall, J., Morton, C. and Bick, D. 2010 Safety in Childbirth and the three 'C's: community, context and culture. *Midwifery* 26/5: 481–2.

Sandall, J., Benoit, C., Wrede, S., Murray, S. F., Van Teijlingen, E. R. and Westfall, R. 2009 Social service professional or market expert? *Current Sociology* 57: 529–53.

Sandel, M. 2012 *What Money Can't Buy: The Moral Limits of the Market*. Allen Lane.

Sandelowski, M. 1991 Compelled to try: the never-enough quality of conceptive technology. *Medical Anthropology Quarterly* 5/1: 29–47.

Sandelowski, M. and de Lacey, S. 2002 The uses of 'disease': infertility as a rhetorical vehicle. In M. Inhorn and F. Van Balen (eds), *Infertility around the Globe: New Thinking on Childlessness, Gender and Reproductive Technologies*. University of California Press, pp. 33–51.

Sandelowski, M., Harris, B. G. and Black, B. P. 1992 Relinquishing infertility: the work of pregnancy for infertile couples. *Qualitative Health Research* 2/3: 282–301.

Sands (Stillbirth and Neonatal Death charity) no date, a *Identifying Pregnancies at Risk of Stillbirth*. [online] At <http://www.uk-sands.org/>.

Sands (Stillbirth and Neonatal Death charity) no date, b *Causes and Risk Factors for Stillbirth*. [online] At <http://www.uk-sands.org/>.

Sands 2010 *Our Major Survey of Bereavement Care Provided by UK Maternity Units to Parents whose Baby Dies*. At <http://www.uk-sands.org/>.

Scamell, M. and Alaszewski, A. 2012 Fateful moments and the categorization of risk: midwifery practice and the ever-narrowing window of normality during childbirth. *Health, Risk and Society* 14/2: 207–21.

Scheff, T. 1966 *Being Mentally Ill*. Aldine Publishing Co.

Scheper-Hughes, N. 1992 *Death Without Weeping: The Violence of Everyday Life in Brazil*. University of California Press.

Schmidt. L. et al. 2005 Communication and coping as predictors of fertility problem stress: cohort study of 816 participants who did not achieve a delivery after 12 months of fertility treatment. *Human Reproduction* 20/11: 3248–56.

Schmied, V., Beake, S., Sheehan, A., McCourt, C. and Dykes, F. 2011a Meta-synthesis of women's perceptions and experiences of breastfeeding support. *Birth: Issues in Perinatal Care* 38: 49–60.

Schmied, V. A., Duff, M., Dahlen, H. G., Mills, A. E. and Kolt, G. S. 2011b 'Not waving but drowning': a study of the experiences and concerns of midwives and other health professionals caring for obese childbearing women. *Midwifery* 24/4: 242–30.

Schmied, V., Gribble, A., Sheehan, V., Taylor, C. and Dykes, F. 2011c 'Ten Steps or climbing a mountain': A study of Australian health professionals' perceptions of implementing the Baby Friendly Health Initiative to protect, promote and support breastfeeding. *Health Services Research* 11: 208.

Schor, J. 2010 *Plenitude: The New Economics of True Wealth*. Penguin.

Schwennesen, N. and Koch, L. 2012 Representing and intervening: 'doing' good care in first trimester prenatal knowledge production and decision-making. *Sociology of Health and Illness* 34/2: 283–98.

Scott, J. 2010 Quantitative methods and gender inequalities. *International Journal of Social Research Methodology* 13/3: 223–36.

Scott, J. 2013 The philosophical basis of objectivity and relativity. In G. Letherby, J. Scott and M. Williams, *Objectivity and Subjectivity in Social Research*. Sage Publications, pp. 13–31.

Scottish Executive Health Department 2002 *Choices and Challenges: The Strategy for Research and Development in Nursing and Midwifery in Scotland*. Stationery Office.

Scottish Government 2011 *A Refreshed Framework for Maternity Care in Scotland*. The Maternity Services Action Group. At <http://www.scotland.gov.uk/>.

Seabrook, J. 2012 Deindustrializing humanity. *New Internationalist* (April): 54–5.

Searle, J. 1996 Fearing the worst – why do pregnant women feel 'at-risk'? *Australian and New Zealand Journal of Obstetrics and Gynaecology* 36/3: 279–86.

Semenic, S., Childerhose, J. E., Lauziere, J. and Groleau, D. 2012 Barriers, facilitators and recommendations related to implementing the Baby-Friendly Initiative (BFI): an integrative review. *Journal of Human Lactation* 28: 317–34.

Sennett, R. 1999 *The Corrosion of Character: The Personal Consequences of Work in the New Capitalism*. WW Norton & Company.

Sennett, R. 2008 *The Craftsman*. Yale University Press.

Shaffer, E. and Brenner, S. 2004 Trade and health care: corporatizing vital human services. In M. M. M. Fort, *Sickness and Wealth: The Corporate Assault on Global Health*. South End Press, pp. 79–94.

Shakespeare, T. 2006 *Disability Rights and Wrongs*. Routledge.

Shapiro, S. 2009 Editorial: explaining risk. A guide for health professionals. *Maturitas* 64: 143–4.

Sharp, K. 1994 Sociology and the nursing curriculum: a note of caution. *Journal of Advanced Nursing* 20: 391–5.

Sharp, K. 2005 What is sociology? In S. Earle and E. Denny (eds), *Sociology for Nurses*. Polity.

Shaw, M. 2010 The regulation of health risks. In B. Heyman, M. Shaw, A. Alasewski and M. Titterton (eds), *Risk, Safety and Clinical Practice: Health Care through the Lens of Risk*. Oxford University Press, pp. 172–93.

Shaw, R. 2003 Theorizing breastfeeding: body ethics, maternal generosity and the gift relation. *Body and Society* 9: 55–73.

Shaw Trust. 2012 *Disability and Employment Statistics* [Online]. At <http://www.shaw-trust.org.uk/>.

Sheldon, A. 2004 Women and disability. In J. Swain, S. French, C. Barnes and C. Thomas (eds), *Disabling Barriers – Enabling Environments*. Sage Publications, pp. 69–74.

Shildrick, M. 1997 *Leaky Bodies and Boundaries, Feminism, Postmodernism and (Bio) Ethics*. Routledge.

Shildrick, M. 2000 Becoming vulnerable: contagious encounters and the ethics of risk. *Journal of Medical Humanities* 21/4: 215–27.

Silverman, D. 2000 *Doing Qualitative Research*. Sage Publications.

Simkin, P. 1992 Just another day in a woman's life? Part II: Nature and consistency of women's long-term memories of their first birth experiences. *Birth* 19/2: 64–81.

Simmons, H. A. and Goldberg, L. S. 2011 'High-risk' pregnancy after perinatal loss: understanding the label. *Midwifery* 27: 452–7.

Simonds, W. and Rothman, B. K. 1992 *Centuries of Solace: Expressions of Maternal Grief in Popular Literature*. Temple University Press.

Simpson, R., Hampshire, K., Iqbal, N. and Bell, M. 2012 *British Pakistani Muslims, Infertility and the New Reproductive Technologies*. ESRC Impact Report, RES-000-23-1488. ESRC.

Sittner, B. J., DeFrain, J. and Hudson, D. B. 2005 Effects of high-risk pregnancies on families. *American Journal of Maternal and Child Nursing* 30/2: 121–6.

Skolbekken, J. 1995 The risk epidemic in medical journals. *Social Science and Medicine* 40: 291–305.

Small, N. 2001 Theories of grief: a critical review. In J. L. Hockey, J. Katz and N. Small (eds), *Grief, Mourning and Death Ritual*. Open University Press, pp. 19–48.

Small, N. 2008 Theories of grief: a critical review. In S. Earle and C. Komaromy, *Death and Dying: A Reader*. Sage Publications.

Smith, B. 1977 *Policy Making in British Government*. Martin Robertson.

Smith, D. 1999 *Writing the Social*. University of Toronto Press.

Smith, P. 1992 *The Emotional Labour of Nursing: Its Impact on Interpersonal Relations, Management, and the Educational Environment in Nursing.* Macmillan Education.

Smith, P. 2008 Compassion and smiles: what's the evidence? *Journal of Research in Nursing* 13/5: 367–70; DOI: 10.1177/1744987108096012.

Snow, D. 2001 Extending and broadening Blumer's conceptualization of symbolic interactionism. *Symbolic Interaction* 24/3: 367–77.

Sobel, H. L., Iellamon, A., Raya, R. R., Padilla, A. A., Olivé, J-M and Nyunt-U, S. 2011 Is unimpeded marketing for breast milk substitutes responsible for the decline in breastfeeding in the Philippines? An exploratory survey and focus group analysis. *Social Science & Medicine* 73: 1445–8.

Sokol, E. 1997 *The Code Handbook: A Guide to Implementing the International Code of Marketing of Breast-milk substitutes.* International Baby Food Action Network.

Solesbury, W. 1976 An illustration of how situations may become political issues and issues may demand responses from government: or how they may not. *Public Administration* 54/4: 379–97.

Souter, V. L. 1998 Patient satisfaction with the management of infertility. *Human Reproduction* 13/7: 1831–6.

Spallone, P. 1989 *Beyond Conception: The New Politics of Reproduction.* Macmillan.

Spencer, L. 2011 With women in perinatal loss. *Canadian Journal of Midwifery Research and Practice* 10/1: 52–8.

Spicker, P. 2006 *Policy Analysis for Practice – Applying Social Policy.* The Policy Press.

Stacey M. (ed.) 1992 *Changing Human Reproduction: Social Science Perspectives.* Sage Publications.

Stahl, K. and Hundley, V. 2003 Risk and risk assessment in pregnancy – do we scare because we care? *Midwifery.* 298–309.

Stainton, M. C., Lohan, M. and Woodhart, L. 2005 Women's experiences of being in high-risk antenatal care day stay and hospital admission. *Australian Midwifery* 18/1: 16–20.

Stanley, L. and Wise, S. 1990 Method, methodology and epistemology in feminist research processes. In L. Stanley (ed.), *Feminist Praxis: Research, Theory and Epistemology.* Routledge, pp. 20–60.

Stanley, L. and Wise, S. 1993 *Breaking Out Again: Feminist Ontology and Epistemology.* Routledge & Kegan Paul.

Stanworth, M. (ed.). 1987 *Reproductive Technologies: Gender, Motherhood and Medicine.* Polity.

Stapleton, H. 1997 Choice in the face of uncertainty. In M. J. Kirkham and E. R. Perkins (eds), *Reflections on Midwifery.* Ballière Tindall, pp. 47–69.

Stapleton, H., Kirkham, M., Thomas, G. and Curtis, P. 2002 Midwives in the middle: balance and vulnerability. *British Journal of Midwifery* 10/10: 607–11.

Stearns, C. A. 1999 Breastfeeding and the good maternal body. *Gender and Society* 13: 308–25.

Stenman, E. 2011 Sustainability: a collective responsibility. *San Diego Business Journal* 32: 41.

Stewart, J. F., Popkin, B. M., Guilkey, D. K., Atkin, J. S., Adair, L. and Flieger, W. 1991 Influences on the extent of breastfeeding: a prospective study in the Philippines. *Demography* 28: 181–99.

Stoeker, R. 1996 *Report to the Community Development Society on the Participatory Research meeting at Melbourne Community Development Society.* At <http://www.comm–dev.htlm>.

Strategic Review of Health Inequalities 2010 *The Marmot Review Strategic Review of Health Inequalities in England post-2010.* At <http://www.instituteof healthequity.org/>.

Strathern, M. 1992 *Reproducing the Future: Essays on Anthropology, Kinship and the New Reproductive Technologies*. Manchester University Press.

Strauss, A. and Corbin, J. 1990 *Basics of Qualitative Research*. Sage Publications.

Stringer, E. 1996 *Action Research: A Handbook for Practitioners*. Sage Publications.

Stronach, I., Corbin, B., McNamara, O. et al. 2002 Towards an uncertain politics of professionalism: teacher and nurse identities in flux. *Journal of Educational Policy* 17: 109–38.

Swinford, S. 2014 Worst hospitals cost NHS £300m. *The Sunday Telegraph*, 23 February, p. 16.

Szasz, T. 1961 *The Myth of Mental Illness*. Free Press.

Szasz, T. 1970 *The Manufacture of Madness*. Routledge & Kegan Paul.

Szerszynski, B. and Urry, J. 2002 Cultures of Cosmopolitanism. *The Sociological Review*. At <http://www.lancs.ac.uk/>.

Taylor, C., Gribble, A., Sheehan, V., Schmied, V. and Dykes, F. 2011 Staff perceptions and experiences of implementing the baby friendly initiative in neonatal intensive care units in Australia. *Journal of Obstetric, Gynecologic, & Neonatal Nursing* 40: 25–34.

Taylor, S. and Field, D. (eds) 2007 *Sociology of Health and Health Care*, 4th edn. Blackwell.

Teijlingen van, E. R. 2003 Dutch midwives: the difference between image and reality. In S. Earle and G. Letherby (eds), *Gender, Identity and Reproduction: Social Perspectives*. Palgrave, pp. 120–34.

Teijlingen, van, E. 2005a A critical analysis of the medical model as used in the study of pregnancy and childbirth. *Sociological Research Online* 10/2. At <http://www.socresonline.org.uk/>.

Teijlingen, van, E. 2005b The profession of medicine. In B. Alder, C. Abraham, E. van Teijlingen and M. Porter (eds), *Psychology and Sociology Applied to Medicine: An Illustrated Colour Text*, 3rd edn. Elsevier Science, pp. 166–7.

Teijlingen, van E. 2012 The state of the world's midwifery (editorial). *International Journal of Childbirth* 1/4: 214–15.

Teijlingen, van, E. R. and van der Hulst, L. 1995 Midwifery in the Netherlands: more than a semi–profession? In G. Larkin, T. Johnson and M. Saks (eds), *Health Professions and the State in Europe*. Routledge, pp. 178–86.

Thomas, C. 1997 The baby and the bathwater: disabled women and motherhood in social context. *Sociology of Health & Illness* 19: 622–43.

Thomas, C. 2007 *Sociologies of Disability and Illness*. Palgrave Macmillan.

Thomas, C. and Curtis, P. 1997 Having a baby: some disabled women's reproductive experiences. *Midwifery* 13: 202–9.

Thomas, G. 2000 Be nice and don't drop the baby. In L. Page and P. Percival (eds), *The New Midwifery: Science and Sensitivity in Practice*. Elsevier, pp. 173–83.

Thomas, H. 2003 Pregnancy, illness and the concept of career. *Sociology of Health & Illness* 25/5: 383–407.

Thomas, H. 2004 Women's postnatal experience following a medically complicated pregnancy. *Health Care for Women International* 25/1: 76–87.

Thomas, S. V. 2006 Management of epilepsy and pregnancy. *Journal of Postgraduate Medicine* 52: 57–64.

Thompson, C. 2005 *Making Parents: The Ontological Choreography of Reproductive Technologies*. MIT Press.

Thompson, D. 2000 *Sociology and Nursing*. Routledge.

Thomson, G., Bilson, A. and Dykes, F. 2012 'Changing hearts and minds': an evaluation of implementation of UNICEF UK Baby Friendly Initiative in the community. *Midwifery* 28: 258–64.

Thomson, G., Dykes, F., Bilson, A., Putsey, J., Whitmore, M. and Dickens, S. 2010 Tackling the infant formula industries: letter. *Public Health Nutrition* 13: 149–50.

Thomson, R. and Kehily, M. J. 2008 *The Making of Modern Motherhood: Memories, Representations, Practices.* The Open University.

Thorne, S., Kirkham, S. and McDonald-Emes, J. 1997 Interpretive description: a noncategorical qualitative alternative for developing nursing knowledge. *Research in Nursing and Health* 20: 169–77.

Throsby, K. 2004 *When IVF Fails: Feminism, Infertility and the Negotiation of Normality.* Palgrave Macmillan.

Throsby, K. and Gill, R. 2004 It's different for men. Masculinity and IVF. *Men and Masculinities* 6/4: 330–48.

Thurber, J. A. 2003 Foreword. In J. W. Kingdon, *Agendas, Alternatives and Public Policies*, 2nd edn. Longman.

Titterton, M. 2005 *Risk and Risk Taking in Health and Social Welfare.* Jessica Kingsley Publishers.

Tjørnhøj-Thomsen, T. 2005 Close encounters with infertility and procreative technology. In R. Jenkins, H. Jessen and V. Steffen (eds), *Managing Uncertainty: Ethnographic Studies of Illness, Risk, and the Struggle for Control.* Museum Tusculanum Press, pp. 71–92.

Toofany, S. 2005 Nurses and health policy. *Nursing Management* 12/3: 26–30.

Towler, J. and Bramhall, J. 1998 *Midwives in History and Society.* Croom Helm.

Tracy, S. 2010 Costing birth as commodity or sustainable public good. In L. Davies, R. Daellenbach and M. Kensington 2010 *Sustainability, Midwifery and Birth.* Routledge, pp. 32–44.

Truman, C. 2003 Ethics and the ruling relations of research. *Sociological Research Online* 8/1. At <www.socresonline.org.uk/>.

Tully, L., Garcia, J., Davidson, L. and Marchant, S. 2002 Role of midwives in depression screening. *British Journal of Midwifery* 10/6: 374–8.

Turner, B. 1995 *Medical Power and Social Knowledge*, 2nd edn. Sage Publications.

Turner, J. H. and Stets, J. E. 2005 *The Sociology of Emotions.* Cambridge University Press.

Turton, P., Badenhorst, W., Pawlby, S., White, S. and Hughes, P. 2009 Psychological vulnerability in children next-born after stillbirth: a case-control follow-up study. *Journal of Child Psychology Psychiatry* 50/12: 1451–8.

Tyler, I. 2011 Pramface girls: the class politics of 'maternal TV'. In B. Skeggs and H. Wood (eds), *Reality Television and Class.* Palgrave Macmillan, pp. 210–24.

UK National Screening Committee 2004 *National Down's Syndrome Screening Programme for England: A Handbook for Staff.* UK National Screening Committee Programmes Directorate.

UNFPA 2011 *The State of the World's Midwifery 2011: Delivering Health, Saving Lives.* World Health Organization.

Unisa, S. 1999 Childlessness in Andhra Pradesh, India: treatment-seeking and consequences. *Reproductive Health Matters* 7/13: 54–64.

United Nations (UN) (ed.) 1993 *Earth Summit: Agenda 21, the United Nations Programme of Action from Rio.* United Nations.

UPIAS 1976 *The Fundamental Principles of Disability.* The Union of Physically Impaired Against Segregation.

Uren, T. H. and Wastell, C. A. 2002 Attachment and meaning-making in perinatal bereavement. *Death Studies* 26/4: 279–308.

Verny, T. and Kelly, J. 1981 *The Secret Life of the Unborn Child.* Sphere Books. Reprinted 2012.

Wackernagel, M. and Rees, W. 1996 *Our Ecological Footprint: Reducing Human Impact on the Earth.* New Society Publishers.

Wagner, M. 1994 *Pursuing the Birth Machine: The Search for Appropriate Birth Technology.* ACE Graphics.

Walby, S. 2009 *Globalization and Inequalities, Complexity and Contested Modernities*. Sage Publications.

Walker, A. and Walker, C. 1997 *Britain Divided: The Growth of Social Exclusion in the 1980s and 1990s*. Child Poverty Action Group.

Walsh, D. 2007 *Improving Maternity Services: Small is Beautiful – Lessons from a Birth Centre*. Radcliffe Publishing Ltd.

Walsh, D. 2009 'Small really is beautiful': tales from a free-standing birth centre. In R. Davis-Floyd, L. Barclay and B. Davis et al. (eds), *Birth Models That Work*. University of California Press, pp. 159–86.

Walsh, D., El-Nemer, A. M. R. and Downe, S. 2008 Rethinking risk and safety in maternity care. In S. Downe (ed.), *Normal Childbirth: Evidence and Debate*, 2nd edn. Churchill Livingstone, pp. 117–28.

Walsh-Gallagher, D., Sinclair, M. and McConkey, R. 2012. The ambiguity of disabled women's experiences of pregnancy, childbirth and motherhood: a phenomenological understanding. *Midwifery* 28: 156–62.

Walter, T. 1994 *The Revival of Death*. Routledge.

Warwick, C. 2011a *Midwives Can't go on Working in a System where Safety is Too Often Compromised*. At <http://www.theguardian.com/>.

Warwick, C. 2011b Midwives must have power to advise commissioning boards. *NursingTimes.net*. At <http://www.nursingtimes.net/>.

Warwick, I., Neville, R. and Smith, K. 2006 My life in Huddersfield: supporting young asylum seekers and refugees to record their experiences of living in Huddersfield. *Social Work Education* 25/2: 129–37.

Watts, S., O'Hara, L. and Trigg, R. 2010 Living with type 1 diabetes: a by-person qualitative exploration. *Psychology & Health* 25/4: 491–506.

Webb, P. and Bain, C. 2011 *Essential Epidemiology: An Introduction for Students and Health Professionals*. Cambridge University Press.

Webber, J. 2011 Nursing and health policy perspectives. *International Nursing Review* 58/2: 145–6.

Weber, M. 1958 *The Protestant Ethic and the Spirit of Capitalism*. W.W. Norton.

Weir, L. 2006 *Pregnancy, Risk and Biopolitics: On the Threshold of the Living Subject*. Routledge.

Wharton, A. S. 1993 The affective consequences of service work managing emotions on the job. *Work and Occupations* 20/2: 205–32.

Whatley, D. 1995 *Birth Mother–Death Mother*. Unpublished. York University.

Whiteford, L. M. and Gonzalez, L. 1995 Stigma: the hidden burden of infertility. *Social Science & Medicine* 40/1: 27–36.

Wiklund, I., Edman, G., Ryding, E.-L. and Andolf, E. 2008 Expectation and experiences of childbirth in primiparae with caesarean section. *British Journal of Obstetrics and Gynaecology* 115: 324–31.

Wiles, R. S., Heath, S. and Crow, G. 2005 *Informed Consent and the Research Process* Manchester: ESRC Research Methods Programme: Methods Briefing 2.

Wilkinson, S. and Kitzinger, C. (eds) 1996 *Representing the Other: A Feminism and Psychology Reader*. Sage Publications.

Wilkinson, R. and Pickett, K. 2010 *The Spirit Level: Why Equality is Better for Everyone*. Penguin.

Williams, A. 2009 Lifecycle influences and opportunities for change. In F. Dykes and V. Moran Hall (eds), *Infant and Young Child Feeding: Challenges to Implementing a Global Strategy*. Wiley-Blackwell, pp.163–80.

Williams, C. 2006 Dilemmas in fetal medicine: premature application of technology or respondong to women's choice. *Sociology of Health & Illness* 28: 1–20.

Williams, C., Alderson, P. and Farsides, B. 2002 Is non-directiveness possible within the context of antenatal screening and testing? *Social Science and Medicine* 54/3: 17–25.

Williams, M. 2005 Situated objectivity. *Journal for the Theory of Social Behaviour* 35/1: 99–120.

Williams, M. 2013 Situated objectivity in sociology. In G. Letherby, J. Scott and M. Williams, *Objectivity and Subjectivity in Social Research*. Sage Publications, pp. 59–78.

Wilson, S. 2007 'When you have children, you're obliged to live': motherhood, chronic illness and biographical disruption. *Sociology of Health & Illness* 29: 610–26.

Wilson, C. L., Fisher, J. R., Hammarberg, K., Amor, D. J. and Halliday, J. L. 2011 Looking downstream: a review of the literature on physical and psychosocial health outcomes in adolescents and young adults who were conceived by ART. *Human Reproduction*; doi: 10.1093/humrep/der041.

Winickoff, J. P., Gottlieb, M. and Mello, M. 2010 Regulation of smoking in public housing. *New England Journal of Medicine* 362 (June): 2319–25.

Witz, A. 1992 *Professions and Patriarchy*. Routledge.

Woodward, B. J., and Norton, W. J. 2006 Lesbian intra-partner oocyte donation: a possible shake-up in the Garden of Eden? *Human Fertility* 9/4: 217–22.

Woolridge, M. 1995 Baby-controlled feeding: biocultural implications. In P. Stuart-Macadam and K. Dettwyler (eds), *Breastfeeding Biocultural Perspectives*. Aldine De Gruyer, pp. 168–217.

World Commission on Environment and Development (WCED) 1987 *Our Common Future*. Oxford University Press.

World Health Organization (WHO) 1948 *What is the WHO Definition of Health?* At <http://www.who.int>.

World Health Organization (WHO) 1981 *International Code of Marketing of Breast Milk Substitutes*. WHO.

World Health Organization (WHO) 1985 *Health Implications of Obesity*. National Institutes of Health Consensus Development Conference Statement. 11–13 February.

World Health Organization/United Nations Children's Fund (WHO/UNICEF) 1989 *Protecting, Promoting and Supporting Breastfeeding: The Special Role of Maternity Services*. WHO and UNICEF.

World Health Organization (WHO) 1990 *Innocenti Declaration on the Protection, Promotion and Support of Breastfeeding*. WHO.

World Health Organization/United Nations Children's Fund (WHO/UNICEF) 1992 Baby Friendly Initiative Part II, Hospital Level Implementation. WHO and UNICEF.

World Health Organization (WHO) 1998 *Obesity: Preventing and Managing the Global Epidemic*. Report of a WHO Consultation on Obesity, 3–5 June. WHO. At <http://whqlibdoc.who.int/>.

World Health Organization (WHO) 2003 *Global Strategy on Infant and Young Child Feeding*. WHO.

World Health Organization 2009 *Gender Disparities in Mental Health*. At <www.who.int/>.

World Health Organization (WHO) 2011a *The Nursing and Midwifery Programme at WHO*. WHO. At <http://www.who.int/nursing>.

World Health Organization (WHO) 2011b *Nursing and Midwifery Services – Strategic Directions 2011–2015*. WHO.

World Health Organization (WHO) 2012 *Maternal Mortality: Factsheet Number 348: May 2012*. [online] At <http://www.who.int/>.

Wray, S. and Deery, R. 2008 The medicalization of body size and women's healthcare. *Health Care for Women International* 29/3: 227–43; doi:10.1080/07399330701738291.

Zadeh, M. A., Khajehei, M., Sharif, F. and Hadzic, M. 2012 High–risk pregnancy: effects on postpartum depression and anxiety. *British Journal of Midwifery* 20/2: 104–13.

Zinn, J. O. 2005 The biographical approach: a better way to understand behaviour in health and illness. *Health, Risk and Society* 7: 1–9.

Zinn, J. O. 2008 Heading into the unknown: everyday strategies for managing risk and uncertainty. *Health, Risk and Society* 10/5: 439–50.

Index